Praise for the Book

"Ulf Mattsson's book is a very comprehensive guidebook that sheds light on the often mystical intersection of cybersecurity and privacy. This book is a must have, must read and must keep for cybersecurity and privacy practitioners and also C-level executives that need to demonstrate both visible and vocal support for their organization's cybersecurity and privacy executives."

—Taiye Lambo, Founder, Holistic Information Security Practitioner Institute (HISPI), eFortresses, CloudeAssurance and Pioneer vCISO

"Ulf Mattsson, whose security insights I have cherished for years, has written the book that C-levels need to read. Data's value to an enterprise is well known, but Ulf explores how it's also a danger. It's a danger to the business in the hands of a cyberthief, it's a danger to the business if it disappears (accidentally or maliciously), it's a danger to business operations if it can't be effectively managed, analyzed, stored and retrieved and it's absolutely a danger to an enterprise when it hurts customers, which is what new data privacy laws are all about. Is data friend or foe? Frustratingly, it's both. Read this book to know how to control data and stop it from controlling you."

—Evan Schuman, Computerworld columnist, cybersecurity writer for McKinsey and founding editor-in-chief of StorefrontBacktalk

"This book navigates the complex intersection of privacy and data security while addressing the challenges of emerging risks posed by Artificial Intelligence, Machine Learning, Quantum Computing. The illustrations are extremely powerful because they describe the technologies being reviewed and how they fit into the overall ecosystem. Practitioners will benefit from the insights and practical advice being offered."

—Renee Guttmann, former CISO at The Coca-Cola Company and VP Information Security and Privacy at Time Warner Inc.

"Rather than a simple walkthrough through how different privacy exploits work, Ulf Mattson goes into fine detail about the importance of privacy regulations, adhering to GDPR, and building a privacy risk management framework. Ulf discusses several instances that took place over the years in cybersecurity and provides a deep understanding of data security and the know-how to build a security framework amid the emerging trends. Another interesting aspect is how it stands out from general academic texts. The book provides practical general advice, strategy outlines, and serves more like a handbook to privacy and data security. I highly recommend the book for any security professional looking to add a privacy and data security guide to their reading list."

—Apu Pavithran, CEO Hexnode

"Privacy has become an ever-evolving landscape of regulation and controls. Ulf Mattsson leverages his decades of experience as a CTO and security expert to show how companies can achieve data compliance without sacrificing operability."

—Jim Ambrosini, CISSP, CRISC, Cybersecurity Consultant and Virtual CISO

"Privacy is not just a something that means help protect individuals and companies. It is the last line of defense for companies to protect customer and companies Crown Jewels. Where algorithms serve as insights and intelligence to growth and manage companies. Not to mention that regulation in this space is becoming ever more complicated. Ulf's book on privacy provides a commonsense approach to establish understand and proactively techniques this protect your organization data."

—Brian Albertson, Director of Programs at ISACA Atlanta Chapter and Technology Manager at State Farm

"In the last five years, the privacy conversation grew in volume and frequency. New standards and requirements certainly drove this conversation as did the increasing complexity of how applications are developed and deployed. Ulf captured the challenges privacy regulations create from the most basic challenges, to working with bleeding edge technologies such as Homomorphic Encryption and Quantum Computing. Any privacy professional should have this book as their reference during daily work."

—Branden Williams, Vice President Ping Identity and former VP/CTO, Security
& Fraud Solutions at First Data Corporation

"Controlling Privacy and the Use of Data Assets *clearly demonstrates that commercial success is tied to protecting data responsibly through collaborative efforts among those heading up privacy, security, technical, business, A Table of Contents and Introduction and legal governance measures. Ulf Mattsson lays out not just the rationale for accountable data governance, he provides clear strategies and tactics that every business leader should know and put into practice. As individuals, citizens and employees, we should all take heart that following his sound thinking can provide us all with a better future."*

—Richard Purcell, CEO Corporate Privacy Group & former Microsoft Chief
Privacy Officer

"Privacy is an increasingly important topic, but many companies either do not understand the importance, or do not understand how to solve the problems. A focus on profits over customer data privacy is particularly problematic. However, both customers and regulatory agencies are increasingly demanding improvements to privacy protection, and this book describes both the issues themselves and the various methods that exist to address them—which is good for everyone."

—Todd Arnold, retired Senior Technical Staff Member and Master Inventor in
cryptographic technology product development at IBM

"With the number of cyber startups going into DLP aka data protection, this book is great to understand what data protection is and where it fits in your cyber program. Got a question on how to secure a data? This book outlines every option you can have. Very pictorial book which is great for visual centric folks. you will not be able to put the book down. For all new CISO/CSO, this will help you to navigate the subject with legal, management, I.T. and the business. For season cyber leaders, this is a great refresher and eye opener to what other industries are doing."

—Alex Tan, Chief Security Officer at Paya & former I.T. Risk & Cybersecurity
Audit Director at Global Payments Inc.

"It is important to capture concepts of privacy over time. Those issues of the past still are relevant, but we also have new challenges to address. We need to understand that when it comes to privacy, no concepts ever really go away, we just keep adding to them. Reading Ulf's Table of Contents, he is covering a wide swath of important privacy topics that are currently relevant and that must be addressed now, and far into the foreseeable future. It looks like a book that those who want to learn more about privacy, and to continue to build upon their knowledge and understanding, will want to read, as well as add to their privacy book collection."

—Rebecca Herold, CEO, The Privacy Professor consultancy / CEO, Privacy &
Security Brainiacs SaaS Services

"Privacy, risk, compliance and security must be understood in context. Without a strong privacy program the company is exposed to billions of dollars of financial exposure, penalties and fines. Without privacy protection we run the risk of falling prey not just to cybercrime but fascism and other autocratic regimes. Ulf's book is timely and allows companies to understand privacy in context."

—Professor Ariel Evans, Chairperson of Cybersecurity Certification at Pace
University and CEO of Cyber Innovative Technologies

Controlling Privacy and the Use of Data Assets

Security, Audit and Leadership Series

Series Editor: Dan Swanson, Dan Swanson and Associates, Ltd.,
Winnipeg, Manitoba, Canada.

The *Security, Audit and Leadership Series* publishes leading-edge books on critical subjects facing security and audit executives as well as business leaders. Key topics addressed include Leadership, Cybersecurity, Security Leadership, Privacy, Strategic Risk Management, Auditing IT, Audit Management and Leadership

The Security Hippie
Barak Engel

Finding Your Granite: My Four Cornerstones of Personal Leadership
Douglas P. Pflug

Strong Security Governance through Integration and Automation: A Practical Guide to Building an Integrated GRC Framework for Your Organization
Priti Sikdar

Say What!? Communicate with Tact and Impact: What to say to get results at any point in an audit
Ann M. Butera

Auditing Information and Cyber Security Governance: A Controls-Based Approach
Robert E. Davis

The Security Leader's Communication Playbook: Bridging the Gap between Security and the Business
Jeffrey W. Brown

Modern Management and Leadership: Best Practice Essentials with CISO/CSO Applications
Mark Tarallo

Rising from the Mailroom to the Boardroom: Unique Insights for Governance, Risk, Compliance and Audit Leaders
Bruce Turner

Operational Auditing: Principles and Techniques for a Changing World (Second Edition)
Hernan Murdock

CyRM^{SM}: Mastering the Management of Cybersecurity
David X Martin

The Complete Guide for CISA Examination Preparation
Richard E. Cascarino

Blockchain for Cybersecurity and Privacy: Architectures, Challenges, and Applications
Yassine Maleh, Mohammad Shojafar, Mamoun Alazab, and Imed Romdhani

For more information about this series, please visit: https://www.routledge.com/Internal-Audit-and-IT-Audit/book-series/CRCINTAUDITA

Controlling Privacy and the Use of Data Assets

Volume 1

Who Owns the New Oil?

Ulf Mattsson

CRC Press
Taylor & Francis Group
Boca Raton London New York

CRC Press is an imprint of the
Taylor & Francis Group, an **informa** business

First Edition published 2022
by CRC Press
6000 Broken Sound Parkway NW, Suite 300, Boca Raton, FL 33487-2742

and by CRC Press
4 Park Square, Milton Park, Abingdon, Oxon, OX14 4RN

CRC Press is an imprint of Taylor & Francis Group, LLC

© 2022 Taylor & Francis Group, LLC

ISBN: 978-1-032-03912-1 (hbk)
ISBN: 978-1-032-03913-8 (pbk)
ISBN: 978-1-003-18966-4 (ebk)

DOI: 10.1201/9781003189664

Typeset in Times
by SPi Technologies India Pvt Ltd (Straive)

To my love and life partner, Catrine, and our children, Johanna and Markus. They are the greatest joys of my life.

Contents

SECTION I   Introduction and Vision

SECTION II   Data Confidentiality and Integrity

SECTION III   Users and Authorization

SECTION IV   Applications

Introduction

Thank you for taking the time to read my book about protecting your data.

This book is about what we learned from the failures of companies to stay on top of Data Privacy. And security and how they responded. It's not about the failure of simply any company, but the good companies—the kinds that many managers have admired and tried to emulate.

Some of them took data privacy and security more seriously than before after security-related incidents. They learned to build short- and long-term plans for better security. Basic core components for data privacy and security can be applied to new use cases and platforms when a new need arises.

Some of them learned before they experienced any major security incident. They learned from other companies in their industry how to implement best practices with granular Data Privacy and Security to achieve a defendable security posture. They assumed that an attacker might soon target their business or already be in their systems. The security landscape is increasingly changing and needs to be monitored to stay vigilant.

The book is a Journey to the Centre of Data Privacy and into the Interior of Data Security. I am painting a picture and a vision for this time in history that is transformative with new ways to think about data privacy and data security. We will review use cases from different industries and discuss data protection options and best practices. I will share inspiring and unforgettable projects in a data privacy and security journey with significant security, cloud, and databases vendors.

The book will review how new and old privacy-preserving techniques can provide practical protection for data in transit, use, and rest. We will position techniques like pseudonymization, anonymization, tokenization, homomorphic encryption, dynamic masking, and more.

The business-oriented Chapters 1–3 cover privacy, risks, threats, trends, evolution, best practices, roadmap, and vision. The rest of the book will describe how different implementations can help control privacy and use of data. It will also review some essential regulations and frameworks.

WHY DO WE NEED THIS BOOK?

This book will help readers grow out of a siloed mentality and into an enterprise risk management approach to regulatory compliance and technical roles, including technical data privacy and security issues.

Over the past five years, there has been an ever-intensifying discussion surrounding data protection and privacy. The European Union's General Data Protection Regulation (GDPR) and the State of California's California Consumer Privacy Act (CCPA) brought the reality of an individual's say in how his/her data is utilized in certain transactions to the forefront of corporate compliance programs. Most books on information security focus on only technical issues or only on high-level privacy issues. They neglect that organizations need to find the right balance between privacy techniques and security controls, which fit within the proscribed regulatory framework. Another element is customer needs and expectations. Customers expect robust security that protects their privacy but wants the process to be efficient and non-intrusive. Security and privacy are two sides of the same trust coin.

Many security experts excel at working with traditional technologies but fall apart in utilizing newer data privacy techniques to balance compliance requirements and the business utility of data.

This book will use practical lessons learned in applying real-life concepts and tools to help security leaders and their teams' craft and implement strategies. These projects deal with a variety of use cases and data types. A common goal is to find the right balance between compliance, privacy requirements, and data's business utility.

This book is based on a good understanding and experience of new and old technologies, emerging trends, and a broad experience from many projects in this domain. This book will provide unique context about the WHY (requirements and drivers), WHAT (what to do), and HOW (how to implement), and review current state and major forces representing challenges or driving change, what you should be trying to achieve, how do you do it, including discussions of different options. We will also discuss WHERE (in systems) and WHEN (roadmap). Unlike other general or academic texts, this book is being written to offer practical general advice, outline actionable strategies, and include templates for immediate use. The book contains matrices and diagrams needed to describe the topic matter.

WHO SHOULD READ THIS BOOK?

The book presents current real-world issues and technological mitigation strategies. The inclusions of the risks to both owners and custodians provide a strong case for why people should care.

The book reflects the perspective of a CTO and Chief Security Strategist. I worked in and with start-ups and some of the largest organizations in the world. The book is for board members, senior decision-makers, and global government policy officials—CISOs, CSOs, CPOs, CTOs, auditors, consultants, investors, and other people interested in data privacy and security. I will also embed a business perspective. Why is this an important topic for the board, audit committee, and senior management regarding achieving business objectives, strategies, and goals and applying the risk appetite and tolerance?

The focus is on Technical Visionary Leaders, including Chief Technology Officer, Chief Data Officer, Chief Privacy Officer, EVP/SVP/VP of Technology, Analytics, Data Architect, Chief Information Officer, EVP/SVP/VP of I.T., Chief Information Security Officer (CISO), Chief Risk Officer, Chief Compliance Officer, Chief Security Officer (CSO), EVP/SVP/VP of Security, Risk Compliance, Governance.

It can also be interesting reading for privacy regulators, especially those in developed nations with specialist privacy oversight agencies (government departments) across their jurisdictions (e.g., federal and state levels).

GUIDE TO READ THE BOOK

The chapters are related to each other, and the business-oriented sections are at the top, and the more technical-oriented chapters are at the bottom. You may start at the top left with Chapter 1 if you are interested in business aspects, Chapter 5 focuses on data protection, Chapter 10 on machine learning and utility, Chapter 9 on applications in hybrid cloud, or Appendix B, which is focused on governance. These are different potential entry points into the book based on interests:

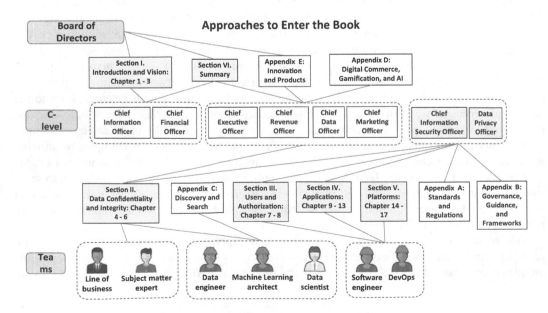

Some suggestions to start reading different chapters:

- You may begin with Chapter 1 if you are interested in business risks and threats to data privacy.
- You may start with Appendix B if you are interested in regulatory compliance or international industry standards. You may begin with Chapter 5 if you are interested in data protection techniques, homomorphic encryption, or quantum computing.
- You may start with Chapter 10 if you are interested in machine learning. You may begin with Chapter 9 if you are interested in applications and hybrid cloud.

Below is an overview of suggestions to start reading different chapters.

Section or Appendix	Title	Chapters	Board of Directors	Chief Information Security Officer	Chief Executive Officer	Chief Data Officer	Chief Revenue Officer	Data Privacy Officer	Chief Information Officer	Chief Marketing Officer	Chief Financial Officer	Line of business	Data scientist	Subject matter expert	DevOps	Data engineer	Machine Learning architect	Software engineer
					C-Level										Teams			
I	Introduction and Vision	1 – 3	y	y							y							
II	Data Confidentiality and Integrity	4 – 6		y				y				y	y	y		y	y	
III	Users and Authorization	7 – 8		y				y							y			y
IV	Applications	9 – 13		y				y							y			y
V	Platforms	14 – 17													y			y
VI	Summary	18	y		y	y	y			y								
A	Standards and Regulations			y				y										
B	Governance, Guidance, and Frameworks			y	y	y	y	y		y				y				
C	Discovery and Search												y			y	y	
D	Digital Commerce, Gamification, and AI		y		y	y	y			y								
E	Innovation and Products		y		y	y	y			y								

THE BUSINESS-ORIENTED CHAPTERS

The business-oriented chapters cover privacy, security, compliance, standards, regulations, trends, and roadmap:

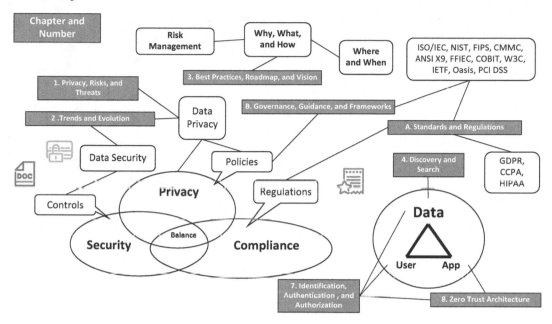

THE TECHNICAL CHAPTERS

The technical chapters cover encryption, cloud, and machine learning:

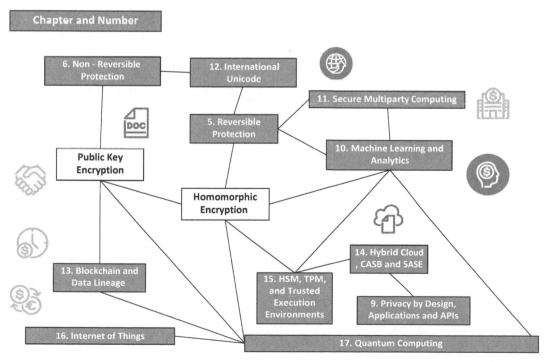

Acknowledgments

This book would not have been possible without the love and support of my wife, Catrine, my son Markus, and my daughter Johanna. They have always been there for me through the ups and downs of taking the leap of faith and moving from Sweden to the United States. It was exciting to build something from the ground up.

This book would have never made it here without my publisher, CRC Press. Especially Dan Swanson. He has been a joy to work with and the person who believed in this book when I pitched him the idea.

Moreover, I'd like to thank members of our team for their help. People on the technology side include Jeffrey Breen, Raul Ortega, Yigal Rozenberg, Nathan Vega, Vic Levy, Clyde Williamson, Joel Kutner, Marco Carmona, Pallavi Suryavanshi, Magnus Sirvio, Anders Lundberg, Thomas Valfridsson, Hans Altsten, Hans Meijer, Tamojit Das, Fredrik Mortberg, and many more.

I'd like to thank members on our business side, including Rick Farnell, Alex Vik, Gustav Vik, Per Johansson, Gordon Rapkin, Bob Fitzgerald, Ulf Dahl, Jan Johansson, David Morris, RJ Singh, and many more.

Moreover, I'd like to thank members of other organizations, including Elaine, Palmer, Sean Schmit, Kathy Kincaid, Bob Picciano, Tom Parenty, Sandeepan Banerjee, Mary Ann Davidson, Patrick Faith, Malcolm McWhinnie, Bart Preneel, Matt Curtin, and many more.

I would also like to thank all the people who have been involved in reviewing my book.

Last but not least, I want to offer my thanks to all of my readers. I appreciate the faith you are placing in me by reading my book

Thank you all. I am very fortunate to have you all in my life.

About the Author

Ulf Mattsson is a recognized information security and data privacy expert with a strong track record of more than two decades implementing cost-effective data security and privacy controls for global Fortune 500 institutions, including Citigroup, Goldman Sachs, GE Capital, BNY Mellon, AIG, Visa USA, Mastercard Worldwide, American Express, The Coca-Cola Company, Wal-Mart, BestBuy, KOHL's, Microsoft, IBM, Informix, Sybase, Teradata, and RSA Security. He is currently the Chief Security Strategist and earlier the Chief Technology Officer at Protegrity, a data security company he co-founded after working 20 years at IBM in software development. Ulf is an inventor of more than 70 issued US patents in data privacy and security.

Ulf is active in the information security industry as a contributor to the development of data privacy and security standards in the Payment Card Industry Data Security Standard (PCI DSS) and American National Standards Institute (ANSI) X9 for the financial industry. He is on the advisory board of directors at several organizations including PACE University, NY, in the area of cloud security and a frequent speaker at various international events and conferences, including the RSA Conference, and the author of more than 100 in-depth professional articles and papers on data privacy and security, including IBM journals, *IEEE Xplore*, *ISSA Journal*, and *ISACA Journal*.

Ulf holds a master's in physics in Engineering from Chalmers University of Technology in Sweden.

Section I

Introduction and Vision

1 Privacy, Risks, and Threats

INTRODUCTION

Why should we care about data privacy? It is often common to think about regulatory compliance as a tedious check-box exercise, but data protection is different. In Europe and other regions data privacy is an important human right we must strive to protect. When we get privacy and data protection wrong, real lives are affected. When privacy is attacked, it can often leave people feeling violated or upset.

"Data risk is the potential for business loss due to poor data governance," according to "What Is Data Risk Management?" Privacy regulations and threats to data are evolving and driving organizations to improve their security postures.

We will discuss this landscape.

IS DATA THE NEW WORLD CURRENCY OR IS TRUST?

The saying "Data is the new oil" was devised based on the growing importance of personal and organizational data according to "Privacy in Practice 2021: Data Privacy Trends, Forecasts":

New data privacy protection concerns are driving new regulations worldwide, and organizations are more mindful of the consequences of data loss. When protecting online data privacy and improving personal data protection, organizations that go beyond just complying with all the new requirements build trust with consumers and users and stand out from their competitors. Given the accelerating pace at which data is created and collected daily, some argue that information "has replaced oil as the world's most valuable resource" according to "Privacy in Practice 2021: Data Privacy Trends, Forecasts." Enterprises that can leverage the data they collect may derive a significant competitive advantage. The patterns, implications, and conclusions revealed by data can yield immense value, and effective data analysis can forecast market trends and indicate customer preferences, helping enterprises pivot to meet demand more successfully.

Data, the New World Currency, and Trust are becoming more and more important for people when sharing personal information.

DATA, USER, AND APP

The book is about "Data, User, App." I think "Data, Users, and Applications" are a central component in Data Privacy and Security.

DOI: 10.1201/9781003189664-2

Businesses have many holdings—sensitive assets—but data may be the most significant. It is studied to provide better services, innovations, and power new revenue feeds according to "About—Protegrity."

THE BALANCE BETWEEN PRIVACY, SECURITY, AND COMPLIANCE

The stakeholders have different interests that we need to balance:

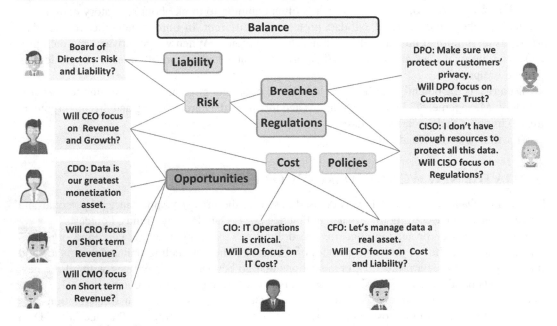

Source: Adapted from Gartner

PRIVACY ENGINEERING TALENT SHORTAGE

Demand for people who can apply detailed privacy requirements to business problems will exceed supply.

Privacy trends all point to a global requirement to design firm's operations around new trusted technology and data-ethics standards that are robust enough to stand up to continual inspection by external stakeholders according to "Privacy megatrend: Privacy engineering talent shortage."

Increasingly, companies will need high-demand staff educated in STEM subjects and those trained in philosophy and ethics. Developers will need privacy expertise, while attorneys will need to be conversant in technology. There's a "dangerous global scarcity of cybersecurity talent, including privacy professionals," according to Cyberseek, which reports that cyber roles take 21% longer to fill than other IT positions.

NEW UNCERTAINTY AND MORE SECURITY BREACHES

Data privacy is creating fear and trust concerns for IT teams, according to a study of 750 cybersecurity and IT professionals worldwide. It found that a makeshift approach to data security, misconfigured services, and confusion around novel cloud security models have created a predicament of confidence that requires making security part of the culture of their business according to "Shifting responsibility is causing uncertainty."

RISK AND TRUST

Risk aversion is common. Organizations risk appetite:

- According to ESG Data Point of the Week, "82% of the business, I.T., and cybersecurity executives believe that cyber-risk is greater today than it was two years ago."

Personal data is increasingly shared with external parties and may be sold to or exploited by different organizations globally. Data that we care about should be continuously protected. New techniques are evolving to enable a more secure sharing of data. I think some level of trust is needed when sharing personal data. We need to find the right balance of benefits and risks when sharing personal data.

THE EDELMAN TRUST BAROMETER

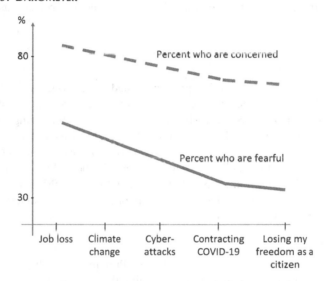

Source: Adapted from 2021 Edelman Trust Barometer

The Edelman Trust Barometer is an online survey that discovered that a nationally representative online sample in developed countries closely mirrors the general population. In nations with low penetration, a nationally representative online sample will be more affluent, educated, and urban than the general population.

PRIVACY AND TRUST

PRIVACY

We will discuss the convergence of data privacy principles, standards, and regulations, including General Data Protection Regulation (GDPR) and California Consumer Privacy Act (CCPA), and the role different technologies can play. We will use a couple of use cases from different industries and talk about different techniques and technologies and how particular data protection techniques can help. Privacy should be a proactive approach that helps organizations increase trust.

"Privacy is becoming a reason for consumers to purchase a product, in the same way, that organic, free trade and cruelty-free labels have driven product sales in the past decade," according to "Gartner Predicts for the Future of Privacy 2020." Recently, Gartner observed a decline in overall customer certification satisfaction, fraud, and increased privacy invasion. We have seen many recent examples in this area.

What Is Data Privacy?

Data privacy requirements exist to help ensure that sensitive consumer data stored by businesses and other organizations is applied for individuals' consent purposes and is otherwise redacted from data storage.

Why Is Data Privacy Important?

Data privacy has become a key concern for consumers. An analysis found that 81% of Americans believe that the risks of data collection by firms outweigh the benefits and that nearly 50% had stopped using a services provider due to privacy concerns according to "Overview – Exterro." Worldwide, a majority believe their data is less secure than it was five years ago. To address these concerns, governments around the world have been enacting privacy and data protection regulations.

Privacy Definitions

- This privacy goal is supported by principles and objectives, with detectable criteria: "Management, Notice, Choice and Consent, Collection, Use, retention and disposal, Access, Disclosure to third parties, Security for Privacy, Quality, Monitoring, and enforcement," according to IAPP (International Association of Privacy Professionals).
- Privacy depends on who you ask. It is the right to be let by yourself without interfering. According to "What is Privacy," information privacy is the right to have some power over how your personal information is collected and used. "What Is Privacy?" Most may think of massive data breaches, wearable tech, social networking, targeted advertising miscues—not to mention the Snowden revelations.

According to GAPP

- Privacy is specified in Generally Accepted Privacy Principles (GAPP) as "the rights and obligations of individuals and organizations concerning the collection, use, retention, disclosure, and disposal of personal information," according to "Service Organization Controls (SOC) Reports."
- GAPP is a structure for Chartered Accountants and Certified Public Accountants in supporting privacy programs. It is a component of SOC 2 according to "SOC 2 Compliance."
- The GAPP framework was previously identified as the AICPA/CICA Privacy Framework and is founded on a single privacy principle. Personally identifiable data must be collected, used, retained, and revealed in compliance with the responsibilities in the entity's privacy notice and with conditions set out in the GAPP issued by the AICPA/CICA.

GDPR and CCPA Definitions of Data (Sensitive and Personal)

In the European Union

The following personal data is defined as "sensitive and is subject to specific processing conditions"

- Personal data revealing racial or ethnic origin, political opinions, religious or philosophical beliefs according to "What personal data is considered sensitive?"
- Trade-union membership
- Genetic data
- Biometric data processed solely to identify a human being
- Health-related data
- Data concerning a person's sex life or sexual orientation

California Consumer Privacy Act

The Personal Information under the California Consumer Privacy Act (CCPA) specifies personal information broadly. It includes data that can identify, relate to, describe, be associated with, or be reasonably capable of being linked with a particular consumer or household.

Who Is Accountable for Privacy?

Gartner asked, who is accountable for privacy in your organization?

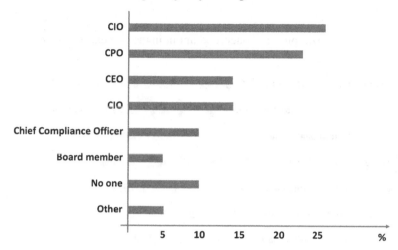

Source: Adapted from Gartner

Good for Business

Privacy Protection

Privacy protection solutions can empower businesses to activate and extract value from sensitive data and create trust by ensuring customers' and employees' privacy is always preserved, across the enterprise, wherever it resides and is accessed. This allows businesses to use sensitive data to fuel advanced analytics, machine learning, and AI—even as those initiatives migrate to cloud environments.

Privacy-Preserving Analytics and Secure Multiparty Computation

Organizations are increasingly worried about data security in numerous scenarios, including collecting and retaining sensitive personal data; processing personal information in external environments, such as the cloud; and information sharing. Commonly implemented solutions do not deliver strong protection from data theft and privacy, according to "Privacy-Preserving Analytics and Secure Multiparty Computation."

Privacy and risk management specialists are particularly concerned about the privacy and security of data used in analytics and shared externally. Compliance with privacy laws such as the US State of California Consumer Privacy Act, the GDPR, and other emerging regulations worldwide require methods for secure handling of sensitive data. New approaches for privacy-preserving computation that are transparent to business procedures can open new openings and help find the proper balance between privacy, security, and compliance.

Encrypting data at rest is not enough to avoid data violations. Data-at-rest encryption produces a "crypto boundary," outside of which data is clear. Because plaintext data is normally needed for processing, this boundary often exists below the point where a compromise is feasible. Data-at-rest encryption also does not support circumstances in which data has to be shared with other busi-nesses. For the data to be valuable, it must be accessible as plaintext within applications, signifi-cantly reducing encryption's protection capacity. A downside of typical data masking techniques is that they do not broadly support transactional or behavioral data protection. These restrictions of data-at-rest encryption and data masking drive an increased focus on finding new techniques for data protection—particularly advanced approaches that can protect data in contexts where traditional encryption and data masking approaches cannot.

RISK

Study about risks that organizations are concerned about in the context of privacy:

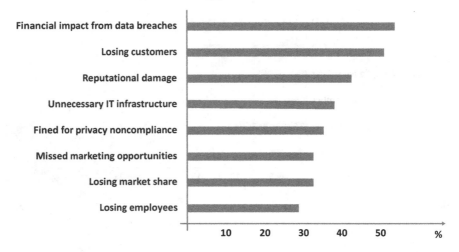

Source: Adapted from Gartner

Cyber-attacks and pandemics are becoming more and more real threats in many people's minds. This is the "Global Risk Perception" from World Economic Forum from 2019:

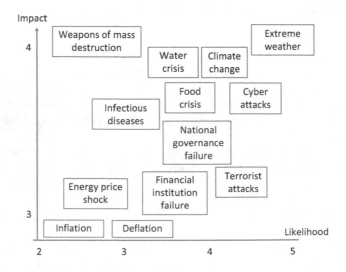

Source: Adapted from World Economic Forum, 2019

Organizations' top risk concerns:

Area	%
Financial impact	46
Losing customers	45
Reputational damage	44

Source: Gartner.

DATA SECURITY IS KEEPING IT PROFESSIONALS CONCERNED

This study found that IT professionals are more concerned about their firm's data security than the security at home. IT professionals are much more concerned about company financials and intellectual property security than their home security, according to "New Study: I.T. Pros Are More Worried About Corporate."

They are concerned about cloud services. Eighty percent are worried that cloud service providers they do business with will become their competitors in their own business.

- "75% of I.T. professionals view the public cloud as more secure than their own data centers, yet 92% of I.T. professionals do not trust their organization is well prepared to secure public cloud services."
- "Nearly 80% of I.T. professionals say that new breaches experienced by other businesses have increased their organization's focus on securing data moving forward."

LEGACY DATA SECURITY APPROACHES LEAVE IT PROFESSIONALS SCRAMBLING

IT professionals use an assortment of different cybersecurity products to try and address data security, but face a difficult battle as these systems are seldom configured correctly, according to "New Study: I.T. Pros Are More Worried About Corporate."

- "78% of organizations use more than 50 discrete cybersecurity products to address security issues; 37% use more than 100 cybersecurity products."

Organizations that discovered misconfigured cloud services experienced ten or more data loss incidents in the last year.

- "59% of organizations shared that employees with privileged cloud accounts have compromised those credentials by a spear-phishing attack."

The most common types of misconfigurations are, according to "New Study: I.T. Pros Are More Worried About Corporate":

- Over-privileged accounts (37%)
- Exposed types of server workloads (35%)
- Lack of multi-factor authentication for access to critical functions (33%)

Organizations are moving more business-critical workloads to the cloud than ever before. Still, growing cloud consumption has created new blind spots as IT teams and cloud service providers work to understand their responsibilities in securing data according to "Shifting responsibility is causing uncertainty." Shifting responsibility is a huge issue, and confusion has left IT security teams scrambling to address a growing threat landscape.

- Nearly 90% of companies are using SaaS, and 76% are using IaaS. Fifty percent expect to move all their data to the cloud in the next two years.

- Shared responsibility security models are confusing. Only 8% of IT security executives state that they fully understand the shared responsibility security model.
- 70% of IT professionals think too many specialized tools are required to secure their public cloud footprint.
- 75% of IT professionals have experienced data loss from a cloud service more than once.

We will discuss this topic more in Volume II of this book.

WHO IS SHARING AND SELLING YOUR DATA?

Who Owns Your Data?

The increasing number of private events and data breaches is destroying brands and customer trust. We will discuss how business prioritization can use a finance-based data risk assessment according to "Gaining Advantage Against Ransomware":

- More than 60 nations have introduced privacy regulations, and by 2023, 65% of the world's inhabitants will have their data covered under fresh privacy regulations, according to Gartner.

Protect Data, Users, and Applications

If your organization collected the data then you are also liable for protection of that data, even if you outsource the operation or storage of that data.

That's Where the Money Is

The man who said that he was robbing banks "because that's where the money is" was named one of the first fugitives to the Top Ten list according to "'Give Me the Money!': Notorious Bank Robberies in Washington."

PRIVACY, SECURITY, AND COMPLIANCE

SECURITY DOES NOT IMPLY PRIVACY

Privacy rules can be defined in a privacy policy. Security controls can enforce a privacy policy. Security does not imply privacy.

Sometimes the overlap between privacy and security is only 10%. Security may be 80% technology, and the rest are people and processes. Privacy may be 30% legal aspects if we think, for example, about GDPR:

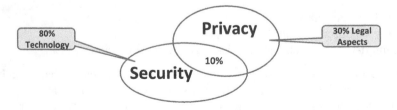

SECURITY CONTROLS CAN ENFORCE A PRIVACY POLICY

Security controls can enforce a privacy policy. Compliance with regulations may require controls to be implemented. A good security posture can be achieved by adding organization-specific controls beyond the regulatory requirements.

The cloud configuration should be validated to enforce the established policy rules and security controls defined by the data subject or owner.

Examples of some of the high-level relations between data, users, apps, privacy, security, and compliance:

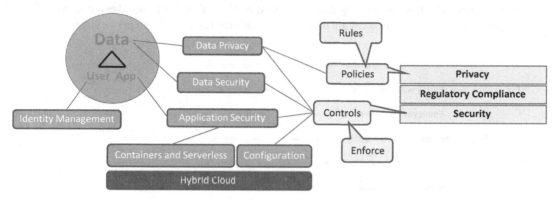

Privacy vs. Security

Data privacy is centered on the use and governance of personal information—things like putting policies in place to ensure that users' personal information is not collected, shared, and used inappropriately. Security centers more on protecting data from evil attacks and the exploitation of taken data for gain. While security is required for protecting data, it's not sufficient for addressing privacy, according to "What Is Privacy."

Asking "Why, What, and How"

I think that is a starting point in asking, "Why, What, and How" before taking the next steps and selecting tools. It is good to have knowledge of the threat landscape and to review privacy regulations that then can define our privacy regulations with rules that we need to implement and enforce via security controls.

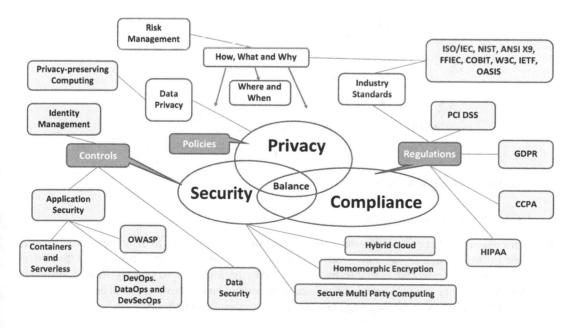

THREATS

CONCERNS OF BREACHES AND SHARING DATA

The global consulting firm FTI reported in 2020 that organizations' two top concerns regarding data privacy are cyber breaches and sharing data with third parties. We will discuss these two areas later in this book. The report cited that organizations' top concerns regarding data privacy were:

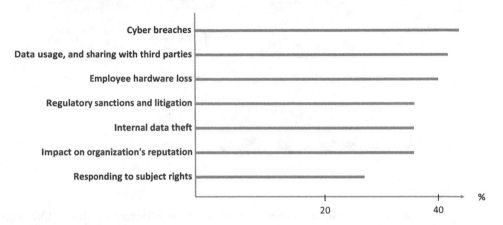

Source: Adapted from FTI

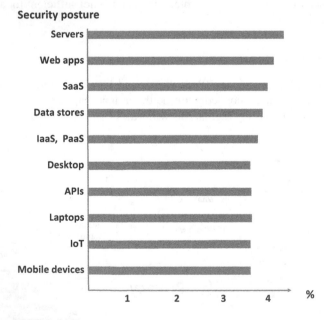

Source: Adapted from (ISC)2, 2021

RANSOMWARE AND OTHER ATTACKS

Attackers may already be in your system and continually find new ways to avoid detection. Ensure that your information is private and protected in transit, in use, in memory, and at rest. Sensitive information can be safe and available by a robust data backup plan to quickly restore systems. Multilayered security can help create a good security posture and discover unusual activity on your sensitive data according to "Protecting Data from Ransomware and Other Attacks."

SUPPLY CHAINS

SolarWinds Attack

Modern software is made using third-party and open-source components. This assembly line of public code packets and third-party APIs is known as a supply chain. According to "Want in on the next $100B in cybersecurity? – TechCrunch," attacks that aim for this construction line are referred to as supply chain attacks.

Existing application-security tools can mitigate some supply chain attacks for open-source dependencies, such as Bridgecrew to automate security engineering and fix misconfigurations and Veracode for security scanning.

But other vulnerabilities can be extremely difficult to detect. Take the supply chain assault that took center stage—the SolarWinds hack of 2020—in which a small piece of code was changed in a SolarWinds update before spreading to 18,000 different companies, all of which relied on SolarWinds software for network monitoring or other services.

SolarWinds hackers gave themselves top administrative privileges to spy on victims undetected.

A Breach for the Ages Went Unnoticed

FireEye declared hackers had taken copies of security testing tools, leading to a broader examination that found the business had been compromised by spyware through an IT management and security platform sold by the software company SolarWinds according to "Cybercrime Never Ends; Nor Should End-to-End Data Protection."

THE THREAT LANDSCAPE

Incidents involving Phishing, Ransomware, Misconfiguration, Stolen credentials, and misdelivery continued to rise in 2020, according to Verizon DBIR, and 10% of all breaches contained ransomware. The US Secret Service noted that most organizations had sufficient information backup. Still, cyber actors shifted their focus to the exfiltration of sensitive data. They threatened to publicize it unless the additional ransom was paid according to "Protecting Data from Ransomware and other Attacks."

The United States had 80% of the ransomware victims in 2020, followed by Australia with 79%, Telecom had 76% of the victims, followed by Education with 73%, according to (ISC)[2]. This is the tendency in ransomware fees, according to Bankinfo Security:

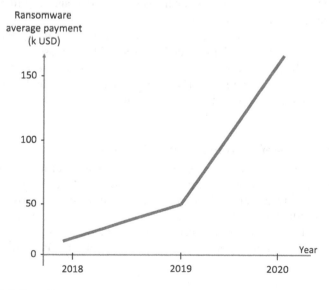

Adapted from BankInfoSecurity.com

In early 2021 ransomware struck " COLONIAL PIPELINE, QUANTA, NATIONAL BASKETBALL ASSOCIATION (NBA), BRENNTAG, ACER, JBS FOODS, AXA, and other victims," according to Illinois.touro.edu. A payment of between US$7.5 million and $50 million was claimed in several of these attacks. The criminal group disrupted gas resources all along the East Coast of the United States, gaining stole to more than 3 TB of data, including Apple product blueprints and other confidential data according to "Protecting Data from Ransomware and other Attacks."

Healthcare Organizations Are Increasingly Targeted

Healthcare organizations are particularly vulnerable and increasingly targeted by ransomware. You should consider instantly protecting PHI (Protected Health Information) and other sensitive data through encryption. "More than 90 percent of all healthcare organizations suffered at least one security breach in the past three years" and ransomware accounted for more than half of those breaches in 2020, according to "The Business Explainer: Encrypted Healthcare Data". Ransomware is also a complicated disruption to business in the short- and long-term. That's why good data governance assures that your healthcare organizations can continue to find new cures, improve one-on-one relationships with patients, and pursue other data-driven initiatives without delay.

Ransomware Is Costly and Disruptive to Operations

The cost of a ransomware attack is exorbitant: IBM estimates it's $4.62 million. According to Sophos, it costs $1.3 million, on average, for a healthcare organization to recover from ransomware, while a single data breach in healthcare costs $9.23 million. To make matters worse, in 2020, a healthcare organization faced anywhere from 15 to 21 days of downtime after an attack, says the ransomware response firm Coveware.

Compliance Risks Can Hamper Business for Years

Beyond a ransomware attack's freeze of data and systems, there are larger ramifications that can pose lasting damage to your organization's financial stability and image, according to "The Business Explainer: Encrypted Healthcare Data."

But all is not lost. Tokenization conceals sensitive data by substituting elements with a randomly generated value that can only be revealed to users with permission. Aside from protecting data, tokenization eases the problems of compliance. Regulators allow pseudonymization, including through tokenization, as an effective form of data encryption. See article 4, paragraph 5 of GDPR and "The Business Explainer: Encrypted Healthcare Data."

Ransomware Poses an Existential Threat to Your Company

Ransomware assaults on patient data and medical systems endanger more than the bottom line: They also inhibit patient care. Increased ransomware assaults come as healthcare organizations rely more than ever on data-driven tools. A ransomware attack delays those efforts. Healthcare is the highly trusted industry to protect data and individual privacy, according to McKinsey. Your ability to end ransomware from interrupting healthcare services will only bolster your organization's reputation to manage sensitive information and pursue new ways of innovating with data.

Organizations targeted by Ransomware attacks:

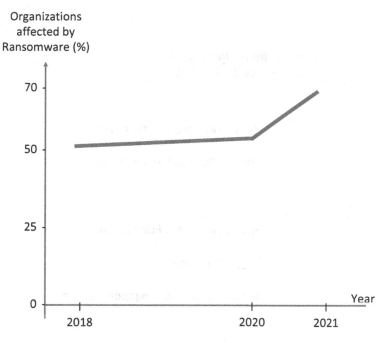

Adapted from (ISC)2

Industries targeted by Ransomware attacks:

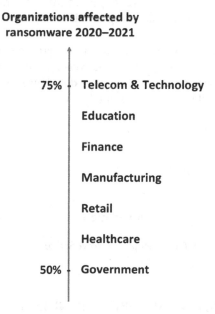

Source: Adapted from isc2.org

Healthcare organizations are particularly vulnerable and severely disrupted by ransomware. Some countries have a larger % of organizations that are targeted by ransomware attacks:

Organizations affected by ransomware 2020–2021

80% — **Australia, USA, Saudi Arabia**

China, Mexico, Turkey, Brazil

Spain, Germany, France, Canada

Italy, Colombia

56% — **South Africa, UK, Singapore, Japan**

Source: Adapted from isc2.org

eCrime Ecosystem

Throughout 2020, major ransomware increasingly threatened organizations in every industry worldwide—and the threat continues according to "Using Threat Intelligence to Get Ahead of Ransomware Attacks."

There is a vast, well-connected eCrime ecosystem with criminal adversaries existing to support enterprise ransomware operations. Many of these adversaries specialize and work in concert with each other, combining malicious services, ransomware distribution methods, and monetization techniques to maximize their overall success and profitability.

Services   **Distribution**   **Monetization**

Source: Adapted from 2021 Global Threat Report, CrowdStrike

BREACHES, DATA LEAKS, AND SECURITY SPENDING

BREACHES AND SECURITY SPENDING

Is there a correlation between number of breaches, data leaks, and security spending budget?

BREACHES AND SECURITY SPENDING

Number of breaches compared to security spending budget. Entertainment, consumer products, technology (software and internet services), and public are in the upper part. Finance is in the bottom part:

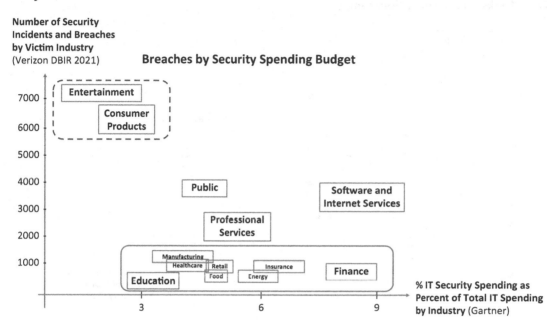

DATA LEAKS PER INDUSTRY

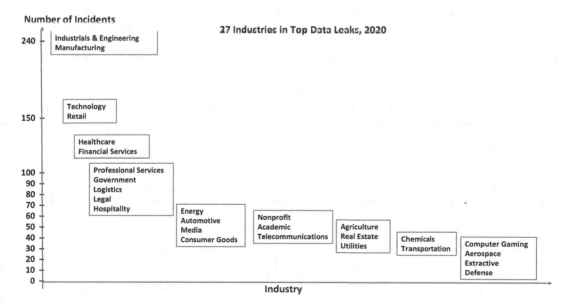

Source: Adopted from Crowdstrike

SECURITY SPENDING AND BREACHES

Is there a correlation between the number of breaches, data leaks, and security spending budget?

DATA LEAKS AND SECURITY SPENDING

The number of data leaks compared to security spending budget. Manufacturing, retail, technology (software and internet services), and healthcare are in the upper part:

Data Leaks and Security Spending

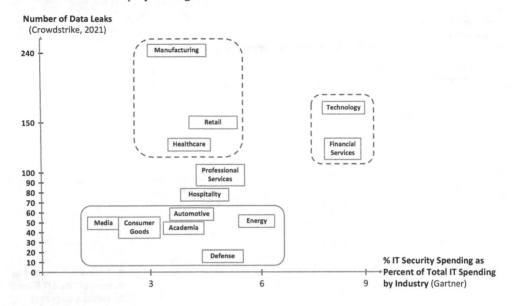

DATA BREACH COSTS INCREASED

Healthcare Data Breach Costs Increased

The healthcare sector keeps very sensitive and private information. Is that data adequately protected?

According to "Healthcare Organizations Are the Top Target for Ransomware Attackers," the healthcare sector was the most targeted vertical for ransomware in 2020. Ransomware attacks seen in the first half of 2021 show a 102% increase from 2020's numbers according to "Ransomware Keeps Healthcare in Crosshairs."

Healthcare data breach costs increased from an average total cost of $7.13 million in 2020 to $9.23 million in 2021, a 29.5% increase. More investments in Healthcare data protection can hopefully lower the loss of sensitive data.

The Cost of a Data Breach Is a 10% Rise

The cost of a data breach in 2021 is US$ 4.24 million. This is a 10% rise from the average cost in 2019, which was $3.86 million according to "What is the Cost of a Data Breach in 2021?" The $180 per record cost of a personally identifiable information breach is higher than payment card data.

The Cost of Doing Business

There is a cost of doing business. For example, the card brands balance easy consumer experience with the cost of security solutions and payment fraud.

Shoplifting and organized retail crime may be higher than computer crime.

The NRSS indicates that the average dollar loss per shoplifting incident was reported as $559 according to "Shedding Light on Retail Theft Statistics."

Protect Your Data from Ransomware

In many cases, the attack's goal isn't just to encrypt data according to "Detect, Protect, Recover: How Modern Backup Applications Can Protect You From Ransomware."

ATTACKS ON DATA

Attacks at Different Layers

Data protection at different layers can protect the data from exposure at each system layer:

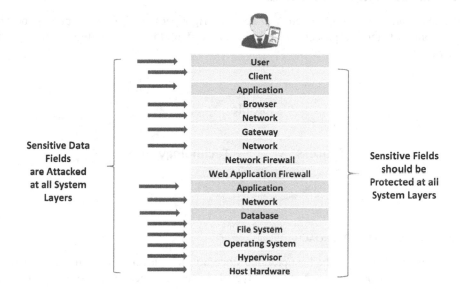

Awareness Training May Not Be Enough

The attack surface is increasing from multiple layers:

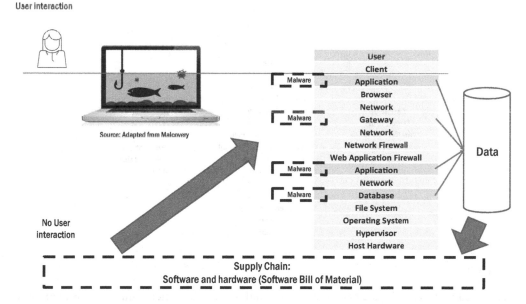

Source: Adapted from Malcovery

SolarWinds' Orion Platform software secretly dispensed malware to spy on the users and extract documents containing sensitive data.

The massive supply chain breach occurred when network management software from SolarWinds had malware inserted into a trusted software update, and this attack has exposed over 18,000 of their customers who used the affected software, many of them government agencies, to potential breaches according to "Life after the SolarWinds supply chain attack."

A BALANCED SECURITY APPROACH

Find a balanced data security approach. You need the right people. You need a process before you can benefit from tools for that process. You may hear a different bias and preference from the teams that are involved:

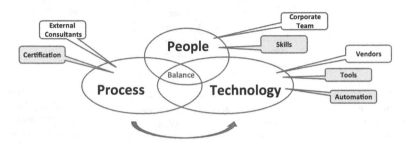

A LAYERED DATA SECURITY APPROACH

A layered security approach is the best practice since no single layer is enough. Data, applications, and users are core for protection. Network layer defenses are becoming less effective when the traditional perimeter changes and zero-knowledge architecture is evolving as a comprehensive defense against many attacks.

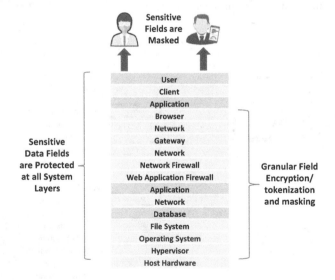

SUMMARY

We discussed why we should care about privacy and that cyber hygiene must start as a board-level conversation. We discussed a top-down approach to create strong ransomware mitigation with zero-trust access and a multilayered defense that can help to create a good security posture.

We discussed the common thinking about regulatory compliance as a tedious check-box exercise, but data protection is different. Data risk is the potential for business loss due to poor data governance and privacy regulations and threats to data are organizations to improve their security postures.

We will discuss these topics in separate chapters of this book.

BIBLIOGRAPHY

1. "Opposition calls for rethink on data storage". *e-Health Insider (UK)*. December 2007. Archived from the originalon.
2. A CEO primer on data privacy strategy, https://www.linkedin.com/pulse/ceo-primer-data-privacy-strategy-jay-cline/?trk=eml-email_series_follow_newsletter_01-hero-1-title_link&midToken=AQFP49 5TjUj8Zg&fromEmail=fromEmail&ut=0pFFRNK_W_Q9U1
3. "German Doctors Say No to Centrally Stored Patient Records". *e-Health Insider (UK)*. January 2008. Archived from the original on 12 October 2008.
4. Fernández-Alemán, J. L., Sánchez-Henarejos, A., Toval, A., Sánchez-García, A. B., Hernández-Hernández, I., and Fernandez-Luque, L. (June 2015). "Analysis of Health Professional Security Behaviors in a Real Clinical Setting: An Empirical Study". *International Journal of Medical Informatics*. 84 (6): 454–467. doi:10.1016/j.ijmedinf.2015.01.010. PMID 25678101.
5. E.U. -What Personal Data is Considered Sensitive?, https://ec.europa.eu/info/law/law-topic/data-protection/reform/rules-business-and-organisations/legal-grounds-processing-data/sensitive-data/what-personal-data-considered-sensitive_en
6. Hackread, https://www.hackread.com/solarwinds-supply-chain-attack-affected-organizations/#:~:text= SolarWinds%20Attack%20In%20December%202020%2C%20the%20cyberworld%20was,to%20 trojanize%20the%20company%E2%80%99s%20most%20widely%20used%20software.
7. Why It's Time for Business Leaders to Take Greater Accountability on Data Privacy, https:// www.darkreading.com/application-security/why-it-s-time-for-business-leaders-to-take-greater-accountability-on-data-privacy?utm_campaign=Oktopost-Rick+Farnell+Protegrity+Coverage& utm_content=Oktopost-LinkedIn&utm_medium=social&utm_source=LinkedIn
8. ESG Data Point of the Week, https://www.esg-global.com/data-point-of-the-week-08-16-21?utm_ campaign=Oktopost-General+industry+News&utm_content=Oktopost-LinkedIn&utm_medium= social&utm_source=LinkedIn
9. https://nvlpubs.nist.gov/nistpubs/SpecialPublications/NIST.SP.1800-26.pdf
10. Using Threat Intelligence to Get Ahead of Ransomware Attacks, https://www.crowdstrike.com/resources/ crowdcasts/exposing-the-ecrime-ecosystem/
11. Best Practices for Lowering Cyber Insurance Costs and Cyber Risk, networkworld.com/arti-cle/3146519/best-practices-for-lowering-cyber-insurance-costs-and-cyber-risk.html#:~:text=If%20 your%20cyber%20insurance%20vendors%20do%20offer%20incentives,in%20reducing%20cyber%20 risk%3A%20Build%20a%20risk-aware%20culture
12. GDPR: Three Ways the World Has Changed in the Privacy Law's First Two Years, https://www.cpomaga-zine.com/data-protection/gdpr-three-ways-the-world-has-changed-in-the-privacy-laws-first-two-years/
13. What Personal data is Considered Sensitive?, https://ec.europa.eu/info/law/law-topic/data-protection/ reform/rules-business-and-organisations/legal-grounds-processing-data/sensitive-data/what-personal-data-considered-sensitive_en
14. Seven Privacy Megatrends: A Roadmap to 2030, https://www.pwc.com/us/en/services/consulting/ cybersecurity-privacy-forensics/library/seven-privacy-megatrends.html
15. The Economist, "The World's Most Valuable Resource Is No Longer Oil, but Data," 6 May 2017, www.economist.com/leaders/2017/05/06/the-worlds-most-valuable-resource-is-no-longer-oil-but-data 33Hautala, L
16. "COVID-19 Contact Tracing Apps Create Privacy Pitfalls Around the World," Cnet, 8 August 2020, www.cnet.com/news/covid-contact-tracing-apps-bring-privacy-pitfalls-around-the-world/
17. 4Hsu, J. "Survey Finds Americans Skeptical of Contact Tracing Apps," *IEEE Spectrum*, 7 July 2020, https://spectrum.ieee.org/the-human-os/biomedical/devices/survey-finds-americans-skeptical-of-contact-tracing-apps
18. "SOC 2 Compliance". Imperva, Retrieved 2019-11-18. https://www.imperva.com/learn/data-security/ soc-2-compliance/
19. Global Threat Report 2021, https://go.crowdstrike.com/rs/281-OBQ-266/images/Report2021GTR.pdf
20. "Generally Accepted Privacy Principles (GAPP) << CIPP Guide", https://www.journalofaccountancy. com/Issues/2011/Jul/20103191.htm
21. Official Website of the European Union, https://ec.europa.eu/info/law/law-topic/data-protection/reform/ rules-business-and-organisations/legal-grounds-processing-data/sensitive-data/what-personal-data-considered-sensitive_en

22. California Consumer Privacy Act FAQs for Covered Businesses, https://www.jacksonlewis.com/publication/california-consumer-privacy-act-faqs-covered-businesses

23. The Business Explainer: Encrypted Healthcare Data Diminishes Ransomware Risk, https://www.protegrity.com/protegrity-blog/the-business-explainer-encrypted-healthcare-data-diminishes-ransomware-risk

24. Privacy-Preserving Analytics and Secure Multiparty Computation, https://sf-prod.isaca.org/resources/isaca-journal/issues/2021/volume-2/privacy-preserving-analytics-and-secure-multiparty-computation

25. Why the OPM Hack Is Far Worse Than You Imagine, https://www.lawfareblog.com/why-opm-hack-far-worse-you-imagine

26. Equifax Data Breach FAQ: What Happened, Who was Affected, What was the Impact?, https://www.csoonline.com/article/3444488/equifax-data-breach-faq-what-happened-who-was-affected-what-was-the-impact.html

27. The OPM Hack Explained: Bad Security Practices Meet China's Captain America, https://www.csoonline.com/article/3318238/the-opm-hack-explained-bad-security-practices-meet-chinas-captain-america.html

28. Willie Sutton, https://www.fbi.gov/history/famous-cases/willie-sutton

29. Theft Types Over Time, https://public.tableau.com/profile/federal.trade.commission#!/vizhome/IdentityTheftReports/TheftTypesOverTime

30. Pro-Privacy Lawmakers Secure a Vote to Protect Browsing Data from Warrantless FBI Collection, https://gizmodo.com/pro-privacy-lawmakers-secure-a-vote-to-protect-browsing-1843632063

31. Board Governance of Cyber Risk, https://normanmarks.wordpress.com/2021/06/28/board-governance-of-cyber-risk/

32. Data Security Still a Major Concern for Most Consumers, https://www.helpnetsecurity.com/2021/06/10/data-security-concern/

33. Shifting Responsibility is Causing Uncertainty, https://www.helpnetsecurity.com/2020/05/18/shifting-responsibility-security/

34. SolarWinds Supply Chain Attack Affected 250 Organizations, https://www.hackread.com/solarwinds-supply-chain-attack-affected-organizations/

35. Life after the SolarWinds supply chain attack, https://www.securelink.com/blog/life-after-the-solarwinds-supply-chain-attack/

36. Edelman Trust Barometer, https://www.edelman.com/sites/g/files/aatuss191/files/2021-01/2021-edelman-trust-barometer.pdf

37. "Give Me the Money!": Notorious Bank Robberies in Washington, https://www.washingtonian.com/2008/10/01/give-me-the-money-notorious-bank-robberies-in-washington/

38. Privacy Megatrend: Privacy Engineering Talent Shortage, https://www.pwc.com/us/en/services/consulting/cybersecurity-privacy-forensics/library/seven-privacy-megatrends/privacy-engineering-talent-shortage.html

39. What Is Data Risk Management?. https://www.datto.com/blog/what-is-data-risk-management

40. Privacy in Practice 2021: Data Privacy Trends, Forecasts, https://www.isaca.org/resources/news-and-trends/isaca-now-blog/2021/privacy-in-practice-2021-data-privacy-trends-forecasts-and-challenges

41. Gartner Predicts for the Future of Privacy 2020, https://www.gartner.com/smarterwithgartner/gartner-predicts-for-the-future-of-privacy-2020

42. Want in on the Next $100B in Cybersecurity?—TechCrunch, https://techcrunch.com/2021/06/23/want-in-on-the-next-100b-in-cybersecurity/

43. Overview—Exterro, https://www.exterro.com/basics-of-data-privacy

44. What is Privacy. https://iapp.org/about/what-is-privacy/

45. New Study: I.T. Pros Are More Worried About Corporate …, https://www.oracle.com/corporate/pressrelease/cloud-threat-report-2020-051420.html

46. Gaining Advantage Against Ransomware, https://www.brighttalk.com/webcast/18768/509029

47. Protecting Data from Ransomware and other Attacks, https://www.globalsecuritymag.com/Protecting-Data-from-Ransomware,20210831,115566.html

48. Service Organization Controls (SOC) Reports, http://sfisaca.org/images/FC15_Presentations/C33.pdf

49. About—Protegrity, https://www.protegrity.com/about

50. Cybercrime Never Ends; Nor Should End-to-End Data Protection, https://www.protegrity.com/protegrity-blog/cybercrime-never-ends-nor-should-end-to-end-data-protection

2 Trends and Evolution

INTRODUCTION

Data risks, privacy regulations, and threats are evolving, and we will discuss this changing landscape. This chapter is divided into sections about data growth, privacy, threats, trust, security, products, and privacy laws that are changing.

DATA GROWTH

We may need to find more effective ways to control data privacy and security for the growing amount of data stored.

Estimated Terabytes of Data Worldwide, 2019–2024

Growth of the Global DataSphere is driven more by the data that we consume and analyze than what we create according to IDC's "Worldwide Global Datasphere Forecast."

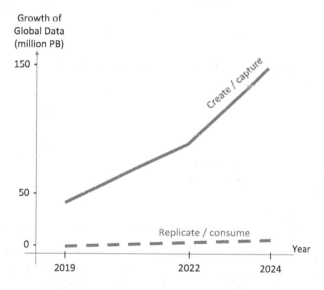

Adapted from IDC Worldwide Global Datasphere Forecast 2020–2024

TRENDS IN CONTROL OF DATA

Over time more data is exposed in an environment that may not be in our corporate control. We may have:

- Contracted providers of SaaS and other services in the cloud
- Outsourced testing of applications
- Individuals that are storing data locally or using services from providers that are not contracted by corporate

DOI: 10.1201/9781003189664-3

More Data Is Outside Corporate Control

This data may be regulated or exposed to attacks:

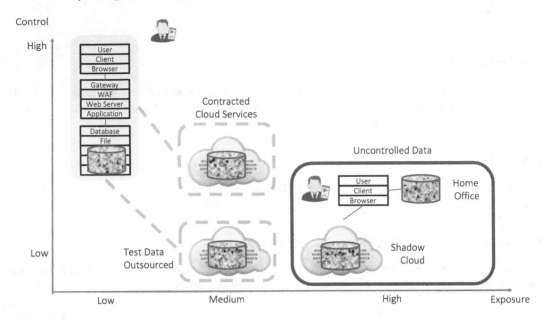

What Can We Do?

We may not be able to control or prevent the data flow, but we can protect sensitive data before it leaves our controlled environment:

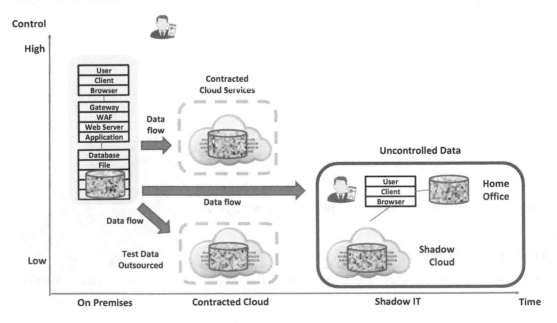

Trends in Data Protection Integration

Major implementations of data protection into networks and data management infrastructures have evolved in steps since 2000.

These are some major Data Protection integration trends:

- Implementations of granular data protection started in 2000 with several major database vendors.
- Tokenization was introduced to PCI DSS and the payment systems industry to provide a higher level of security control, flexibility, and application transparency. Tokenization was increasingly used for PII data to provide a higher level of security control and separation of duties.
- Integration into networks with CASB solutions followed that.
- They were later followed by integration with data discovery tools and database catalogs.

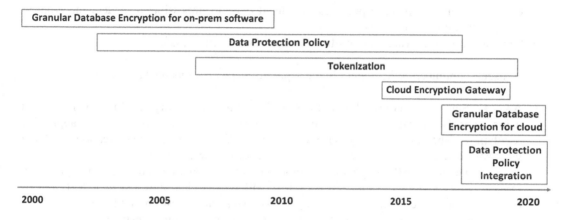

Automation of integration and policy management followed these milestones. We will discuss this more in separate chapters and in Volume II of this book.

Confluence of Data Security Controls

Amalgamation of more comprehensive Data Security Platforms (DSP):

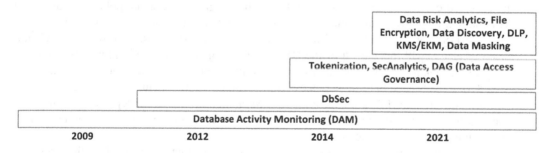

Source: Adopted from Gartner, 2021

DSP Future State

This will be DSP Future State according to Gartner:

1. Consistent visibility on (sensitive) data, data stores, policies and applicable regulations.
2. High levels of integration capability and simplified deployment models.
3. Ease of administration via a consolidated policy control plane.
4. Democratized access to the technologies required to secure data thoroughly.
5. Roles moving from being focused on a single product or technology to being multidimensional.
6. Data stores for AI and ML, for example data lakes, will increase in importance.

7. Complex administration using disparate products that frequently have no API integration.
8. Rudimentary or nonexistent sensitive-data visibility and control.
9. Lack of hybrid cloud capabilities. DSPs that are partially still not ready for cloud or solutions that lack support for on-premises data stores.
10. Very long planning and implementation cycles. The implementation of a new data security product takes one year or longer. Eventually it delivers only part of what was envisioned.
11. Immature or nonexistent capabilities for privacy enhanced computation technologies (PECT).
12. Not all vendors currently address the full set of required and recommended DSP capabilities illustrated in Figure above.
13. Pattern-driven data discovery capabilities that find patterns or well-known identifiers without considering the context.
14. Frustrating amount of false positives making it close to impossible to understand what is really happening to your data.
15. Separate and siloed teams responsible for each data security capability.

We will discuss a number of these areas in the separate chapters of this book, for example:

- Area #1: Sensitive-data visibility and control is a critical capability of DSP. This is enabled using a consistent overview of data silos, data security policies, controls and the applicable regulations. The best DSPs will have semantic capabilities for data classification—judging what something really is, rather than relying on preconfigured identifiers.
- Area #2: The use of API integration and cloud-delivered services will increase in importance. DSP provides a number of integration options with popular data stores, such as API integration, agent software or network gateways. Customers can choose the DSP implementation architecture that is least/noninvasive in their environment. Customers can choose to position enforcement points as close to data assets as possible. This will maximize protection, while minimizing user impact.
- Area #3: The DSP management control plane is decoupled from data types and control objects, allowing centralized administration. The administrative interface will allow data security policy to be managed from a single console and applied regardless of the data silo or the required control objective. AI and ML will be integral to automate policy creation. Full API enablement allows automation and integration with existing processes and tools.
- Area #4: DSPs are available as stand-alone tools and cloud-based service offerings. Cloud-based offerings will make most of the DSP security objects available via low threshold API integration, making best in class data security controls achievable and affordable for many.
- Area #10: Clients need to bring in place complex (product) architectures and processes before they can configure the first policies or reports. Meaningful proof of concepts has become rare. Vendors frequently shore up prices through feature licenses or complex licensing constructs that no mere mortal can understand.
- Area #11: Established vendors frequently do not have the adoption of PECT on the roadmaps of their DSP, whereas newer products from startup companies frequently have PECT capabilities included. On either side, the benefits, scope, and limitations of PECT are not communicated well making it difficult for clients to adopt them.
- Area #12: Some DSP offerings only focus on adapting traditional product platforms rather than replatforming their data security capabilities entirely. DSPs sometimes provide only a partial set of capabilities or have cobbled them together from different acquisitions; multiple control centers, appliances, gateways, or agents may be required.
- Area #13: Data discovery rarely makes use of AI/ML support to do semantic analysis to find out what something really is. For example, depending on the context, a date can be a date of birth, a transaction date, or the dateline of a newspaper article. Each data type will need the appropriate level of protection.

Major Changes in Regulations, Attacks, and Use of Data

1. Regulations: GDPR documents where data came from, how data is used and shared. CCPA identifiers of households
2. Changing Attack Vectors: Supply chain attacks data, Ransomware stealing data
3. Increasing use of data and at more granular levels

CHANGING SECURITY POSTURES

Enforcement of Security Compliance

I think that enforcement is important, and checklists are not enough for a good security posture. PCI DSS implemented a strict enforcement program that drove the organization to encrypt cardholder data.

Similar enforcement for PII data security could drive organizations to a good security posture. Organizations in group A may focus resources to comply with a minimal checklist of regulations. This may divert resources from security posture beyond the checklists. A good security posture goes beyond basic checklists and may lead to compliance with basic security best practices. Illustration of Organizations in group A that focus resources to comply with a minimal checklist of regulations:

EVOLVING TECHNOLOGIES FOR DATA PROTECTION

New tools for data protection can arm innovative businesses to win in an ever-changing, more and more competitive digital economy. Responsible firms believe their customers and employees have a right to privacy—they value those relationships, after all. Unfortunately, now and in the future, success in safeguarding privacy will not be guaranteed by a wish to do so. The countless regulations already enacted, compounded by the many others that are sure to come, only stress the need for businesses to protect the privacy of anyone and everyone whose personally identifiable information resides in corporate data according to "Privacy-Preserving Analytics and Secure Multiparty."

Privacy-Preserving Techniques

New methods for data protection create opportunities to exploit the sensitive data that is demonstrated to be most effective in triggering advanced analytics, machine learning, and AI homomorphic encryption, which permits calculations on encrypted data, and machine learning are increasing in popularity. We will examine new homomorphic encryption algorithms that are safe from Quantum Computer-Based Attacks and machine-learning algorithm that can be optimized for Quantum Computers according to "New technologies for data protection that arm innovative businesses to win."

Privacy-preserving techniques for AI—such as differential privacy or k-anonymity—can safeguard an individual's sensitive data while also decreasing bias in AI algorithms. We will study international privacy standards, including reversible techniques and non-reversible one-methods, and review how differential privacy provides a formal guarantee that individual-level information about participants in the database is not leaked.

Evolution of Fine-Grained Data Protection

The evolution of data protection brought techniques that are more transparent to applications and databases. Key management and distribution of encryption keys became easier when applications could perform some operations on data protected with FPE or tokenization.

This section illustrates some examples that can be expected when running different protection techniques. Parsing of input or output data and other housekeeping procedures may add overhead.

Comparing TCO and Performance of Some Data Protection Techniques

I was comparing the TCO (Total Cost of Ownership) of some Data Protection Techniques. TCO includes licensing, implementation, design, test, administration, audit, compliance, and monitoring. Compliance can, for example, be for PCI DSS.

TCO (Total Cost of Ownership) improved over time:

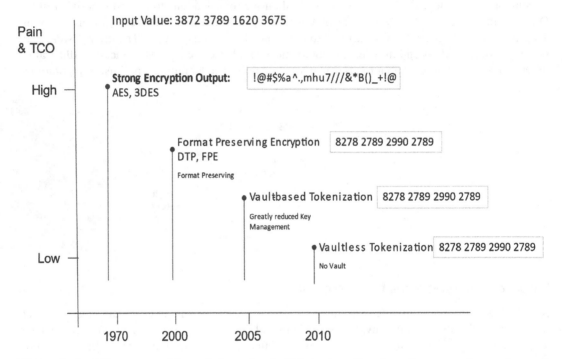

The evolution of cryptographic tools brought algorithms that allow broader types of operations on data encrypted with homomorphic encryption schemes:

	Operations				
Cryptographic Tool	Addition	Multiplication	Division	Match	Only Integers
Tokenization	No	No	No	Yes	No
AES symmetric block cipher encryption	No	No	No	Yes	No
Format Preserving Encryption (FPE)	No	No	No	Yes	No
Order-preserving encryption	No	No	No	Yes	No
RSA public key encryption (PKE)	No	Yes	No	Yes	Yes
PHE (Partially Homomorphic encryption)	Addition or multiplication	Addition or multiplication	No	Yes	Yes
SWHE (Some What H homomorphic encryption)	Yes	Yes	No	Yes	Yes
Fully homomorphic encryption (FHE)	Yes	Yes	Yes	Yes	Yes

Hybrid Cloud

Data must move without obstacle through an enterprise's numerous cloud-based databases and applications. Businesses want the cloud to place workloads in development containers according to "New technologies for data protection." They need the cloud to tap AI and reinvent how they make decisions. The most critical data types in driving innovation—with advanced analytics, machine learning, and AI—are considered most sensitive and must be safeguarded. A common worry with cloud hosting is the danger of vendor lock-in and a failure to migrate to a different cloud service provider when features or pricing shifts. Firms often implement a "best of breed" cloud approach and end up with several providers. Some businesses understand the liabilities implied by a "shared security model" or simply do not trust their hosting vendors to fully control critical components like data security, user accounts, and systems.

So most firms want to have the complete power of data security policies and encryption keys and are very acquainted with their on-premises encryption and key management systems, so they often prefer to leverage the same means and skills throughout multiple clouds. We will discuss a unified data security policy and encryption key management to leverage the same tool and skills throughout multiple clouds and on-premises systems.

Machine Learning

Machine learning models and information in trusted execution environments (TEE) bring confidence that sensitive data is secure. Businesses can rapidly extract value, apply insights in real-time, and predict outcomes that accelerate growth, and "You don't want me to know what stocks you're trading, and I don't want you to know the algorithm." Operating on clear text information inside a TEE can also increase the speed compared to operating on homomorphically encryption data and provide scalability close to what you expect in a cloud environment. We will examine how you can shield machine learning models and data in TEE.

Responsible Use of AI and Trends

"Disruption is unsettling, but it can also catalyze innovation and change. We have now entered the area of AI-augmented work and decision throughout all the functional areas of a business," Jyoti, group VP for AI and automation research, said in a statement. "Responsible creation and use of AI solutions that can sense, predict, respond, and adapt at speed is an important business imperative," according to "IDC: AI spending will reach $342B in 2021."

Companies could spend nearly $342 billion on AI software, hardware, and services in 2021. That's corresponding to the latest edition of IDC's Worldwide Semiannual Artificial Intelligence Tracker, which forecast that the AI market will accelerate in 2022, with 18.8% growth, and remain on the path to break the $500 billion mark by 2024 according to IDC 2021:

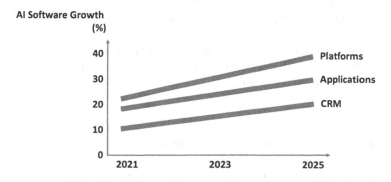

Source: Adapted from IDC, 2021

For its story, IDC surveyed over 700 large enterprises across a total of 27 countries and five rest-of regions. While the report suggests the competitive AI landscape remains highly fragmented, 2020 was the year that strengthened the value of enterprise AI, according to IDC.

Automation by AI Could Raise Productivity Growth Globally

Other reports agree with IDC's top-level finding: AI technologies are becoming common in enterprises worldwide. While the adoption rate differs between businesses, most of them—95% in a recent S&P Global report—consider AI to be important in their digital transformation efforts. The benefits could be enormous. McKinsey predicts automation only could raise productivity growth globally by 0.8% to 1.4% annually.

DATA SECURITY ROLES ARE CHANGING

Data and Security Governance (DSG) Converge (Gartner):

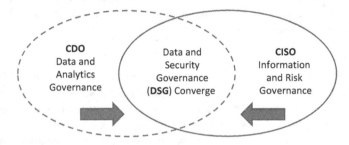

Source: Adapted from Gartner

We will discuss governance and roles in a separate chapter.

PRIVACY

THE FUTURE OF PRIVACY

Privacy laws and regulations appear to be evolving as quickly as the technology landscape. New and emerging technologies may be used for privacy-related tasks. Privacy laws and regulations seem to be growing as soon as the technology environment. New and emerging technologies may be used for privacy-related according to "Privacy in Practice 2021: Data Privacy Trends, Forecasts." Thirty-one percent of respondents say their enterprises already use AI or plan to use it to perform privacy-related tasks. However, there seems to be some resistance to using AI for this purpose—42% of respondents say that their enterprises have no plans to use AI for privacy-related tasks at this time:

- Overall, respondents are optimistic about their ability to avoid a material privacy breach in the next year. Only 17% say that a violation is very likely or likely, and 27% say it is very unlikely or unlikely.
- There is some ambiguity about the likelihood of a material privacy breach in the next 12 months: Nineteen percent of respondents report not knowing the possibility of a breach in the next year, and 13% prefer not to answer.

Evolving Global Privacy

In 2020, privacy entered everyday conversations, a year when individual companies took more strident efforts to roll out privacy-friendly products. And regulation has spread to protect more of the earth population whose data is protected by standard security requirements is expected to increase from 61% in 2020 to 82% by the end of 2021, according to "Seven privacy megatrends—A roadmap to 2030." What's coming in the next decade? Companies will fight for trust, safety, and integrity.

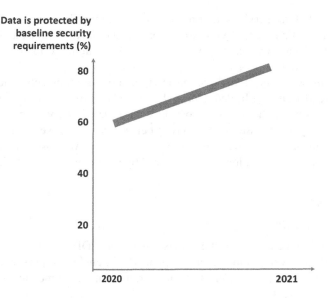

Source: Adapted from PWC

- Transforming data into benefit, securely and ethically, is the corporate imperative for the following decade. The companies that most effectively take responsibility of their data life cycle will have the most significant opportunities for success.
- Nation-states have been especially aggressive in seeking to steal data related to the research and development, manufacturer, and distribution of SARS-CoV-2. Increasing implementation of artificial intelligence, robotics, and other technologies will create new data-ethics risks, including privacy, manipulation, and bias.
- European regulators want to activate the General Data Protection Regulation (GDPR) provisions for privacy certification provisions. In the United States, the Federal Trade Commission (FTC) and a leading consumer advocacy journal have developed privacy labs to evaluate products, mobile apps, and websites. Fifty-nine percent of the employee had concerns about exposure of personal data to third parties, according to PwC.
- The companies that will face the most significant challenges adapting to emerging standards will be technology and data practices. We will discuss what companies will be affected first.

Privacy Laws Are Changing

Actions Needed by Organizations

A shorter list of points that can lead to specific action by an organization. For example:

1. The notion of a "right to privacy" varies across jurisdictions. Therefore, FIs (financial institutions) should be aware that they may hold personally identifiable information (PII) and financial information about individuals and organizations who reside in places with stronger protection than those afforded to residents of the country or state the FI has its operations.
2. This is a rapidly evolving field. FIs should have a "legal and regulatory watch" function, probably under the legal department or the chief data officer (if there is one) to monitor the evolution of applicable laws and regulations, including GDPR in the European Union, CPRA in California, PIPEDA in Canada, and many more, if they hold accounts for residents of any of those geographical entities.
3. All data held by an FI that poses potential privacy issues should be identified and rated for the severity of its potential loss or misuse.

4. The adoption of cloud services, and migration between such services, should include a risk assessment about the potential violation of privacy laws, regulations, and customer expectations (the latter because adverse publicity can be as damaging to the FI's business as regulatory or legal penalties).

5. FIs should consider encryption, de-identification, or obfuscation techniques for data placed in the cloud to render any exfiltrated data useless for identifying customers and their assets.

6. FIs should be aware of the potential costs of data breaches, brand impact, and, if appropriate (as determined by a risk assessment), buy cyber insurance to cover those costs; in particular, parametric insurance should be considered as a way to recover costs without having to debate or prove the actual financial loss, as is required by traditional indemnity insurance policies.

GDPR Is Changing

GDPR under "Schrems II"

The cloud hosting of data can violate the provisions of the GDPR, considering the risk of access requests by authorities. Several court orders suspended all transfers of personal data to the US and other third countries since the companies did not implement supplementary measures to provide adequate protection for the data.

- We will discuss solutions hosted by US cloud hosting providers that were approved by the court to be sufficient to protect data under the EU GDPR.
- We will discuss how to select and apply adequate protection for the data that can satisfy the requirements for cross-border data transfer.

Privacy in Transition

Data Privacy by the Numbers

- By 2023, Gartner predicts that 65% of the world's population will have its data included under modern privacy laws, up 10% from 2020. As cyber-attackers continue to develop increasingly advanced hacking methods, organizations must prioritize modernizing their data privacy standards and tools according to "Data Privacy Day 2021: Data-Protection Tips for Business."

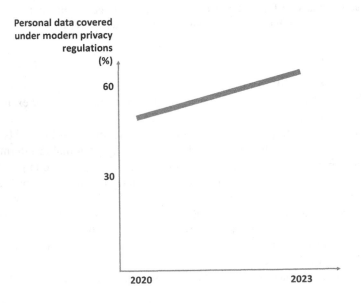

Source: Adapted from Gartner

- Seventy percent of organizations surveyed by Cisco said they had seen "significant" business benefits—including operational efficiency, agility, and innovation—from highlighting data privacy. Preserving data privacy does not impede innovation. Organizations can confidently use their data to push advanced analytics and AI initiatives when data privacy is done right.
- Smart use of data drives results. By incorporating secure AI into customer experience (CX) schemes and marketing initiatives, 24% of companies examined by the IBM Institute for Business Value said they could make faster, more informed choices. A promise to protect customers' sensitive data must underpin every CX initiative.

RISE OF PRIVACY ENFORCEMENT

Privacy enforcement participants will use automated technologies to bolster their powers according to "Privacy megatrend: Rise of privacy enforcement."

Why Will It Happen?

Regulators are resource-strapped and pressured to execute. Several now have larger enforcement authority and can impose greater upper limit fines and penalties. Plaintiffs' law companies are seeking new revenue streams, publications need new audiences to stay afloat, and advocates struggle to remain relevant.

European regulators want to activate the General Data Protection Regulation (GDPR) provisions for privacy certification agreements. In the United States, the FTC and a leading consumer advocacy journal have developed privacy labs to evaluate products, mobile apps, and websites. Participants can now continually probe companies for privacy vulnerabilities using a new bot and AI technologies and relationships with third-party accreditation systems with these capabilities.

What's Driving the Pace of This Trend?

1. Data-intensive technology innovation.
2. Heightened government need for revenue.
3. The heightened law firm, publication, advocate needs for revenue and relevance.
4. Sharing and collaboration are rising among regulators.
5. Increasing enforcement.
6. Successful class-action lawsuits.
7. Community sentiment.

Data Privacy Enforcement Actions Worldwide

There is an increase of data privacy enforcement actions worldwide reported by PwC in recent years:

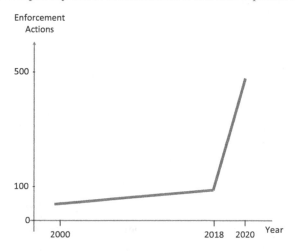

Source: Adapted from The PwC Privacy Policy Database, Data Privacy Enforcement Actions Worldwide reported PwC

THREATS

TRENDS IN THREATS, PRIVACY, AND TRUST

The Threat Landscapes

The recent trends in fraud and identity thefts are alarming. What is the data/statistics telling us? Attackers are stealing your data.

TRENDS IN BREACHES

It may take a long time before we discover that an attacker is inside and stealing our data. There are various ways that attackers get inside, and the SolarWinds attack against the supply chain illustrates this increasing issue. Discovery in months or more still accounts for over a quarter of breaches, according to Verizon DBIR. The increase of ransomware is impacting these numbers since discovery is often immediate. Ransomware is increasingly also taking a copy of the data and pressuring the victims into paying up:

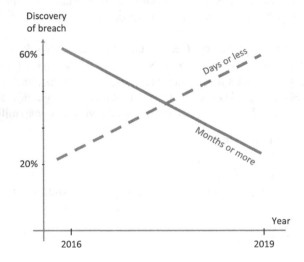

Source: Adapted from Discovery of breaches according to Verizon DBIR

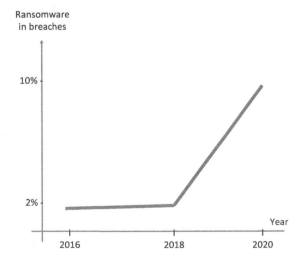

Source: Adapted from Verizon DBIR

Ransomware has many ways of gaining a foothold in your business: hacking, malware, phishing, credentials, misuse, physical intrusion, and errors.
Focus on Restoring Operations:

- Focus on restoring the operation, not shutting down data pipes
- Resilience delivered through disaster recovery

Protection that follows:

- Your data
- Persistent data protection that eliminates data value
- Persistent privacy protection that protects your customers

Gives Control Back to the Business

- Removes a major source of ransom value
- Reduces or eliminates the need for announcing customer data loss

Action Varieties in Breaches over Time

Attackers become increasingly efficient and lean more toward attacks such as phishing and credential theft. Misconfiguration that leads to data theft increased, for example, in Amazon AWS S3 cloud services:

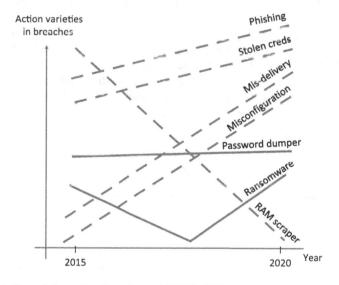

Source: Verizon Data Breach Investigations Report DBIR 2020

Threatening to Publicize the Data

In 2020, cyber actors increased malware attacks against US victims during the pandemic, including the healthcare and public health segment. The US Secret Service noticed a marked uptick in the number of ransomware assaults, ranging from a small dollar to multimillion-dollar ransom demands, according to "Verizon Data Breach Investigations Report 2021." While most companies had adequate data backup solutions to mitigate these attacks, cyber actors focused on the exfiltration of sensitive data. These cyber actors often organized criminal groups, monetized the theft by threatening to publicize the data unless the additional ransom was paid.

Incident vs. Breach Definitions in the DBIR Report

We talk about incidents and breaches and use the following definitions:

- Incident: A security event that compromises the integrity, confidentiality, or availability of an information asset.
- Breach: An incident that causes in the confirmed disclosure—not only potential exposure—of data to an unauthorized party.

UNDER CONTROL? IS THE SITUATION GETTING WORSE?

1. How do we control the privacy of Test Data? By using prod data? Outsourced testing?
2. Do we have increasingly less control over distributed data when working from home? Is our attack surface increasing?
3. Is compliance under control? Is the situation getting worse?
4. How much is endpoint security helping? How can we protect against supply chain attacks? Solarwinds?

IDENTITY THEFTS

According to newly released data, the FTC received more than 2.1 million fraud reports from consumers in 2020. Scams remain the most widespread type of fraud reported to the agency according to "FTC 2020 Data Shows Consumer Fraud Hit 2.2 Million."

Online shopping was the second-most widespread fraud category told by consumers, rounded out the upper five fraud types according to "New Data Shows FTC Received 2.2 Million Fraud Reports from Consumers."

Consumers stated losing more than $3.3 billion to fraud in 2020, up from $1.8 billion in 2019. Nearly $1.2 billion of losses described last year were due to imposter scams, while online spending reported for about $246 million in reported losses from consumers.

Thirty-four percent of all consumers who filed a fraud article with the FTC—reported losing money, up from just 23% in 2019. This is a list of the steady increase of identity thefts (and synthetic identity fraud) reported to the US FTC over the years:

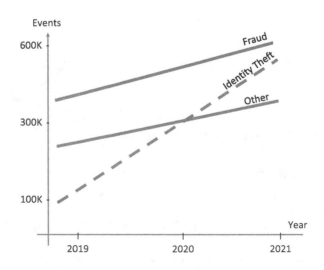

Source: Adapted from FTC Identity Thefts Report, US Federal Trade Commission (FTC)

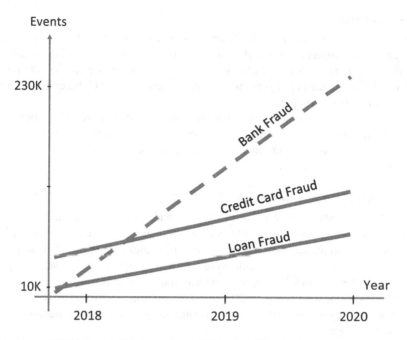

Source: Adapted from FTC Identity Thefts Report, US Federal Trade Commission (FTC)

The trend of data theft continues. This is a list of the steady increase of Identity Thefts reported to the US FTC over the last 20 years:

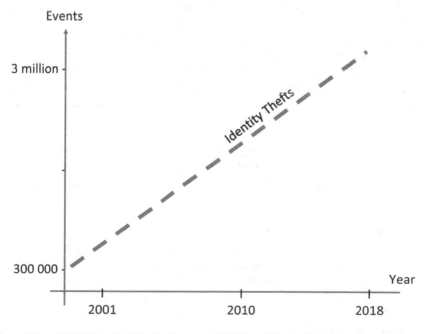

Source: Adapted from FTC Identity Thefts Report, US Federal Trade Commission (FTC)

Cybercrime Never Ends

Recently found breaches of critical business and government infrastructure uncovered the fundamental vulnerability of connected networks. In two separate instances, hackers attached to Russia and China exploited the network monitoring software of the company SolarWinds to break into the systems of several US government agencies and firms according to "Cybercrime Never Ends; Nor Should End-to-End Data Protection."

The breaches serve as a remembrance of the inescapability of cybercrime. More than three billion people had their data stolen in just two of the top 15 largest breaches of the twenty-first century. In comparison, the smallest incident since 2000 involved the data of a mere 134 million people, according to CSO.

Sixty-Three Percent of Companies Had Suffered a Breach

A Dell study in 2020 showed that 63% of businesses had suffered a breach within the past year. According to Bitdefender, endpoint misconfigurations of security policies caused a third of all recent security incidents, and inadequate remote-management policies account for hundreds of thousands of exposed systems. Bitdefender found employees defy even the most alert security policies, with 93% of surveyed workers acknowledging to recycling old passwords.

The typical total cost of a breach in 2020 was $3.86 million, according to IBM. It's too soon to estimate fiscal harm from the huge hack of US government agencies and companies or whether there will be significant damage at all.

Potential Cloud Barriers

Businesses are rapidly turning to the cloud to achieve speedier analytics outcomes at scale. In fact, according to Gartner, end-user expenditure on public cloud services is projected to increase by more than 18% in 2021 to total $304.9 billion.

Barriers to Increased Cloud Adoption

When asked about barriers they anticipate to increased cloud adoption, 39% of executives cited inadequate employee skills to properly move data to cloud systems. This is followed closely by budgetary constraints (38%) and the risk of unsecured data in transit to the cloud being breached (38%). Other potential hurdles to cloud adoption include compliance with privacy regulations (26%) and reliance on on-premises environments (24%).

Several industry- and country-specific privacy regulations have emerged in recent years, substantially impacting how businesses use and safeguard their data. In response to these new and developing laws, 55% of surveyed executives recognized compliance with data privacy regulations as a leading priority for the coming year according to "Most businesses to accelerate data security investments."

Additionally, 76% of executives stated they are worried about the effect that new, state-specific data privacy laws—such as California's CCPA and Virginia's CDPA—will have on their company's data initiatives. US State Privacy Legislation Tracker from IAPP can provide updated information for this topic.

Need for Businesses to Protect the Privacy

Rick Farnell, CEO of Protegrity, said, "Global enterprises today face a multitude of data privacy regulations, which will only be compounded by approaching regulations that are coming down the pike." This new reality further emphasizes the need for businesses to safeguard the privacy of personally identifiable information that resides with their company data ecosystem. Only then can companies consistently and reliably make the best of their data while staying in pace with compliance both now and in the future."

TRUST

TRUST IN COMPANIES AND NATIONAL GOVERNMENT

The PwC Privacy Policy Database, 2021, reports Trust in companies' headquarters in different regions:

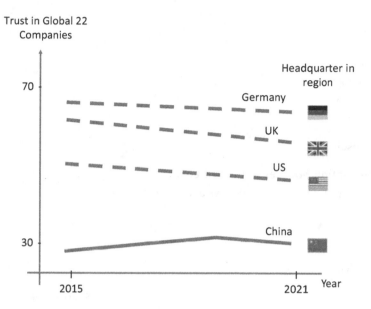

Source: Adapted from The PwC Privacy Policy Database, 2021, reports Trust in companies

The PwC Privacy Policy Database, 2021, reports Trust in national government in different regions:

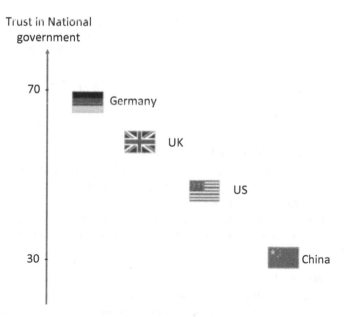

Source: Adapted from The PwC Privacy Policy Database, 2021, reports Trust in national government in different regions

TRUST IS CENTRAL TO DIGITAL TRANSFORMATION

Nine Characteristics of a Trusted Organization

By 2023, organizations that instill Trust will participate in 50% more ecosystems to expand revenue generation opportunities (Source: Gartner). Trust factors include:

1. Honest
2. Communicative
3. Competent
4. Transparent
5. Customer-centric
6. Financially viable
7. Socially responsible
8. Innovative
9. Privacy-conscious

Trust in all Information Sources at Record Lows

Percent trust in each source for general news and information:

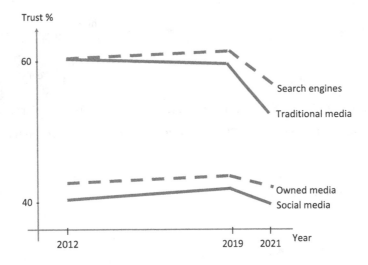

Source: Adapted from 2021 Edelman Trust Barometer

The Emergence of Trusted Technology First Movers

A confluence of security Chapter 2. Trends and Evolution megatrends will create once-in-a-generation opportunities to establish trusted technology standards according to "Privacy megatrend: Emergence of trusted technology first movers."

Attitudes about socially acceptable technology are expected to continue to evolve and sometimes conflict, hinging on how technology innovation, public opinion, and regulation interrelate across the three privacy regulatory poles.

Rise of Privacy Enforcement

Privacy enforcement sponsors will use automated technologies to strengthen their powers according to "Privacy megatrend: Rise of privacy enforcement." Regulators are resource-strapped and pressured to perform. Several now have greater enforcement authority and can impose higher maximum fines and penalties. Plaintiffs' law firms seek new revenue flows, publications need new audiences to stay afloat, and advocates struggle to remain relevant.

SECURITY

LAYERED SECURITY

You should stick to a layered security approach for protecting your company. It is essential to make sure that you are using updated applications and operating systems. Thus, patch administration is very important for any business. You should also set up spam detecting and antivirus on every computer. Also, you should use a firewall for safeguarding your network according to "5 Ways to Improve IT Security on a Limited Budget."

You should also use data encryption to protect your data. Encryption means playing vital data in safeguarding your information from hackers. This will make certain that only and your clients can access your data.

Digital Technologies and Innovation

Digital technologies are accelerators of innovation. They can enhance efficiency, power new tools and services, enable new business patterns, and distort the boundaries between industries.

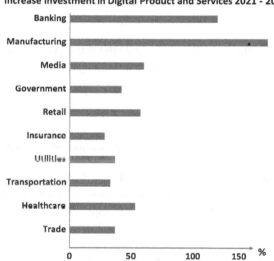

Increase Investment in Digital Product and Services 2021 - 2022

Source: Adapted from Gartner, 2021

We will discuss more about this topic in Volume II of this book.

EVOLVING IT SECURITY TECHNOLOGIES

The war between data defenders and data crooks has been described as a cat-and-mouse game according to "Top 5 emerging information security technologies." As rapidly as the white hats counter one form of black-hat evil behavior, another malevolent form rears its ugly head.

- The shortcomings of usernames and passwords are well understood. A more reliable form of authentication is necessary. One technique is to bake authentication into a user's hardware.
- When somebody's username and password are compromised, whoever has them can waltz onto a network and engage in all kinds of malicious behavior. That behavior can trigger off a red flag to system defenders if they're using user behavior analytics (UBA). The technology uses big data analytics to detect abnormal behavior by a user.
- A key to data loss prevention is tools such as encryption and tokenization. They can safeguard data down to field and subfield levels, which can gain an enterprise in several ways.

Hybrid or Multi-Cloud

Most companies are practicing a hybrid or multi-cloud strategy these days for several reasons, including integration of multiple services, agility, accelerated innovation, and corporate continuity.

- Seventy-one percent of firms that responded to the study said they were taking these approaches, while only 27% said they relied on single cloud implementation. Those using hybrid or multi-cloud were about evenly split between the two methods according to "3 best practices for locking down your hybrid cloud."

While the hybrid and multi-cloud approaches offer many business benefits, they also come with their own set of security concerns according to "3 best practices for locking down your hybrid cloud."

- Fifty-eight percent of respondents, one of the biggest challenges when working with a multi-cloud environment is ensuring data protection and privacy for each domain.
- For 67% of cybersecurity professionals, misconfiguration of cloud security remains the largest cloud security danger.
- This is followed by exfiltration of sensitive information (59%), and unauthorized access and insecure interfaces/APIs, tied at 49%.

Another major question (according to 57% of respondents) is the skills to deploy and manage a full solution across all cloud environments, followed by struggling with how the different solutions all fit together (52%). And with cloud overall, 53% told that a lack of visibility was hampering cloud implementation.

Cloud-forward all the way.

- Thirty-three percent of surveyed organizations are running more than 50% of workloads in the cloud;
- In the next year, the survey found that figure will grow to 56%.
- That's for the reason that cloud computing is delivering on its original promises; organizations are experiencing quicker time to market (53%), improved responsiveness (51%), and cost reductions (41%).

Consider locating and right-size your security controls to a cloud-based platform.

SECURITY SPENDING

IT budgets are come to be tighter with time. Thus, it is hard for most companies to improve their security. According to a story by IBM security, more than 69% of IT professionals think that their funding is inadequate.

But, security threats are evolving with time. Hackers are using complicated attacks to steal organizational data. Thus, it is also important to improve your IT security. It will help you in safeguarding your data from hacks. There are some minor modifications that you can do to increase your security.

Data Security Investment on the Rise

Gartner's research found that more than nine in ten businesses plan to increase their data security investments in 2021. The top data security investments proposed for 2021 include cloud data security (67%), training for employees (54%), and data security for SaaS environments (50%), according to "Most businesses to accelerate data security investments."

Amid solid interest in data security investments, some respondents cited potential implementation barriers. These include the extreme amount of time required to deploy new data security technologies (47%), insufficient employee skills to implement new data security technologies (39%), and budgetary constraints (39%). Privacy and security managers were more likely (42%) to cite insufficient skills as barriers to data security implementation than data and AI executives (35%), according to "Most businesses to accelerate data security investments."

Many organizations anticipate significant benefits despite likely implementation challenges due to greater investment in data security technology and practices. Interestingly, the most widely agreed-upon benefit of data security was improved customer feel, as cited by 70% of respondents.

Additional anticipated benefits include reduced financial risk due to a data breach (64%), reduced reputational business risk due to a data breach (61%), and a greater ability to utilize secure data for AI and advanced analytics initiatives (59%). Data and AI executives were more keenly aware (69%) of data security's potential impact on AI and analytics timelines than their security and privacy counterparts (54%).

IT Security Spending as Percent of Total IT Spending by Industry (Gartner, 2020):

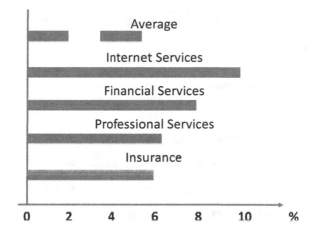

Source: Adapted from Gartner

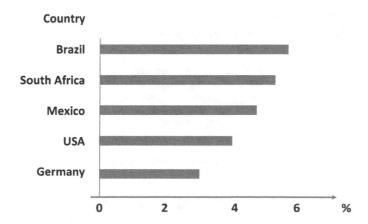

Source: Adapted from (ISC)2, 2021

We will discuss healthcare security in a separate chapter.

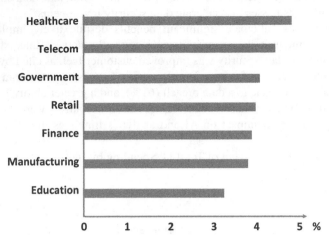

Source: Adapted from (ISC)2, 2021

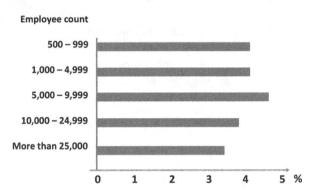

Source: Adapted from (ISC)2

Security in Three to Five Years

Factors impacting Information Security Functions in Three to Five Years:

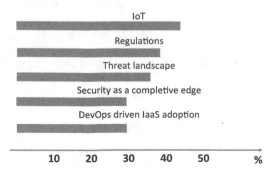

Source: Adapted from Gartner

We will discuss IoT, regulations, threats, and DevOps in separate chapters.

Currently in production

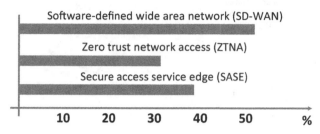

Source: Adapted from (ISC)2, 2021

We will discuss zero Trust and SASE in separate chapters.

Planning to implement

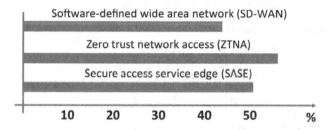

Source: Adapted from (ISC)2, 2021

Cybersecurity Market

"The cybersecurity market was valued at USD 156.24 billion in 2020, and it is expected to reach USD 352.25 billion by 2026, registering a CAGR of 14.5% during 2021–2026," according to "Cybersecurity Market Trends."

- The trends for IoT, BYOD, AI, and machine learning in cybersecurity are growing.
- For instance, machine learning provides benefits in outlier detection, much to the benefit of cybersecurity.

Quickly increasing cybersecurity incidents and regulations requiring their coverage are driving the cybersecurity market. Cybercrimes, which involve "damage and destruction of data, stolen money, lost property, intellectual property theft, and other areas, currently cost the world almost USD 600 billion each year, or 0.8% of the global GDP" according to "Cybersecurity Market Trends."

By 2025, it is estimated that there may be just about 30 global smart cities, and 50% of these may be located in North America and Europe, which may demand high cybersecurity.

High reliance on conventional authentication methods and low preparedness are challenging the market to grow. In a market scenario where security professionals recommend identity-management solutions, such as facial recognition and biometric identification, most businesses in the region (over 80%) still use usernames and passwords as the sole means of logging in.

The global cybersecurity market is predicted to grow from $167.1B in 2019 to $248.26B by 2023, attaining a 10.4% CAGR, according to Statista. Worldwide security spending on Identity Access Management reached $10.58B in 2019. This data from Mordor Intelligence Analysis:

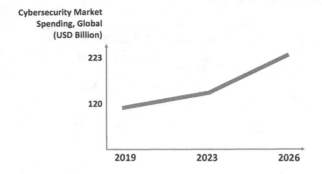

Source: Adapted from Mordor Intelligence Analysis

TECHNOLOGY USE

PLAN FOR DATA PROTECTION

We will discuss applications and APIs in a separate chapter.

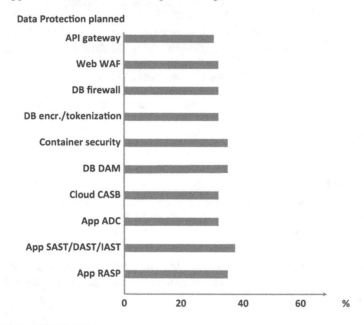

Source: Adapted from (ISC)2, 2021

SUMMARY

We have discussed data growth, privacy, threats, trust, security, products, and changing privacy laws. The breaches serve as a reminder of the inescapability of cybercrime. As stunning as the hacks were, more will undoubtedly come, and no one is safe, not even in the workplace, where hackers hope human error or negligence opens the door to networks and files.

We will discuss this topic more in Volume II of this book.

BIBLIOGRAPHY

1. Seven Privacy Megatrends: A Roadmap to 2030, https://www.pwc.com/us/en/services/consulting/cybersecurity-privacy-forensics/library/seven-privacy-megatrends.html

2. Information-security, https://information-security.enterprisesecuritymag.com/vendors/top-information-security-consulting-service-companies.html#:~:text=The%20war%20between%20data%20defenders%20and%20data%20thieves,the%20main%20challenge%20for%20many%20organizations%20in%202019

3. Most notable Cybersecurity Unicorns in the United States, https://www.vcbay.news/2021/07/24/most-notable-cybersecurity-unicorns-in-the-united-states/#:~:text=In%202020%2C%20the%20Cybersecurity%20market%20was%20valued%20at,threats%20and%20report%20to%20keep%20their%20data%20confidential

4. Privacy Megatrend: Emergence of Trusted Technology First Movers, https://www.pwc.com/us/en/services/consulting/cybersecurity-privacy-forensics/library/seven-privacy-megatrends/emergence-trusted-technology-first-overs.html

5. GDPR: Three Ways the World Has Changed in the Privacy Law's First Two Years, https://www.cpomagazine.com/data-protection/gdpr-three-ways-the-world-has-changed-in-the-privacy-laws-first-two-years/

6. US State Privacy Legislation Tracker, https://iapp.org/resources/article/us-state-privacy-legislation-tracker/

7. Cybersecurity Market – Growth, https://www.mordorintelligence.com/industry-reports/cyber-security-market

8. FTC 2020 Data Shows Consumer Fraud Hit 2.2 Million, https://www.pymnts.com/news/security-and-risk/2021/ftc-2020-data-shows-consumer-fraud-hit-2-2-million/#:~:text=The%20Federal%20Trade%20Commission%20%28FTC%29%20received%20more%20than,with%20online%20shopping%20the%20second-most%20common%20fraud%20category

9. 3 Best Practices for Locking Down your Hybrid Cloud Security Approach, https://techbeacon.com/security/3-best-practices-locking-down-your-hybrid-cloud-security-approach

10. Digital Transformation, https://www2.deloitte.com/us/en/insights/topics/digital-transformation.html?icid=top_digital-transformation

11. Leading the Cloud Transformation of Space, http://spacebelt.com/

12. "Are Satellites the Key to Cybersecurity in the Cloud? - Via Satellite –". *Via Satellite*. 2017-07-19. Retrieved 2018-02-24.

13. 5 Ways to Improve IT Security on a Limited Budget, https://bleuwire.com/improve-it-security-limited-budget/

14. "Just Try and Steal Cryptocurrency from Space, Hackers". *Motherboard*. 2016-09-16. Retrieved 2017-12-08.

15. "SolarCoin Selects Cloud Constellation's SpaceBelt for Secure Space-based Storage and Transaction". *ElectriCChain*. Retrieved 2017-12-08.

16. "Satellite Cloud Startup Inks Deal for Space-based Cryptocurrency Platform". *Ars Technica*. Retrieved 2017-12-08.

17. Sheetz, Michael (2017-09-14). "Virgin Orbit Announces Contract to Launch a Dozen Cloud Constellation Satellites". *CNBC*. Retrieved 2018-01-24.

18. "Space-based Cryptocurrency coming in 2018". Archived from *the original* on 2018-01-23. Retrieved 2018-01-25. Solarcoin, a currency that rewards users for generating solar electricity, has just signed a deal to house its multibillion dollar cold storage treasury in data centers orbiting the earth.

19. "Satellites the Key to Cybersecurity in the Cloud? - Via Satellite". *Via Satellite*. 2017-07-19. Retrieved 2018-02-24.

20. Henry, Caleb (2016-09-20). "Cloud Constellation Gains SolarCoin as Customer for Forthcoming SpaceBelt Network - Via Satellite". *Via Satellite*. Retrieved 2017-12-08.

21. Data Creation and Replication Will Grow at a Faster Rate Than Installed Storage Capacity, According to the IDC Global DataSphere and StorageSphere Forecasts, https://www.tmcnet.com/usubmit/2021/03/24/9331644.htm

22. New Technologies for Data Protection that Arm Innovative Businesses to Win, https://www.globalsecuritymag.com/New-technologies-for-data,20210605,112451.html

23. Data Security Still a Major Concern for Most Consumers, https://www.helpnetsecurity.com/2021/06/10/data-security-concern/

24. Worldwide Global DataSphere Forecast, 2021–2025: The World, https://www.marketresearch.com/IDC-v2477/Worldwide-Global-DataSphere-Forecast-Keeps-14315439/

25. "Privacy-Preserving Analytics and Secure Multiparty …, https://engage.isaca.org/swedenchapter/events/eventdescription?CalendarEventKey=dabd556d-0105-4cd9-af8a-55fbf9cbd5c1&CommunityKey=6592afac-ec0b-41ca-b0c4-1e2dbb4d9da3&Home=%2fcommunities%2fcommunity-home%2frecent-community-events

26. New Technologies for Data Protection, https://www.universe.com/events/new-technologies-for-data-protection-that-arm-innovative-businesses-to-win-tickets-15PYDT

27. IDC: AI Spending Will Reach $342B in 2021 | VentureBeat, https://venturebeat.com/2021/08/04/idc-ai-spending-will-reach-342b-in-2021/

28. Privacy in Practice 2021: Data Privacy Trends, Forecasts …, https://www.isaca.org/resources/news-and-trends/isaca-now-blog/2021/privacy-in-practice-2021-data-privacy-trends-forecasts-and-challenges

29. Data Privacy Day 2021: Data-Protection Tips for Business …, https://www.protegrity.com/protegrity-blog/data-privacy-day-2021-data-protection-tips-for-business-and-consumers

30. New Data Shows FTC Received 2.2 Million Fraud Reports from Consumers, https://www.ftc.gov/news-events/press-releases/2021/02/new-data-shows-ftc-received-2-2-million-fraud-reports-consumers. https://resources.ordr.net/blog/verizon-data-breach-investigations-report-2021-what-we-found-fascinating

31. Most Businesses to Accelerate Data Security Investments, https://www.helpnetsecurity.com/2021/06/25/data-security-investments/

32. Cybersecurity Market Trends, Sizel Industry Growth 2021 to …, https://www.mordorintelligence.com/industry-reports/cyber-security-market

3 Best Practices, Roadmap, and Vision

INTRODUCTION

We will discuss practical ways to implement data privacy, suggested best practices, a roadmap, and vision going forward. A multilayer defense can help create a good security posture and discover unusual activity on your sensitive data. We will discuss how sensitive data can be protected, how a central enterprise policy can control encryption keys, and what data protection techniques are used for different types of data.

PROTECT YOUR BUSINESS

Protect your business by protecting your data, users, and applications. This core is a foundation in your IT Systems:

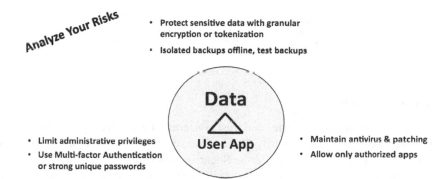

These steps can be parts of a Zero Trust Architecture to protect your assets and help to protect you from ransomware and other attacks.

PEOPLE, PROCESS, AND TECHNOLOGY

- People: Staff Training and Awareness. Professional Skills and Qualifications,
- Process: Management System, Governance, Frameworks, Best Practices, and IT Audit.
- Technology: You cannot deploy technology without competent people, support processes, or an overall plan.

People
Process
Technology

DOI: 10.1201/9781003189664-4

Examples:

- AI technology can automate tasks and help competent people in making decisions, supported by processes.
- Security needs to be integrated DevOps CI (Continuous Integration) process. DevOps is a mindset, and many legacy tools can be integrated with that process.

WE NEED A COMMON LANGUAGE FOR SECURITY

Do we need to use a common language to discuss data privacy and security across the different teams?

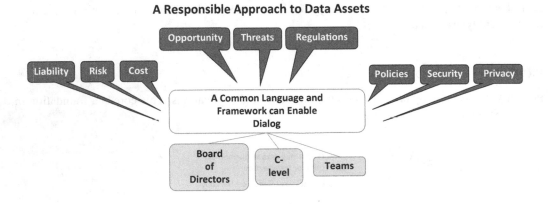

A Responsible Approach to Data Assets

A SECURITY-FIRST APPROACH

To address increasing data security worries and trust concerns, cloud service providers and IT teams need to work collectively to build a security-first culture according to "78% of Organizations Use More than 50 Cybersecurity Products to Address Security Issues."

This involves hiring, training, and retaining skilled IT security professionals and constantly enhancing processes and technologies to help mitigate threats in a gradually expanding digital world.

- Sixty-nine percent of companies report that their CISO reactively responds and gets involved in public cloud projects only after a cybersecurity incident.
- Seventy-three percent of organizations have or plan to hire a CISO with more cloud security skills; over half of organizations (53%) have added a brand new role called the Business Information Security Officer (BISO) to collaborate with the CISO and assist incorporate security culture into the business.
- Eighty-eight percent of IT professionals think that within the next three years, the greater part of their cloud will use smart and automated patching and updating to enhance security.
- Eighty-seven percent of IT professionals see AI/ML capabilities as a "must-have" for new security purchases to improve protection against things like fraud, malware, and misconfigurations.

The lift-and-shift of critical data to the cloud over the last few of years has shown good promise, but the hodgepodge of security tools and processes has led to a steady cadence of costly misconfigurations and data leaks. Positive progress is being made, though, according to "New Study: IT Pros Are More Worried about Corporate."

Best-Practice Behavior

According to *Harvard Business Review*, to foster a security-aware organizational culture, senior leaders and managers must lead by example and promote best-practice behavior. This could be anything from ensuring sensitive information is secure at all times (whether online or in physical spaces) or something as simple as not leaving your PC unattended and unlocked.

Your Best Defense against Cyberattacks

A report covering 31 countries—60% of the world population and a corresponding 85% of global GDP—assessed the financial loss of online scams in 2019 to be €36 billion according to "Your Employees Are Your Best Defense against Cyberattacks."

Leaders logically depend on their security department to safeguard an organization's information and investment decisions about the correct means to do so. But this approach is too thin. For a security-aware culture, all community members must be sincerely and wholeheartedly dedicated—beyond simply doing the one- to two-day security training that most companies mandate. Creating such a security-aware culture is enabled when leaders can influence their team members to adopt certain mindsets and actions.

THE STAKEHOLDERS

Gadgets can bring malware into the corporate network. In the following years, battles over the future of online Privacy—and therefore the nature of data ownership—will come to a head. Finding the right Balance and Protecting data in ways that are transparent to business processes and compliant with regulations:

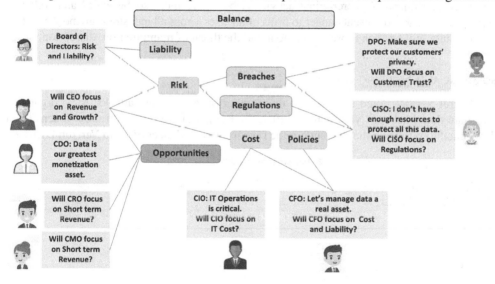

Source: Adapted from Gartner

Security does not imply Privacy. Some Privacy rules can be enforced by basic Security Controls. Privacy can be defined in a policy with people, processes, and technology.

$$\frac{Privacy}{Security}$$

The Customer Is Responsible for Data Security in Cloud

The customer/user that collected the data is always responsible for data security in all cloud service models, SaaS, IaaS, and PaaS. Cloud service providers follow a shared security responsibility model, which means your security team maintains some responsibilities for security as you move applications, data, containers, and workloads to the cloud, while the provider takes some responsibility, but not all according to "Shared Responsibility Model Explained."

If your organization collected the data, then you are also liable for that data, even if you outsource the operation or storage of that data to a cloud provider.

In general, my view is that the customer is responsible for data, users, applications, and configuration. For example, security configuration of Amazon AWS S3 buckets and Application Containers. Configuration is defined as code in software and may include containers and other application components. The cloud provider is responsible for infrastructure. This can be hardware, communication, hypervisor, physical security.

Applications, Data and Users
Configuration as Code (Software)
Cloud Provider Infrastructure

We will discuss more details about security for data, users, and applications for SaaS, IaaS, and PaaS cloud models in later sections of the book.

ADDRESSING THE THREAT LANDSCAPE

Everyone is looking at for new ways to innovate, from fast-growing startups to legacy enterprises and—yes—even cybercriminals. Cybercriminal activity is becoming more sophisticated and well funded, which presents a clear and present danger to firms of all sizes across all industries around the globe.

Securing data will be even more critical to avoid the threat of manipulation, disruption, or worse.

RANSOMWARE AND SECURING DATA

The US Secret Service noted an uptick in the number of ransomware attacks. Most organizations had adequate data backup. Cyber actors shifted their emphasis to the exfiltration of sensitive data and threatened to publicize the data unless the ransom was paid, according to Verizon DBIR.

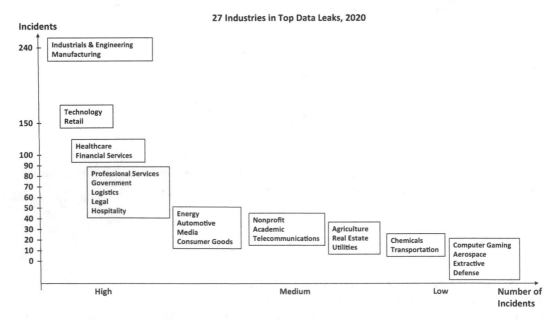

Source: Adopted from Crowdstrike

Top industries attacked by ransomware:

Industry	Percentage
Telecom & Tech	75%
Education	73%
Finance	65%
Manufacturing	62%
Retail	60%
Health Care	59%

Source: Adopted from The International Information System Security Certification Consortium (ISC)2

PREVENTING ATTACKS

According to NIST IR 8374 "CYBERSECURITY FRAMEWORK FOR RANSOMWARE RISK MANAGEMENT," these are steps that companies can take right now to help recover from an upcoming ransomware incident:

1. Build and implement an incident recovery plan with specified roles and strategies for decision-making.
2. Meticulously plan, implement, and test a data backup and restoration strategy—and secure and isolate backups of crucial data.
3. Keep an up-to-date directory of internal and external connections.

PREVENT ATTACKS

1. Maintain antivirus and patching
2. Allow only authorized apps
3. Limit personally owned devices
4. Limit administrative privileges
5. Limit personal apps
6. Avoid unknown files or links
7. Block ransomware sites

RECOVER AFTER ATTACKS

According to NIST, organizations can recover after attacks by implementing:

1. Verify emergency contacts
2. Isolated backups offline, test backups
3. Follow recovery plan

SECURE DATA

LIMIT DATA EXPOSURE

According to NIST SP 800-207, a Zero Trust Architecture (ZTA) can provide the following ENTERPRISE SECURITY CHARACTERISTICS:

1. Maintaining data defense at rest and in transit
2. Remediating device weaknesses that could result in unauthorized access to information stored on or accessed by the device, and misuse of the device

3. Extenuating malware execution on the device can result in unauthorized access to information stored on or accessed by the device, and abuse of the device
4. Extenuating the risk of data loss through accidental, deliberate, or malicious deletion or obfuscation of data stored on the device
5. Sustaining awareness of and responding to suspicious or malicious events within and against the device to stop or detect a compromise of the device

Defending users and resources in ZTA is based on continuous validation of User Context and doesn't just trust the user ID that is logged in. Validate context of each user request and segment sensitive data into separate environments or network segments:

1. Understanding who the users are, which applications they are using and how they are connecting
2. Apply policy that ensures secure access to your data
3. Controls close to the protected surface as possible, creating a micro perimeter around it
4. This micro-perimeter pushes with the protect surface wherever it goes
5. Keep on to monitor and maintain in real-time

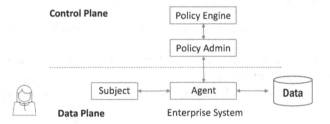

Source: Adopted from NIST

ZTA can be based on a policy that enforces attribute-based dynamic access control for your data. A CASB can enforce the policy and control access to cloud data:

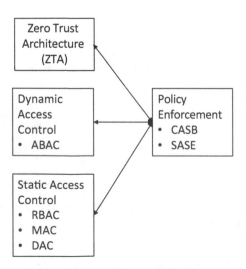

Maintaining Data Protection at Rest and in Transit

Store data in a form that supports the use cases and for each specific type of data. The structure of data is important to consider:

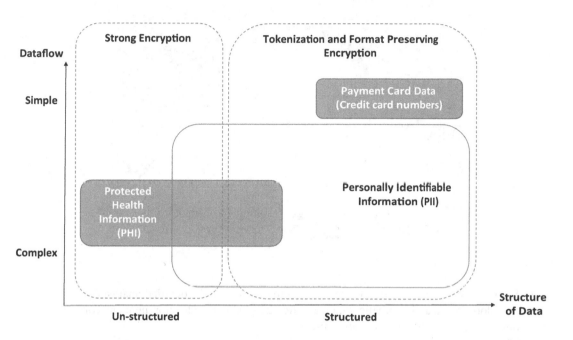

Store data in a form that provides a balance between protection and usability for the use cases of different business applications:

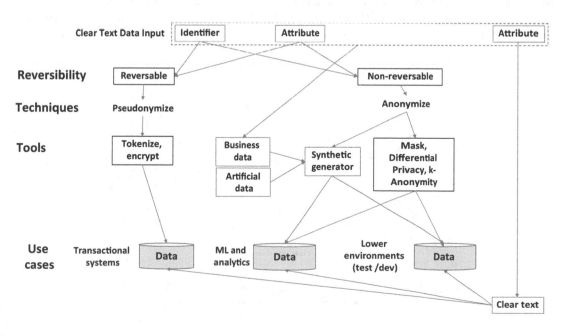

Use cases in transactional business applications may require protected data to be reversed in some operations:

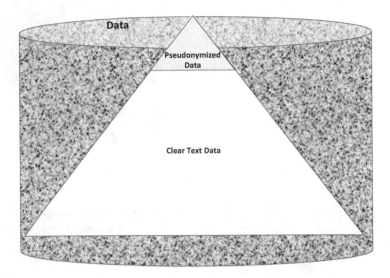

Use cases:

- Some use cases may require protected data to be reversed for detailed analysis.
- Pseudonymized and synthetic data may often be used in test/development environments, with anonymized data being very rarely used.
- The analytics use case would involve both pseudonymized and anonymized Data, with an emerging role of synthetic data for this use case.
- Synthetic data may often be used in test/development environments, with anonymized data being very rarely used.
- The analytics use case would involve both pseudonymized and anonymized data.

Synthetic, pseudonymized, and anonymized data will be discussed in Chapters 5 and 6.

Use cases in analytical and test/development environments may not require most protected data to be reversed:

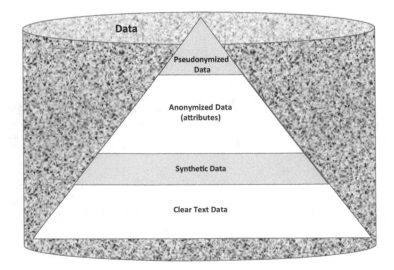

Some use cases may require protected data to be reversed for detailed analysis. This may take place in a staging environment.

Data Inference Leakage

Data inference leakage is the question about "Could the rest of the attributes be sufficient de-anonymize the data?"

Two models are particularly important to protect private information

- Differential privacy (DP) applies to randomized computations executed against a dataset and returning an aggregate result for the entire set. It prevents inference about specific records by requiring that the result of the computation yield nearly identical distributions for similar data sets. DP is one of the meticulous privacy concepts, which received widespread interest for sharing summary statistics from genomic datasets while protecting Privacy. DP permits only indirect observation of data through noisy measurement. Obtain approximately the same substantive results while simultaneously protecting the Privacy according to "Probabilistic Inference and Differential Privacy."
- K-anonymity has become one of the most important models to protect private information in data publication. For each combination of values of quasi-identifiers in the k-anonymous table, there are at least k records that share those values. K-anonymity protects data against linking attacks according to "Toward inference attacks for k-anonymity."

DATA AT REST PROTECTION

TOKENIZATION

Considerations:

1. If the correspondence between the pseudonyms and the actual names needs to be kept, then where is it stored, and is that table secure? Could a hacker get hold of both the pseudonymized data and the conversion table?
2. Could the rest of the attributes be sufficient de de-anonymize the data? If this is a medical dataset, and "Mary Smith" is the pseudonym for a 43-year old Asian woman with advanced melanoma living in ZIP code 12345-6789, how many people meeting that description are there? (Full US ZIP codes are quite specific to small areas.)

This is hard. It requires an assessment or audit by people who know the structure and semantics of the data. Some professionals would detect the risk immediately; some wouldn't. Employing a white-hat hacker (on-site, under control) would be a good test that the data is protected enough. You give them a challenge such as "if you spend a day at our office trying to de-anonymize records from a dataset we give you, and you fail, we pay for your time. If you manage to de-anonymize some records, we pay you 10x that amount."

The mapping between pseudonyms and the actual names needs to be kept secure:

Could a hacker get hold of both the pseudonymized data and the conversion table?
A Secret is unique to each data item/field/column.

Best practices:

- A Secret can be unique to a branch office. A Secret is stored encrypted with a key that can be kept on-premises in an HSM.
- User credentials are granular with limited access. User behavior is monitored.

COARSE-GRAINED VS. FINE-GRAINED ENCRYPTION

Coarse-grained encryption may comply with regulations and other requirements. This takes the form of platform-based encryption (such as on AWS, Azure, volume encryption, database encryption).

- Some organizations use File Encryption with some use cases (like protecting a landing zone) that require separation of duties.
- "Best Practice" to have Fine-Grained Data Protection (encryption/tokenization).

PCI DSS evolved from encryption of the PAN (Primary Account Number) to recommending tokenization:

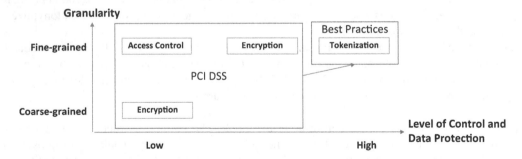

The IBM Security Framework for EU GDPR mentions tokenization and encryption to protect data:

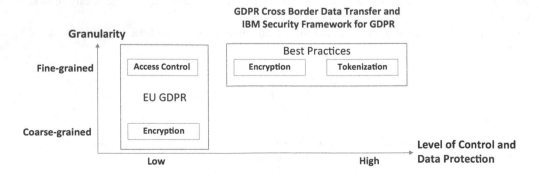

A risk evaluation may suggest encryption even if, for example, US HIPAA does not require general encryption:

TOKENIZATION

The correspondence table should obviously be encrypted on a secure server, and access to it should probably be protected through MFA, with one of the factors possibly being a hardware token held by the person who is accountable for the protection of that data (then there is the issue of what happens if that physical token is lost, so there probably need to be 2–3, and the organization needs to know who has them. Or lock that token in a safe, with only a few people having the combination to the safe, and so on (typical issues).

We will discuss this topic in separate chapters.

APPLICATION SECURITY

WEB APPLICATION SECURITY RISKS

According to Verizon DBIR, Web applications are targeted in many attacks.

Top Three Web Application Security Risks

According to OWASP, the top three Web Application security risks are:

1. A1:2017-Injection: Injection mistakes, such as SQL, NoSQL, OS, and LDAP injection, happen when untrusted information is sent to an interpreter as part of a command or query. The attacker's antagonistic information can trick the interpreter into executing unintended commands or accessing data without proper authorization.
2. A2:2017-Broken Authentication: Application functions connected to authentication and session management are frequently applied incorrectly, allowing aggressors to compromise passwords, keys, or session tokens or to exploit other implementation flaws to assume other users' identities provisionally or permanently.
3. A3:2017-Sensitive Data Exposure: Many web applications and APIs do not appropriately protect sensitive information, such as financial, healthcare, and PII.

Attackers may steal or modify such weakly guarded data to conduct credit card fraud, identity theft, or other violations. Sensitive information may be compromised without extra protection, such as encryption at rest or in transit, and involves special precautions when exchanged with the browser.

Data is attacked at different system layers:

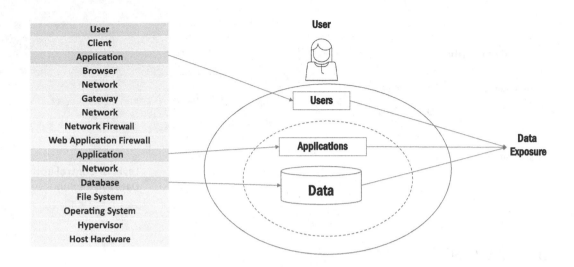

Data can be protected at different system layers:

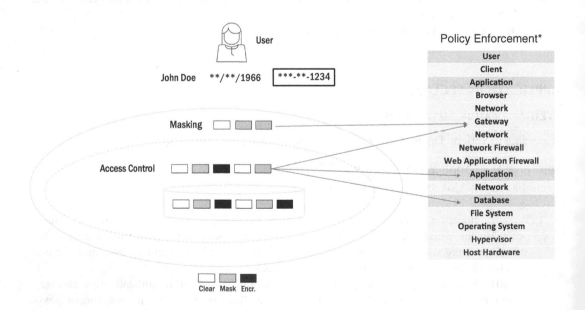

CLOUD DATA

Data must move without interruption through an enterprise's many cloud-based databases and applications. Companies need the cloud to place workloads in development containers. The most crucial data types in pushing innovation—with advanced analytics, machine learning, and AI—are those held most sensitive and must be protected.

Naturally, sensitive information chronicles how customers and employees engage, and, once harnessed, reveal insights and outcomes that are game-changers for your business. Such intelligence, once reined, optimizes experiences in real-time while creating a blueprint for quick growth. Privacy and innovation go together. You cannot have one with not the other, and neither is optional anymore. Organizations are quite aware of their on-premises encryption and key management systems, so they often prefer to leverage the same systems and services across multiple clouds. Companies often adopt a "best of breed" cloud attitude. A common concern is vendor lock-in and an inability to migrate to another cloud service provider:

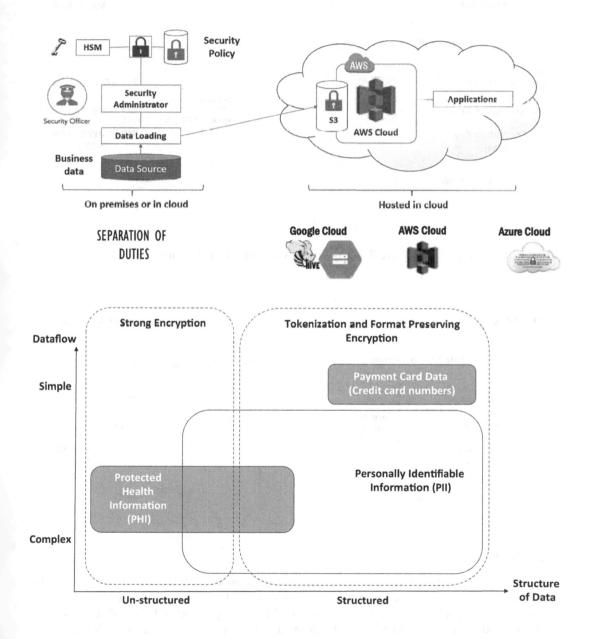

This is an example of the separation of duties for cloud data security. The enterprise policy and key management system are separated from the data administration in the cloud.

KEEPING KEYS UNDER CONTROL

Customers increasingly are concerned about trust in the cloud provider, and organizations want consistency in key management across environments, keeping the encryption keys under my control.

Hybrid Data Security Architecture Security Policy Management on-premises:

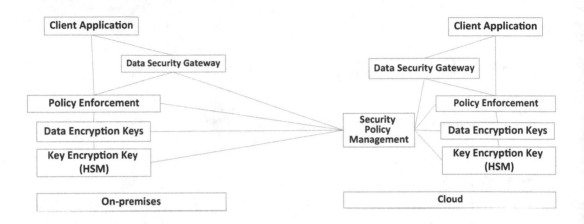

Hybrid Data Security Architecture Security Policy Management in the Cloud:

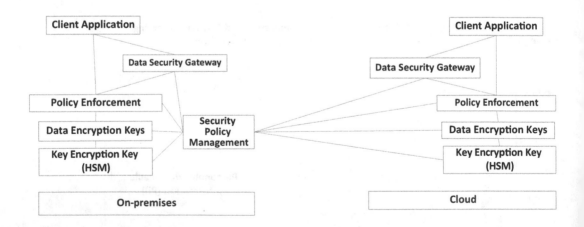

DATA IS MORE DISTRIBUTED

This is what it used to look like in a typical corporate environment. We had cloud systems and on-premises systems managed by corporate, including laptops and the backups of different databases.

Contracts with hosting providers may include the shared responsibility for cloud resources. As a cloud user/client, you are still responsible for the data since you collected the data. You can out-source your operations, but you're still liable for the data.

PEOPLE INCREASINGLY WORK FROM HOME

Over time and particularly with the COVID pandemic, more people started to work from home, and more data started to be hosted in the cloud and stored in different local environments.

These additional systems are not managed by corporate. Users choose to use new cloud-based applications that store additional types of personal and corporate data. Users also stored local copies of data. Our mobile phone data is usually stored and backed up into the cloud. Data is more distributed less controlled by corporate:

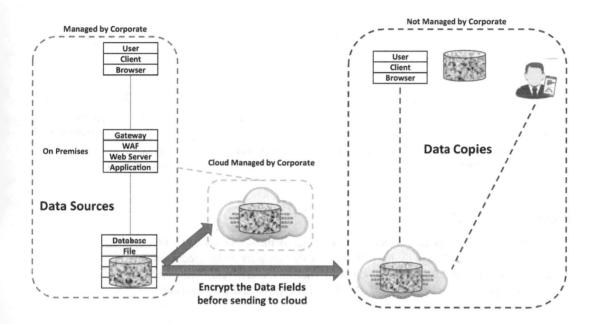

EFFECTIVE DATA SECURITY STRATEGY

For an effective data security strategy, organizations need the ability to use the right protection method, for the right use case, at the right time.

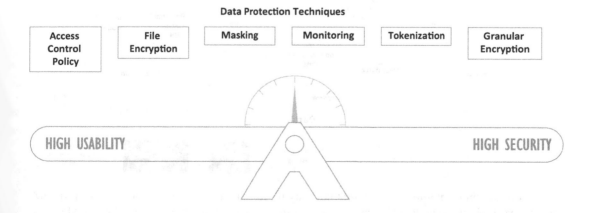

ROADMAP

Organizations can start quickly with low hanging fruit among data protection methods and advance to more effective data protection over time:

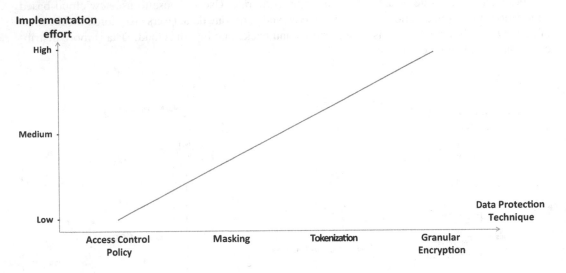

PROTECT SENSITIVE DATA

Ensure that your data is private and protected from manipulation by applying fine-grained data encryption or tokenization to limit exfiltration by ransomware and protect from other attacks on your data. This will protect data in transit, in use, in memory, and at rest. These are the general characteristics of fine-grained data protection, including encryption and tokenization:

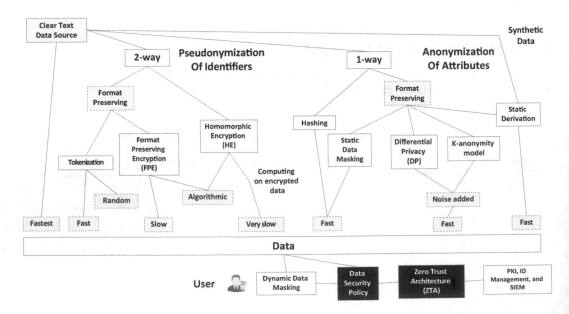

Data protection techniques are different but may initially look the same. Some are very fast, and some are very slow. Some techniques are aggregating data or adding noise to the data to "dummy down" the data. Some protection techniques are non-reversible "One-way" transformations like hashing, static data masking, differential privacy, and K anonymity.

In Test/Dev environments or Analytics environments, you may replace some of your business data with synthetic "fake" data. Synthetic data can be generated or derived from your business data, and you can mix these approaches. In the separate chapters of this book, we will discuss how new techniques for data protection create opportunities to harness sensitive data.

If you want the protected data format preserved, you may use tokenization or format-preserving encryption (FPE). FPE is typically ten times slower than AES encryption. AES encryption performance can be similar to Vaultless tokenization. Tokenization in the cloud can, for example, scale up to 180 million transactions per second.

Examples of basic performance can be found in Chapter 3.

ROADMAP

I call this "The Road to Data Privacy and Security," and I think that different people have their own starting point and destination and may take their own road in this journey:

| Area | The Road to Data Privacy and Security | | | |
	Risk Management	Define Privacy Policies	Specify Security Controls	Operate
	Review Threats Landscape	Specify Regulations Requirements	Vendor Selection & Implement Tools	Manage
	Find Opportunities			
Activity	Apply Regulations	Select Industry Standards	Select Industry Standards	Monitor
	Define Risk Appetite		Implement Privacy by Design	Audit
	Address Certifications		Select Data Protection Techniques	Report

COMPLIANCE WITH GDPR CROSS-BORDER PRIVACY RESTRICTIONS

This is an example of cross-border data privacy using tokenization. A major international bank performed a consolidation of all European operational data sources to Italy:

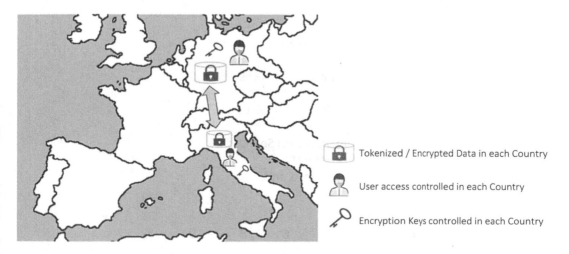

Tokenized / Encrypted Data in each Country

User access controlled in each Country

Encryption Keys controlled in each Country

Source: Gartner Forecast: Information Security and Risk Management, Worldwide (G00385345)

Financial data and Personally Identifiable Information (PII) is handled in compliance with the EU Cross Border Data Protection Laws, specifically Datenschutzgesetz 2000 (DSG 2000) in Austria and Bundesdatenschutzgesetz in Germany. This required access to Austrian and German customer data to be restricted to only requesters in each respective country. They achieved compliance with EU Cross Border Data Security laws and implemented country-specific data access restrictions.

INFORMATION SECURITY SPENDING

Gartner reported in 2020 that organizations would prioritize two top areas for Security Investments in Encryption Software and Cloud Access Security Brokers (CASB) in the next few years. We will discuss these two technologies later in this book.

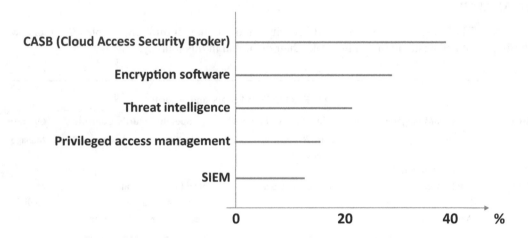

Source: Adapted from Gartner

SPENDING BY INDUSTRY

IT Security Spending as Percent of Total IT Spending by industry:

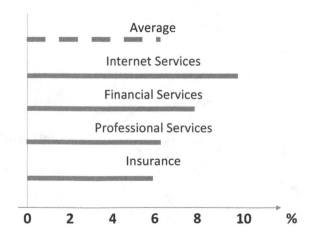

Source: Adapted from Gartner

IT Security Spending as Percent of Total IT Spending by country:

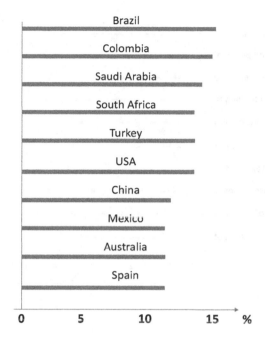

Source: Adapted from (ISC)2, 2021

USE OF COMMON DATA PROTECTION TECHNIQUES

What controls are you using beyond what is legally required?

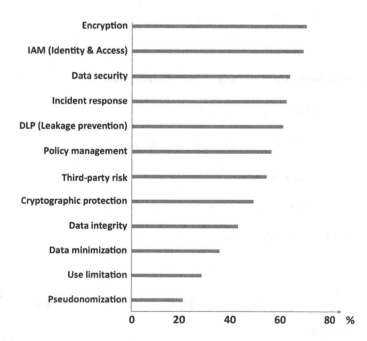

Source: Adapted from Gartner, 2021

What are the barriers to establishing effective security defenses?:

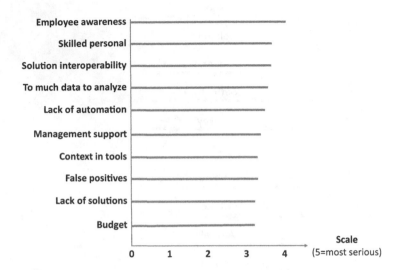

Source: Adapted from (ISC)2

What data protection are you currently using?:

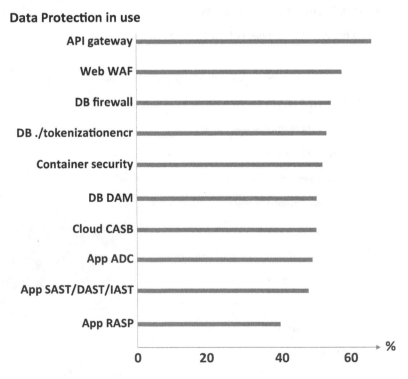

Source: Adapted from (ISC)2

What are your major budget areas for the next two years?:

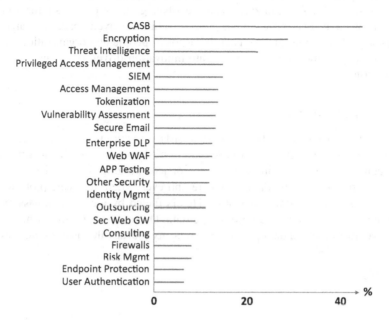

Source: Adapted from Gartner

How much of your IT budget is allocated to security?:

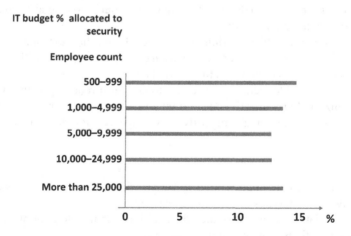

Source: Adapted from Gartner

VISION

I have a vision of equality and hope for Data Privacy. We can use data-security solutions to provide data privacy and protect your personal data and the world's most sensitive data. Organizations can overcome the obstacle and create trust with their customers by securing their sensitive data and maintaining the top level of data privacy and compliance. The data security industry has a storied history of innovation in data privacy and security. This heritage grounds us as the industry works jointly to consistently transform solutions that provide enterprises with the best data-security capabilities. For over three decades, organizations have evolved granular protection for some of the most sensitive data. Throughout this journey, data privacy solutions stayed apace with an ever-changing technology industry, always adapting to meet the needs of people and organizations. In that regard, old data protection approaches are reimagined into innovation-driven solutions built atop a proven and solid foundation.

PROTECT SENSITIVE DATA ANYWHERE

We must continuously strive towards global standards for ubiquitous data protection. We must empower intelligence-driven companies to use data to push innovation with security analytics and artificial intelligence without violating compliance or jeopardizing privacy. To make this vision a reality, we should protect sensitive data anywhere and everywhere to create protected data agility that aligns with the speed of modern business. This is fueled by a collective passion for building software that allows users to innovate with secure data. Our industry is partnering with innovative users to ensure we always lead a data privacy and security journey that is constantly evolving.

STEPS IN THE VISION

Extract value from protected data

- New solutions arm innovative businesses to win in an ever-changing, increasingly competitive digital economy. These solutions can empower businesses to activate and obtain value from sensitive data and engender trust by ensuring the privacy of customers and employees is always kept.
- This allows businesses to private use data—including its application in advanced analytics, machine learning, and AI—to do excellent things without worrying about putting customers, employees, or intellectual property at risk.
- We will discuss how machine learning on protected data that arm innovative businesses to win. We will also discuss how recent advances in quantum computers will significantly impact opportunities and threats to new and historical data.
- We will discuss available technologies and a longer-term roadmap with future technologies that can optimize and protect ML code current and future computers. All of this propels businesses forward by giving you a competitive advantage over less innovative competitors.

Secure AI

- Secure AI solutions create opportunities to harness the sensitive data that is most effective in activating advanced analytics and machine learning.
- Secure sensitive data wherever it is and whatever it is—in the cloud or on-premises.
- Data knows no confines, nor should data protection.

SUMMARY

We discussed how implementing a multilayer defense can help create a good security posture and how sensitive data can be protected and how a central enterprise policy can control encryption keys and what data protection techniques are used for different types of data.

We discussed practical ways to implement data privacy, suggested best practices, a roadmap, and vision going forward. We also discussed how sensitive data can be protected, how a central enterprise policy can control encryption keys, and what data protection techniques are used for different types of data.

More of this will be discussed in Volume II of this book.

BIBLIOGRAPHY

1. Zero Trust Architecture (ZTA), https://nvlpubs.nist.gov/nistpubs/SpecialPublications/NIST.SP.800-207.pdf
2. OWASP, https://owasp.org/www-project-proactive-controls/
3. OWASP Top Ten, https://owasp.org/www-project-top-ten/
4. How to Prevent Internal and External Attacks on Data - Securing the Enterprise Data Flow Against Advanced Attacks, http://papers.ssrn.com/sol3/papers.cfm?abstract_id=1144290
5. A New Scalable Approach to Data Tokenization, http://ssrn.com/abstract=1627284
6. Focus Your Attention on Data Security, Zero-trust and Supply Chains, https://techcrunch.com/2021/06/23/want-in-on-the-next-100b-in-cybersecurity/?utm_campaign=Oktopost-Rick+Farnell+General+Industry+News&utm_content=Oktopost-linkedin&utm_medium=social&utm_source=linkedin
7. Privacy-Preserving Analytics and Secure Multiparty Computation, https://sf-prod.isaca.org/resources/isaca-journal/issues/2021/volume-2/privacy-preserving-analytics-and-secure-multiparty-computation
8. Payment Card Data - Know Your Defense Options, http://papers.ssrn.com/sol3/papers.cfm?abstract_id=126002
9. Probabilistic Inference and Differential Privacy, https://proceedings.neurips.cc/paper/2010/file/fb60d411a5c5b72b2e7d3527cfc84fd0-Paper.pdf
10. The Good, the Bad and the Ugly of Protecting Data in a Retail Environment, http://papers.ssrn.com/sol3/papers.cfm?abstract_id=1104320
11. Toward Inference Attacks for k-Anonymity, https://link.springer.com/article/10.1007/s00779-014-0787-y
12. Verizon DBIR, https://www.verizon.com/business/resources/reports/dbir/
13. Shared Responsibility Model Explained, https://cloudsecurityalliance.org/blog/2020/08/26/shared-responsibility-model-explained/#:~:text=Cloud%20service%20providers%20adhere%20to%20a%20shared%20security,the%20provider%20takes%20some%20responsibility%2C%20but%20not%20all
14. 78% of Organizations Use More than 50 Cybersecurity Products to Address Security Issues, https://www.securitymagazine.com/articles/92395-of-organizations-use-more-than-50-cybersecurity-products-to-address-security-issues#:~:text=To%20address%20increasing%20data%20security%20concerns%20and%20trust,mitigate%20threats%20in%20an%20increasingly%20expanding%20digital%20world.
15. Data Security for PCI and Beyond, http://papers.ssrn.com/sol3/papers.cfm?abstract_id=974957
16. Your Employees Are Your Best Defense Against Cyberattacks, https://hbr.org/2021/08/your-employees-are-your-best-defense-against-cyberattacks?utm_campaign=Oktopost-Rick+Farnell+Personal&utm_content=Oktopost-LinkedIn&utm_medium=social&utm_source=LinkedIn
17. Risk-Based Classification Process, http://papers.ssrn.com/sol3/papers.cfm?abstract_id=1365522
18. Information Security, https://en.wikipedia.org/wiki/Information_security
19. k-Anonymity: A Model for Protecting Privacy, https://dataprivacylab.org/dataprivacy/projects/kanonymity/kanonymity.pdf
20. Statistically Valid Inferences from Privacy Protected Data, https://gking.harvard.edu/dp
21. New Study: IT Pros Are More Worried About Corporate ..., https://www.oracle.com/corporate/pressrelease/cloud-threat-report-2020-051420.html

Section II

Data Confidentiality and Integrity

4 Computing on Encrypted Data

INTRODUCTION

Traditional encryption methods, such as AES, are high-speed and allow data to be stored in encrypted form.

Encryption of data in the cloud needs secret keys that may lead to security worries. Homomorphic encryption resolves this problem, allowing the cloud service to perform the computations while protecting sensitive data.

In this chapter, we will discuss homomorphic encryption use cases, technology, and how it can be used to support computing in the cloud and other environments that may be untrusted.

PROTECTING SENSITIVE DATA IN THE CLOUD

Protecting sensitive data in the cloud, outsourced, or shared is increasingly essential. While traditional encryption methods can be applied to privately outsource information storage to the cloud, the information cannot be used for computations without first decrypting it. This results in a massive loss of utility. For example, a secure cloud service may involve users downloading their encrypted information, decrypting it locally, and performing needed computations instead of returning an encrypted result to the user.

DATA PROTECTION TECHNIQUES OVERVIEW

Traditional data protection schemes can provide reversible (2-way) or irreversible (1-way) encryption of data. Some of these are preserving the format of the input data. The speed characteristics vary between these data protection techniques. Homomorphic encryption (HE) use cases are focused on performing operations on the encrypted data values:

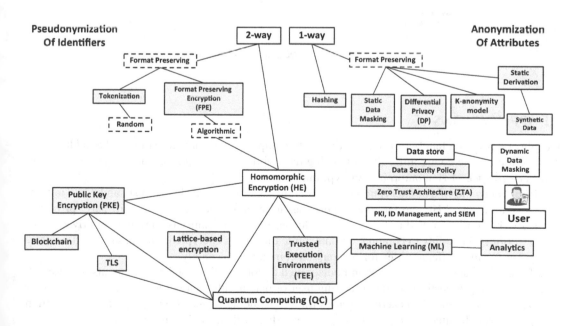

DOI: 10.1201/9781003189664-6

HOMOMORPHIC ENCRYPTION

The cloud sees encrypted information, and only the customer can uncover the computation result. One of the benefits of the lattice-based cryptosystems mentioned earlier is building methods that securely and privately carry computation on encrypted information. Homomorphic encryption allows operations on encrypted data. Standard cryptosystems in use these days don't have this property. The result will be gibberish if you try to add two ciphertexts (encrypted texts) encrypted using the Advanced Encryption Standard (AES). Homomorphic encryption differentiates itself by maintaining the structure of the information. It encodes data in a mathematical body and then encrypts it to don't affect the contained information. Homomorphic encryption is vital because it allows consumers and enterprises to store their sensitive data in the cloud in encrypted form. The cloud can compute the data in its encrypted form and then return encrypted predictions or analytics, all without ever decrypting the data or learning anything about the client's sensitive information. A consortium of researchers from industry, government, and academia focuses on standardizing this new cryptographic primitive. HomomorphicEncryption.org is an open association of industry, government, and academia to standardize homomorphic encryption.

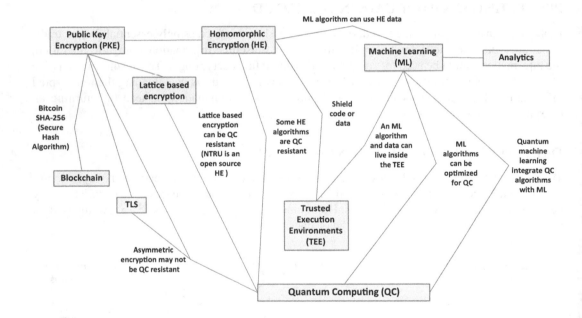

HE APPLICATIONS

HE plays a part in a family of privacy-preserving computation techniques (PPCT) that address and remove the classic compromise of distributing data while retaining privacy, according to "Security and Performance of Homomorphic Encryption."

HE expands the role of encryption by broadening its reach from "data at rest" and "data in transit" to "data in use." HE can facilitate enterprises to leverage the services of third-party providers (typically but not controlled to the cloud) by decreasing or (in some cases) removing privacy worries. HE offers the ability to compute on data while the data is encrypted. This has enabled industry and government to offer abilities for outsourced computation securely.

HE permits data to be encrypted and outsourced to commercial cloud environments for research and data-sharing objectives while protecting user or patient information privacy. It can be used for companies and organizations across various trades, including financial services, retail, information technology, and healthcare, to permit people to use data without seeing its unencrypted values.

Fully homomorphic encryption has numerous applications. For instance, it facilitates private queries to a search engine—the user submits an encrypted query. The search engine computes a concise encrypted answer without ever looking at the query in the clear. It also enables searching on encrypted information—a user stores encrypted files on a remote file server and can, later on, have the server recover only files that (when decrypted) fulfill some Boolean constraint, even though the server cannot decrypt the files on its own.

Domain	Genomics	Health	National Security	Education	Social Security	Business Analytics	Cloud
Sample topics	GWAS	Billing	Smart grid	School dropouts	Credit history	Prediction	Sharing
Data owner	Medical institutions	Clinics	Nodes	Welfare	Government	Owners	Clients
Why HE?	HIPAA	Insurance	Privacy	FERPA	Cyber crimes	Data is valuable	Untrusted servers
Who pays?	Health insurance	Hospital	Energy company	DoE	Government	Owners	Clients

Source: Adapted from Homomorphicencryption.or.g

HOMOMORPHIC ENCRYPTION CAN BE USED TO SIMPLIFY

Low-cost cloud computing and cloud storage have fundamentally changed how businesses and people use and manage their information. Conventional encryption methods, such as AES, are extremely fast and allow information to be stored easily in encrypted form. The cloud can use the encrypted data and return only the encrypted result to the owner of the information. More complicated application scenarios can involve several parties with private information that a third party can run on and return the result to one or more members to be decrypted according to "Security and Performance of Homomorphic Encryption."

CATEGORIES OF HE TECHNOLOGIES

HE is a cryptographic method that facilitates third parties to process encrypted data and return an encrypted product to the data owner while providing no knowledge about the data or the results according to "Top Strategic Technology Trends for 2021."

HE enables algorithm suppliers to shield proprietary algorithms and data owners to keep information private Partially homomorphic encryption (PHE) permits just one operation on the encrypted data (i.e., either addition or multiplication but not both). Somewhat homomorphic encryption (SWHE) allows a limited number of the data's addition or multiplication operations, but not both.

1. Fully homomorphic encryption (FHE) refers to "a class of encryption methods envisioned by Rivest, Adleman, and Dertouzos already in 1978, and first constructed by Craig Gentry in 2009" according to "Introduction—Homomorphic Encryption Standardization."

History of HE Algorithms

DH '76	RSA '78	RAD '78	GM '82	El-Gamal '85	Benalon '94	Pallier '99	SYY '00	BGN '05	IP '07	Gen '09
				PHE				SWHE		FHE
1976										2015

Source: Adapted form Homomorphicencryption.org.

Specific Use Cases

Fully homomorphic encryption permits an unlimited number of both addition and multiplication operations. Amongst the spectrum of HE tools, FHE has the greatest potential industry influence. However, practical implementations have puzzled technologists for decades. In practice, these days, fully homomorphic encryption is not fast adequate for most business implementations. Partially homomorphic encryption is a highly practical implementation, and fully homomorphic encryption is suitable for specific use cases.

FULLY HOMOMORPHIC AND OTHER HE ALGORITHMS

FHE permits you to do an unbounded number of operations. SHE (also called SWHE) is more universal than "PHE in the sense that it supports homomorphic operations with additions and multiplications" according to "Security and Performance of Homomorphic Encryption." PHE (Partially Homomorphic Encryption) systems are generally more economical than SHE and FHE, primarily since they are homomorphic with respect to only one kind of operation: addition or multiplication. SHE and PHE may not be suitable for data sharing scenarios that require a broader set of operations.

HE Quantum-Safe Lattice-Based Cryptography

Lattice-based cryptography is built on cryptographic systems such as Learning With Errors (LWE). "Lattice-based cryptography has been published and analyzed increasingly during 2011 to 2020 in more than 180 papers" according to "Security and Performance of Homomorphic Encryption":

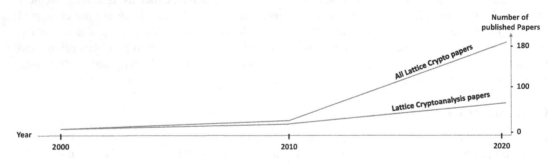

Source: Adapted from CSA (Cloud Security Alliance)

A Sample Program for HE Multiplication

A homomorphic multiplication program may start with the client encrypting a first plaintext and a second plaintext and sending it to a server. The server is then performing the homomorphic multiplication and sending the encrypted result back to the client. The client is then decrypting the result of multiplications to get the clear text result of the multiplication operation:

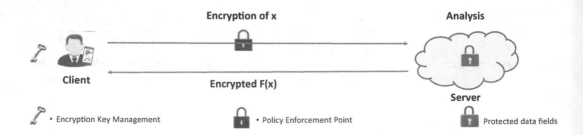

HE PERFORMANCE

While substantial improvements have been made in the latest years, general fully HE-based (FHE) processing stays 1,000 to 1,000,000 times slower than comparable plaintext operations, according to "Security and Performance of Homomorphic Encryption."

One instance (using 128-bit security) with the NTRU public-key-based lattice encryption reported 55 k crypto operations per second compared to 8 k for RSA and 4 k for ECC.

The Centre for Secure Information Technologies (CSIT), Queen's University Belfast, Northern Ireland, reported the following approximated timings for multiplication and small-size encryption on different processors using FHE Gentry–based lattice-based cryptography:

Processor Platform	Multiplication (millisecond)	Encryption (seconds)
TSMC	8	2
GPU	1	2
GTX	0.5	0.01

Source: Adapted form The Centre for Secure Information Technologies.

COMPARING ENCRYPTION PERFORMANCE

The TSMC company provides advanced semiconductor process technology. GPU (graphics processing unit) is a specialized electronic circuit intended to alter memory to accelerate the creation of images. GTX 16 is a gaming supercharger to accelerate graphics performance.

Cases comparing file encryption and decryption of a 50KB file the RSA algorithm and the ancient homomorphic El-Gamal asymmetric key encryption algorithm and Paillier asymmetric algorithm stated the resulting process time for decrypting a 123KB file was on RSA (60 sec), ElGamal (10 sec), and Paillier (150 seconds). Hardware acceleration can improve performance according to "Security and Performance of Homomorphic Encryption":

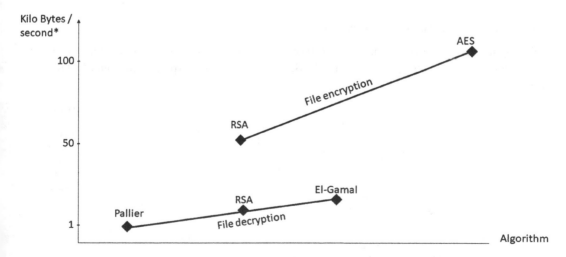

Source: Adapted from Homomorphicencryption.org *: Speed will depend on the configuration

Comparing Scalability and Performance

This figure compares scalability aspects and performance of HE algorithms with some field encryption algorithms and tokenization:

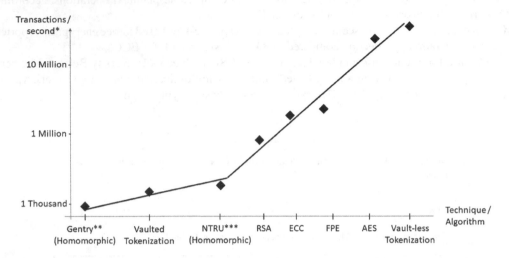

Source: Adapted from Homomorphicencryption.org *: Speed will depend on the configuration

The figure below shows examples of performance of operations (decryption, encryption, and addition) in bytes per second on longer data messages (files):

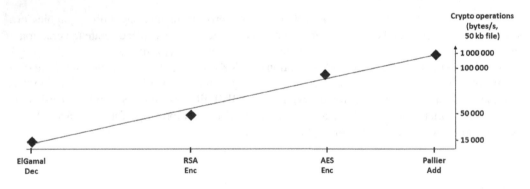

Source: Adapted from Homomorphicencryption.org

The figure below shows examples of performance of operations per second on short data (20+ bytes) encryption and multiplication with AES, RSA, and homomorphic algorithms (NTRU and Gentry):

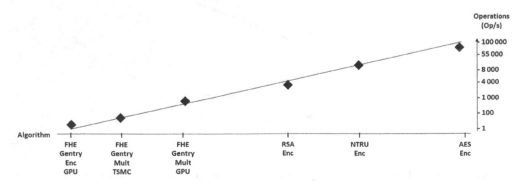

Source: Adapted from Homomorphicencryption.org

Let's discuss some popular schemes, including Fully Homomorphic Encryption over the Torus (TFHE), Brakerski/Fan-Vercauteren (BFV), and Cheon-Kim-Kim-Song (CKKS):

Library	FHEW	TFHE	BGV	BFV	CKSS
cuFHE		y			
FHEW	y				
FV-Nflib				y	
HEAAN					y
Helib			y		(y)
PALISADE			y	y	(y)
SEAL				y	Y

Source: Adapted form Homomorphicencryption.org.

IBM is supporting CKKS in HElib library. Duality is using BFV and CKKS in PALISADE library. Microsoft is using BFV and CKKS in SEAL library.

HE Operations	BGV	BFV	CKKS
Addition	y	y	y
Multiplication	y	y	y
Division	n	n	n
No exponentiation	n	n	n
No non-polynomial	n	n	n
Only integers	y	y	y

Source: Adapted form Homomorphicencryption.org.

The figure above shows that division, exponentiation, and non-polynomial operations are not supported.

HE Programs

Below is an abbreviated example that illustrates some aspects of programming in HE applications. The first step is to define the chosen security level by declaring a Context, for example, with a modulus size (65537) and a security level (128) that will be used when you generate a pair of asymmetric encryption keys:

```
Int plaintextModulus = 65537;
Double sigma = 3.2;
SecurityLevel securityLevel = HEStd_128_classic;
Unit32_depth = 2;
...
```

Next step is the encoding end encryption of plain text vectors:

For example, the ciphertext2 is using the cryptoContext to use the keyPair publicKey to encrypt plaintext2:

```
// First plaintext vector is encoded
std::vector<uint64_t> vectorOfInts1 = {1,2,3,4,5,6,7,8,9,10,11,12};
Plaintext plaintext1 = cryptoContext->MakePackedPlaintext(vectorOfInts1);
// Second plaintext vector is encoded
std::vector<uint64_t> vectorOfInts2 = {3,2,1,4,5,6,7,8,9,10,11,12};
Plaintext plaintext2 = cryptoContext->MakePackedPlaintext(vectorOfInts2);
// Third plaintext vector is encoded
std::vector<uint64_t> vectorOfInts3 = {1,2,5,2,5,6,7,8,9,10,11,12};
Plaintext plaintext3 = cryptoContext->MakePackedPlaintext(vectorOfInts3);
// The encoded vectors are encrypted
auto ciphertext1 = cryptoContext->Encrypt(keyPair.publicKey, plaintext1);
auto ciphertext2 = cryptoContext->Encrypt(keyPair.publicKey, plaintext2);
auto ciphertext3 = cryptoContext->Encrypt(keyPair.publicKey, plaintext3);
```

Next step is the addition of cipher texts. We evaluate by adding using EvalAdd of ciphertext1 and ciphertext2:

```
// Homomorphic additions
auto ciphertextAdd12 = cryptoContext->EvalAdd(ciphertext1,ciphertext2);
auto ciphertextAddResult = cryptoContext->EvalAdd(ciphertextAdd12,ciphertext3);
// Homomorphic multiplications
auto ciphertextMul12 = cryptoContext->EvalMult(ciphertext1,ciphertext2);
auto ciphertextMultResult = cryptoContext->EvalMult(ciphertextMul12,ciphertext3);
```

The next step is the decryption of results. Then we decrypt the result of additions by using the cryptoContext to Decrypt with the secretKey on the ciphertext of the added result and similarly on the multiplicated result:

```
// Decrypt the result of additions
Plaintext plaintextAddResult;
cryptoContext->Decrypt(keyPair.secretKey, ciphertextAddResult,
&plaintextAddResult);
```

```
// Decrypt the result of multiplications
Plaintext plaintextMultResult;
cryptoContext->Decrypt(keyPair.secretKey, ciphertextMultResult,
&plaintextMultResult);
```

```
// Output results
cout << plaintextAddResult << endl;
cout << plaintextMultResult << endl;
```

HE SECURITY

The security of the best practical homomorphic encryption schemes is built on the "Ring-Learning With Errors (RLWE) problem, which is a hard mathematical problem related to high-dimensional lattices" according to "Security and Performance of Homomorphic Encryption. The RLWE question is closely linked to famous hard lattice problems currently considered secure against quantum computers. Similarly, RLWE and, subsequently, most homomorphic encryption methods are secure against quantum computers. This makes them more secure than factorization and discrete logarithm-based systems such as RSA and many forms of elliptic curve cryptography.

NIST's post-quantum cryptography standardization project had several proposals based on hard lattice problems like what modern day homomorphic encryption utilizes. The NIST report describes the second-round candidates' evaluation and selection process based on public feedback and internal review. The third-round runner-up public-key encryption and key-establishment algorithms are Classic McEliece, CRYSTALS-KYBER, NTRU, and SABER.

FACTORS THAT MAY INHIBIT HE ADOPTION

While massive enhancements have been made in late years, general FHE-based processing remains several thousand times slower than equivalent plaintext efforts. Therefore, the computational overhead remains too heavy for FHE in most typical computing scenarios.

We need to simplify and standardize APIs and SDKs. The overwhelming majority of historical HE research has come from elite corporate and academic cryptographic experts. As a result, most of the HE libraries remain too difficult for mainstream IT providers and customers to leverage without intensive training. HE technology must be abstracted and simplified to succeed among mainstream end-user and TSP organizations by incorporating it into familiar developer languages, frameworks, and platforms. The future of this technology is tied to the increasing role of open innovation that can counter the secrecy and silo mentality of some research labs.

HE SOFTWARE AND ALGORITHMS

EXAMPLES OF POPULAR LIBRARIES AND ALGORITHMS

Algorithms supported in crypto libraries:

Algorithm	BGV	BFV	CKKS
Library/Scheme			
FV-NFLib		y	
HEAAN			y
Helib (IBM)	y		y
PALISDE (Duality)	y	y	y
DEAL (Microsoft)		y	y
TFHE		y	y

Source: Adopted from UTMSR (UTHealth-Microsoft Research).

Optimized data types:

Algorithm	BGV	BFV	CKKS
Operation			
Fast integers	y	y	
Fast integers vectors	y	y	
Fast real numbers vectors	y		y
Fast polymons	y	y	y
Fast scalar multiplications	y	y	

Source: Adopted from UTMSR (UTHealth-Microsoft Research).

Addition, multiplication, and other operations:

HE Operations	BGV	BFV	CKKS
Addition	y	y	y
Multiplication	y	y	y
Division	n	n	n
No exponentiation	n	n	n
No non-polynomial	n	n	n
Only integers	y	y	y

Source: Adopted from UTMSR (UTHealth-Microsoft Research).

Examples of HE Vendors

The software industry is complex to navigate. In the majority of cases, when selecting a software vendor, there are many options to choose from, ranging from larger established software companies to smaller, yet reputable, companies. When evaluating potential software vendors, it's essential to understand the various trade-offs between larger and smaller software companies, according to "Deciding Between Large vs. Small Software Vendors." The smaller vendors may have a focus on specific industries or use cases. They may also have a bundle of related features for machine learning (ML) or data privacy techniques.

Examples of features from larger and smaller HE Vendors:

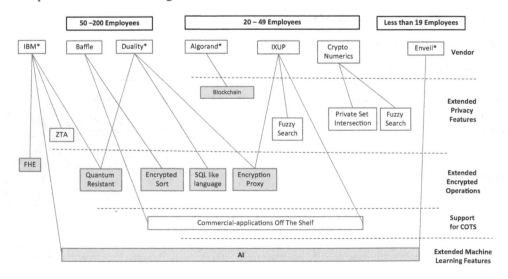

*: Members of Homomorphicencryption.org

Examples of operations supported by some algorithms:

Cryptographic Tool	Operat.ions				
	Addition	Multiplication	Division	Match	Only integers
Tokenization	No	No	No	Yes	No
AES symmetric block cipher encryption	No	No	No	Yes	No
Format Preserving Encryption (FPE)	No	No	No	Yes	No
Order-preserving encryption	No	No	No	Yes	No
RSA public key encryption (PKE)	No	Yes	No	Yes	Yes
PHE (Partially Homomorphic Encryption)	Addition or Multiplication	Addition or Multiplication	No	Yes	Yes
SWHE (Some What H homomorphic Encryption)	Yes	Yes	No	Yes	Yes
Fully homomorphic encryption (FHE)	Yes	Yes	Yes	Yes	Yes

DATA PROTECTION FOR SECURE ANALYTICS IN CLOUD

Organizations have privacy concerns that prohibit analytics involving sensitive data by using cloud services. We will discuss how to address this problem by using fast HE techniques. We will compare the time and memory requirements of the secure computing pipeline with the non-secure methods. The research team for this study included the Center for Secure Artificial intelligence For hEalthcare (SAFE), School of Biomedical Informatics, University of Texas Health Science Center, Houston, USA.

USE CASE IN HEALTH CARE

The use case is based on health care data involving genotype imputation by utilizing HE that can evaluate millions of imputation models in seconds according to "Ultrafast homomorphic encryption models enable secure outsourcing of genotype imputation."

In HE-based methods, the genotype data and result is end-to-end encrypted, that is, encrypted in transit, at rest, and, most significantly, in analysis, and can be decrypted only by the information owner. SAFE compared secure imputation with three other state-of-the-art non-secure methods under different settings. It was found that HE-based methods provide full genetic data security with comparable or slightly lower accuracy. In addition, HE-based methods have time and memory needs that are comparable to the non-secure methods. SAFE provides five different implementations and workflows that use three cutting-edge HE schemes (BFV, CKKS, TFHE).

Mathematically Provable

The methods use the HE formalism that offers mathematically provable and potentially the deepest security guarantees for protecting genotype data. At the same time, imputation is executed in an untrusted system. To include a thorough set of approaches, we focus on three state-of-the-art HE cryptosystems, namely Brakerski/Fan-Vercauteren (BFV), Cheon-Kim-Kim-Song (CKKS), and Fully Homomorphic Encryption over the Torus (TFHE). In the HE-based framework, genotype data is encrypted by the data owner before outsourcing the information. After this point, data stays continually encrypted, that is, encrypted in-transit, in-use, and at rest; it is never decrypted until the results are sent to the information owner. The strength of the HE-based framework stems from the fact that the genotype data remains encrypted even while the imputation is being performed.

The Strongest Form of Security for Outsourcing

The HE framework provides the strongest security for outsourcing genotype imputation compared to other approaches under the same adversarial model. HE-based frameworks have been judged impractical since their inception. Therefore, in comparison to other cryptographically secure methods, such as multiparty computation and trusted execution environments, HE-based frameworks have received little attention. Recent theoretical discoveries in the HE literature and a strong community effort have since rendered HE-based systems practical. However, many of these improvements are only beginning to be reflected in practical implementations and applications of HE algorithms.

Detailed Benchmarking

SAFE performed detailed benchmarking of the time and memory requirements of HE-based imputation methods and demonstrated the feasibility of large-scale secure imputation.

Secure Methods

- The UTMSR (UTHealth-Microsoft Research) team uses a linear model with the nearby tag variants as features for each target variant. The plaintext model training uses the GSL library according to "Ultrafast homomorphic encryption models enable secure."
- Chimera-TFHE. The Chimera team used multi-class logistic regression (logreg) models trained over one-hot encoded tag features: each tag SNP variant is mapped to three Boolean variables.
- EPFL-CKKS. EPFL uses a multinomial logistic regression model.
- SNU-CKKS. The SNU team applies one-hidden layer neural network for the genotype imputation.

The total time with the different implementations and workflows using three cutting-edge HE schemes (BFV, CKKS, TFHE) was:

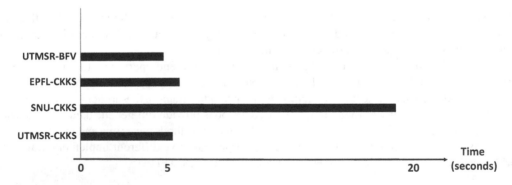

Source: Adopted from UTMSR (UTHealth-Microsodt Research)

Non-Secure Methods

The non-secure methods were run on a Linux workstation with 769 Gigabytes of main memory on an Intel Xeon Platinum 8168 CPU at 2.7 GHz with 96 cores.

- **Beagle** is the JAR formatted Java executable file for Beagle. The "population panel (1,500 individuals) and the testing panel data are converted into VCF file format as required by Beagle" according to "Ultrafast homomorphic encryption models enable secure."

- **IMPUTE2** with haplotype, legend, genotype, and the population panels are converted into specific formats that IMPUTE2 requires.
- **Minimac3** in a combination of "Eagle+Minimac3" is used in the Michigan Imputation Server's pipeline that is served for public use.

Beagle, IMPUTE2, and Minimac3 are similar. Minimac3 is an algorithm for genotypic imputation designed to handle extremely large reference panels in a more computationally economical way with no loss of accuracy.

The whole pipeline timing was:

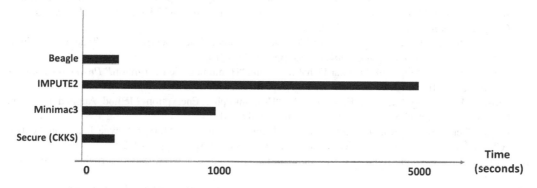

Source: Adopted from UTMSR (UTHealth-Microsoft Research)

SUMMARY

We discussed one way to protect sensitive data in the cloud, outsourced, or shared and allow computations without decrypting it. Homomorphic encryption (HE) use cases are becoming more important when sharing data that require performing operations on the encrypted data values. HE can be used to support computing in the cloud and other environments that may be untrusted.

We discussed the lack of standardization that inhibits consistency to create an economy of scope and scale.

We will discuss this topic more in Volume II of this book.

BIBLIOGRAPHY

1. Gentry, C. "A Fully Homomorphic Encryption Scheme." Stanford University. September 2009, https://crypto.stanford.edu/craig/craig-thesis.pdf
2. Ultrafast Homomorphic Encryption Models Enable Secure Outsourcing of Genotype Imputation, https://www.sciencedirect.com/science/article/pii/S240547122100288X
3. Homomorphic Encryption and Data Security in the Cloud, http://docs.udc.edu/seas/Faculty/Oladunni-Homomorphic_Encryption_and_Data_Security_in_the_Cloud.pdf
4. Homomorphic Encryption Standardization, Academic Consortium to Advance Secure Computation, https://homomorphicencryption.org/standards-meetings/
5. Homomorphic Encryption Standardization, https://homomorphicencryption.org/
6. Homomorphic Encryption, https://brilliant.org/wiki/homomorphic-encryption/
7. Deciding between Large vs Small Software Vendors, https://www.softwarepundit.com/deciding-between-large-vs-small-software-vendors
8. Security and Performance of Homomorphic Encryption, https://www.globalsecuritymag.com/Security-and-Performance-of,20210601,112333.html

9. Top Strategic Technology Trends for 2021, https://www.converge.com/wp-content/uploads/2021/01/top-tech-trends-ebook-2021.pdf#:~:text=Homomorphic%20encryption%20%28HE%29%20is%20a%20cryptographic%20method%20that,is%20not%20fast%20enough%20for%20most%20business%20implementations

10. Hrestak, Darko and Picek, Stjepan (2014). "Homomorphic Encryption in the Cloud." *Information and Communication Technology, Electronics and Microelectronics (MIPRO), 2014 37th International Convention on*, vol., no., pp. 1400–1404, 26–30 May 2014, pp. 1400–1404, 26–30.

11. Louk, M. and Lim, Hyotaek. "Homomorphic Encryption in Mobile Multi Cloud Computing." *Information Networking (ICOIN)*, pp. 493–497, 12–14, January 2015.

12. Li, Jian, Song, Danjie, Chen, Sicong, and Lu, Xiaofeng. "A simp Cloud Computing and Intelligent Systems (CCIS), *2012 IEEE 2nd International Conference*, vol. 1, pp. 214–217, 2012.

13. Chen, Baohua and Zhao, Na. "Fully Homomorphic Encryption Application in Cloud Computing," *Wavelet Active Media Technology and Information Processing (ICCWAMTIP), 11th International Computer Conference*, pp. 471–474, 2014.

14. Bouti, Adil and Keller, Jorg. "Towards Practical Homomorphic Encryption in Cloud Computing." *Network Cloud Computing and Applications*, pp. 67–74, 2015.

15. Turner, Claude and Ogburn, Pushkar Dahal Monique. "Homomorphic Encryption." *Procedia Computer Science*, 502–509, 2013.

16. Tebaa, M., El Hajji, S., and El Ghazi, A. "Homomorphic Encryption Method Applied to Cloud Computing." *Network Security and Systems*, pp. 86–89, 2012.

17. Begna, Geremew, Nwafor, Ebelechukwu, Blackstone, Jeremy, and Murray, Wayne Patterson Acklyn. "Cloud Service Security & Application Vulnerability." *SoutheastCon*, pp. 1–9, 2015.

18. Introduction—Homomorphic Encryption Standardization, https://homomorphicencryption.org/introduction/

19. Togan, Mihai and Plesca, Cezar. "Comparison-Based Computations Over Fully Homomorphic Encrypted Data." *Communications (COMM)*, pp. 1–6, 29–31, 2014.

20. Moore, C., O'Neill, M., O'Sullivan, E., Doroz, Y., and Sunar, B. "Practical Homomorphic Encryption: A survey." *Circuits and Systems (ISCAS)*, pp. 2792–2795, 2014.

21. Li, Xing, Yu, Jianping, Zhang, Peng, and Sun, Xiaoqiang. "A (Leveled) Fully Homomorphic Encryption Scheme based on Error-free Approximate GCD." *Electronics Information and Emergency Communication (ICEIEC)*, pp. 224–227, 14–16, 2015.

5 Reversible Data Protection Techniques

INTRODUCTION

This chapter will discuss reversible data protection techniques and use cases focused on granular protecting data fields that need to be recovered back to clear text from the encrypted data values. Examples include identifiers like names and account numbers.

DATA PROTECTION TECHNIQUES OVERVIEW

PROTECTION AT A FINE-GRAINED LEVEL

Traditional cybersecurity investment has been at the network level, building walls to keep the villains out of the business space. The difficulty is that once criminals get through some of those barriers, criminals have access to it and put organizations at risk if data is not protected at a fine-grained level, according to "Protegrity protects kinetic data by making it worthless."

Different data protection schemes can provide reversible (2-way) or irreversible (1-way) encryption of data. Some of these preserve the input data format, and some are based on an encryption algorithm and keys. The following figure illustrates some characteristics of different protection approaches and major use cases:

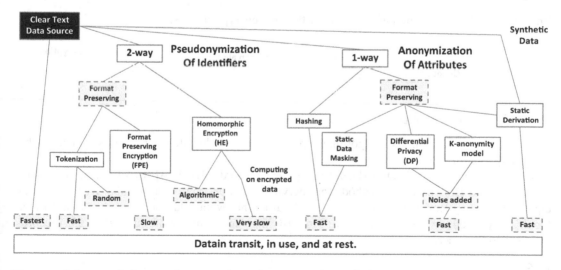

The speed characteristics vary between these data protection techniques.

DOI: 10.1201/9781003189664-7

PERFORMANCE

The speed is an important characteristic and varies between reversible data protection Techniques. This aspect is critical for some use cases. For example, Vaultless Tokenization can be run parallel and operates in memory without accessing a vault for token storage. This example can help when estimating performance aspects of different data protection techniques:

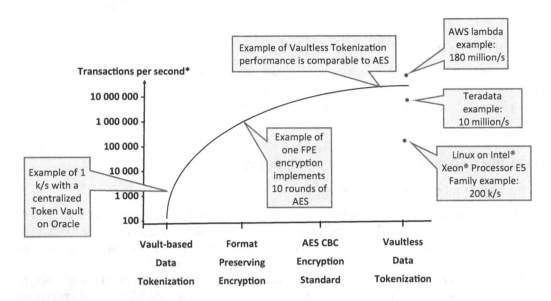

*: Speed will depend on the configuration.

ENCRYPTION

Encryption is based on a mathematical algorithm and encryption keys:

BLOCK CIPHER AND MODES

Block ciphers are deterministic algorithms operating on fixed-length groups of bits, called blocks, using a symmetric key.

Examples include RC5, DES (Data Encryption Standard), 3DES, AES (Advanced Encryption Standard), and Blowfish. The methods for encryption and decryption are similar. RC5 is a block cipher devised by Ronald Rivest in 1994 which, different several additional ciphers, has a variable block size (32, 64, or 128 bits), key size (0 to 2040 bits), and a number of rounds (0 to 255) according to "Block cipher."

DES

DES has a block size of 64 bits and a key size of 56 bits. 64-bit blocks come to be popular in block cipher designs after DES. The key length varied on several factors, including government regulation. DES, Triple DES, triple-encrypts each block with either two independent keys (112-bit key and 80-bit security) or three independent keys (168-bit key and 112-bit security). It was widely adopted as a replacement.

AES and DES

Advanced Encryption Standard (AES) has a block size of 128 bits and a key size of 128–256 bits with a block size of a maximum of 256 bits according to "Format Preserving Encryption: A Survey."

AES can, in some configurations, be three times faster than Triple-DES (DES3). Encryption time for DES and AES with different modes and key lengths (mins) in this example can help when estimating performance aspects of different block cipher algorithms. This is an example of encryption time in minutes for DES and AES running in CBC (Cipher Block Chaining) and ECB (Electronic Code Book) modes:

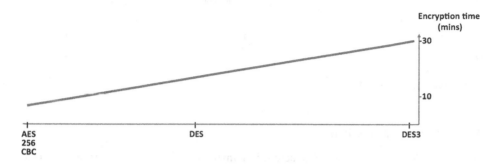

Mode of an Encryption Operation

- CBC is a cipher mode of operation that takes input from previous blocks in a chaining process to make the output depending on all data from the input string, providing added security.
- ECB mode creates an Electronic Code Book of individual characters and is not taking any input from previous characters in the input string. This makes each output character independent of other data from the input string, providing a lower level of security.

Performance of AES on Different Processors

The graph below is a speed comparison example of AES in CBC mode for key lengths 128 bits and 256 bits on different processors. This is a comparison example that can help when estimating performance aspects of different processors running AES:

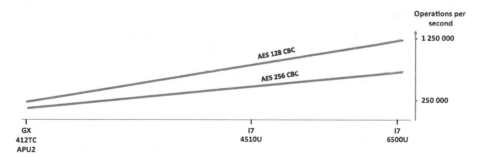

Source: Adapted from OpenSSL

OpenSSL is an open sources software package that is popular to use for general AES encryption operations on data for communication or storage.

Clock Cycles per Byte of AES

This is a comparison example of the number of clock cycles needed to execute AES for key lengths 128, 192, and 256 bits in hardware (assembly) and software implementations. AES with a 256-bit key length in CBC mode performs 16 clock cycles per byte running in software. This is a comparison example that can help when estimating performance aspects of different key lengths with AES:

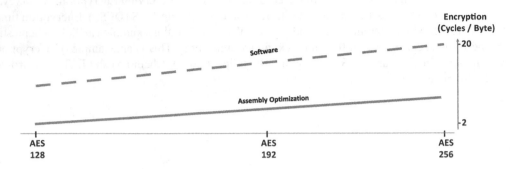

Source: Adapted from OpenSSL

AES NI Instruction Set on Intel

An example of Intel® AES NI (AES acceleration instructions on Intel) performance testing on Linux/Java Stack observed consistent and significant performance improvement in application file encryption/decryption. Specifically, 38% (average) for encryption and 37.5% (average) for decryption, over a wide range of key sizes and file sizes.

Format Preserving Encryption

Format Preserving Encryption (FPE) is a type of encryption algorithm that preserves the format of the information. At the same time, it is being encrypted according to "What is Format Preserving Encryption (FPE)? Is Format Preserving Encryption secure?"

FPE is weaker than the standard Advanced Encryption Standard (AES), but FPE can preserve the length of the data and its format.

A block cipher mode of operation defines how an algorithm should operate for the cryptographic transformation of data.

For instance, a Social Security number (SSN) consists of nine decimal numerals, so it is an integer that is less than one billion.

There are various techniques applied for the Format Preserving Encryption like Prefix cipher, Cycle walking, Feistel mechanism, Feistel modes, and more according to "Format Preserving Encryption: A Survey."

Credit card number input with output in FPE and strong cipher:

Feistel Finite Set Encryption Mode (FFSEM) allows encryption of a value ranging from 0..n with resultant ciphertext in that same span.

FFSEM has two sub-functions: FFSEM-PRF, a Pseudo-Random Function built on some block cipher, and FFSEM-ROUND, an individual Feistel round.

- Advantages: No Cipher text Expansion, Randomization
- Disadvantages: Non-deterministic Performance, No authentication

NIST Special Publication 800-38G, "Recommendation for Block Cipher Modes of Operation: Methods for Format-Preserving Encryption" specifies FF1 and FF3 according to "Recommendation for Block Cipher Modes of Operation."

A third mode, FF2—submitted to NIST under the name VAES3—was included in the initial draft did not necessarily provide strong assurance that individuals cannot be re-identified according to "Recommendation for Block Cipher Modes of Operation."

FPE VULNERABLE TO GUESSING ATTACKS

The values of the parameters, for example, radix, minlen, and maxlen affect the security that FF1 and FF3 be able to offer since, as for any FPE method, encrypted data may be vulnerable to guessing attacks when the number of possible inputs is necessarily small according to "NIST SP 800-38G – Appendix." Example of general security aspects for different size input:

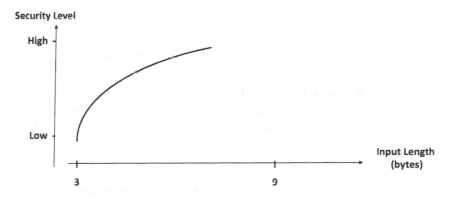

*: Example with a specific tweak

Tweaking is done by incorporating the tweak as an input to the round functions in FPE.

Blowfish

Blowfish has a 64-bit block size and a variable key length from 1 bit up to 448 bits according to "BLOWFISH ALGORITHM." It is a 16-round Feistel cipher and uses large key-dependent S-boxes. Notable features of the design include the key-dependent Sboxes and a highly complex key schedule. Feistel cipher is also used in Format Preserving Encryption algorithms.

Example of modes of operation:

* Electronic Codebook mode (ECB)
* Cipher Block Chaining mode (CBC)
* Cipher Feedback mode (CFB)

TOKENIZATION AND FORMAT PRESERVING ENCRYPTION

PARTIAL TRANSFORMATION

Tokenization and Format Preserving Encryption may be used for partial transformation, for example, leaving the leading four characters in clear text:

	Input	Output
Tokenization	1234-5678	1234-4277

Examples of encrypted and tokenized data:

	Input	Output
Encryption	1234-5678	a1D46Ghi78*$#+
Tokenization	1234-5678	9087-4277

Partial Transformation of Credit Card

Tokenization and Format Preserving Encryption may be used for partial transformation of a credit card number. For example, leaving the leading six characters in the clear text makes it easy for applications to route payment transactions to different banks for settlement. The upper output in the figure below is an example of this type of formatting. The lower output would require this type of application to first decrypt the data before using the first six characters for routing the transaction:

Tokenization and FPE for Many Types of Data

Tokenization and Format Preserving Encryption are typically used for many data fields with numerical data or characters. Traditional strong encryption like AES is suited for most types of data, including unstructured files like x-ray images:

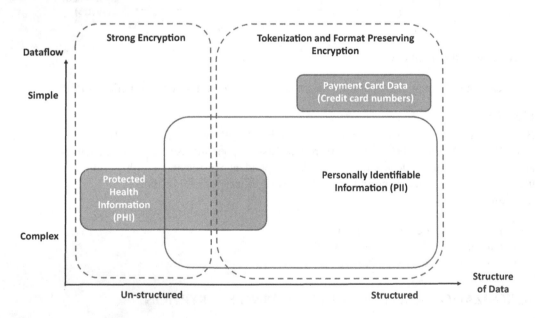

LOWER RISK WITH HIGHER PRODUCTIVITY

A Balance between Usefulness and Protection

Partial transformation, leaving some characters in clear text, can balance the usefulness and protection of data.

- Lower productivity and creativity can be the result if by providing users access only to a minimum set of data to perform a task.

Lower risk with higher productivity and creativity can be achieved by providing users access to more data in transformed and partially protected forms:

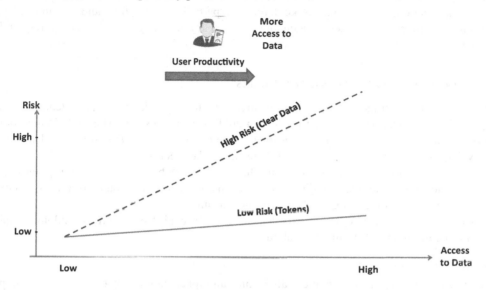

TOKENIZATION

TOKENIZATION REPLACES SENSITIVE DATA WITH USELESS ONES

When applied to data security, tokenization is the process of replacing a sensitive data element with a non-sensitive equivalent, described as a token that has no extrinsic or exploitable value or value.

DIFFERENCE FROM ENCRYPTION

Tokenization is a non-mathematical approach that substitutes sensitive data with non-sensitive substitutes without altering the type or length of data. This is an essential distinction from strong encryption (not FPE) because changes in data length and type can make data unreadable in intermediate systems such as databases. Tokenized data can still be handled by legacy systems which makes tokenization more flexible than classic encryption.

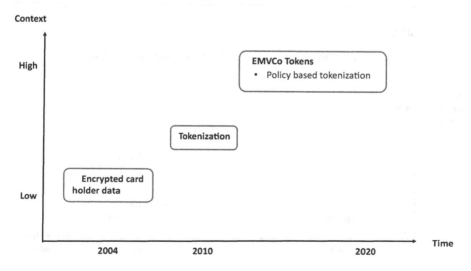

Tokens Require Significantly Less Computational Resources

Tokens require significantly less computing, according to "Tokenization (data security)."

With tokenization, specific data is kept fully or partially visible for handling and analytics, while sensitive information is kept hidden and can be a key advantage in systems that rely on high performance.

VALIDATION BY THIRD-PARTY ENCRYPTION EXPERTS

Tokenization may be utilized to safeguard sensitive data, for example, personally identifiable information (PII). Tokenization is frequently used in credit card processing. The PCI Council defines tokenization as "a process by which the primary account number (PAN) is substituted with a surrogate value called a token 'according to' Tokenization (data security)."

Methods to tokenize and encryption must have validation by third-party encryption experts. Great examples would include a credible university that invents encryption algorithms or an expert that broke the security of a recognized encryption algorithm.

A tokenization scheme can provide excellent security since it is based on fully randomized tables. Read more in Volume II of this book about this.

Lookups of Random Values

Encryption is based on a mathematical algorithm, and tokenization can be based on lookups of random values:

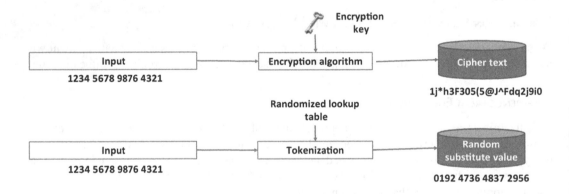

OPERATIONAL ASPECTS

Positioning of significant operational aspects of different tokenization techniques:

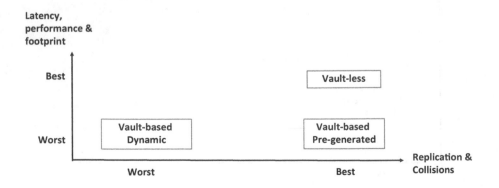

Tokenization lookup tables can be stored in a vault (vault-based) or memory (vault-less). Examples of operational aspects of different tokenization techniques:

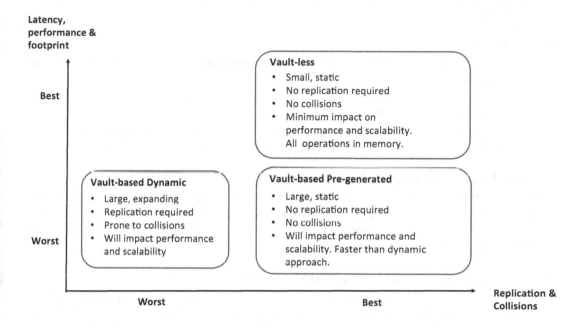

TYPES OF TOKENS

Tokens can be: single or multi-use, cryptographic or non-cryptographic, reversible or irreversible, authenticable or non-authenticable, and different combinations. In the context of payments, the disparity between high and low-value tokens plays a significant role according to "Tokenization (data security) – WikiMili."

High-Value Tokens (HVTs)

HVTs serve as substitutes for actual PANs in payment operations and are used as an instrument for completing a payment transaction according to "Tokenization (data security)."

To work, they must look like actual PANs. Multiple HVTs can map back to a single PAN and a single physical credit card with no owner being aware of it.

Low-Value Tokens (LVTs) or Security Tokens

LVTs also act as substitutes for actual PANs in payment transactions. However, they serve a different purpose. LVTs cannot be used by themselves to complete a payment transaction. For an LVT to function, it must be feasible to match it back to the actual PAN it represents, albeit only in a tightly controlled fashion.

Irreversible Tokens

These can never be converted back to the original PAN. In any circumstance, no party can obtain a PAN from its irreversible token, either through analysis or through any kind of stored information extraction. Within this classification, tokens may be "authenticatable" or "non-authenticatable."

AUTHENTICATABLE IRREVERSIBLE TOKENS

Non-Authenticatable Irreversible Tokens

Irreversible tokens that are not authenticatable represent little to no risk for the disclosure of PAN. For example, they can never be linked to a specific PAN, but they may be related to a customer or account within the business.

Reversible Tokens

Reversible tokens can become a PAN again by means of de-tokenization. Reversible tokens can be plotted to a unique PAN.

Reversible Cryptographic Tokens

Reversible cryptographic tokens are tokens generated from PANs using strong cryptography. In this instance, the PAN is never stored; only the cryptographic key is stored.

Reversible Non-Cryptographic Tokens

Acquiring the PAN from its token is only by an information lookup in a card data vault (CDV), which would then typically retrieve the PAN from a PAN-to-token table. The only factor that should be kept secret is the relationship between the PAN and its token according to "Tokenization Product Security Guidelines."

Transactions Are More Secure due to TOKENIZATION

Payment transactions are highly secure due to the model of Payment Tokenization. The Payment Tokenization Specification provides an interoperable Technical Framework that will benefit Acquirers, Merchants, Card Issuers, and Cardholders. This Technical Framework describes a global Payment Tokenization ecosystem that overlays and interoperates with existing payment ecosystems to support digital commerce and new techniques of payment.

Example of Application of Token Domain Restriction Controls:

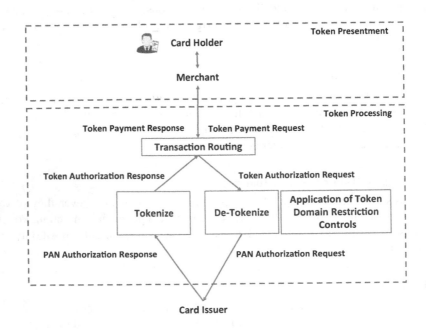

Source: Adapted from EMVCo

What Does EMVCo Do?

EMVCo manages and evolves EMV Specifications according to "Overview of EMVCo" to facilitate a standardized payments infrastructure. EMVCo does not establish obligations, requirements, or otherwise for the implementation of its specifications. EMVCo does not mandate or enforce EMV compliance or the implementation policies for issuers, merchants, and acquirers, which are handled by payment networks independently outside of EMVCo.

We will talk more about this topic in Volume II of this book, including the evolving PCI DSS.

Microsharding

Microsharding splits a file into multiple pieces, but the pieces are very small, with just a few bytes according to "MICROSHARDING: AN INNOVATIVE WAY TO PROTECT CLOUD DATA."

Each microshards is stored in different locations or multiple cloud providers. Sharding has improved performance by splitting files or volumes into numerous pieces that are a few thousand bytes or larger.

SUMMARY

We discussed reversible data protection Techniques and that utility balanced with speed is an essential characteristic and even critical for some use cases when data fields need to be recovered back to clear text from the encrypted data values.

We reviewed examples when Vaultless Tokenization performs better than some encryption schemes and traditional vault-based tokenization methods.

BIBLIOGRAPHY

1. Smith, H. E. and Brightwell, M. 1997. Using Datatype Preserving Encryption to Enhance Data Warehouse Security, *NIST 20th National Information Systems Security Conference*, pp. 141.
2. Your Official Source for Developing on Intel® Hardware and Software, https://software.intel.com/content/www/us/en/develop/home.html
3. Microsharding: An innovative Way to Protect Cloud Data, https://shardsecure.com/blog/microsharding-an-innovative-way-to-protect-cloud-data#:~:text=Normally%20these%20pieces%20are%20a%20few%20thousand%20to,of%20these%20microshards%20are%20stored%20in%20different%20locations.
4. Overview of EMVCo, https://search.yahoo.com/search?fr=mcafee&type=E211US739G0&p=MVCo+manages+and+evolves+EMV+Specifications+and+supporting+testing+programm
5. Black, J. and Rogaway, P. (2002). Ciphers with Arbitrary Finite J. Black and P. Rogaway. Ciphers with Arbitrary Finite Domains. *RSA Data Security Conference, Cryptographer's Track (RSA CT '02), Lecture Notes in Computer Science*, vol. 2271, pp. 114–130, Springer.
7. Spies, Terence. (2008). "Feistel finite set encryption mode." NIST Proposed Encryption Mode.
8. Bellare, M., Ristenpart, T., Rogaway, P., and Stegers, T. (2009). *Format Preserving Encryption*. Springer.
9. A New Approach To Data Privacy, https://shardsecure.com/blog/microsharding-an-innovative-way-to-protect-cloud-data
10. Bellare, Mihir, Rogaway, Phillip, and Spies, Terence. (2010). "The FFX Mode of Operation for Format-Preserving Encryption" NIST, February 20, 2010. © March 2016 | IJIRT | Volume 2 Issue 10 | ISSN: 2349-6002 IJIRT 143299 International Journal Of Innovative Research In Technology 17
11. Liu, Zheli, Jia, Chunfu, Li, Jingwei and Cheng, Xiaochun. (2010). *Format-Preserving Encryption for Date Time* IEEE.
12. Phillip Rogaway. (2010). "A Synopsis of Format-Preserving Encryption" March 27.
13. Vance, J. (2011). "VAES3 Scheme for FFX: An Addendum to the FFX Mode of Operation for Format Preserving Encryption" NIST. Eric Brier, Thomas Peyrin and Jacques Stern" BPS: A Format-Preserving Encryption Proposal" NIST
14. Format Preserving Encryption: A Survey, http://ijirt.org/master/publishedpaper/IJIRT143299_PAPER.pdf

15. Blowfish Algorithm, https://www.academia.edu/16734455/BLOWFISH_ALGORITHM#:~:text= Blowfish%20was%20designed%20in%201993%20by%20Bruce%20Schneier,to%20use%20for%20 any%20one%20is%20any%20situation
16. What is Format Preserving Encryption (FPE)? Is Format Preserving Encryption Secure?, https://www. encryptionconsulting.com/education-center/what-is-fpe/
17. GDPR and Protecting Data Privacy with Cryptographic Pseudonyms, https://www.ibm.com/blogs/ insights-on-business/gbs-strategy/gdpr-protecting-data-privacy-cryptographic-pseudonyms/
18. ISO/IEC 29101:2013 (Information Technology – Security Techniques – Privacy Architecture Framework)
19. ISO/IEC 19592-1:2016 (Information Technology – Security Techniques – Secret Sharing – Part 1: General)
20. UN Privacy Preserving Techniques Handbook, https://marketplace.officialstatistics.org/privacy-preserving-techniques-handbook#:~:text=UN%20Privacy%20Preserving%20Techniques%20 Handbook%20In%20this%20UN,and%20enabling%20Big%20Data%20Collaborations%20Across%20 Multiple%20NSOs. cISO/IEC 29101:2013 Information technology – Security techniques – Privacy architecture framework, https://www.iso.org/standard/45124.html
21. NIST SP 800-38G – Appendix, https://compliance360software.com/category/nist-special-publication-800-38g/
22. ISO/IEC 19592-2:2017 (Information Technology – Security Techniques – Secret Sharing – Part 2: Fundamental Mechanisms
23. The Future of Cryptography, https://qeprize.org/news/the-future-of-cryptography/#:~:text=%20 The%20Future%20of%20Cryptography%20%201%20An,the%20lattice-based%20cryptosystems%20 mentioned%20earlier%20is…%20More%20
24. NIST Special Publication 800-38G, "Recommendation for Block Cipher Modes of Operation: Methods for Format-Preserving Encryption" https://nvlpubs.nist.gov/nistpubs/SpecialPublications/NIST.SP.800-38G.pdf
25. Protegrity Protects Kinetic Data by Making it Worthless in …, https://siliconangle.com/2021/06/17/ protegrity-protects-kinetic-data-by-making-it-worthless-in-the-wrong-hands-awsshowcase2q21/
26. Block cipher – HandWiki, https://handwiki.org/wiki/Block_cipher
27. Recommendation for Block Cipher Modes of Operation …, https://nvlpubs.nist.gov/nistpubs/Special Publications/NIST.SP.800-38G.pdf
28. Tokenization (data security) – Wikipedia, https://en.wikipedia.org/wiki/Tokenization_(data_security)
29. Tokenization (data security) – WikiMili, The Best …, https://wikimili.com/en/Tokenization_(data_security)
30. Tokenization Product Security Guidelines, https://www.pcisecuritystandards.org/documents/ Tokenization_Product_Security_Guidelines.pdf

6 Non-Reversible Data Protection Techniques

INTRODUCTION

This chapter will discuss non-reversible data protection techniques focused on granular protection of data fields. These are useful for use cases that do not need the data to be recovered back to clear text from the transformed data values. Examples include passwords, analytics, and data in test environments.

OVERVIEW OF DATA PROTECTION TECHNIQUES

Traditional encryption schemes can provide reversible (2-way) or non-reversible (1-way) encryption of data. We will discuss some newer non-reversible data protection techniques that are important for the anonymization of attributes. This can help with compliance to data privacy regulations like EU GDPR and US CCPA/CPRA. We will, for example, discuss different types of masking, differential privacy, k-anonymity, and synthetic data.

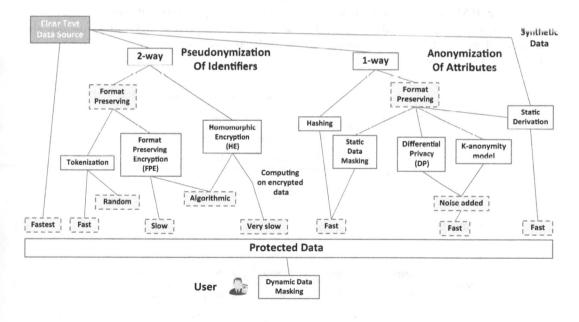

Conventional cybersecurity investment in current years has been at the network level, creating walls to keep bad actors out of the business space. The problem is that once offenders get through some of those barriers, if data is not protected at a fine-grained level, crooks have access to it and put businesses at risk. Some of these preserve the input data format and some are based on an encryption algorithm and keys. The speed characteristics vary between these data protection techniques.

DOI: 10.1201/9781003189664-8

SOME MAJOR ATTACKS ON DATA

New York City (NYC) Taxi and Limousine Commission released a data set with every taxi ride in NYC during 2013, including details about each ride. Analysis re-identified drivers and exposed privacy about drivers and passengers. Netflix published a half-million movie ratings that re-identified some users.

MEDICAL RECORDS CAN BE RE-IDENTIFIED

In 1997, Latanaya Sweeny showed how de-identification of medical records could be re-identified to the tune of 87% of the US population with a linkage attack, having birth date, gender, and a five-digit postal code (US Zip):

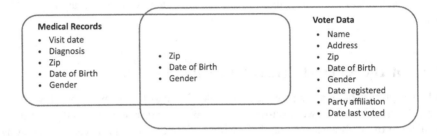

WHY ANONYMIZE?

Privacy Regulations like EU GDR, US HIPAA, and CPPA may render data that is anonymized as Out of Scope. IIAP have great resources for this discussion at https://iapp.org/resources/.

Anonymization requires analysis of the full data set. Multiple passes and transformations are required until an ideal balance between privacy and utilization is found.

Example of data masking:

Original Data			Masked Data		
Name	SSN	Age	Name	SSN	Age
Brown	180-80-0724	54	Michaels	111-22-3333	52
Duncan	252-38-1786	24	Lee	111-222-3334	22

Example of data generalization:

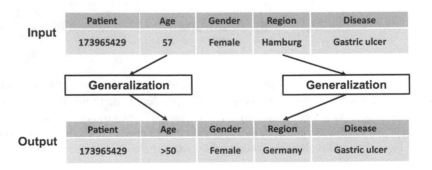

RANDOMIZATION TECHNIQUES

GENERAL

The term "randomization" refers to a category of de-identification techniques in which values of an attribute are changed so that their new values randomly differ from their true values. Such a process reduces the ability of an attacker to deduce the value of an attribute from the values of other attributes in the same data record, thereby reducing the effectiveness of inference attempts. Such tailoring involves a detailed understanding of the nature of the data and the choice of appropriate parameters for the selected randomization techniques (and typically involves performing a statistical evaluation). The output of randomization is microdata.

Certain randomization techniques, such as permutation, apply to both numerical and non-numerical data attributes. Specific approaches to randomization are described below.

NOISE ADDITION

Noise addition is a randomization technique that modifies a dataset by adding random values, "random noise," to the values of a selected attribute with continuous values while as much as possible retaining the original statistical properties of the attribute across all records in the dataset. Such statistical properties include the distribution, mean, variance, standard deviation, covariance, and attribute correlation.

Noise addition to a selected continuous attribute is performed by adding, or multiplying by, a stochastic or randomized number. Many different noise addition algorithms have been developed with the goal of preserving the statistical properties of the de-identified data and its usefulness for different use cases according to INTERNATIONAL STANDARD ISO/IEC 20889.

For example, the stochastic value can be chosen from a normal distribution with zero mean and a small standard deviation, such as changing a student's numeric grade from 3.33 to 3.53.

PERMUTATION

Permutation is a technique for reordering the values of a selected attribute across the records in a dataset without values' modification. As a result, permutation retains the exact statistical distribution of the selected attribute across all records in the dataset.

Permutation techniques apply to both numeric and non-numeric values. Special considerations need to be taken to ensure that the resulting dataset is consistent and realistic, because observable inconsistencies can help reconstruct the permutation algorithm. For example, it is to be expected that men are taller than women on average; it is also to be expected that first or given names typically correspond to the listed gender.

Permutation approaches or algorithms differ both in their approach and their complexity. Some algorithms are based on repeatedly swapping values between records until all values are replaced for the selected attribute; others follow logic designed for the specific application needs. In order to preserve the correlation among the distributions of selected attributes (i.e., selected columns in a table), the same perturbation algorithm needs to be applied to all these attributes.

Knowledge of a deterministic permutation algorithm typically allows the data to be restored to its original state by back-tracking the algorithm, which makes a controlled re-identification possible. On the other hand, using a non-deterministic permutation algorithm (i.e. an algorithm that employs a degree of randomness as part of its logic) makes the re-identification process less trivial and more resilient to re-identification attacks.

Because of this, specific organizational objectives for controlled re-identification and appropriate technical and organizational measures to safeguard the knowledge of the algorithms from unwarranted access need to be taken into consideration while choosing or designing the algorithm.

MICROAGGREGATION

The term "microaggregation" refers to a category of de-identification techniques that replace all values of continuous attributes with their averages computed in a certain algorithmic way. For each continuous attribute (or for a selected set of continuous attributes), all records in the dataset are grouped such that the records with closest values of the attribute (or attributes) belong to the same group and there are at least k records in each group, for a sufficiently large value of k. The new value of each attribute is then computed to be the average of the attribute's values in the group. The closer the values in each group are, the more data usefulness is preserved. The output of microaggregation is microdata. Microaggregation does not preserve data truthfulness, according to INTERNATIONAL STANDARD ISO/IEC 20889.

STATISTICAL TOOLS

General

Statistical tools are methods of a statistical nature that change the overall structure of the data. Such methods are commonly used to either de-identify datasets or to enhance the effectiveness of de-identification techniques.

Sampling

Data sampling is an arithmetic analysis technique that selects a representative subgroup to reduce the risk of re-identification; random sample is performed on data principals according to "Data Privacy."

Performing a random sampling adds uncertainty about the dataset. For example, by merely matching attributes of a certain record from the sample with external information, an attacker cannot be sure that the record corresponds to the specific data principal since there is no certainty that the data principal is present in the sample dataset. More generally, applying generalization or randomization techniques on a sample, rather than on a whole population, can increase the effectiveness of these de-identification techniques.

The methods for drawing samples from data vary broadly and their selection depends on the dataset and the anticipated use cases. An example of a common algorithm is a simple probability sampling. Random numbers are used to select the records in a dataset, ensuring no correlation among the records in the resultant sample. The output of sampling used in this way is microdata according to INTERNATIONAL STANDARD ISO/IEC 20889.

Aggregation

Aggregation involves the combination of related attributes or attribute values.

- Aggregation of attribute values comprises the set of broadly used arithmetical functions that produce results representing all the records in the original dataset when applied to an attribute in microdata. The resulting statistical aggregated values are intended to be useful for reporting on or analyzing the data without revealing any individual records.
- Aggregation of related attributes includes attributes resulting aggregated attributes remain within their original records.

If done effectively, aggregation reduces the ability of an attacker to single out, link, or deduce the value of an attribute. The output of aggregation is macrodata (i.e., data that is aggregated in frequency or magnitude) according to INTERNATIONAL STANDARD ISO/IEC 20889.

PSEUDONYMIZATION VS. ANONYMIZATION

ANONYMIZED DATA SUPPORTS AI AND ANALYTICS INITIATIVES

Anonymization has become a popular method of protection because it can advance data-intensive business applications, such as analytics. Anonymized data satisfies stringent data regulations and high customer expectations on privacy—thresholds that can either float or sink a company's AI pursuits.

By adjusting privacy settings to a user's specifications, an effective data-protection platform can strip bare data elements that shouldn't be seen by information analysts, business partners, or data marketplaces.

A CMO, for instance, can anonymize aspects of a customer's personal information. Or a research hospital can anonymize sensitive personal data.

PROTECTED DATA DRIVES REVENUE AND SATISFIES CUSTOMERS

Anonymization and pseudonymization answer organizations' pressing imperatives to keep sensitive data private. While keeping it open enough to inform corporate decision making, product development, customer service, and just about every aspect of business, according to "They're Not Just Long Words: Anonymization."

De-identifying data of sensitive elements fully protect the data as it moves across diverse cloud and on-premises environments. This is enabling organizations to use data to inform AI, machine learning, analytics, and many other data-driven initiatives that offer a competitive edge in our highly competitive digital world, according to "They're Not Just Long Words: Anonymization."

PSEUDONYMIZATION

Pseudonymization is recognized as a valuable method for privacy protection of PII, including personal health information.

Application areas include according to ISO 25237:2017—Health informatics–Pseudonymization":

1. Indirect use of clinical data (e.g., research);
2. clinical trials and post-marketing surveillance;
3. pseudonymous care;
4. patient identification systems;
5. public health monitoring and assessment;
6. confidential patient-safety reporting (e.g., adverse drug effects);
7. comparative quality indicator reporting;
8. peer review;
9. consumer groups;
10. field service.

ANONYMIZATION

Anonymization is the method and set of tools used where no longitudinal consistency is needed. The anonymization process is also used where pseudonymization has been used to address the remaining data attributes according to "Anonymization."

Anonymization can lead to a reduced possibility of linkage. Each element allowed to pass should be justified. Each element should present minimal risk, given the intended use of the resulting dataset. Thus, where the intended use of the resulting dataset does not require fine-grain codes, a grouping of codes might be used.

We will discuss more in Volume II of this book.

DIFFERENTIAL PRIVACY

Differential privacy is a form of field-level data masking designed such that data can be used for querying aggregate statistics while limiting the exposure of individuals' specific information.

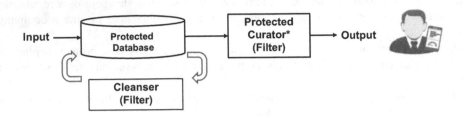

Differential privacy is a rigorous mathematical definition that analyzes a dataset and computes information's mean, variance, median, mode, and more and gives a formal guarantee that individual-level information about participants in the database is not leaked according to "Differential Privacy."

This approach supports data sharing scenarios and has the applicability of processing data in untrusted environments.

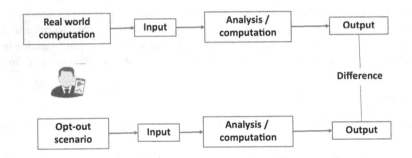

Use Case of Differential Privacy and k-Anonymity

A bank wanted to broaden access to its data lake without compromising data privacy, preserving the data's analytical value, and at reasonable infrastructure costs. Current approaches to de-identify data did not fulfill the compliance requirements and business needs, which had led to several bank projects being stopped. The issue with these techniques, like masking, tokenization, and aggregation, was that they did not sufficiently protect the data without overly degrading data quality.

This approach allows creating privacy-protected datasets that retain their analytical value for data science and business applications. The solution automatically enforced the compliance policies before the data was consumed by data science and business teams from the data lake. The analytical quality of the data was preserved for machine learning purposes by using AI and leveraging privacy models like differential privacy and k-anonymity.

Improved data access for teams increased the business' bottom line without adding high infrastructure costs while reducing consumer information exposure risk.

Examples of Differential Privacy Models

Six Different Types of Transformation Algorithms

The figure below illustrates that differential privacy can be implemented in six different transformation algorithms suitable for different use cases. They provide mathematical definitions of how the algorithms hide the presence or absence of any individual's data in a dataset.

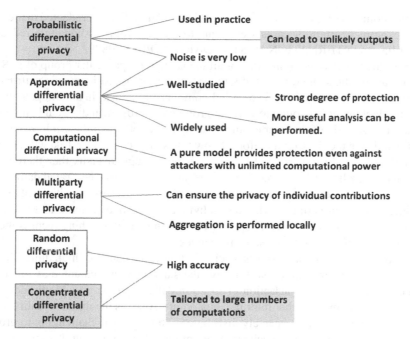

Source: Adapted from INTERNATIONAL STANDARD ISO/IEC 20889

k-Anonymity Model

For k-anonymity to be achieved, there need to be at least k individuals in the dataset who share the set of elements that might become identifying for each individual. K-anonymity might be described as a "hiding in the crowd" guarantee: if each individual is part of a larger group, then any of the records in this group could correspond to a single person according to "Generating high-fidelity synthetic patient data."

The k-anonymity model ensures that groups lesser than k individuals cannot be identified. Queries will give back at least k number of records. K-anonymity is a formal privacy measurement model that ensures a corresponding equivalence class containing at least K records for each identifier.

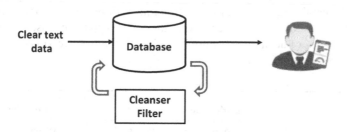

L-diversity is an enhancement to K-anonymity designed to protect against deterministic inference. This variant of K-anonymity is subject to attacks, which have led to the development of T-closeness. T-closeness is an improvement to L-diversity for datasets with attributes that are unevenly distributed, belong to a small-scale range of values, or are categorical.

While k-anonymity can provide some valuable guarantees, the technique comes with the following conditions:

The sensitive columns of interest must not reveal information that was redacted in the generalized columns. For example, certain diseases are unique to men or women, showing a redacted gender attribute according to INTERNATIONAL STANDARD ISO/IEC 20889.

The values in the sensitive columns are not all the same for a particular group of k. Suppose the sensitive values are all the same for a set of k records that share quasi-identifying attributes. In that case, this dataset is still vulnerable to a so-called homogeneity attack. In a homogeneity attack, the attacker uses the fact that it is enough to find the group of records the individual belongs to if all of them have the same sensitive value. For example, all men over 60 in our dataset have cancer; I know Bob is over 60 and is in the dataset; therefore, I now know Bob has cancer. Likewise, even if not all the values are the identical for a group of k, if there is not enough diversity then there is still a high chance that I discover a little more about Bob according to "No charge best rated dating online sites for women." If about 90% of the records in the group all have the same sensitive value, an attacker can at least infer with high certainty what the individual's sensitive attribute is. Measures such as l-diversity and t-closeness can be used to specify that among any k matching records there must be a given amount of diversity among the sensitive values.

The dimensionality of the data must be sufficiently low. If the data is of high dimensionality, such as time series data, it becomes quite hard to give the same privacy guarantee as low dimensional data. For types of data such as transaction or location data, it can be possible to identify an individual uniquely by stringing together multiple data points. Also, as the dimensionality of data often increases, the data points are very sparsely distributed. This makes it challenging to group records without heavily distorting the data to achieve k-anonymity. By combining this approach with data minimization and only releasing the columns people really need, the dimensionality can be reduced to manageable levels (at the cost of making different releases for different purposes).

K-anonymization is still a powerful tool when applied appropriately and with the right safeguards in place, such as access control and contractual safeguards. It forms an essential part of the arsenal of privacy-enhancing technologies, alongside alternative techniques such as differentially private algorithms. As big data becomes the norm rather than the exception, we see increasing dimensionality of data and more and more public datasets that can aid re-identification efforts.

ANONYMIZATION

K-anonymity can be used to add noise to generalize data. The k-anonymity model ensures that groups smaller than k individuals cannot be identified. Queries will return at least k number of records. K-anonymity is a formal privacy measurement model that ensures a corresponding equivalence class containing at least K records for each identifier. Synthetic example of k-anonymous microaggregation in published data with k = 3, relating various demographic attributes acting as quasi-identifiers. For k-anonymity to be achieved, there needs to be at least "k" individuals in the data set who share the set of attributes that might be identifying for everyone. The figure shows an example of k-anonymity sample data set:

Identifier	Quasi Identifiers			Confidential Attribute	
Civil #	Gender	Age	Post Code	Wage	Affiliation
125-55-1321	M	22	94123	22	Socialist
321-33-4321	F	26	94321	33	Conservation
876-89-6543	M	24	94654	44	Conservation
245-56-6789	M	40	90222	55	Socialist
876-34-4322	F	38	90654	43	Conservative
837-45-1256	F	42	90876	32	Socialist

K-anonymity might be described as a "hiding in the crowd" guarantee. If each individual is part of a larger group, then any of the records in this group could correspond to a single person. The figure shows the data anonymized. This is achieved by generalizing some quasi-identifier attributes and redacting some others. K-Anonymity applied to a dataset:

Identifier	Quasi Identifiers			Confidential Attribute	
Civil #	Gender	Age	Post Code	Wage	Affiliation
*	M	40	94***	22	Socialist
*	M	38	94***	33	Conservation
*	M	42	94***	44	Conservation
*	F	22	90***	55	Socialist
*	F	26	90***	43	Conservative
*	F	24	90***	32	Socialist

Read more about dynamic masking, static data masking, and synthetic data in Volume II of this book.

SYNTHETIC DATA

Synthetic data are used for a non-reversible approach to generating microdata artificially to represent a predefined statistical data model. By definition, a synthetic data set does not contain any data collected from or about existing data principals, but the data look realistic for the intended purposes. If the synthetic data fit the original data too closely, it can reveal genuine data principals, such as personal data. There are various ways to create synthetic data. Theoretically, data can be randomly generated based on several selected statistical properties. Key characteristics of such a model are the distributions of each attribute (overall and in subpopulations) and the internal relationships among the attributes. In practice, synthetic data generation can involve multiple or continuous transformations on real data sets using randomization techniques and sampling. Typically, synthetic data is used for testing tools and applications, for developing queries, and as a surrogate for real data in some applications. A data curator should reproduce queries performed on synthetic data on actual data to ensure that inferences drawn on the synthetic data are correct when drawn on actual data. The privacy guarantees of synthetic data can be evaluated using the differential privacy model.

Synthetic data is an approach to generating microdata artificially to represent a predefined statistical data model. By definition, a synthetic dataset does not contain any data collected from or about existing data principals, but looks realistic for the intended purposes. Synthetic data fitting the original data too closely can reveal genuine data principals, such as personal data. There are various ways to create synthetic data. Theoretically, data can be randomly generated based on several selected statistical properties. Key characteristics of such a model are the distributions of each attribute (overall and in subpopulations) and the internal relationships among the attributes. In practice, synthetic data generation can involve multiple or continuous transformations on real datasets using randomization techniques and sampling. Typically, synthetic data is used for testing tools and applications. Synthetic data can be used for developing queries. In some applications, synthetic data can be used as a surrogate for real data: in these cases, the data curator should reproduce queries performed on synthetic data on actual data to ensure that inferences drawn on the synthetic data are correct when drawn on actual data. The privacy guarantees of synthetic data can be evaluated using the differential privacy model.

Synthetic Data in Fintech

When past data is not available or when the available data is not sufficient because of lack of quality or diversity, companies rely on synthetic data to build models. You can generate a random sample of any distribution such as normal, exponential, chi-square, t, lognormal, and uniform. The utility of synthetic data varies depending on the analyst's degree of knowledge about a specific data environment. Fitting real data to a known distribution by generating synthetic data can be done with the Monte Carlo method to generate synthetic data. Static derivation of real data to synthetic data can provide data that is not regulated but highly useful for sharing with third parties according to Sarkar in "Synthetic Data Generation—A Must-Have Skill for New Data Scientists":

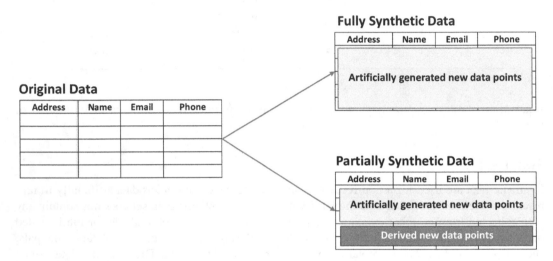

Source: Adopted from Sarkar

Example of Synthetic Data

Synthetic Data retains the structure of the original data but is not identical:

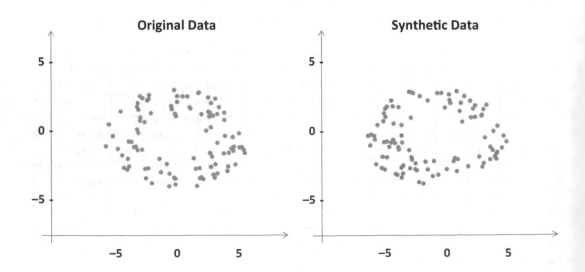

Maximizing Access While Maintaining Privacy

Veeramachaneni and his team at MIT had been tasked with analyzing a large amount of information from the online learning program edX, and wanted to bring in some MIT students to help according to "The real promise of synthetic data."

Perfecting the Formula—and Handling Constraints

In 2013, Veeramachaneni's team gave themselves two weeks to create a data pool they could use for that edX project. They realized that if they built a series of synthetic data generators, they could make the process quicker for everyone else.

The team finished an algorithm that correctly captures relationships between the different fields in a real dataset—think a patient's age, blood pressure, and heart rate—and creates a synthetic dataset that preserves those relationships without identifying information.

Artificial Data Give the Same Results

Even though data scientists can gain great insights from large data sets—and can finally use these insights to tackle most important challenges—achieving this is much easier said than done, according to "Artificial data give the same results as real data—without compromising privacy."

HASHING

Hashing is a form of encryption is based on a mathematical algorithm and may use encryption keys (HMAC hashing for creating Message Authentication Codes). This is a speed comparison example for different input and output lengths of SHA hashing algorithms. The longest output in this example is 512 bits. This comparison example can help estimate performance aspects of different hashing key lengths with SHA. Example on 64-bit Windows 10 with 1 core Intel i7 2.60GHz and 16GB RAM:

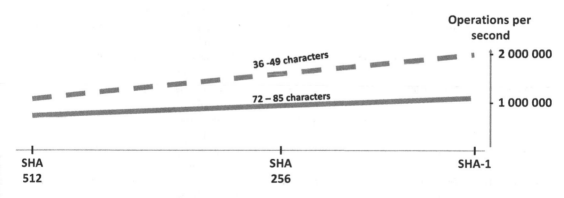

Source: Adapted from OpenSSL

SUMMARY OF DATA PROTECTION TECHNIQUES

Data Protected at a Fine-Grained Level

Traditional cybersecurity investment has been at the network level, building walls to keep the villains out of the business space. The difficulty is that once criminals get through some of those barriers, if data is not protected at a fine-grained level, offenders have access to it and put organizations at risk, according to "Protegrity protects kinetic data by making it worthless."

INTERNATIONAL STANDARD

INTERNATIONAL STANDARD ISO/IEC 20889 provides a comparison of how different Data Protection Techniques can reduce risk of linking, inference, singling,-out and other aspects:

De-Identification Technique		Use Case			Truthful At Record	Applicable	Reduces Risk		
		Transit	In Use	At Rest			Singling Out	Linking	Inference
Pseudonymization	Tokenization	Yes	Yes	Yes	Yes	Direct identifiers	No	Part	No
Cryptographic tools	Deterministic encryption	Yes	No	Yes	Yes	All attributes	No	Part	No
	Order-preserving encryption	Part	Part	Part	Yes	All attributes	No	Part	No
	Homomorphic encryption	Yes	Yes	Yes	Yes	All attributes	No	No	No
Suppression	Masking	Yes	Yes	Yes	Yes	Local identifiers	Yes	Part	No
	Local suppression	Yes	Yes	Yes	Yes	Identifying attributes	Part	Part	Part
	Record suppression	Yes	Yes	Yes	Yes	All attributes	Yes	Yes	Yes
	Sampling	Part	Part	Part	Yes	All attributes	Part	Part	Part
Generalization	Generalization	Yes	Yes	Yes	Yes	Identifying attributes	Part	Part	Part
	Rounding	Yes	Yes	Yes	Yes	Identifying attributes	No	Part	Part
	Top and bottom coding	Yes	Yes	Yes	Yes	Identifying attributes	No	Part	Part
Randomization	Noise addition	Yes	Yes	Yes	No	Identifying attributes	Part	Part	Part
	Permutation	Yes	Yes	Yes	No	Identifying attributes	Part	Part	Part
	Microaggregation	Yes	Yes	Yes	No	Identifying attributes	No	Yes	Part
Privacy models	Differential privacy	No	Yes	Yes	No	Identifying attributes	Yes	Yes	Part
	k-Anonymity	No	Yes	Yes	Yes	Quasi Identifier	Yes	Part	No

Source: Adapted from INTERNATIONAL STANDARD ISO/IEC 20889.

PRIVACY-PRESERVING DATA MINING

This is an overview of privacy-preserving data mining techniques according to "The Hitchhikers Guide to Privacy by Design":

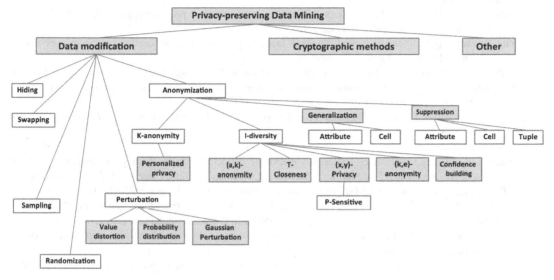

Source: Adapted from The Hitchhiker's Guide to Privacy by Design

SUMMARY

This chapter discussed non-reversible data protection techniques that are increasingly important for the anonymization of attributes and can help with compliance with data privacy regulations like EU GDPR and US CCPA/CPRA.

These non-reversible data protection techniques provide granular protection of data fields that are useful data not needed to be recovered back to clear text. We discussed different types of masking, differential privacy, k-anonymity, synthetic data, and more.

We will discuss this topic more in Volume II of this book.

BIBLIOGRAPHY

1. International Standard ISO/IEC 20889, https://webstore.ansi.org/Standards/ISO/ISOIEC208892018?gcl id=EAIaIQobChMIvI-k3sXd5gIVw56zCh0Y0QeeEAAYASAAEgLVKfD_BwE
2. The Hitchhikers Guide to Privacy by Design, Barbara Peruskovic, https://issuu.com/protegrity/docs/the_hitchhiker_s_guide_to_privacy_b
3. Artificial Data Give the Same Results As Real Data—Without Compromising Privacy, https://news.mit.edu/2017/artificial-data-give-same-results-as-real-data-0303
4. Anonymization, https://www.sciencedirect.com/topics/biochemistry-genetics-and-molecular-biology/anonymization
5. The Real Promise of Synthetic Data, https://news.mit.edu/2020/real-promise-synthetic-data-1016
6. GDPR and Protecting Data Privacy with Cryptographic Pseudonyms, https://www.ibm.com/blogs/insights-on-business/gbs-strategy/gdpr-protecting-data-privacy-cryptographic-pseudonyms/
7. Synthetic data, https://en.wikipedia.org/wiki/Synthetic_data

8. "Synthetic data". McGraw-Hill Dictionary of Scientific and Technical Terms, The real promise of synthetic data, https://news.mit.edu/2020/real-promise-synthetic-data-1016

9. k-Anonymity: An Introduction, https://www.privitar.com/blog/k-anonymity-an-introduction/

10. Dynamic Data Masking (DDM), https://www.gartner.com/en/information-technology/glossary/dynamic-data-masking-ddm

11. Data De-identification: Possibilities, Progress, and Perils, https://forge.duke.edu/blog/data-de-identification-possibilities-progress-and-perils

12. The Privacy Myth of De-Identified Medical Data, https://medium.com/healthwizz/the-privacy-myth-of-de-identified-medical-data-10b9678e4bea

13. Sarkar, T. "Synthetic Data Generation—A Must-Have Skill for New Data Scientists." Towards Data Science, 19 December 2018, https://towardsdatascience.com/synthetic-data-generation-a-must-have-skill-for-new-data-scientists-915896c0c1ae

14. Reiter, J. P. "Using CART to Generate Partially Synthetic, Public Use Microdata." *Journal of Official Statistics*, 21, 3, January 2005

15. IIAP, https://iapp.org/resources/

16. Watson, A. "Using Generative, Differentially-Private Models to Build Privacy-Enhancing, Synthetic Datasets from Real Data." *Medium*, 2 March 2020, https://medium.com/gretel-ai/using-generative-differentially-private-models-to-build-privacy-enhancing-synthetic-datasets-c0633856184

17. Protegrity Protects Kinetic Data by Making it Worthless in …, https://siliconangle.com/2021/06/17/protegrity-protects-kinetic-data-by-making-it-worthless-in-the-wrong-hands-awsshowcase2q21/

18. Data Privacy, cdn.ymaws.com. https://cdn.ymaws.com/www.members.issa.org/resource/resmgr/journalpdfs/data_privacy-de-id_issa0520.pdf

19. Differential Privacy|Harvard University Privacy Tools …, https://privacytools.seas.harvard.edu/differential-privacy

20. ISO 25237:2017 – Health Informatics – Pseudonymization, https://standards.iteh.ai/catalog/standards/iso/c32d71a0-fa2f-44b6-8ab4-22ae74c8fbb3/iso-25237-2017

21. Generating High-Fidelity Synthetic Patient Data for …, https://www.nature.com/articles/s41746-020-00353-9

22. No Charge Best Rated Dating Online Sites for Women, https://geneflux.net.my/no-charge-best-rated-dating-online-sites-for-women-in-london/

23. They're Not Just Long Words: Anonymization, https://www.protegrity.com/protegrity-blog/theyre-not-just-long-words-anonymization-and-pseudonymization-protect-data-driven-business

Section III

Users and Authorization

7 Access Control

INTRODUCTION

In this chapter, we will discuss technologies for identification, authentication, and authorization. We will cover some evolving standards and different access control models. These components are critical for providing privacy and controlling confidentiality and access to data.

Identification is the user reference. Authentication will prove that you are this user. Authorization is defining the rights to perform different operations on specific data and other resources:

> Identification
> Authentication
> Authorization

ACCESS TO DATA

Management of PII and controls can be layered in privacy, access, and data:

Privacy	Policy communication			PII Categorization	
	Consent Management			Privacy Management	
Access	Identity Management			Pseudonymization scheme	
	Access control		Authentication		Authorization
PII	PII Management		PII Transfer		PII Validation
	PII Pseudonymization	PII Anonymization	Secret sharing		PII Encryption
	PII Use	PII Inventory	PII Archiving		Audit logging

Source: ISO/IEC

IDENTIFICATION AND AUTHENTICATION

When logging into a system, a user is validated via authentication and may receive an authenticator, for example, a token and credentials, such as a user name. They are allowed to access a resource based on an authorization policy or via more authenticators according to "6 the European central bank ECB has defined strong."

PASSWORDS AND BIOMETRICS

Passwords

At times, a password called a passcode is a memorized secret, typically a string of characters usually used to confirm a user's identity. Using the language of the NIST Digital Identity Guidelines, the secret is memorized by a party called the claimant, while the party verifying the claimant's identity is called the verifier.

DOI: 10.1201/9781003189664-10

A passphrase can be a sequence of words to control a computer system, program, or data entry. A passphrase is comparable to a password in usage, but it usually is longer for added security. Passphrases may derive an encryption key from a passphrase according to "passphrase - Ask Leo!"

A password manager is a computer system that stores passwords. It shows the passwords that are put or created in the password manager, typically used to store several passwords as a person may forget some passwords.

Biometrics

Biometrics can be more suitable for user identification instead of authentication. For example, unlocking a mobile device frequently and less frequently asking for a password to validate the user. Weaknesses of biometrics: Biometrics is a more complex and more expensive technology. If biometric information is ever compromised, it will be a much bigger problem than with passwords because you cannot change your biometrics information. A password can be easier to change than biometrics.

Multi-Factor Authentication

Multi-factor Authentication (MFA) is an electronic authentication method in which a user is granted access to a website or application only after successfully presenting several pieces of evidence (or factors) to an authentication mechanism: information (something only the user knows), possession, and inherence. MFA protects the user from an unknown person trying to access their data such as personal ID details or financial assets according to "How to set up MFA for your Microsoft 365 account."

Pooled Database Connections

The phrase "pooled connection" means that connections to the database stay open and are shared (Application User X) between multiple users (User 1 and User 2) according to "Configuring Database Connections." This represents a significant performance improvement over non-pooled connections as the establishment of a database connection is a relatively expensive operation:

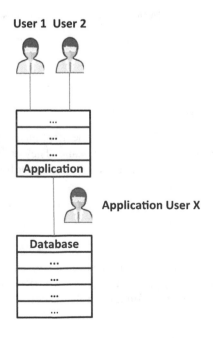

Example with a typical system stack:

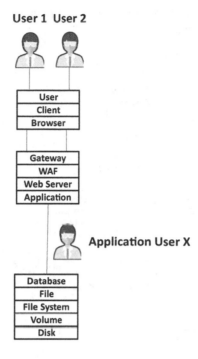

Authorization

Most modern-day multi-user operating systems involve role-based access control (RBAC) and depend on the authorization. Access control also uses authentication to confirm the identity of consumers. As soon as a consumer attempts to access a resource, the process verifies that the consumer has been authorized to use that resource, according to "Authorization":

Who Should See the Data?

Different roles need access to various information in our sample data record, including e-mail address and telephone number:

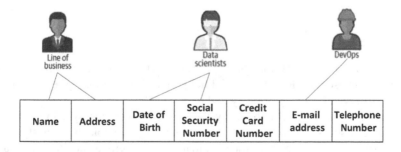

Access Control

In computer security, general access control includes identification, authorization, authentication, access approval, and audit according to "Computer access control."

A narrower description of access control would cover only access approval, whereby the system decides to grant or reject an access call from an already authenticated subject based on what the subject is authorized to access.

A Distributed Approach with a Central Point of Control

A mature data protection system should provide a central point of control for data protection systems at the application, database, and file levels.

Access Control Architecture

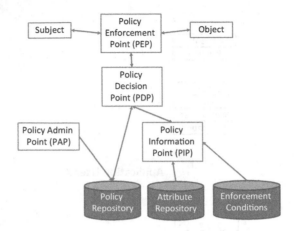

ACCESS CONTROL MODELS

MANDATORY ACCESS CONTROL

Mandatory access control (MAC) refers to the ability of a subject or initiator to access or usually perform some sort of function on an object or target according to "Mandatory access control."

A user or subject is usually a process or thread, and traditionally, MAC has been closely associated with multilevel security (MLS) and specialized military systems.

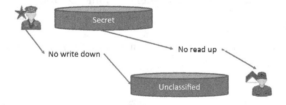

DISCRETIONARY ACCESS CONTROL

Discretionary Access Control (DAC) is the way to go to let people manage the content they own. DAC is excellent to let users of an online social network choose who accesses their data. It allows people to revoke or forward privileges easily and immediately.

DAC is a type of access control defined by the Trusted Computer System Evaluation Criteria as a means of limiting access to objects based on the identity of subjects or groups to which they belong. The controls are discretionary in the idea that a subject with a specific access authorization is capable of passing that permission (perhaps indirectly) on to any other subject, according to "HC3 Intelligence Briefing Access Control."

ROLE-BASED ACCESS CONTROL

Role-based access control (RBAC) is "a form of access control which as you said is appropriate to separate responsibilities" in a system where multiple roles are fulfilled according to "What is

Role-Based Access Control (RBAC)? Examples, Benefits, and More." RBAC is designed to separate duties by letting users select the roles they need for a specific task.

Issues with a Role-Based Access Control

RBAC employs pre-defined roles that have a specific set of privileges. Examples:

- Lack of policies that express a complicated Boolean rule set that can evaluate several different attributes.

Example of a Role-Based Access Control (RBAC)

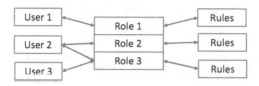

ATTRIBUTE-BASED ACCESS CONTROL

Attribute-based access control (ABAC) defines an access control paradigm whereby access rights are granted to users using policies that combine attributes. The policies can use any attribute (user attributes, resource attributes, object, environment attributes, etc.). This model supports Boolean logic, in which rules contain "IF, THEN" statements about who is making the request, the resource, and the action.

Unlike RBAC, which employs pre-defined roles that carry a specific set of privileges associated with them and to which subjects are assigned, the critical difference with ABAC is the concept of policies that express a complex Boolean rule set that can evaluate many different attributes according to "Authorization Models: ACL, DAC, MAC, RBAC, ABAC." Attribute-based access control is sometimes referred to as policy-based access control (PBAC) or claims-based access control (CBAC).

ABAC is an effort to "shift the paradigm of granting resource access" to a specific user to granting access based on the value of a user's attributes according to "A Basic ABAC (Attribute-Based Access Control) Primer."

While user authentication is still required, access is no longer granted via a particular ACL. Instead, a decision is made based on the value of specific attributes whether or not access should be granted at the point of authentication. This approach substantially decreases the administration required to maintain data security.

ABAC System Definitions

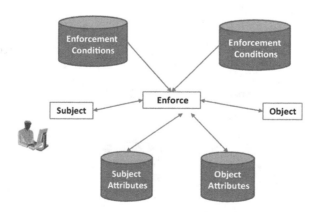

RBAC – ABAC Hybrid

Why do customers want ABAC in addition to RBAC?

- RBAC Is Easy to Configure
  o RBAC Systems provide coarse grain access controls based on users' roles, making them easy to configure.
- ABAC Systems provide fine-grained access controls.
  o ABAC allows targeted security with authorization associated with the context of data consumption.
- RBAC + ABAC allows the ease of role-based security with the option of targeted security
  o Supports targeted use cases for restricting access to some data based on their role and other required factors.

Deployment effort is minimized in a system where both are present for the customer allowing one method to evaluate both types of restrictions:

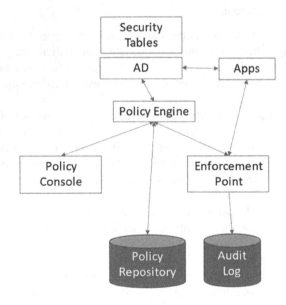

RBAC + ABAC Integration

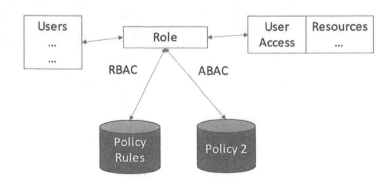

RBAC + ABAC Service Data Flow Diagram

A simple RBAC + ABAC Service Data can Flow Diagram:

User Defined Functions (UDF) can be used to implement the RBAC and ABAC logic:

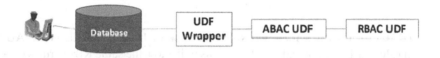

The RBAC service is filtered through an ABAC Service to additional context rules:

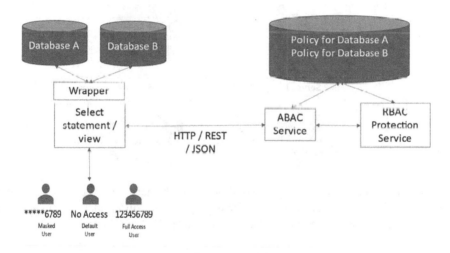

In this example, RBAC defines rules for Role and Data Element. ABAC represents context-oriented rules for Location and Database:

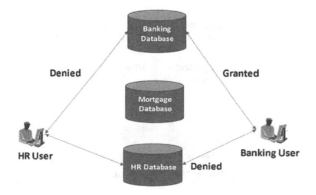

An example with RBAC and context-based ABAC rules:

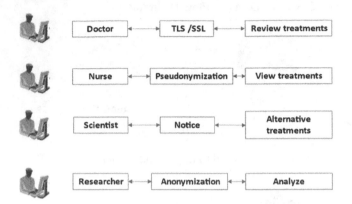

The static RBAC defines rules for User Role and Type of Data (Data Element). ABAC adds context-oriented rules for Location and Database. This will allow the same RBAC rules to be used in different situations where the ABAC rules will change the behavior. In this example, the PEP (Policy Enforcement Point) Servers will enforce the RBAC and ABAC rules that the Admin Service builds:

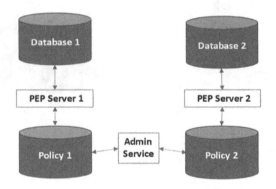

The user is granted access, for example, based on where the access originated. The context may consider where and when the access occurs, for example, from different locations or on special weekdays. This is an example of adding ABAC context to an RBAC policy:

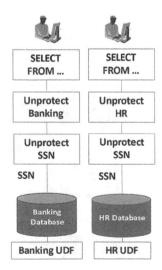

This is a simple "No-code" example that can provide a Yes/no response implemented in a UDF wrapper:

This is a simple "Low-code" data transformation by a UDF wrapper:

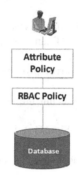

SUMMARY

In this chapter, we discussed technologies for identification, authentication, and authorization. These components are critical to separate for providing privacy and controlling confidentiality and access to data.

Identification is only the user reference, and authentication will prove that you are this user. We discussed how authorization models like RBAC, ABAC, MAC, and DAC could allow different operations on specific data fields and records in specific dynamic access situations.

We discussed some evolving standards and different access control models critical for providing privacy and controlling confidentiality and access to data.

We will debate more about this topic in Volume II of this book.

BIBLIOGRAPHY

1. Sovrin™: A Protocol and Token for SelfSovereign Identity and Decentralized Trust, https://sovrin.org/wp-content/uploads/2018/03/Sovrin-Protocol-and-Token-White-Paper.pdf
2. Biometric device, en.wikipedia.org/wiki/Biometric_device
3. W3C Publishes Working Draft of the W3C Accessibility Guidelines (WCAG) 3.0, https://www.access-board.gov/news/2021/01/21/w3c-publishes-working-draft-of-the-web-content-accessibility-guidelines-wcag-3-0/#:~:text=The%20World%20Wide%20Web%20Consortium%20%28W3C%29%20Web%20Accessibility,cooperation%20with%20individuals%20and%20organizations%20around%20the%20world
4. Unified Access Management, https://en.wikipedia.org/wiki/Unified_access_management
5. Password Management, https://en.wikipedia.org/wiki/Password_management
6. A Basic ABAC (Attribute Based Access Control) Primer, https://www.idmworks.com/identity-access-management-concepts/attribute-based-access-control-primer/#:~:text=What%20is%20ABAC%3F%20Attribute%20Based%20Access%20Control%20is,is%20no%20longer%20granted%20via%20a%20specific%20ACL
7. 6 the European Central Bank ECB has Defined Strong, https://www.coursehero.com/file/p37h8jln/6-The-European-Central-Bank-ECB-has-defined-strong-authentication-as-a/

8. Authorization Models: ACL, DAC, MAC, RBAC, ABAC, https://dinolai.com/notes/others/authorization-models-acl-dac-mac-rbac-abac.html#:~:text=ABAC%20%28Attribute-Based%20Access%20Control%29%20Unlike%20role-based%20access%20control,rule%20set%20that%20can%20evaluate%20many%20different%20attributes

9. Directory System Agent, https://docs.microsoft.com/en-us/windows/win32/ad/directory-system-agent?redirectedfrom=MSDN

10. Lightweight Directory Access Protocol (LDAP), https://tools.ietf.org/rfc/rfc4511.txt

11. Computer Access Control, https://en.wikipedia.org/wiki/Computer_access_control

12. Server Administration Application – Configuring Database Connections, https://hub.verj.io/ebase/doc/Server_Admin_Database.htm#:~:text=The%20term%20pooled%20connectionmeans%20that%20connections%20to%20the,a%20database%20connection%20is%20a%20relatively%20expensive%20operation

13. Mandatory Access Control, https://en.wikipedia.org/wiki/Mandatory_access_control

14. What is Role-Based Access Control (RBAC)? Examples, Benefits, and More, https://www.upguard.com/blog/rbac#:~:text=Role-based%20access%20control%20%28RBAC%29%2C%20also%20known%20as%20role-based,that%20is%20less%20error-prone%20than%20individually%20assigning%20permissions

15. How to Setup MFA for your Microsoft 365 Account, https://www.ravenscroftonline.com/knowledge-base/mfa365/

16. "What's the Difference b/w SSO (Single Sign On) & LDAP?". JumpCloud. 2019-05-14. Retrieved 2020-10-27.

17. "SSO and LDAP Authentication". Authenticationworld.com. Archived from the original on 2014-05-23. Retrieved 2014-05-23.

18. "Two-factor Authentication: What you Need to Know (FAQ) – CNET". CNET. Retrieved 2015-10-31.

19. Jacomme, Charlie and Kremer, Steve (2021-02-01), "An Extensive Formal Analysis of Multi-factor Authentication Protocols," *ACM Transactions on Privacy and Security*. 24 (2): 1–34. doi:10.1145/3440712. ISSN 2471-2566. S2CID 231791299.

20. Trusted Computer System Evaluation Criteria. United States Department of Defense. December 1985. DoD Standard 5200.28-STD. Archived from the original on 2006-05-27.

21. http://fedoraproject.org/wiki/Features/RemoveSETUID – Fedora 15 set to remove SETUID in favor of (Linux kernel) capabilities.

22. Belim, S. V. and Belim, S. Yu. (December 2018). "Implementation of Mandatory Access Control in Distributed Systems." *Automatic Control and Computer Sciences*. 52: (8), 1124–1126. doi:10.3103/S0146411618080357. ISSN:0146-4116.

23. http://csrc.nist.gov/publications/history/dod85.pdf

24. "Technical Rational Behind CSC-STD-003-85: Computer Security Requirements". (1985-06-25). Archived from the original on July 15, 2007. Retrieved 2008-03-15.

25. "The Common Criteria Portal". Archived from the original on 2006-07-18. Retrieved 2008-03-15.

26. US Department of Defense (December 1985). "DoD 5200.28-STD: Trusted Computer System Evaluation Criteria". Retrieved 2008-03-15.

27. "Controlled Access Protection Profile, Version 1.d". National Security Agency. 1999-10-08. Archived from the original on 2012-02-07. Retrieved 2008-03-15.

28. Passphrase - Ask Leo!, https://askleo.com/glossary/passphrase/

29. Configuring Database Connections, https://hub.verj.io/ebase/doc/Server_Admin_Database.htm

30. Authorization, https://en.wikipedia.org/wiki/Authorization_(computer_access_control)

31. HC3 Intelligence Briefing Access Control, https://www.hhs.gov/sites/default/files/hc3-intelligence-briefing-access-control-on-health-information-systems.pdf

8 Zero Trust Architecture

INTRODUCTION

Zero Trust Architecture (ZTA) was created before remote working became popular and organizations' traditional perimeter-based security models broke up.

This chapter will discuss the concepts of ZTA, CASB, and SASE and how they can help with data privacy and security.

THE OLD SECURITY MODEL

The old security model of "inside means trusted" and "outside means untrusted" is no longer valid. When users became mobile and when business partners on the "outside" where required to access, virtual private networks (VPNs) and demilitarized zones (DMZs) became common according to "Gartner: Market Guide for Zero Trust Network Access."

KEY OBJECTIVES

In the zero trust model, there are key goals when it comes to securing your networks according to "Secure networks with Zero Trust":

- Be ready to handle attacks and minimize the extent of the damage
- Increase the difficulty of compromising your system

Zero trust assumes that anyone accessing your system, devices, etc., is a bad actor for those getting up to speed. Zero trust helps prevent successful data breaches by eliminating the concept of trust.

- Zero trust can help secure remote users, bring your own device (BYOD), and cloud-based assets not located within an enterprise.
- Zero trust is a shift of network defenses toward a more comprehensive IT security model that allows organizations to restrict access controls to networks, applications, and the environment.
- Zero trust defined: Instead of assuming everything behind the corporate firewall is safe, the zero trust model assumes breach and verifies each request as though it originates from an open environment.

ZERO TRUST STRATEGY ASSUMES BREACHES ARE INEVITABLE

Zero trust assumes breaches are unavoidable, and you must verify each request as if it originates from an uncontrolled network—identity management plays a crucial role in this.

POINT OF CONTROL MOVES TO THE DATA LAYER

Doing this at range requires intelligent passive mapping, along with rules to pull the signal from the noise in an increasingly data-rich world according to "Focus your attention on data security, zero-trust, and supply chains."

Dynamic Security Rules

The new NIST SP 800-207 publication defines Zero Trust Architecture (ZTA) as a collection of concepts and ideas designed to reduce the uncertainty in enforcing accurate, per-request access decisions.

DOI: 10.1201/9781003189664-11

Data is not a new thesis, but the change in data stacks from an initial cybersecurity lens according to "Want in on the next $100B in cybersecurity?"

For instance, data is expanding faster than we can secure it. We need first to know where the information is situated.

Zero Trust, Network Segmentation, and PCI DSS

Network segmentation is an architecture that divides a network into smaller sections or subnets. Each network segment acts as its own network. Segmentation divides a computer network into lesser parts.

Zero trust is a cornerstone for compliance with access control requirements in data privacy regulations like GDPR and CCPA. New US privacy laws are modeled after these principles.

A zero trust model can help manage risk and provide a dynamic instead of static security rules and enforcement. Static network segmentation is often used to segment Cardholder Data Environment for PCI DSS scope.

Secure Networks with Zero Trust

In a zero trust approach, networks are instead segmented into smaller islands with their own ingress and egress controls to minimize the "blast radius" of unauthorized access to data.

TO MAKE THIS HAPPEN, FOLLOW THESE PRINCIPLES

- Validate explicitly.
- Constantly authenticate and authorize based on all available data points.
- Use least-privileged access.
- Limit user access with Just-In-Time.
- Assume breach. Minimize blast radius.

Data Privacy and Zero Trust Architecture

Data security controls data privacy regulations, and Zero Trust Architecture are connected in a data security policy that is governing access to resources:

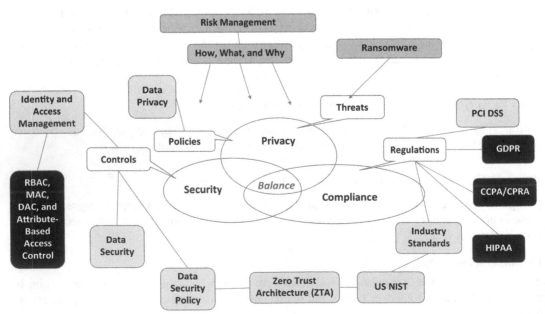

Protection techniques are related to Zero Trust Architecture and connected in a data security policy that is controlling the use of different data protection techniques and access to data:

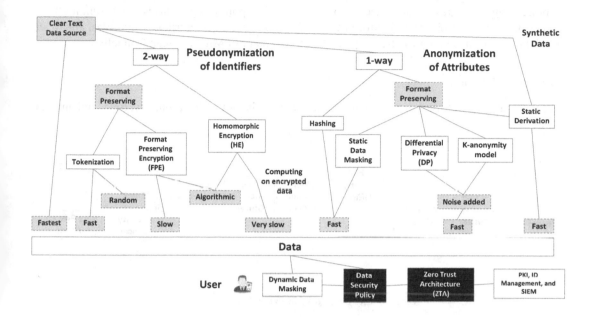

Zero Trust *Protects Resources, Not Network Segments*

Zero trust assumes no implicit trust is granted that includes remote users, bring your own device (BYOD), and cloud-based assets not located within an enterprise-owned network boundary. Zero trust protects data and other resources.

It goes more granular and dynamic than traditional network segments.

The network location is no longer seen as the prime component to the security posture of the resource. In the abstract model of access, a subject needs access to an enterprise resource.

Access is granted through a policy decision point (PDP) and corresponding policy enforcement point (PEP) according to IETF Rfc3198 at "Scott Rose Oliver Borchert Stu Mitchell Sean Connelly":

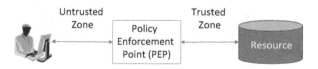

Source: Adopted from NIST

ZERO TRUST CENTRALIZES THE ACCESS MECHANISMS

The zero trust grants access based on the identity of the humans and their devices, plus other attributes and context (such as time/date, geolocation, and device posture), and adaptively offers relevant trust required at the time according to "Device Integrity and the Zero Trust Framework." The result is improved flexibility and better monitoring. ZTNA is useful for organizations looking for more flexibility.

TRUST ALGORITHM

For an enterprise with a ZTA deployment, the policy engine is the brain and the PE's trust algorithm as its primary thought process. According to Cyber-Ark, the trust algorithm (TA) is the process for the policy engine to grant or deny access to a resource. The policy engine takes input from multiple sources database with observable information about subjects, subject attributes and roles, and other metadata sources according to "Scott Rose Oliver Borchert Stu Mitchell Sean Connelly."

CONTEXT OF REQUEST

Access to data can be based on the context of the request, including location, day, time, and amount of records.

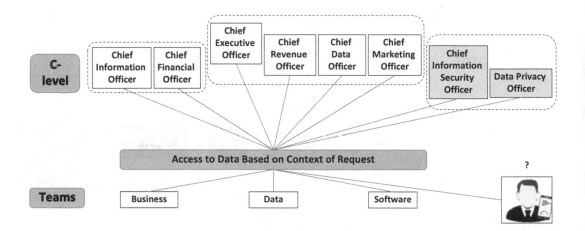

Enterprise with Contracted Services or Nonemployee Access

Another use case is an enterprise that includes on-site visitors or contracted service providers. They may require limited access to enterprise resources to do their work, according to NIST.SP.800-207. A Zero Trust Architecture will allow these devices and any visiting service technician access to the internet while obscuring enterprise resources. Example of an Enterprise Campus Network:

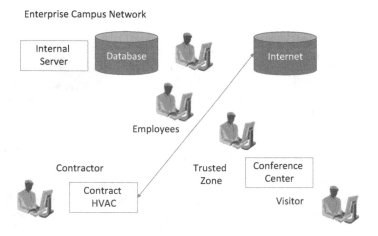

Source: Adopted from NIST

There are different parts and a distinct control plane, while application data is communicated on a data plane.

Example of Device Agent/Gateway-Based Deployment

The PEP is here using a gateway in front as a proxy for the resource:

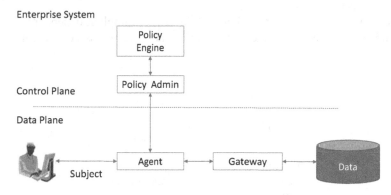

Source: Adopted from NIST

User Access Validation and Segmentation

Don't trust the user ID. Validate context of each user request and segment sensitive data into separate environments or network segments:

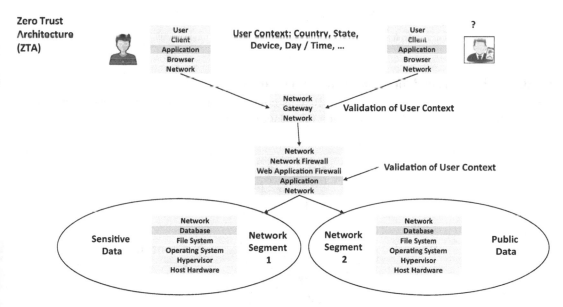

Zero Trust, CASB, and SASE

Enterprises commonly have isolated processes for networking-related and security-related functions, creating inefficiencies and preventing an end-to-end view. Gartner forecasts that 80% of new digital business applications opened up to ecosystem partners will be accessed through ZTNA by 2022. It estimates that 60% of enterprises will phase out most of their remote access virtual private networks (VPNs) in favor of ZTNA by 2023.

SASE will experience a compound annual growth rate (CAGR) of 42% from 2019 to 2024, when it approaches $11 billion. It also says that 40% of enterprises will have explicit strategies to adopt SASE by 2024, according to "Why SASE And ZTNA Are Even Better Together When Tightly Integrated."

According to Gartner, "Zero Trust Network Access (ZTNA) augments conventional VPN technologies for application access and removes the excessive trust once required to allow employees and partners to connect and collaborate."

The relation between SASE and Zero Trust Architecture is implicit dependence, with zero trust projects forming part of a SASE strategy. Dynamic and static access control can be enforced in CASB or SASE:

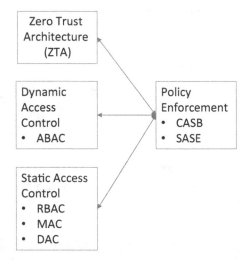

ABAC Provides a Foundation for a Data-Oriented ZTA

RBAC is static and data-oriented while ABAC is context-oriented, for example, based on current user location, ABAC provides a foundation for a data-oriented ZTA:

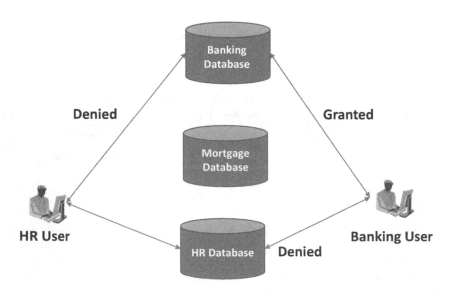

The Relation between SASE and CASB

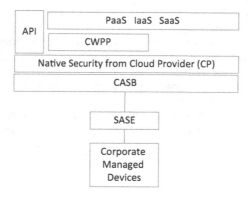

SUMMARY

In this chapter, we examined the concept of Zero Trust given data privacy and security policies and how it can divide a computer network into smaller parts to improve network performance and security.

Zero trust is a cornerstone for compliance with access control requirements in data privacy regulations like EU GDPR and US CCPA.

This chapter also discussed how ZTA, CASB, and SASE are related and how they can help with data security.

We will discuss this topic more in Volume II of this book.

BIBLIOGRAPHY

1. The Ransomware Epidemic: How Zero Trust Security Can Help, https://www.forbes.com/sites/forbestech-council/2021/04/23/the-ransomware-epidemic-how-zero-trust-security-can-help/?sh=5bef7cd72dc7
2. Five Practical Steps to Implement a Zero-Trust Network, https://cisomag.eccouncil.org/implementing-zero-trust-network/
3. NIST sp800-207, https://csrc.nist.gov/publications/
4. IETF Address Allocation for Private Internets, https://www.ietf.org/rfc/rfc3198.txt
5. Information Systems Security, https://bus206.pressbooks.com/chapter/chapter-6-information-systems-security/
6. Gartner Market Guide for Zero Trust Network Access, Published 8 June 2020 and revised 16 June 2020 by Steve Riley, Neil MacDonald and Lawrence Orans.
7. Elisity Fundamentally Changes Enterprise Security Model with New Security Paradigm Combining Zero Trust Network Access with Software-Defined Perimeter, https://www.businesswire.com/news/home/20200812005170/en/Elisity-Fundamentally-Changes-Enterprise-Security-Model-with-New-Security-Paradigm-Combining-Zero-Trust-Network-Access-with-Software-Defined-Perimeter
8. Focus Your Attention on Data Security, Zero-trust and Supply Chains, https://techcrunch.com/2021/06/23/want-in-on-the-next-100b-in-cybersecurity/
9. Mutual TLS: Securing Microservices in Service Mesh, https://thenewstack.io/mutual-tls-microservices-encryption-for-service-mesh/
10. Zero Trust Architecture, https://www.nist.gov/publications/zero-trust-architecture
11. Network Architectures, https://www.ncsc.gov.uk/collection/device-security-guidance/infrastructure/network-architectures
12. Passphrase - Ask Leo!, https://askleo.com/glossary/passphrase/
13. Configuring Database Connections, https://hub.verj.io/ebase/doc/Server_Admin_Database.htm
14. Authorization, https://en.wikipedia.org/wiki/Authorization_(computer_access_control)

15. HC3 Intelligence Briefing Access Control, https://www.hhs.gov/sites/default/files/hc3-intelligence-briefing-access-control-on-health-information-systems.pdf

16. Want in on the next $100B in Cybersecurity? – TechCrunch, https://techcrunch.com/2021/06/23/want-in-on-the-next-100b-in-cybersecurity/

17. Secure Networks with Zero Trust, https://docs.microsoft.com/en-us/security/zero-trust/deploy/networks

18. Scott Rose Oliver Borchert Stu Mitchell Sean Connelly, https://tsapps.nist.gov/publication/get_pdf.cfm?pub_id=930420

19. Device Integrity and the Zero Trust Framework – Eclypsium, https://eclypsium.com/2020/07/21/device-integrity-and-the-zero-trust-framework/

20. Why SASE and ZTNA Are Even Better Together When Tightly Integrated, https://www.forbes.com/sites/forbestechcouncil/2021/10/01/why-sase-and-ztna-are-even-better-together-when-tightly-integrated/?sh=6dace8e47e97

Section IV

Applications

9 Applications, APIs, and Privacy by Design

INTRODUCTION

Privacy by design is an important aspect of data privacy regulations like GDPR and impacts how security functions are integrated into applications and data. The evolving API Ecosystem is changing the way we implement Applications.

We will discuss protecting applications, the software supply chain, and three increasingly used techniques for the security and privacy of data and computation in cloud environments.

THE API ECONOMY

We live in an API economy, a collection of business patterns and channels based on secure access to functionality and data exchange according to "Integration and APIs: Two Sides of the Same Coin."

APIs make it simpler to integrate and connect people, places, systems, data, things, and algorithms, creating new user involvements, according to "Welcome to the API Economy."

An API is a software element that—in terms of its procedures, inputs, outputs, and underlying data types—employs a function that is independent of its "host" app according to "Serverless and APIs: Rethinking Curriculum in Higher Education." Tech news sites have frequently featured in-depth articles on the API economy for years. Business publications are now doing the same (see "Why the API Economy Is Exploding," *Forbes*).

Providers of technology and services have also launched major marketing campaigns based on their API offerings. But what is the API economy? Is it a real "economy"? Are real companies making real money from APIs? This article, and the research highlighted within, will answer those questions and provide clarification. It is helpful to first remind ourselves what an economy is—and the generally agreed definition is: "A processor system by which goods and services are produced, sold and bought in a country or region." So in the API economy, the products are the APIs, and the market is global, not generally confined by a country or a region. However, most of the money generated by the API economy is not made by directly charging for APIs. Revenue is made through business opportunities enabled by the APIs and the app constructs (see "The App and Its Impact on Software Design") through which they are consumed, while the APIs themselves are free, at least initially. In the API economy, most of the goods and services are traditional ones that the companies involved already produced, sold, and bought well before the API economy was talked about, typically on traditional channels.

DEFINITION OF THE API ECONOMY

"A set of business models and channels—based on secure access of functionality and exchange of data to an ecosystem of developers and the users of the app constructs they build—through an API, either within a company or on the Internet with business partners and customers." Strictly speaking, by that definition, internal API programs are also part of the API economy according to "Digital Business." In some cases, companies also cross-charge other internal departments to use their APIs. Having said all that, the main manifestation of the API economy is still clearly between a company and its business partners, clients, and general consumers, according to "Digital Business."

In this model, API providers publish an API to a target constituency of developers (whether they be inside the company, their business partners, or simply independent Web and mobile app developers). The more business-sensitive the API, the more tightly these developers are targeted, vetted, and managed. When an API provider decides to publish an API, it needs to make sure there are app developers who are interested in using it because they need to either:

- Get paid for it
- Improve their own productivity
- Open new business opportunities (for either the API developer or the app developer or the company they work for—or all of them

When the application construct that consumes the API (for example, a mobile app that allows you to change your address for a utility) is ready (and tested by the API provider), it is distributed to end-users. Suppose end users find the app construct of value. In that case, its use will multiply, multiplying the value that the API provider initially aimed at when it decided to publish the API. That is the foundation of the API economy.

The main rule here is that the app construct must be valuable to both the users and the API provider to hit the multiplication and get the value system going.

The API gateway:

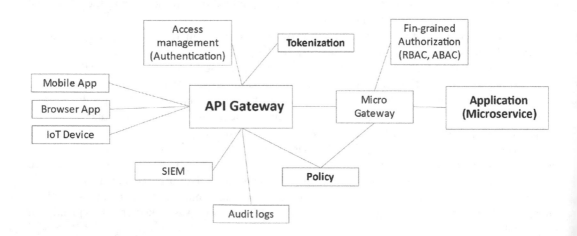

APPLICATIONS AND APIs

We already live in an API economy, and Application Programming Interfaces (APIs) are done through API calls according to "APIs Are at the Heart of Digital Business."

Privacy System Design

The ICT system of the PII principal focuses on but is not limited to communicating the privacy policy, handling consent management, and PII collection.

Since the PII principal is the party that provides PII to the overall system, the ICT system in use by the PII principal should contain components for securing PII during collection. According to "ISO/IEC 29101," these techniques can include pseudonymization, anonymization, encryption, and secret sharing.

The architecture for the ICT system of the PII principal:

Privacy	Policy communication		PII Categorization	
	Consent Management		Privacy Management	
Access	Identity Management		Pseudonymization scheme	
	Access control	Authentication		Authorization
PII	PII Management	PII Transfer		PII Validation
	PII Pseudonymization	PII Anonymization	Secret sharing	PII Encryption
	PII Use	PII Inventory	PII Archiving	Audit logging

Source: ISO/IEC

THE Design and Investigating involve input from multiple organizational departments, according to "Tackling Privacy by Design: Practical Advice." Suppose your company has avoided being subject to one of the new consumer privacy laws and has not by now been forced to discover answers to the above questions, such as through data mapping.

Basic Principles

More than two decades ago, when most of us technology people just worried about Y2K or the Internet collapsing, the true visionary Dr. Ann Cavoukian realized that those doom scenarios are not the ones to be worried about. Working as the Canadian privacy expert and Commissioner for Ontario and with a background in psychology, criminology, and law, she realized that the systemic effects of ever-growing information systems will affect our lives in much more profound ways than we ever imagined. To realize the true benefits of this technology growth, she recognized the need to incorporate the social and human value norms into the design of those technology systems. She developed the Privacy by Design framework—an approach that is characterized by proactive, positive-sum (full functionality) measures. The objectives of this framework are not just to ensure privacy and personal control over one's information but also to gain a sustainable competitive advantage for the organizations themselves by doing so.

Privacy by design consists of these principles according to "The Hitchhikers Guide to Privacy by Design":

1. Proactive not reactive; preventative not remedial
   • Privacy-invasive events are anticipated and prevented before they happen. Focus is on before-the-fact prevention, not remediation after a problem (e.g., data breach) occurs.
2. Privacy as the default setting
   • This means maximum privacy protection is offered as a baseline—the maximum degree of privacy is ensured by automatically protecting personal data in any given IT system or business practice.
3. Privacy embedded into the design
   • Implant privacy into the design and architecture of IT systems and business practices by treating it as any other system requirement (e.g., usability, performance). This way, privacy becomes an essential component of the core functionality being delivered.
4. Full functionality—positive-sum, not zero-sum
   • Implementation of privacy is not compromising business goals. A win-win manner without unnecessary trade-off. It is an approach of "and" vs. "or," having to, for example, accommodate for privacy and security.
5. End-to-end security—full lifecycle protection
   • The security measurement is to be implemented through the whole information management lifecycle and embedded into the system before collecting the information. All data is to be securely retained and then securely destroyed at the end of the process in a timely fashion.
6. Visibility and transparency—keep it open
   • All stakeholders must operate according to any stated promises and objectives and must be subject to independent verification. Systems parts and operations must remain visible and transparent to all actors, users, and providers alike.
7. Respect for user privacy—offering privacy options.

PRIVACY BY DESIGN IS KEY TO CLOUD

Within a typical company, "data streams across multiple regions and multi-cloud environments that combine vendors and programming languages according to "Tackling Privacy by Design: Practical."

Cloud-centric organizations, especially, face steep challenges. Clouds can't replace all legacy systems or remove the need for data warehouses and even data centers. According to "The Hitchhiker's Guide to Privacy by Design," they simply add another layer to the enterprise data framework.

DATA PROTECTION

This tactic leads to a privacy-by-design framework that emphasizes maximum data security, compliance, and operational requirements. It also simplifies inherently difficult security tasks, such as masking data elements but ensuring their usability according to "Privacy by Design Key to Cloud-migration Success."

As companies pursue rapid innovation that focuses on agility, flexibility, and DevOps—typically through multi-cloud environments and an increasing array of IoT data—this approach delivers highly automated controls over data from top to bottom and across an enterprise.

AGILE DEVELOPMENT

THE TEAM AND THE PROCESS

Agile is a way of thinking and more about how the Team works regardless of your tools.

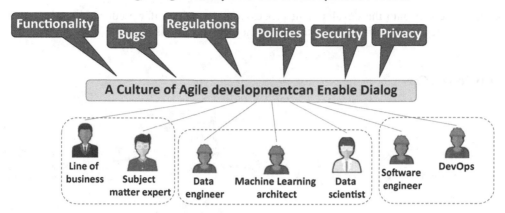

Integrating Security into the Development Process

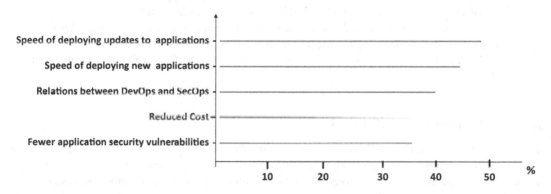

BENEFITS OF EMBRACING DEVSECOPS

Source: Adapted from ISC2

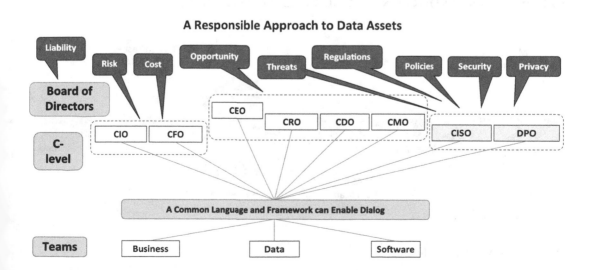

A Responsible Approach to Data Assets

INTEGRATING SECURITY INTO THE DEVELOPMENT PROCESS

Integrating security into the development process can be helped if we educate developers about security and integrate security into the tools that they are already using.

Security in DevOps

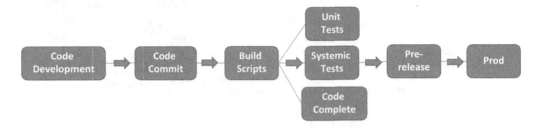

Security Reviews

- Security reviews of source code can be effective for larger application monoliths (a million lines of code) since context can be found within a single code component.
- Security review of source code is less effective for smaller applications since less context can be found within a single code component. Runtime security testing with the interaction between different APIs can be more effective for smaller application components or microservices.

SOFTWARE BILL OF MATERIALS

A software bill of materials (SBOM) is a list of components in a piece of software and should be declared when using any product. This becomes more important from a security point of view when applications tend to include more than 80% of their functionality from imported functions, for example, from open-source libraries. Software vendors often create products by assembling open-source and commercial software components.

APPLICATION TESTING AND QUALITY ASSURANCE (QA)

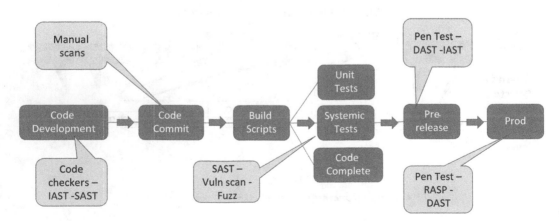

Domains of Application Testing:

1. DAST—Dynamic Application Self Testing
2. IAST—Dynamic Application Security Testing
3. Fuzz—Throwing lots of random garbage as input
4. Vulnerability Analysis
5. RAST—Runtime Application Self Protection

API TRENDS FOR SECURITY IN DEVOPS

More Microservices

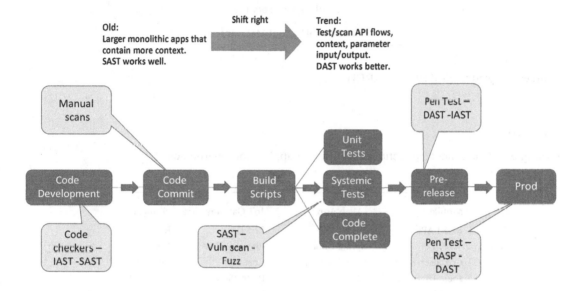

Effective Testing with Application Microservices

Interactive Application Security Testing and other approaches:

- Interactive Application Self-Testing (IAST) provides execution path scanning, monitoring, and embedded application whitelisting according to "What is IAST? All About Interactive Application Security Testing."
- Static Application Security Testing (SAST) examines all code—or runtime binaries (less effective for Microservices).
- Vulnerability analysis including platform configuration, patch levels, or application composition to detect known vulnerabilities.
- Fuzz testing is essentially throwing lots of random garbage at applications, seeing whether any (type of) garbage causes errors.
- Runtime Application Self Protection (RASP) provides execution path scanning, monitoring, and embedded application whitelisting (effective for microservices).
- Regression testing enhances the visibility of your build quality before putting it in production. Examples: Full Regressions, Overnight Targeted Checks, and Smoke Checks executed with manual, automation, crowdsourcing, and artificial intelligence and allow a software development team to quickly validate their UI and API and load test it.

PORTABILITY FOR HYBRID CLOUD

Portability can be an important aspect of Hybrid Cloud deployments. Containers provide a high degree of when compared to serverless functions:

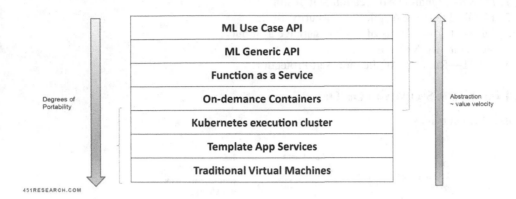

Source: Adapted from 451REASEARCH

FLEXIBILITY

Example of Container architectures for different application environments:

Mobile	Web App	IoT Gateway	Tomcat
REST API	REST API	REST API	REST API
Node JS	Spring Boot	Jboss DB EAP	Node JS
Container	Container	Container	Container
Jboss DB Store	MySQL store	PostgreSQL	MongoDB
Containers	Containers	Containers	Containers

VIRTUALIZATION

Example of applications with runtime files in a virtualized environment:

App	App	App	App
	Runtime files	Runtime files	
		Host OS	

CONTAINERS

DOCKER AND KUBERNETES

Kubernetes is an open-source container-orchestration system for automating computer application deployment, scaling, and management according to "Accelerating Kubernetes with NVIDIA Operators."

It was originally designed by Google and is now maintained by the Cloud Native Computing Foundation. It aims to provide a platform for automating the deployment, scaling, and operations of database management systems. It works with various container tools and runs containers in a cluster, often with images built using Docker.

Containers in Kubernetes:

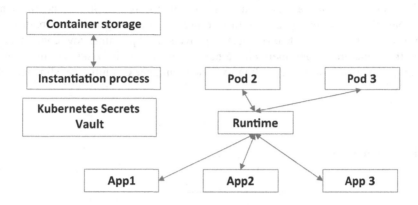

Example of applications with a Data Store included in the container image:

App	App	App
Guest OS	Guest OS	Guest OS
	Hypervisor	
	Host OS	
Jboss DB Store	Jboss DB Store	Jboss DB Store
Containers	Containers	Containers

Kubernetes Security and Compliance Frameworks

The challenge of administering security and maintaining compliance in a Kubernetes ecosystem is typically the same: an increasingly dynamic, changing landscape, be it new approaches of cyberattacks or adhering to changing regulations.

According to "A Practical Guide to the Different Compliance Kubernetes Security Frameworks and How They Fit Together," Kubernetes security requires a complex and multifaceted approach since an effective strategy needs to:

1. Ensure clean code
2. Provide full observability
3. Prevent the exchange of information with untrusted services
4. Produce digital signatures for clean code and trusted applications

According to "A Practical Guide to the Different Compliance Kubernetes Security Frameworks and How They Fit Together," security and compliance are often mistaken as two separate requirements; their objectives are the same. While organizations may choose how they administer security, regulatory bodies are the ones who set and enforce mandatory compliance standards. Adhering to these regulations is also crucial in terms of ensuring business continuity, protecting reputation, and determining an application's level of risk. To help with this, various institutions offer standardized frameworks and guidelines for administering security in a complex, dynamic Kubernetes ecosystem.

Compliance for Containers

Containerized architecture has significantly changed the way software is developed, tested, and deployed. There are major challenges in ensuring containers are compliant, and applying compliant security controls to this new type of infrastructure. Most regulations were created before containers were prevalent, and do not have specific provisions explaining how containers should be protected. At the same time, containers create new types of security risks that must be addressed to prevent compliance violations, according to "The Container Compliance Almanac: NIST, PCI, GDPR and CIS."

SERVER-LESS

Lambda Functions in AWS

Redshift	Snowflake
	Amazon API Gatewae
Lambda function	Lambda function
Protect function	Protect function
Customer's AWS Account (outside VPC)	
Security Service	
Lambda Layers	

DATA PRIVACY AND SECURITY IN A SERVERLESS CLOUD ENVIRONMENT

Data privacy and security can be implemented at different system layers on-premises and cloud. Separation of duties, security policy, and key management architectures can be implemented in a serverless environment using AWS, Azure, IBM Cloud, and GCP:

We will discuss more API and Modern application development in Volume II of this book.

ENTERPRISE ARCHITECTURE FRAMEWORK (EAF)

An Enterprise Architecture Framework (EAF) maps all the software development processes within the organization and how they relate and interact to fulfill the enterprise's mission. It provides organizations with the ability to understand and analyze weaknesses or inconsistencies to be identified and addressed. Several already-established EAFs are in use today; some of these frameworks were developed for very specific areas, whereas others have broader functionality according to "Enterprise Architecture."

ZACHMAN FRAMEWORK FOR ENTERPRISE ARCHITECTURE

John Zachman published the Zachman Framework, and it is based around the principles of classical architecture that establish a common vocabulary and set of perspectives for describing complex enterprise systems. The Zachman Framework has six perspectives or views according to "A COMPARISON OF ENTERPRISE ARCHITECTURE FRAMEWORKS":

1. Planner,
2. Owner,
3. Designer,
4. Builder,
5. Subcontractor, and
6. User.

The second dimension of Zachman"s Framework deals with the six basic questions: what, how, where, who, when, and why [6]. The framework does not guide sequence, process, or implementation but rather focuses on ensuring that all views are well established, ensuring a complete system regardless of the order in which they were established. The Zachman Framework has no explicit compliance rules since it is not a standard written by or for a professional organization.

WEB APPLICATION FIREWALL

Web application firewalls (WAF) are a specialized version of a network-based appliance that acts as a reverse proxy, inspecting traffic before being forwarded to an associated server according to "Application Firewall":

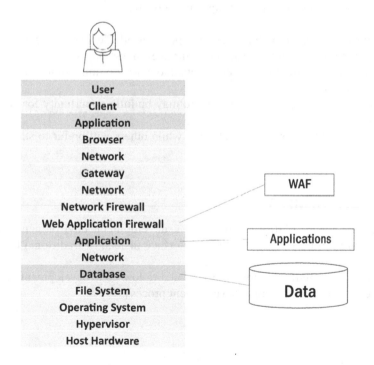

A WAF is a specific form of application firewall that filters, monitors, and blocks HTTP traffic to and from a web service according to "Create a Holiday Readiness Plan Unit I Salesforce Trailhead." By inspecting HTTP traffic, it can prevent attacks like SQL injection and cross-site scripting.

A WAF does not have much context about operations on specific data since it is a network-based device that inspects traffic before being forwarded to an associated server and application.

APPLICATION DEVELOPMENT

OWASP API Security Top 10

OWASP API Security Project: focuses on strategies and solutions to understand and mitigate the unique vulnerabilities and security risks of Application Programming Interfaces (APIs) according to "OWASP."

The OWASP Top 10 2017 includes the following examples according to "What Is the OWASP Top 10 and How Does It Work?"

3. Sensitive Data Exposure. Sensitive data exposure is when important stored or transmitted data (such as social security numbers) is compromised.
5. Broken Access Control. Broken access control is when an attacker can get access to user accounts. The attacker can operate as the user or as an administrator in the system.
7. Cross-Site Scripting (XSS). XSS attacks occur when an application includes untrusted data on a webpage. Attackers inject client-side scripts into this webpage.
9. Using Components with Known Vulnerabilities. This vulnerability's title states its nature; it describes when applications are built and run using known vulnerabilities components.

THE PACE OF CHANGE IN THE SOFTWARE DEVELOPMENT INDUSTRY

With the move to modern software development on web, mobile, and cloud, new languages, frameworks, plug-ins, modules, and components appear almost weekly.

- How can developers keep on top of all the options available, and how can developers ensure the choices made of which to use are the right ones in the long term?
- Building a new generation of modern applications may require significant reskilling of the development team.
- For maintaining existing applications, there may be little opportunity for developers to add new skills.
- Some developers will embrace the change, while others will prefer to stick with what they know.

LOW-CODE DEVELOPMENT

A low-code development platform provides a development environment used to create application software through a graphical user interface instead of traditional hand-coded computer code.

No-code development platforms are closely related to low-code development platforms as both are designed to expedite the application development process.

Trends

1. Faster development.
2. Writing less code means more apps can be built faster than ever before.
3. Digital transformation.
4. Transformation of manual and paper-based processes into the cloud, desktop, web and mobile applications for better efficiency, productivity, data accuracy, and customer service.

5. Reducing the maintenance burden.
6. By simplifying application maintenance and development, overall lifecycle costs can be reduced, and resources freed up to build new applications.
7. Move to mobile.
8. Satisfy the increasing demand for mobile applications across the business.
9. Cloud computing.
10. Improve availability while cutting operational costs by quickly moving applications or parts of applications to the cloud for better agility and elasticity.
11. Skills management.
12. Eliminate pockets of expertise and specialized skills. Allow any developers to work on any part of an application. Eliminate resource shortages and conflicts.
13. Combating shadow IT.
14. Accelerate the deployment of applications so that business users don't feel they need to take matters into their own hands. Deliver apps in days or weeks instead of months or years.

SECURITY METRICS

Security metrics can be collected automatically from tools in the DevOps testing cycle to report on trends in vulnerabilities:

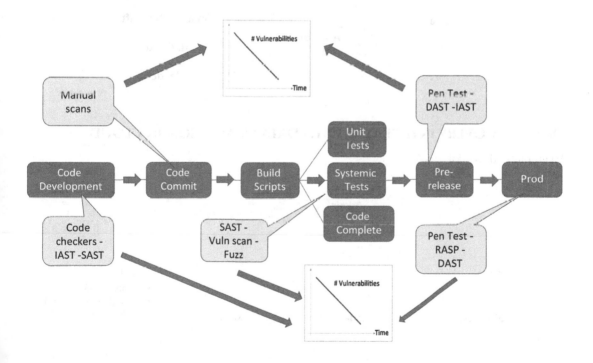

KAFKA

Kafka is a framework implementation of a software bus using stream-processing according to "Kafka." It is an open-source software platform developed by the Apache Software Foundation written in Scala and Java. The project aims to provide a unified, high-throughput, low-latency platform for real-time handling data feeds.

Kafka and Data Lakes:

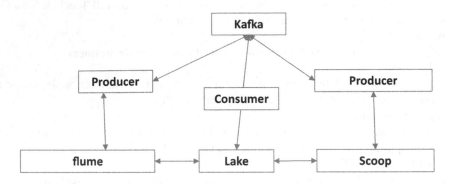

Kafka and Amazon AWS:
A data lake is a vast pool of raw data, the purpose for which is not yet defined.

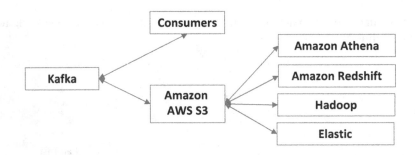

DATA DISCOVERY INTEGRATED WITH DATA PROTECTION IN CLOUD

Example with Kafka:

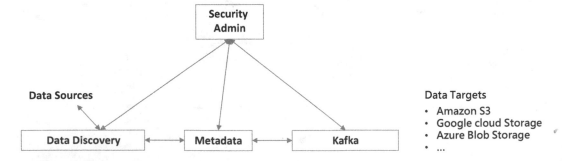

DATA LAKE VS. DATA WAREHOUSE

Data lakes and data warehouses are extensively used to store big data, but they are not interchangeable, according to "Data Lake vs. Data Warehouse." A data lake is a vast pool of raw data, the purpose for which is not yet defined. A data warehouse is a repository for structured, filtered data that has already been processed for a specific purpose, according to "An Introduction to Data Lakes | Severalnines." The two types of data storage are often mistaken, but the distinction is important because they serve different objectives and require different eyes to be properly optimized.

PRIVACY-PRESERVING DATA MINING

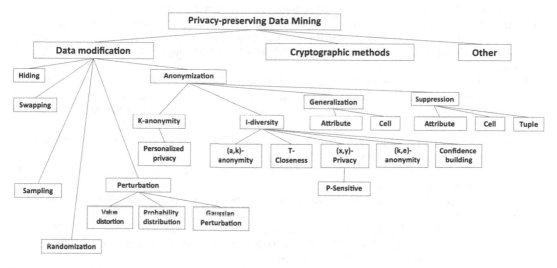

Source: Adapted from The Hitchhiker's Guide to Privacy-Privacy by Design

SUMMARY

We discussed protecting data in applications, the software supply chain, and the trend toward an API economy.

Privacy by design is an important aspect of data privacy regulations. It is impacting how security functions are integrated, and the evolving API Ecosystem is changing the way we implement applications, the software supply chain, and three increasingly used techniques for the security and privacy of data and computation in cloud environments.

We will talk more about this topic in Volume II of this book and also cover Infrastructure/service bill of materials (IBOM).

BIBLIOGRAPHY

1. Kafka, https://en.wikipedia.org/wiki/Apache_Kafka#:~:text=From%20Wikipedia%2C%20the%20free%20encyclopedia%20Apache%20Kafka%20is,high-throughput%2C%20low-latency%20platform%20for%20handling%20real-time%20data%20feeds

2. Data Lake vs Data Warehouse, https://www.talend.com/resources/data-lake-vs-data-warehouse/#:~:text=Data%20lakes%20and%20data%20warehouses%20are%20both%20widely,has%20already%20been%20processed%20for%20a%20specific%20purpose

3. Low-code Development, https://en.wikipedia.org/wiki/Low-code_development_platform

4. Open Web Application Security Project Top 10 (OWASP Top 10), https://www.synopsys.com/glossary/what-is-owasp-top-10.html

5. The Hitchhikers Guide to Privacy by Design, Barbara Peruskovic, https://issuu.com/protegrity/docs/the_hitchhiker_s_guide_to_privacy_b

6. MITRE Privacy Engineering Framework, https://www.mitre.org/publications/systems-engineering-guide/enterprise-engineering/engineering-informationintensive

7. GDPR Privacy by Design, https://gdpr-info.eu/issues/privacy-by-design/

8. Tackling Privacy by Design: Practical Advice, https://www.cpomagazine.com/data-privacy/tackling-privacy-by-design-practical-advice-following-multiple-implementations/:

9. New Enterprise Application and Data Security Challenges and Solutions, https://www.brighttalk.com/webinar/new-enterprise-application-and-data-security-challenges-and-solutions/

10. Open Source API Gateways, https://www.tecmint.com/open-source-api-gateways-and-management-tools/#:~:text=Goku%20API%20Gateway%20is%20an%20open-source%20microservice%20gateway,and%20as%20a%20unified%20platform%20for%20third-party%20APIs

11. APIs Are at the Heart of Digital Business, https://www.gartner.com/smarterwithgartner/apis-are-at-the-heart-of-digital-business#:~:text=APIs%20are%20minimizing%20the%20friction%20caused%20by%20bimodal,ticket%20online%20%20E2%80%94%20are%20completed%20through%20API%20calls

12. 'Privacy by Design' Key to Cloud-migration Success, https://www.protegrity.com/protegrity-blog/privacy-by-design-key-to-cloud-migration-success#:~:text=Maximum%20Data%20Protection%20This%20approach%20leads%20to%20a,as%20masking%20data%20elements%20but%20ensuring%20their%20usability

13. What is IAST? All About Interactive Application Security Testing, https://hdivsecurity.com/bornsecure/what-is-iast-interactive-application-security-testing/

14. Accelerating Kubernetes with NVIDIA Operators, https://developer.nvidia.com/blog/accelerating-kubernetes-with-nvidia-operators/

15. Integration and APIs: Two Sides of the Same Coin, https://www.jitterbit.com/blog/integration-apis-two-sides-coin-2/

16. Application Firewall, https://en.wikipedia.org/wiki/Application_firewall#:~:text=Web%20application%20firewalls%20%28WAF%29%20are%20a%20specialized%20version,traffic%20before%20being%20forwarded%20to%20an%20associated%20server

17. What is Kubernetes?, https://kubernetes.io/docs/concepts/overview/what-is-kubernetes/

18. Welcome to the API Economy, https://www.gartner.com/smarterwithgartner/welcome-to-the-api-economy

19. Digitale Identiteit, https://www.overons.kpn/en/kpn-in-the-netherlands/innovation/digital-identity

20. Serverless and APIs: Rethinking Curriculum in Higher Education, https://simon.rochester.edu/download.aspx?id=16631

21. Enterprise Architecture – CIO Wiki, https://cio-wiki.org/wiki/Enterprise_Architecture

22. A Comparison of Enterprise Architecture Frameworks, http://ggatz.com/images/SOA_COMPARE.pdf

23. Create a Holiday Readiness Plan Unit | Salesforce Trailhead, https://trailhead.salesforce.com/en/content/learn/modules/b2c-holiday-season-ready/b2c-holiday-ready-plan

24. OWASP – Wikipedia, https://en.wikipedia.org/wiki/Open_Web_Application_Security_Project

25. What Is the OWASP Top 10 and How Does It Work?, https://www.synopsys.com/glossary/what-is-owasp-top-10.html

26. The Container Compliance Almanac: NIST, PCI, GDPR and CIS, https://www.aquasec.com/cloud-native-academy/container-security/container-compliance/

27. A Practical Guide to the Different Compliance Kubernetes Security Frameworks and How They Fit Together, https://www.armosec.io/blog/kubernetes-security-frameworks-and-guidance

10 Machine Learning and Analytics

INTRODUCTION

This chapter will discuss a range of new emerging technologies for privacy and confidentiality in machine learning and data analytics. Machine learning automates the workflow to quickly provide more comprehensive insights.

USING AI TO GAIN COMPETITIVE ADVANTAGE

These approaches are deployed for using IT to gain competitive advantage:

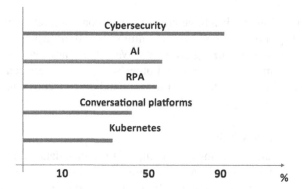

Source: Adapted from Gartner

DATA AND TECHNOLOGY ARE DRIVING BUSINESS CHANGE

As data volumes grow and new machine learning rises, leaders need to gain the benefits according to "Legacy Companies Need to Become More Data Driven—Fast."

Here are five tactics leaders should consider:

1. Know your business and prioritize data.
2. Link technology investments to objectives.
3. Centralize data infrastructure, decentralize customer management.
4. Educate the C-Suite on the value of machine learning and AI.
5. Start small and recognize that transformational changes often take decades.

DATA PRIVACY IS GOOD FOR BUSINESS

Just as CISOs and other security-minded business leaders wrap their heads around the so-called SolarWinds hack—a massive cyberattack that the US government believes was the work of Russia—they must now contend with the news of a second intrusion on a popular cloud service: Microsoft email.

DOI: 10.1201/9781003189664-14

Data Privacy Can Boost the Bottom Line

Protected data has also enabled retailers, increase online sales to homebound customers who don't yet want to venture into stores, according to "As Facebook Hack Shows, Data Privacy is Good for Business."

How Innovative Enterprises Win with Secure Machine Learning

New solutions help innovative enterprises succeed in an ever-changing, increasingly competitive digital economy. These solutions can empower enterprises to activate and extract value from sensitive data and engender trust by preserving the privacy of customers and employees. This enables enterprises to effectively use private data—including its application in advanced analytics, machine learning (ML), and artificial intelligence (AI)—without worrying about putting customers, employees, or intellectual property at risk.

Enterprises can gain an edge over less innovated competitors by understanding how using ML on protected data is beneficial, how recent advances in quantum computing will significantly impact opportunities and threats to new and historical data, and how current and future technologies and longer-term road map with future technologies can optimize and protect ML code. All of this propels enterprises forward by giving them a competitive advantage over less innovative competitors.

Quantum machine learning and is a huge area of discussion, research, development, and experimenting. We are now beginning to see more quantum algorithms which are the fabrication and tapestry for the future of machine learning programs. We will discuss analytics that utilizes machine learning (ML) models. Quantum computers and other strong computers can break algorithms and patterns in encrypted data. We can instead use random numbers to secure sensitive data with tokens. We will discuss how these techniques are related.

Race to Own the Data-Value Chain

Deals and alliances will escalate as companies compete to control data along their value chains.

Converting data into value, securely and ethically, is the business imperative for better data-valuation models to better understand how much profits depend on data sourced through third parties and acquire or partner with the best-valued information assets. Nearly 75% of IT leaders in the United States and the United Kingdom now rely heavily on data for business decisions, according to "Privacy megatrend: Race to own the data-value chain."

MACHINE LEARNING AND AI

According to "Artificial Intelligence vs Machine Learning," "machine learning is a step-step process and journey to figure out improved approaches to the problem at hand."

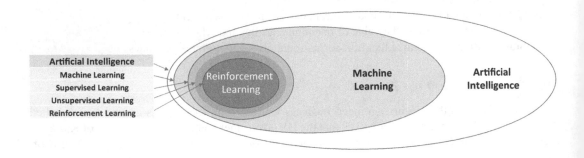

THE DIFFERENCE BETWEEN AI AND MACHINE LEARNING

Machine Learning is a subset of AI. ML is a set of algorithms built to achieve AI: those algorithms require the ability to learn from data, alter themselves when exposed to more data, and achieve a goal without being explicitly programmed according to "Machine-learning-vs-artificial-intelligence-difference-between-ml-and-ai."

Supervised vs. Unsupervised Learning and Deep Learning

A supervised learning algorithm can map a conclusion based on the typical path from input to output and will be able to identify that type of data based on identifiers that can be classified into categories. On the other hand, an unsupervised learning algorithm tries to find cohesions without any human involvement to gain insights according to "Artificial Intelligence vs. Machine Learning."

We will also discuss these topics in Volume II of this book.

GAINING A SENSE OF SECURITY

Adding more devices and software solutions falls short of securing AI and machine learning (ML) data. Increasingly data privacy and security must be built into the data flow according to "Gaining a Sense of Security About Secure Data and Algorithms."

CRACKING OPEN THE BLACK BOX OF AUTOMATED MACHINE LEARNING

MIT has developed an interactive tool that, for the first time, lets users see and control how increasingly popular automated machine-learning (AutoML) systems work according to "Cracking open the black box of automated machine learning."

SECURE AI AND ML

SECURE AI DEFINED

A starting is to understand the two building blocks of a data framework: secure data and secure algorithms.

Secure Data

The techniques include data tokenization and homomorphic encryption that substitutes an actual value, differential privacy, or k-anonymity, which adds "noise" and generalizes information.

Synthetic data substitutes statistical properties and can combine with derivations from the original data. According to "Gaining a Sense of Security About Secure Data and Algorithms," you can combine these techniques.

AI under Assault

Attacks on AI are coming, and Gartner stated that 30% of all AI cyberattacks by 2022 will leverage training data according to "Gaining a Sense of Security About Secure Data and Algorithms."

Protection Is Key

Critical is for business also focus on educating and training teams cross-functionally to know data generation techniques, protection approaches, and how data contamination can occur according to "Gaining a Sense of Security About Secure Data and Algorithms." Mitre offers solutions on AI risks at GitHub.

Whole Slide Imaging (WSI) is enabling us to quickly digitize pathology images to high-resolution files, and more and more businesses build automated diagnostics with machine learning based on WSI data according to "Automating Digital Pathology Image Analysis with Machine":

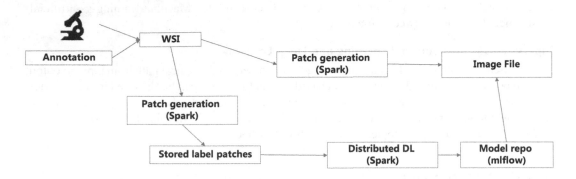

MATCHING GOVERNANCE WITH RISK LEVEL

Governance is not a free lunch; it takes effort, discipline, and time. From the business stakeholders' perspective, governance is likely to slow down the delivery of new models, which may cost the business money. It can look like a lot of bureaucracy for data scientists that erodes their ability to get things done. In contrast, those responsible for managing risk and the DevOps team managing deployment would argue that strict governance across the board should be mandatory.

SECURE AI—EXTRACT VALUE FROM PROTECTED DATA

Secure AI solutions create opportunities to harness the sensitive data that is most effective in activating advanced analytics and machine learning. When sensitive data is protected, businesses can quickly extract value, apply insights in real time, and predict outcomes that accelerate growth and operate in the cloud or on-premises.

Data knows no boundaries, and data protection must follow the data according to "Cracking open the black box of automated machine learning."

Decades ago, a central repository served as a starting point for any type of data analysis and business decision, but today, data resides everywhere and crosses company lines.

Businesses are increasingly exploring ways to share and pool data among a group of organizations for specific use-cases. This makes it possible to build a common AI model and deliver benefits to everyone. According to "Cracking open the black box of automated machine learning."

A New Era Emerges—AI on Protected Data

The overworked security staff can now secure data faster, innovate, and operate better and automate many data protection tasks. Access to protected data it can avoid lengthy verification processes for trade secrets and PII records, according to "Data privacy must evolve in an AI-centric world."

Putting Protection into Play

Start to define what techniques for protecting critical data and map them to the different business use-cases according to "Data privacy must evolve in an AI-centric world."

Most Companies Still Aren't Set Up to Support AI and ML Initiatives

Specify the flow for collecting information; implement AI platforms that can use protected information; that ensure data in motion can remain protected according to "Data privacy must evolve in an AI-centric world."

Secure AI—Extracting Value from Protected Data

Secure AI solutions create opportunities to harness the sensitive data proven to be most effective in activating advanced analytics and ML. With the confidence that sensitive data are protected, enterprises can rapidly extract value, apply insights in real time, and predict outcomes that accelerate growth. Sensitive data should be secured wherever it is and whatever it is—in the cloud or on-premises, at rest or in use—so it can be leveraged across the enterprise by frontline employees, analytics teams, and anyone who needs the information to make business decisions. Data know no boundaries, nor should data protection. Whether encrypting, tokenizing, or applying privacy methods, the solution should secure the data behind the many operating systems that drive the day-to-day functions of the enterprise and the analytical systems behind decision making, personalized customer experiences, and AI modeling.

Responsible AI

Responsible businesses give a right to privacy—safeguarding privacy, now and in the future, must be guaranteed. The desire to do so is a big undertaking, according to "Preserving Privacy With New Technologies."

To achieve success, we need to broaden the scope of people participating in the creation of these capabilities and do so diversely and inclusively. Example of what Responsible AI involves:

- Explainability to ensure we don't have impenetrable black-box
- Models that can explain themselves and allow individuals to say it's wrong causes harm or involve a risk of harm
- Creating a culture of transparency
- Global governance of data and AI

Responsible AI and Confidential AI

Responsible AI aims to define the trust and ethics related to decisions made by AI models:

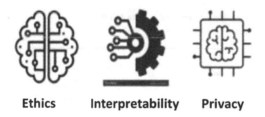

Ethics   **Interpretability**   **Privacy**

We will discuss the applicable data protection techniques in separate chapters in the book:

Generalization   **Synthetic Data**   **Private AI Models**

Algorithmic Trust Models

Algorithmic trust models can help ensure data privacy, and Gartner identifies a set of emerging technologies tied to algorithmic trust:

1. Secure access service edge (SASE)
2. Explainable AI
3. Responsible AI
4. Bring your own identity
5. Differential privacy
6. Authenticated provenance

Responsible AI and Confidential AI can be integrated

Responsible AI and confidential AI can be integrated with data security into enterprise platforms by using a gateway. We will discuss the gateway in a separate chapter in the book. Data protection techniques are applied early in the process:

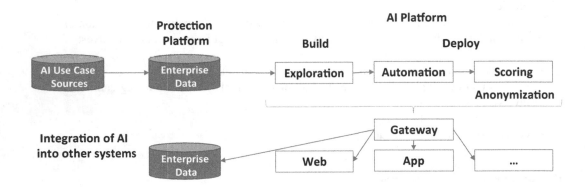

Privacy-Preserving Data Mining

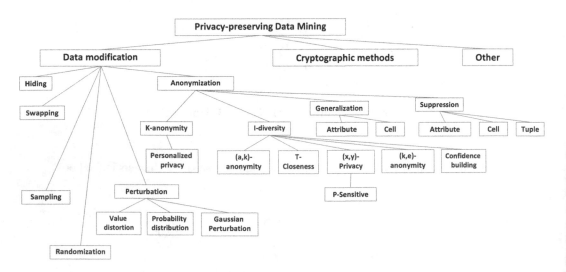

Source: Adapted from The Hitchhiker's Guide to Privacy-Privacy by Design

We will discuss more this topic and tools in Volume II of this book.

MLOPS

MLOps (machine learning operations) is a discipline that enables data scientists and IT professionals to collaborate and communicate while automating machine learning algorithms, and it is important to find the right balance between getting the job done efficiently and protecting against all possible threats according to "What Is MLOps?"

There are several dimensions to consider when assessing risk, including:

1. The audience for the ML model
2. The lifetime of the model and its outcomes
3. The impact of the outcomes

This assessment should determine the governance measures applied and drive the complete MLOps development and deployment tool chain.

MACHINE LEARNING AND CLOUD

AMAZON AWS AND MACHINE LEARNING

AWS pre-trained AI Services provide ready-made intelligence for your applications and workflows according to "Artificial Intelligence Services."

GOOGLE CLOUD AI AND MACHINE LEARNING

AI Hub is a hosted repository of plug-and-play AI components, encourages experimentation and collaboration within your organization. AI building blocks make it easy for developers to add sight, language, conversation, and structured data to their applications according to "ai—Vlybok."

MICROSOFT AZURE AND MACHINE LEARNING

Microsoft Azure Machine Learning (Azure ML) service is part of Cortana Intelligence Suite that enables predictive analytics and interaction with data using natural language and speech through Cortana according to "Hosting Neo4j in the Cloud—Developer Guides."

CASE STUDIES

USE CASE: DIGITAL PATHOLOGY IMAGE ANALYSIS

Whole Slide Imaging (WSI) has been at the center of this transformation, enabling us to rapidly digitize pathology slides into high-resolution images. WSI has enhanced sharing and facilitated enhanced education and remote pathology services according to "Automating Digital Pathology Image Analysis with Machine."

USE CASE: INSILICO MEDICINE

This provides an alternative to animal testing for research and development programs in the pharmaceutical industry, according to Insilco. With ML, Insilico is able to analyze how a compound will affect cells and what drugs can be used to treat the cells in addition to possible side effects according to "This Biotech Startup Just Raised $255 Million."

A comprehensive drug discovery engine, discover signatures of disease and identify the most promising targets for a very a large number of molecules that already exist or can be generated de novo with the desired set of parameters:

Source: Adapted from silico

De-identifying techniques for Data protection can be applied in different areas:

	Data Protection	
Area	Pseudonymized	Anonymized
Diagnostics	Pseudonymized	
Research		Anonymized
Real-time Analysis	Pseudonymized	Anonymized
Training		Anonymized
Predictive Analytics	Pseudonymized	Anonymized
Treatments	Pseudonymized	Anonymized

USE CASE: REDUCING FINTECH RISK WITH MACHINE LEARNING

Anonymization can minimize the risk of identification. In this example, a bank requiring credit card approval for a transaction by a customer reduced the privacy risk from 26% to 8% and provided 98% accuracy compared to the initial ML model.

Anonymization is a non-reversible method of protection because it can advance data-intensive business applications, such as analytics, by using differential privacy or k-anonymity. Pseudonymization is a reversible approach that can be based on encryption or tokenization. Encryption uses mathematical algorithms and cryptographic keys to change data into binary cyphertext. Tokenization substitutes cleartext data with a deterministic random string of characters. The figure illustrates where anonymization is integrated to reduce the risk of identification:

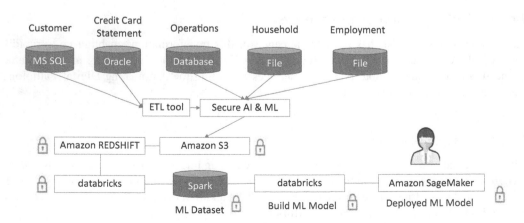

This approach can be used for analysis, insight, dashboarding, reporting, predictions, forecasts, simulation, and optimization with values to be expected in savings and revenue adds. The approach uses pseudonymization and anonymization to protect data that are used in ML models:

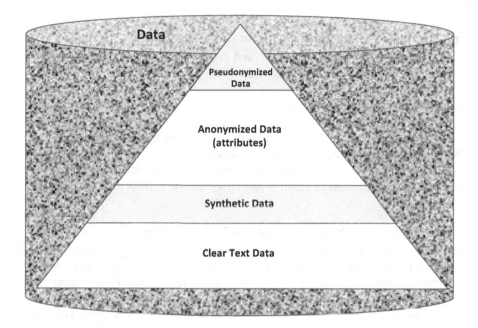

The figure above illustrates some different protection approaches and a typical example of the amount of data for each technique. These are discussed in separate chapters.

DATA LEADERS AND DATA LAGGARDS

HOW INNOVATIVE BUSINESSES WIN WITH SECURE MACHINE LEARNING

New solutions arm innovative businesses to win in an ever-changing, increasingly competitive digital economy. These solutions can empower businesses to activate and extract value from sensitive data and engender trust by ensuring the privacy of customers and employees is always preserved according to "Solutions—Protegrity,

We will discuss how machine learning on protected data that arm innovative businesses to win. We will also discuss how recent advances in quantum computers will significantly impact opportunities and threats to new and historical data. We will discuss available technologies and a longer-term roadmap with future technologies that can optimize and protect ML code current and future computers.

MLOPS FOR RESPONSIBLE AI

Responsible use of machine learning (more commonly referred to as Responsible AI) covers two main dimensions. Intentionality ensuring that models are designed and behave in ways aligned with their purpose. This includes the assurance that data used for AI projects comes from compliant and unbiased sources, plus a collaborative approach to AI projects that ensures multiple checks and balances on the potential model bias.

Intentionality also MLOps to mitigate risk includes explainability, meaning the results of AI systems should be explainable by humans (ideally, not just the humans who created the system).

A Growing Divide between Data Leaders and Data Laggards

There is a growing divide between data leaders and data laggards. MIT Sloan discusses six analytics and AI trends that all data leaders should consider:

1. Companies are continuing bold AI momentum.
2. Customer experience analytics are taking center stage.
3. Those who leverage external data outperform competitors by double digits.
4. CDOs are leading the charge toward a data-driven culture.
5. Data science is losing its luster (in favor of demonstrating business value).
6. Data can expose wide gaps in equity—and also empower change.

Data Privacy Requires the Creation of a Top-to-Bottom Culture

Data privacy isn't a software function, a button you can press to make everything right. No, data privacy requires the creation of a top-to-bottom culture of data security that's reinforced by a data-protection platform that simplifies the work of policy management and administration. When organizations can make sense of all the data they create and share, they have a clear perspective on which data is sensitive and needs to be protected. According to "As Facebook Hack Shows, Data Privacy is Good for Business," it can only be called private—and, thus, effectively useless should it ever be accessed in a breach, according to "As Facebook Hack Shows, Data Privacy is Good for Business."

Impact of New Technologies

Edelman Trust Barometer listed people feelings about the impact of new technologies, including 44% positive versus 20% negative impact of AI:

Area	%			
	Positive	Negative	Don't know	Equal
Personalization medicine	50	10	25	15
Driverless cars	44	20	26	11
AI	44	20	26	11
Gene editing	41	14	27	19
Blockchain	35	18	25	21

Source: Adapted from Edelman Trust Barometer.

Compliance Sets the Tone

Consumers don't mind sharing their personal information for sales, marketing, and other commercial purposes, as long as the organization that uses their data respects individual privacy. Governments, meanwhile, are ensuring data privacy becomes a way of business. More than a dozen

US state governments are currently drafting or are about to vote on compliance legislation that codifies privacy, building upon a foundation of established regulations such as GDPR, HIPAA, PCI DSS, and Sarbanes-Oxley. Virginia, in February 2021, passed a data privacy law, the Customer Data Protection Act (CDPA), that experts say hews mostly to the California Consumer Privacy Act—a widely applauded privacy initiative that took effect in 2018—but differs from California's law in that only the Virginia attorney general can enforce violations, leaving consumers in that state no private right of action according to "As Facebook Hack Shows, Data Privacy is Good for Business."

Protect the Power of Data

Protected data allows organizations to pursue—without the worry of running afoul of regulations—AI-supported analytics and machine learning, DevOps and containerization, IoT, and many traditional digital applications for sales, operations, customer satisfaction, development, production, employee productivity, and engagement.

Homomorphic encryption, which allows computations on encrypted data and machine learning, are growing in popularity. New homomorphic encryption algorithms can be secure from quantum computer–based attacks, and machine-learning algorithms can be optimized for quantum computers according to "Privacy-Preserving Analytics."

ANALYTICS MARKET

AI spending will reach $342B in 2021, and the AI market will accelerate even more in 2022, with 18.8% growth according to IDC.

AI at an enterprise level has grown 270%. First AI replaced humans and reduced costs according to "How Businesses Use AI to Boost Revenue" and more lately to increase revenue.

TAKING DATA TO THE CLOUD

With the explosion of data, every application is now a data application. Learn why hundreds of software teams build their applications in the cloud across multiple use cases and industries.

THE GLOBAL HADOOP BIG DATA ANALYTICS MARKET IS GROWING

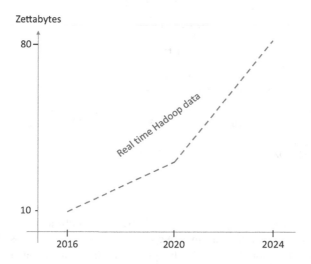

Source: Adapted from Maximize Market Research

THE GLOBAL HADOOP BIG DATA ANALYTICS MARKET

The global Hadoop big data analytics market grows according to "Analytics Market Research Reports & Consulting":

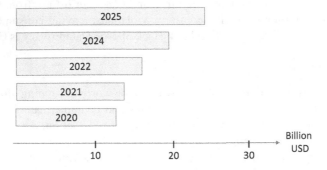

Source: Adapted from Maximize Market Research

This data may be spread over different platforms.

ROBOTIC PROCESS AUTOMATION (RPA) VS. ML

The fundamental difference between RPA and ML is based on Doing and Thinking. While RPA is associated with "doing," ML is related to "thinking" and "learning" and acts accordingly. RPA is used for automating repetitive tasks like sending emails or downloading the attachments, retrieving the subject according to "Robotic Process Automation (RPA) vs Machine Learning (ML)."

ML IS SECURITY PRODUCTS

Preference to use AI in Security Products:

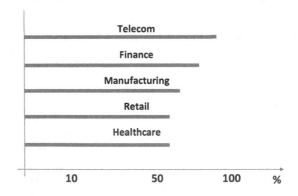

Source: Adapted from (ISC)2

SUMMARY

Innovative enterprises can stay competitive by implementing solutions that help extract value from sensitive data. New techniques like TEE and tokenization fabrics make it possible for enterprises to securely use private information—including its application in advanced analytics, ML, and AI—to be successful without worrying about putting customers, employees, or intellectual property at risk.

Commonly implemented solutions do not provide strong protection from quantum computers. Proper planning for and understanding of available technologies like tokenization fabrics and enhancement options offered by evolving technologies quantum computers can provide realistic approaches to data protection that give enterprises a competitive advantage over less innovative competitors.

We will discuss this topic more in Volume II of this book.

BIBLIOGRAPHY

1. Data Privacy Must Evolve in An AI-centric World, https://www.itproportal.com/features/data-privacy-must-evolve-in-an-ai-centric-world/

2. IDC: AI Spending Will Reach $342B in 2021, https://venturebeat.com/2021/08/04/idc-ai-spending-will-reach-342b-in-2021/?utm_campaign=Oktopost-General+industry+News&utm_content=Oktopost-LinkedIn&utm_medium=social&utm_source=LinkedIn

3. 6 Trends in Data and Artificial Intelligence for 2021 and Beyond, https://mitsloan.mit.edu/ideas-made-to-matter/6-trends-data-and-artificial-intelligence-2021-and-beyond?utm_campaign=Oktopost-Rick+Farnell+General+Industry+News&utm_content=Oktopost-linkedin&utm_medium=social&utm_source=linkedin

4. Insilico Medicine and Usynova Announce Strategic Partnership on Accelerating R&D of Small Molecule Innovative Drugs with AI, https://finance.yahoo.com/news/insilico-medicine-usynova-announce-strategic-095000185.html?fr=sycsrp_catchall

5. Moving From Raw Data to Business Impact, https://content.dataiku.com/getting-the-most-out-of-ai-2021/moving-from-raw-data?lb_email=&utm_campaign=NAM%20NE%20Database%20Email%20Campaigns%202021&utm_medium=email&_hsmi=130987205&_hsenc=p2ANqtz-_x2T7Ur-WhR6wYRaIykyIn5pv2U134SfEYFTxKnL0cbrSRvf

6. Current Regulations Driving MLOps Governance, https://content.dataiku.com/getting-the-most-out-of-ai-2021/oreilly-ml-ops?lb_email=&utm_campaign=NAM%20NE%20Database%20Email%20Campaigns%202021&utm_medium=email&_hsmi=130987205&_hsenc=p2ANqtz-_x2T7Ur-WhR6wYRaIykyIn5pv2U134SfEYFTxKnL0cbrSRvf

7. Gaining a Sense of Security About Secure Data and Algorithms, https://www.protegrity.com/protegrity-blog/gaining-a-sense-of-security-about-secure-data-and-algorithms#:~:text=Secure%20Algorithms%20In%20the%20AI%20world%2C%20the%20term,but%20it%20has%20built-in%20protection%20from%20undesired%20access

8. 5 Big Myths of AI and Machine Learning Debunked, https://www.splunk.com/pdfs/ebooks/5-big-myths-of-ai-and-machine-learning-debunked.pdf

9. Insilico, https://insilico.com/

10. What Is MLOps?, https://www.oreilly.com/library/view/what-is-mlops/9781492093626/ch04.html

11. Machine-learning-vs-artificial-intelligence-difference-between-ml-and-ai, https://www.smlease.com/entries/technology/machine-learning-vs-artificial-intelligence-difference-between-ml-and-ai/#:~:text=Machine%20learning%20is%20a%20subset%20of%20artificial%20intelligence,a%20pattern%20in%20data%20and%20doing%20predictions%20accordingly

12. Analytics Market Research Reports & Consulting, https://www.marketsandmarkets.com/analytics-market-research-206.html#:~:text=The%20Hadoop%20Big%20Data%20Analytics%20Market%20is%20expected,a%20CAGR%20of%2013.0%25%20during%20the%20forecast%20period

13. Legacy Companies Need to Become More Data Driven—Fast, https://hbr.org/2021/06/legacy-companies-need-to-become-more-data-driven-fast

14. RSA Conference Blog, https://www.rsaconference.com/Library/blog

15. How Businesses Use AI to Boost Revenue, https://www.entrepreneur.com/article/381444

16. Privacy Megatrend: Race to Own the Data-Value Chain: PwC, https://www.pwc.com/us/en/services/consulting/cybersecurity-privacy-forensics/library/seven-privacy-megatrends/data-value-chain.html

17. Artificial Intelligence vs Machine Learning | BigID, https://bigid.com/blog/artificial-intelligence-vs-machine-learning/

18. Gaining a Sense of Security About Secure Data and Algorithms, https://www.protegrity.com/protegrity-blog/gaining-a-sense-of-security-about-secure-data-and-algorithms

19. Cracking Open the Black Box of Automated Machine Learning …, https://news.mit.edu/2019/atmseer-machine-learning-black-box-0531

20. Preserving Privacy with New Technologies, https://www.isaca.org/resources/news-and-trends/isaca-now-blog/2021/preserving-privacy-with-new-technologies

21. Automating Digital Pathology Image Analysis with Machine Learning on Databricks, https://databricks.com/blog/2020/01/31/automating-digital-pathology-image-analysis-with-machine-learning-on-databricks.html

22. Artificial Intelligence Services, https://aws.amazon.com/machine-learning/ai-services/

23. ai—Vlybok, http://www.imqsyc.co/ai/

24. Hosting Neo4j in the Cloud—Developer Guides, https://neo4j.com/developer/guide-cloud-deployment/

25. This Biotech Startup Just Raised $255 Million, https://onlinemarketingscoops.com/this-biotech-startup-just-raised-255-million-to-make-its-ai-designed-drug-a-reality/

26. Solutions—Protegrity, https://www.protegrity.com/solutions

27. As Facebook Hack Shows, Data Privacy is Good for Business, https://www.protegrity.com/protegrity-blog/data-privacy-is-good-for-business

28. Privacy-Preserving Analytics, https://engage.isaca.org/swedenchapter/events/eventdescription?CalendarEventKey=dabd556d-0105-4cd9-af8a-55fbf9cbd5c1&CommunityKey=6592afac-ec0b-41ca-b0c4-1e2dbb4d9da3&Home=%2fcommunities%2fcommunity-home%2frecent-community-events

29. Robotic Process Automation (RPA) vs Machine Learning (ML), https://www.techindiatoday.com/rpa-vs-machine-learning/#:~:text=The%20fundamental%20difference%20between%20RPA%20and%20ML%20is,emails%20or%20downloading%20the%20attachments%2C%20retrieving%20the%20subject

11 Secure Multiparty Computing

INTRODUCTION

We will discuss different approaches and technologies that can help to facilitate secure multiparty computing (SMPC). They support different use cases, and some technologies are slowly emerging. How can parties handle confidential data if they do not trust everyone involved?

It is often the case that mutually skeptical parties need to perform a joint computation, for example, during auctions, data mining, voting, negotiations, and business analytics according to "Secure Multiparty Computation."

A TRADITIONAL MODEL

Secure multiparty computation (also known as secure computation, multiparty computation [MPC], to create methods for parties to jointly compute while keeping those inputs private according to "Secure multi-party computation – Wiki."

A traditional model can use a central authority for sharing information. Another approach is to share information on a peer-to-peer basis. The shared information is protected in this example of secure multiparty computing:

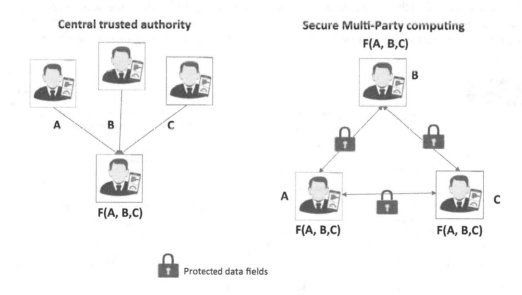

USE CASES

Different techniques for privacy-preserving computing are useful in specific use cases for secure multiparty computation:

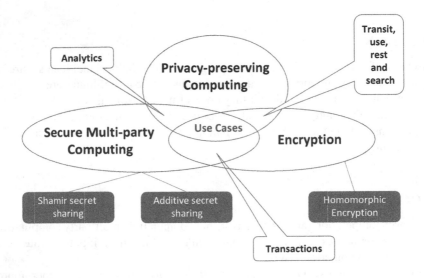

DATA SCIENCE

Secure multiparty computation enables solutions to manage your internal data pipeline's privacy for data science and orchestrate collaborative data analytics legally, without the need to collocate or move the data. There is no need to collocate or move the data and allow businesses to use sensitive data to fuel advanced analytics, machine learning, and AI—even as those initiatives migrate to cloud environments.

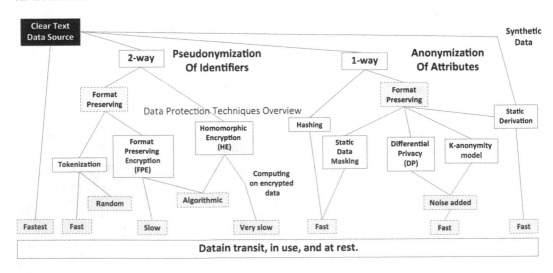

Data must move through an enterprise's many cloud-based databases and applications. The most critical data types in driving innovation—with advanced analytics, machine learning, and AI—are those deemed most sensitive and must be safeguarded. You can shield machine learning models and data in trusted execution environments. This is a complement of encryption of the machine learning models and data for outsourced environments, like different cloud models.

SECURE MULTIPARTY COMPUTATION PROTECTS PRIVACY

In the example below, Jill calculates the average salary across six people by adding a secret number (874,346) to her salary and then adding each person. The average salary will then be the total sum minus 874,346 divided by six people:

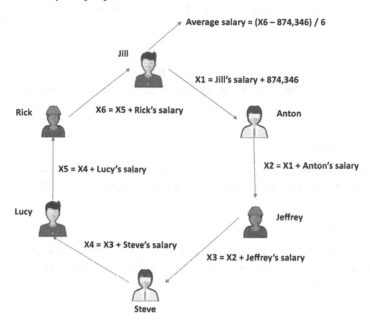

In traditional basic cryptographic tasks, cryptography assures security and integrity of communication and storage.

Secure multiparty computation prevents eavesdropping and protects participants' privacy from each other according to "Secure multi-party computation – Wiki."

Secure multiparty computation can be one source of information for analytics:

Increased need for data analytics drives requirements.

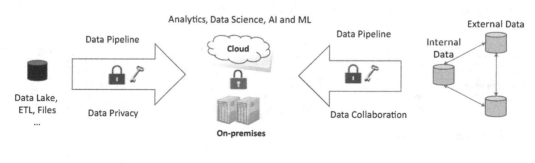

BASIC PROPERTIES

The only information that can be inferred about the private data is what could be inferred from seeing the function's output alone.

SECURITY OF AN MPC PROTOCOL

The security of an MPC protocol can rely on different assumptions according to "Secure multi-party computation – Wiki":

- It can be based on some mathematical problem, like factoring.

PROTOCOLS

Protocols proposed for two-party computation and multiparty computation (MPC) are different, and special-purpose protocols differ from the generic ones according to "Secure multi-party computation – Wiki."

TWO-PARTY COMPUTATION

The two-party setting was first from one of the two papers of Yao, although not actually containing what is now known as Yao's garbled circuit protocol according to "Searcher."

YAO-BASED PROTOCOLS

An issue with Yao-based protocols is that the function must be represented in XOR and AND gates. Since most real-world programs contain loops and complex data structures, this is a highly nontrivial task according to "Secure multi-party computation – Wiki."

SHAMIR SECRET SHARING

Secret sharing like Shamir secret sharing shares are random elements added to the field and look randomly distributed according to "Secure multi-party computation – Wiki."

PRIVATE SET INTERSECTION

Private Set Intersection (PSI) is a special case of multiparty computation, in which each party has a set of items, and the goal is to learn the intersection of those sets. PSI identifies the common customers without disclosing any other information. According to "A Brief Overview of Private Set Intersection," this replaces one-way hashing functions that are susceptible to dictionary attacks according to "A Brief Overview of Private Set Intersection":

ID	Amount Spent (A)
345-237-5744	500
422-475-1552	513
901-488-9720	892
055-381-2751	200
334-718-8888	298

ID	Amount Spent (B)
901-488-9720	200
055-381-2751	298
934-718-8888	100
345-237-5744	713
422-475-1552	202

ID	Amount Spent (C)
855-381-2751	892
934-718-8778	200
345-237-5744	298
901-488-9720	100
055-381-2751	713

Source: Adopted from NIST

HOMOMORPHIC ENCRYPTION

Tokenization, data masking and anonymization, and data de-identification are all valuable tools that aren't ideal for some use cases in sharing with partners.

Homomorphic encryption supports systems to process encrypted data without exposing what's underneath, according to "Homomorphic Encryption Will Take on the Challenge of AI."

DATA MARKETPLACES

According to World Economic Forum, data marketplaces offer a future direction and an opportunity to build trust in society.

PSEUDONYMIZATION AND SMART CONTRACTS

Trust in data marketplaces currently can exist and is scalable according to "Data marketplaces can transform economies." Fourth Industrial Revolution (4IR or Industry 4.0) can be used to better control how data is used by designing a robust governance structure that builds trust, according to "Data marketplaces can transform economies."

Building an Ethical and Secure Data Sharing Ecosystem

Opportunities for trust in data-sharing systems are discussed in "Data marketplaces can transform economies." In contrast to traditionally siloed data sharing, data marketplaces allow data to be leveraged to build trust, according to "Data marketplaces can transform economies."

| Connect contributors and consumers to data | Ethical use | Unlock data from source | Recognize benefits and risks | Harness technologies |

Source: Adopted from The World Economic Forum

According to "Data marketplaces can transform economies," the current global regime on data permissions is disconnected and, in many ways, broken, and 4IR aims to reimagine consent and permissions by looking at ways to ensure privacy, for example, in improving the predictability of outcomes using smart contracts and pseudonymization.

Scope of Processing Through Pseudonymization

Inspiring trust requires that data use be limited to permission purposes and not used for further unauthorized processing.

Pseudonymization has been recognized in GDPR to separate information from identities:

1. It protects various classes of identifiers.
2. It protects at the record and data-set level.
3. It protects against unauthorized re-identification.

This prevents the re-identification from ensuring that data is "anonymous" and made available only under controlled situations.

Security of Data Will Be Critical

The security of data will be critical to participation in data exchanges and to their continuation. As increasing amounts of value are exchanged in them, they will become increasingly more attractive to dishonest operators, resulting in a rapidly changing threat landscape. Security takes on a new meaning in an "open" data exchange environment, especially when placed in the context of data marketplaces that store or use citizen data or are involved in the delivery of critical national services. Technical, policy, commercial, and governance mechanisms will become crucial to effectively coordinate and manage security for the data marketplaces.

Adjusting Security Approaches to Meet Data Marketplace

Traditionally, data security has focused on two main states of data: data in motion and data at rest, according to "How to Protect Data in Motion." When designing data exchanges, however, two new states of data, data during processing and data post-use, also require security

The Expanded Focus of a Secure Data Exchange

Data exchange and/or marketplace			
States of data: Expanded focus		States of data: Traditional focus	
Data during processing	Data post-use	Data in motion	Data at rest
This is required because data may be processed remotely and potentially used for unintended purposes. Examples include GDPR	From a regulatory perspective, this will include the Emerging regulatory approaches to privacy frameworks	This ensures the security of data while it is transferred from point A to point B	This ensures the security of data while it is not being used and is stored; traditionally a database.

Source: Adopted from The World Economic Forum

SHAREMIND MPC PLATFORM

Sharemind™ is an example of a system that works on encrypted data without decrypting it and providing secret sharing, similar to encryption without a key. According to "Secure Multiparty Computation and Secret Sharing," no plaintext value leaves data owner's premises unencrypted according to "Secure Multiparty Computation and Secret Sharing."

A simple example shows how three servers can add two secret numbers without seeing them. All operations in the example are made on two-digit numbers. For example, (99 + 1 = 100 0, 3–8 = –5):

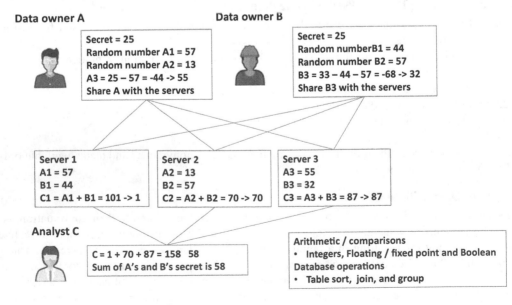

Source: Adopted from Sharemind

SUMMARY

We discussed different approaches and technologies that can help to facilitate secure multiparty computing in different use cases and how parties can handle confidential data if they do not trust everyone involved, for example, during auctions, data mining, voting, negotiations, and business analytics.

We will talk more about this topic in Volume II of this book.

BIBLIOGRAPHY

1. Shamir, R. Rivest, and L. Adleman. "Mental Poker", Technical Report LCS/TR-125, Massachusetts Institute of Technology, April 1979. Secure Multiparty Computation and Secret Sharing.
2. A Free, AI-powered Research Tool for Scientific Literature, www.semanticscholar.org
3. Data-driven Economies: Foundations for Our Common Future, https://www.weforum.org/whitepapers/b77d0ac8-89f2-485a-a821-727e694eb2d3
4. Privacy Ecosystem, https://repo.cyber.ee/sharemind/www/files/technology/sharemind-technical-overview.pdf
5. Outsourcing Multi-Party Computation, https://www.microsoft.com/en-us/research/publication/outsourcing-multi-party-computation-2/, https://www.microsoft.com/en-us/research/wp-content/uploads/2011/05/272.pdf
6. How to Protect Data in Motion, https://www.endpointprotector.com/blog/how-to-protect-data-in-motion/
7. Yao, Andrew C. Protocols for Secure Computations (extended abstract), https://research.cs.wisc.edu/areas/sec/yao1982-ocr.pdf
8. Yao, Andrew Chi-Chih (1986). "How to Generate and Exchange Secrets (Extended Abstract). *FOCS*, pp. 162–167.
9. Goldreich, Oded, Micali, Silvio, and Wigderson, Avi (1987). "How to Play any Mental Game or A Completeness Theorem for Protocols with Honest Majority". *STOC*, pp. 218–229.
10. Galil, Zvi, Haber, Stuart, and Yung, Moti (1987). "Cryptographic Computation: Secure Fault-Tolerant Protocols and the Public-Key Model". *CRYPTO*, pp. 135–155.
11. Chaum, David, Damgård, Ivan, and van de Graaf, Jeroen. "Multi-party Computations Ensuring Privacy of Each Party's Input and Correctness of the Result, pp. 87–119.
12. Jump up to: [ab]Abascal, Jackson, Faghihi Sereshgi, Mohammad Hossein, Hazay, Carmit, Ishai, Yuval, and Venkitasubramaniam, Muthuramakrishnan. (2020-10-30). "Is the Classical GMW Paradigm Practical? The Case of Non-Interactive Actively Secure 2PC". *Proceedings of the 2020 ACM SIGSAC Conference on Computer and Communications Security. CCS '20. Virtual Event, USA: Association for Computing Machinery: 1591–1605.* doi:10.1145/3372297.3423366. ISBN:978-1-4503-7089-9.
13. The Fourth Industrial Revolution (4IR or Industry 4.0), https://iap.unido.org/articles/what-fourth-industrial-revolution
14. Kilian, Joe (1988). "Founding Cryptography on Oblivious Transfer". *STOC*, pp. 20–31.
15. Chaum, D., Crepeau, C., and Damgard, I. (1988). "Multi-Party Unconditionally Secure Protocols". *STOC*.
16. Ben-Or, Michael, Goldwasser, Shafi, and Wigderson, Avi (1988). "Completeness Theorems for Non-Cryptographic Fault-Tolerant Distributed Computation (Extended Abstract)". *STOC*, pp. 1–10.
17. Rabin, Tal and Ben-Or, Michael (1989). "Verifiable Secret Sharing and Multiparty Protocols with Honest Majority (Extended Abstract)". *STOC*, pp. 73–85.
18. Dolev, Danny, Dwork, Cynthia, Waarts, Orli, and Yung, Moti (1993). "Perfectly Secure Message Transmission. *J. ACM* 40(1): 17–47.
19. Ostrovsky, Rafail and Yung, Moti (1991). "How to Withstand Mobile Virus Attacks". *PODC*, pp. 51–59.
20. Bogetoft, Peter, Christensen, Dan Lund, Damgård, Ivan, Geisler, Martin, Jakobsen, Thomas, Krøigaard, Mikkel, Nielsen, Janus Dam, Nielsen, Jesper Buus, Nielse, Kurt, Pagter, Jakob, Schwartzbach, Michael, and Toft, Tomas (2008). "Multiparty Computation Goes Live". Cryptology ePrint Archive (Report 2008/068).
21. Yung, Moti 2015. From Mental Poker to Core Business: Why and How to Deploy Secure Computation Protocols? *ACM Conference on Computer and Communications Security*, pp. 1–2, https://dl.acm.org/citation.cfm?doid=2810103.2812701

22. Data Marketplaces Can Transform Economies. Here's how, https://www.weforum.org/agenda/2021/08/data-marketplaces-can-transform-economies/

23. Backes, Michael, Pfitzmann, Birgit, and Waidner, Michael (2004). "A General Composition Theorem for Secure Reactive Systems." In *Theory of Cryptography Conference*, pp. 336–354. Springer, Berlin, Heidelberg, https://link.springer.com/chapter/10.1007/978-3-540-24638-1_19

24. Aumann, Y. and Lindell, Y. (2007). "Security Against Covert Adversaries". *TCC*.

25. Yao, Andrew C. (1986). "How to generate and exchange secrets." *SFCS '86 Proceedings of the 27th Annual Symposium on Foundations of Computer Science*, pp. 162–167.

26. Ben-Or, Michael, Goldwasser, Shafi, and Wigderson, Avi (1988-01-01). "Completeness Theorems for Non-cryptographic Fault-tolerant Distributed Computation. *ACM*, pp. 1–10. doi:10.1145/62212.62213. ISBN 978-0897912648. S2CID 207554159.

27. A Brief Overview of Private Set Intersection, https://csrc.nist.gov/presentations/2021/a-brief-overview-of-private-set-intersection#:~:text=Description%20Private%20set%20intersection%20%28PSI%29%20is%20a%20special,state%20of%20the%20art%20for%20PSI%20protocol%20techniques

28. I. Damgård, V. Pastro, N. Smart, and S. Zakarias (2012). "Multi-party computation from somewhat homomorphic encryption". Crypto 2012, vol. Springer LNCS 7417, pp. 643–662.

29. Secure Multi-party Computation – Microsoft Research, https://www.microsoft.com/en-us/research/project/multi-party-computation/#!overview

30. Secure Multi-party Computation – Wiki, https://en.wikipedia.org/wiki/Secure_multi-party_computation

31. Searcher, https://searcher.com/computation

12 Encryption and Tokenization of International Unicode Data

INTRODUCTION

Protecting the increasing use of International Unicode characters is required by a growing number of privacy laws in many countries and general privacy concerns with private data. Data protection should also be universal. No matter the language, data protection should render data useless if it is breached in a hack or ransomware attack.

Unicode is an international standard for encoding in the world's writing systems, both modern and ancient according to "Entering Unicode characters into Prism" providing the basis for processing in any language according to "Unicode: Name a Language, And We'll Protect the Data."

Current approaches may return data in new and unexpected languages, increasing the size, and changing the data formats. This will break many applications and slow down business operations.

We will discuss how new approaches with significantly higher performance will solve these issues, and a memory footprint can be customizable and fit on small IoT devices. New approaches will also improve portability, security, performance, memory footprint, and language preservation, and provide granular data protection for all languages.

OLD APPROACHES

Many old approaches to protect International Unicode characters will increase the size and change the data formats. This will break many applications and slow down business operations. Current approaches may also randomly return data in new and unexpected languages. According to "Webinar Series," the new approach with significantly higher performance and a memory footprint can be customizable and fit on small IoT devices according to "Webinar Series."

Major Issues

Increasing use of International Unicode characters and privacy concerns according to "New privacy technologies for Unicode" and old approaches will typically increase the size and change the formats to break many applications and slow down business applications. Old approaches may randomly return data in new and unexpected languages:

| Input | → | RadixConversion* | → | Tokenization | → | RadixConversion* | → | Output |

*: Conversion between base 10, 62, and 64, and 114

The Long Journey to a New Approach

Chaining three characters of languages with less than 100 characters in the alphabet that you want to tokenize can result in small randomized lookup tables. You would need 100*100*100 = 1,000,000 rows to cover all permutations. This lookup table will give you a one-in-a-million chance to guess the right row.

DOI: 10.1201/9781003189664-16

Example of changing with a block size of three characters. Each block can overlap with two characters to gain process input from previous characters in the input string. This will allow input strings of three characters and longer:

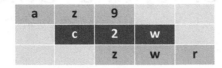

For shorter input strings padding can be applied. The chaining process can inject initialization vectors in the steps and be performed from left to right and back again to gain process input from all characters in the input string.

The details of this tokenization process can be found in US Patent application Ser. No. 12/659,200, filed March 1, 2010, now US Patent 9,639,716. The process is stateless and can run within a medium-sized amount of memory across distributed systems and without I/O (input/output) operations to a storage system.

The title is "Distributed tokenization using several substitution steps." https://uspto.report/patent/app/20110213807

BILLIONS OF ROWS

Chaining three characters of languages with less than 1,000 characters in the alphabet you want to tokenize would need 1,000*1,000*1,000 = 1,000,000,000 rows to cover all permutations. This lookup table will give you 1 billion rows. Permutations of the characters from the five Japanese languages that can be found in a mailing address would require even larger tables to store the permutations of the characters from the five languages. A different approach will be required.

THE NEW APPROACH

Look at design aspects required for languages with around 1,000 characters in the alphabet and input that is mixing multiple Unicode scripts. Japanese would be a good example.

The new approach must support five languages for a Japanese address label. Example of six characters in the input string with five languages:

The approach is to link Unicode code points of the characters in fabric instead of chaining blocks of characters.

- Lookup tables will store the selected alphabet from each Unicode script.
- Chaining each input character via multiple steps will generate each final output character.

The chaining can inject initialization vectors in the steps and be performed from left to right and back again to gain process input from all characters in the input string:

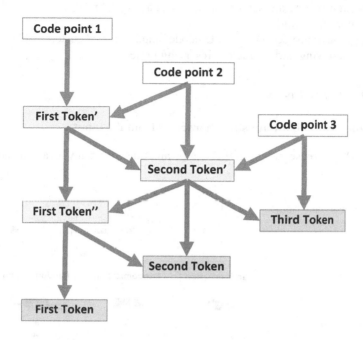

Linking characters in a fabric can be flexible for mixing different scripts, for example, with the five Japanese languages:

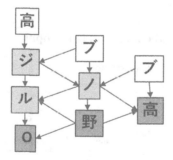

EXAMPLES OF STANDARDS USED IN JAPAN

The new approach must consider five languages and five standards used in Japan:

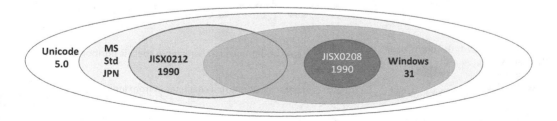

BENEFITS OF THE NEW APPROACH

- Significantly higher performance. Tokenization of 3 million characters per second was reported on smaller standard servers operating in a single thread.
- A small memory footprint.
- Portability, granular protection for all Unicode languages, and customizable alphabets.
- Byte length preserving and character preserving protection.

SECURITY AND DESIGN ASPECTS

I am avoiding leaks about unusual characters from the input.

An example of a 40% increase of length that can be an issue with many legacy databases:

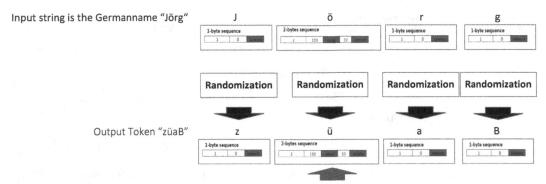

German umlauts: ä, ö, ü

Avoiding leaks about unusual characters from input.

Approach 1: Randomly Shuffle the output string

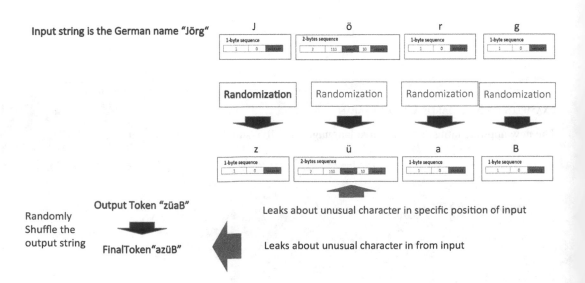

Avoiding leaks

Approach 2: Randomize the full input string

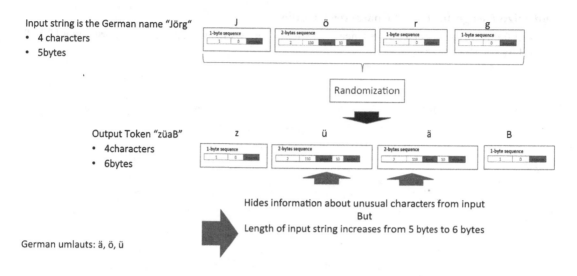

Input string is the German name "Jörg"
- 4 characters
- 5bytes

Output Token "züaB"
- 4characters
- 6bytes

German umlauts: ä, ö, ü

Output token 40% longer

Avoiding increasing the byte length of the output string.

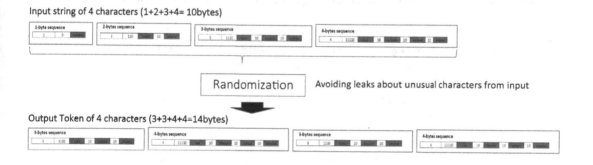

Input string of 4 characters (1+2+3+4= 10bytes)

Randomization   Avoiding leaks about unusual characters from input

Output Token of 4 characters (3+3+4+4=14bytes)

Validation by third-party encryption experts

Sensitive data involving personally identifiable information (PII) and primary account number (PAN) can be replaced with values called tokens according to "Tokenization (data security)."

Third-party encryption experts must validate methods to tokenize or encrypt. Great examples would include a credible university that invented encryption algorithms or an expert that broke the security of a recognized encryption algorithm.

A tokenization scheme can provide excellent security since it is based on fully randomized tables.

Unicode Character Encoding Standard

Unicode is information technology in most of the world's writing systems according to "What is Unicode and how is it used?" The Unicode has 143,859 characters, with Unicode 13.0 (these characters consist of 143,696 graphic characters and 163 format characters) covering 154 modern and historical scripts and multiple symbols set emoji. The character repertoire of the Unicode Standard is synchronized with ISO/IEC 10646, each being code-for-code identical with the other according to "ASCII, ISO 8859, and Unicode – Base64 Decode and Encode."

Different Character Encodings Can Implement Unicode

Unicode Transformation Formats most commonly used are UTF-8, UTF-16, and UCS-2 (a precursor of UTF-16 without full support for Unicode) according to "Unicode – Wikipedia."

Optimize Design for UTF-8 Character Encoding

We will focus this paper on UTF-8 since character encodings for websites 2020 reported that UTF-8 is used by 95.4%:

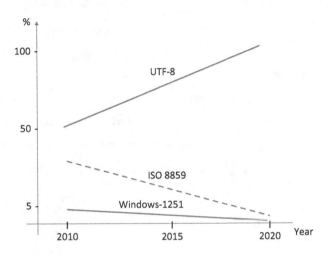

Source: Adapted from Wikipedia.

Some other alternatives to character encodings are minor in use and in decline:

Encoding	2010	2017	2018	2019	2020
UTF-8	21	88	91	93	96
ISO-8859	28	6	4	4	2
Windiws-1251	4	2	1	1	1
Windiws-1251	3	1	1	1	0
GB2312	3	1	0	0	0
ShiftJS	2	0	0	0	0
GBK	1	0	0	0	0
EUC-KR	0	0	0	0	0
ISO-8859-9	0	0	0	0	0

Read more about this topic in Volume II of this book.

SUMMARY

We discussed that a growing number privacy regulations require data protection and an increasing use of International Unicode characters. Many of the old approaches to protect Unicode characters may return data in new and unexpected languages, increasing the size, and changing the data formats. This will break many applications and slow down business operations.

New approaches with significantly higher performance will solve these issues, and a memory footprint can be customizable and fit on small IoT devices.

New approaches will also improve portability, security, performance, memory footprint, and language preservation, and provide granular data protection for all languages.

BIBLIOGRAPHY

1. UTF-16, An Encoding of ISO 10646, https://www.ietf.org/rfc/rfc2781.txt
2. What is Unicode and How Is It Used?, https://philosophy-question.com/library/lecture/read/406812-what-is-unicode-and-how-is-it-used
3. Unicode, https://en.wikipedia.org/wiki/Unicode
4. "The Unicode Standard: A Technical Introduction", https://www.unicode.org/standard/principles.html
5. Entering Unicode characters into Prism, https://www.graphpad.com/support/faq/entering-unicode-characters-into-prism/
6. "Usage Survey of Character Encodings broken down by Ranking", w3techs.com
7. "Conformance" (PDF). The Unicode Standard, https://www.unicode.org/versions/Unicode13.0.0/ch03.pdf#I1.36559
8. "UAX #29: Unicode Text Segmentation §3 Grapheme Cluster Boundaries", unicode.org. https://unicode.org/reports/tr29/#Grapheme_Cluster_Boundaries
9. Webinar Series, https://www.protegrity.com/webinar-series
10. New Privacy Technologies for Unicode, https://www.slideshare.net/ulfmattsson/jun-29-new-privacy-technologies-for-unicode-and-international-data-standards-2021-jun28b
11. ASCII, ISO 8859, and Unicode – Base64 Decode and Encode, https://www.base64code.com/knowledgebase/ascii-iso8859-unicode/

13 Blockchain and Data Lineage

INTRODUCTION

We will discuss blockchain positioning and start a discussion about blockchain technology and security. We are more and more dependent on data, and it is becoming increasingly important to use a ledger or other means in tracking data to where it moves and how it is transformed as it moves through various stages. Business workflows involve transactions and custody of value in the form of digital assets, and organizations are increasingly using blockchain in B2B use cases to reduce cost and increase security.

DATA LINEAGE AND PROVENANCE

Data lineage and provenance typically refer to the way or the steps a dataset came to its current state data lineage, as well as all copies or derivatives. Recent studies suggest that most companies are still struggling to make sense of their data. If you want to drive real value from your data, you must first understand where it is coming from, where it has been, how it is being used, and who is using it—that's what data lineage is all about, according to "A beginner's guide to answer, what is data lineage?"

WHAT IS BLOCKCHAIN?

Blockchain has five elements according to "How blockchain will evolve until 2030 and today's hype versus reality":

1. Distribution: Blockchain participants are located physically apart from each other and are connected on a network according to "The CIO's Guide to Blockchain."
2. Encryption: Public and private keys to record the data in the blocks securely and semi-anonymously
3. Immutability: Transactions are cryptographically signed, time-stamped, and sequentially added to the ledger
4. Tokenization: Transactions involve the secure exchange of value
5. Decentralization: Both network information and the rules for how the network operates are maintained by nodes on the distributed network due to a consensus mechanism

BLOCKCHAIN ENABLES TRUSTED DATA

Blockchain enables a single source of data, and Master Data Management (MDM) projects identify three different approaches to allowing "single source of truth" and blockchain enables a distributed "MDM" according to "Data and Trending Technologies: Data":

BLOCKCHAIN DELIVERS DATA LINEAGE BY DEFAULT

One of the key challenges in data management is establishing data lineage. Blockchain provides a distributed and permanent record of transactions that can be encrypted to provide different levels of access to viewers, and new transactions are added and verified according to protocols that prevent duplication and ensure consensus.

DOI: 10.1201/9781003189664-17

BLOCKCHAIN-BASED SOLUTIONS

An example of a blockchain-based solution for vaccine distribution

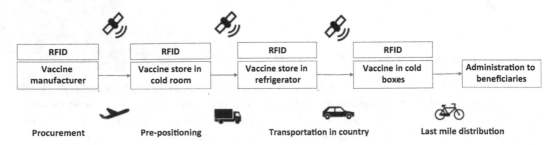

Source: Adopted from Springer

BLOCKCHAIN HAS THE POTENTIAL TO RESHAPE INDUSTRIES

Blockchain can enable trust and provide transparency, and enabling value exchange across business ecosystems potentially lowering costs, reducing transaction settlement times, and improving cash flow according to "Top 10 Strategic Technology Trends":

1. Assets can be traced to their origin, significantly reducing the opportunities for substitutions with counterfeit goods.
2. Asset tracking also has value in other areas, such as tracing food across a supply chain to identify the origin of contamination more easily or tracking individual parts to assist in product recalls.
3. Another area in which blockchain has potential is identity management.
4. Smart contracts can be programmed into the blockchain, where events can trigger actions.

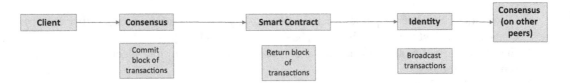

The business value of blockchain will increase significantly, according to Gartner.

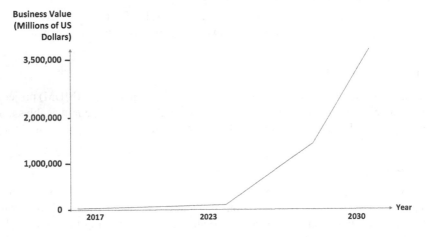

Source: Adapted from Gartner

HEALTHCARE PROVIDER DIRECTORY TO ILLUSTRATE INTEROPERABILITY

US Veteran Affairs (VA) is conducting a pilot evaluating AI and Virtual Reality technology utilizing a DL-based blockchain. VA is providing healthcare for Veterans. The Veterans Health Administration is America's largest integrated healthcare system, providing care at 1,293 healthcare facilities.

CURRENT STATE OF PROVIDER DIRECTORY UPDATES

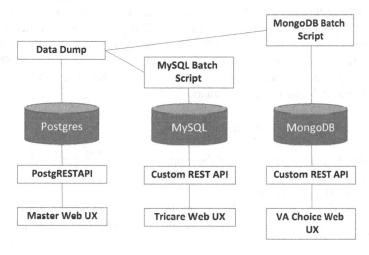

Source: Adapted from VA NAII's 2020–2021 AI Tech Sprint

INTEROPERABILITY AS AN ARCHITECTURAL LAYER

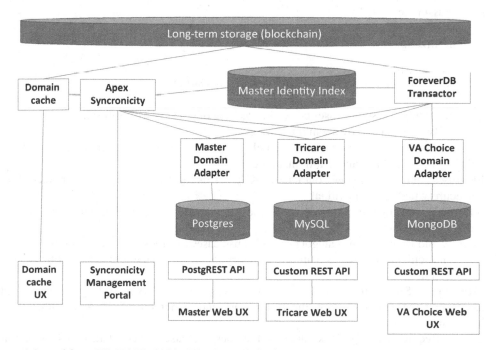

Source: Adapted from VA NAII's 2020–2021 AI Tech Sprint

A PLATFORM FOR DIGITAL TRANSFORMATION

POPULAR PLATFORMS

Hyperledger, Ethereum Corda, Bitcoin, and Quorum

According to *Forbes*, Hyperledger is used by 28 organizations, Ethereum by 23, Corda by 9, Bitcoin by 9, and Quorum by 6:

- Amazon, Anthem, Baidu, BMW, Broadridge, Cargill, China Construction Bank, Citigroup, Coinbase, Credit Suisse, Daimler, De Beers, Depository Trust & Clearing, Dole Foods, Facebook, Foxconn, General Electric, Google, Honeywell, HSBC, Enterprise, IBM, ING Group, Intercontinental Exchange, JPMorgan, Mastercard, Microsoft, Nasdaq, National Settlement Depository, Nestlé, Optum, Overstock, Ripple, Royal Dutch Shell, Samsung, Santander, Signature Bank, Silvergate Bank, Square, Tencent, T-Mobile, UBS, United Nations, Vanguard, VMware, and Walmart.

Typical blockchain platforms for different industries:

- Large banks: Hyperledger Fabric, Ethereum, and Corda. Potentially also with: Axcore, Symbiont Assembly, and Quorum.
- Insurance: Hyperledger Fabric.
- Retailers: Hyperledger Fabric and Ethereum. Potentially also Bitcoin, Ravencoin, and Florin.
- Automotive: Hyperledger, Corda, and Ethereum. Potentially also Quorum, Corda, and Tezos.

Blockchain Provides an Alternative Trust Model

1. Distributed trust
2. Asset provenance
3. Programmability
4. Native asset creation
5. Digital asset representation
6. Decentralization

Blockchain Use Cases according to "IoT use cases" and Gartner:

1. Asset Tracking. These use cases cover the tracking of physical assets through the supply chain to identify location and ownership accurately.
2. Claims. This category covers automated claims processing in areas such as automobile, agriculture, travel, and life and health insurance.
3. Identity Management/Know Your Client (KYC). This category covers use where records must be securely tied to an individual.
4. Internal Record Keeping. In these use cases, the data to be secured remains within an individual organization.
5. Loyalty and Reward. This category includes use cases for tracking loyalty points.
6. Payment/Settlement. Use cases in this category involve a payment between parties or settlement of a trade.
7. Provenance. Similar to the asset-tracking use case, this covers recording the movement of assets, but the aim is to show the full history and ownership of the asset rather than its location.
8. Shared Record Keeping. This category includes use cases where data needs to be shared securely between multiple participants.

9. Smart Cities/the IoT. This group includes use cases that use blockchain to provide data tracking and to control functions for smart spaces or IoT solutions.
10. Trade Finance. These use cases aim to streamline the process of financing trades, including managing letters of credit, simplifying trade finance, and facilitating cross-border trade.
11. Trading. Use cases in this group aim to improve the process for buying and selling assets, including dealing in derivatives, trading of private equity, and sports trading.

TOKENIZATION IN BLOCKCHAIN

Paintings, company stocks to real estate can be tokenized on blockchain to guarantee that the ownership information is immutable according to "What is tokenization in blockchain?"

Unfortunately, one problem stems from the fact that no country has a solid regulation for cryptocurrency so far. For example, they have no legal rights on the property and thus are not protected by the law. According to "What is tokenization in blockchain?" it brings us back to some sort of centralization, especially with smart contracts.

Convert a Digital Value into a Digital Token

Tokenization can be implemented locally to the data tokenized or offloaded to the cloud and in the cloud to provide a lower total cost of ownership by sharing resources implementation and administration. A high level of security can be provided by separating the tokenization system into a container that is separated from the processing of data. The container can run on-premises or isolated in a remote private cloud according to "What is tokenization in blockchain?"

HYPERLEDGER ARCHITECTURE AND SECURITY

It is essential to establish a set of security controls such as the ones based on NIST, ISO 27002 according to "Security Controls for Blockchain Applications." This is notably important when serving industries as highly regulated as financial services or healthcare according to "Security Controls for Blockchain Applications."

HYPERLEDGER FABRIC

As with any blockchain, Hyperledger Fabric 2.0 leverages cryptographic primitives at its core to operate. According to "Demystifying the blockchain," these cryptographic artifacts are used to sign transactions and create hashes of data like block headers and Merkle trees, according to "Demystifying the blockchain." The field of cryptography is constantly evolving, researching, and developing new algorithms for artifacts like hash functions and digital signatures.

Workflow for Trade Finance Use Case:

Source: Adapted from CSA

Risk by the Rating of Vulnerabilities

Risks can be rated by the "Likelihood and Impact of the Vulnerabilities" according to "Cloud Security Alliance Hyperledger Fabric":

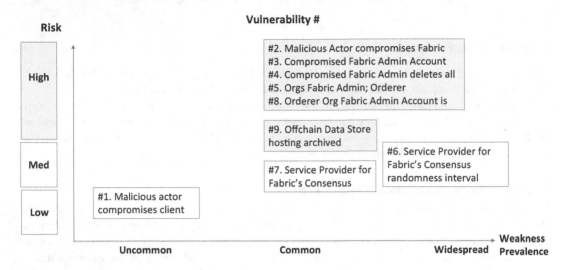

Source: Adapted from CSA

Descriptions of Vulnerabilities by Reference number (Ref #) in the figure:

1. Malicious actor compromises client; injects unauthorized list of Peer Nodes as endorsing peers in Endorsing Policy via chain code
2. Malicious actor compromises Fabric Admin Account; gains access to Fabric Admin Credentials of Orderer Org from Endorsement Policy
3. Compromised Fabric Admin Account used to instantiate untrusted chain codes
4. Compromised Fabric Admin deletes all logs detailing malicious activity
5. Orgs Fabric Admin; Orderer Fabric Admins digital credentials compromised while being transmitted out of band to Client Org Fabric Admin
6. Service Provider for Fabric's Consensus Mechanism could manipulate RAFT's Leader Election Process by modifying the randomness interval, in turn affecting the Consistency and Availability of the Consensus (Ordering) Service
7. Service Provider for Fabric's Consensus Mechanism could manipulate RAFT's Leader Election Process by modifying the randomness interval, in turn affecting the Consistency and Availability of the Consensus (Ordering) Service
8. Orderer Org Fabric Admin Account is compromised to gain unauthorized access to the Replication Logs of the Orderer Leader node running RAFT Consensus mechanism, causing a Confidentiality Breach
9. Off-chain Data Store hosting archived Replication Logs of the Orderer Leader node running RAFT Consensus mechanism is compromised causing Confidentiality Breach

Risk, Detectability, and Technical Impact of the Vulnerabilities:

Vulnerability	Risk	Weakness Detectability	Technical Impact
2. Malicious Actor compromises Fabric	9	3	3
3. Compromised Fabric Admin Account	9	3	3
4. Compromised Fabric Admin deleted all	9	3	3
5. Orgs Fabric Admin; Orderer	9	3	3
8. Orderer Org Fabric Admin Account is	9	2	3
9. Offchain Data Store hosting archived	7	2	3
6. Service Provider for Fabric's Consensus randomness interval	6	1	3
7. Service Provider for Fabric's Consensus	4	1	3
1. Malicious actor compromises client	1	1	1

Source: Adapted from CSA.

The vulnerabilities identified using STRIDE are rated for their likelihood and impact, and the risk of compromise to the Fabric 2.0 Network is determined according to "Threat modeling and stride." The risk rating methodology is not a quantitative risk calculation but a qualitative one. The use of qualitative methods to support refining the results of threat models, such as the ones produced by STRIDE, is an industry practice for deriving insights as per technical factors present during design (Jones, 2019). The actors behind the attack vectors are considered to be Advanced Persistent Threats13 (APT) as per industry reports (Allianz, 2021) (Crowdstrike, 2021) (Verizon, 2020). APT-type threats are assumed to have a relatively high contact frequency which simplifies the risk calculation.

Risk and Weakness Prevalence of the Vulnerabilities:

Vulnerability	Ref	Attack Vector	Weakness Prevalence	Weakness Detectability	Technical Impact	Risk
Malicious Actor compromises Fabric	2	3	3	3	3	9
Compromised Fabric Admin Account	3	3	3	3	3	9
Compromised Fabric Admin deleted all	4	3	3	3	3	9
Orgs Fabric Admin; Orderer	5	3	3	3	3	9
Orderer Org Fabric Admin Account is	8	2	3	2	3	9
Offchain Data Store hosting archived	9	2	3	2	3	7
Service Provider for Fabric's Consensus randomness interval	6	2	4	1	3	6
Service Provider for Fabric's Consensus	7	1	3	1	3	4
Malicious actor compromises client	1	1	1	1	1	1

Source: Adapted from CSA.

Read about security aspects in Volume II of this book.

FINANCIAL FUNCTIONS, DEFI, AND WEB3

DECENTRALIZED APPLICATIONS (DAPPS)

DeFi revolves around decentralized applications, also known as DApps, that perform financial functions on distributed ledgers called blockchains, a technology that was first made famous by Bitcoin and has since been adopted more broadly. Rather than transactions being made through a centralized intermediary such as a cryptocurrency exchange or a traditional securities exchange on Wall Street, transactions are directly made between participants, mediated by smart contract programs.

SMART CONTRACTS AND DEFI

These smart contract programs, or DeFi protocols, typically run using open-source software that is built and maintained by a community of developers.

NAP—A TRUE CROSS-BLOCKCHAIN TOKEN

This project contains a proof of concept implementation of a true cross-blockchain token. That is, holders of the token can decide on which blockchains they want to hold their tokens with the ability to freely transfer tokens from one chain to another.

    The token differs from atomic swaps in the sense that tokens are not exchanged between two different users on different blockchains, but rather the same token can be transferred to another blockchain with no other user involved, according to "NAP – A true cross-blockchain token."

DAPPS AND WEB3

DApps are typically accessed through a Web3-enabled browser extension or application, such as MetaMask, which allows users to directly interact with the Ethereum blockchain through a digital wallet. Many of these DApps can interoperate to create complex financial services. For example, stablecoin holders can lend assets like USD Coin or DAI to a liquidity pool in a borrow/lending protocol like Aave, and allow others to borrow those digital assets by depositing their own collateral, typically more than the amount of the loan. The protocol automatically adjusts interest rates based on the moment-to-moment demand for the asset according to "DeFi and Web3."

BLOCKCHAIN SHARDING

"Sharding is a database partitioning technique that will be used to dramatically scale ethereum's blockchain and enable it to process more transactions per second." The definition is quite accurate. However, the sharding technique is not the prerogative of the Ethereum network, according to "What Is Blockchain Sharding?"

    Lack of scalability is the worst nightmare of any distributed ledger. Many decentralized networks strive to introduce a single solution to a sensitive issue. Sharding is a promising concept that has the potential to finally resolve the scalability problem while saving the decentralized nature of blockchains.

SUMMARY

We discussed Blockchain, DeFi, and Web3 technologies and that we are more and more dependent on data. One of the key challenges in data management is establishing data lineage and how this solves the "data lineage" problem of data management. Blockchain provides different levels of access to viewers and how blockchain ensures the verifiability of data among its peers.

    We will discuss more regarding this topic in Volume II of this book.

BIBLIOGRAPHY

1. VA NAII's 2020-2021 AI Tech Sprint, HIMSS Blockchain handout-46_57.
2. NAP – A true cross-blockchain token, https://github.com/pantos-io/nap-token/blob/master/README.md
3. Blockchain Provides an Alternative Trust Model, https://www.gartner.com/smarterwithgartner/cios-cant-ignore-these-5-realities-of-blockchain/
4. Security Controls for Blockchain Applications, Deloitte, https://www2.deloitte.com/ch/en/pages/risk/articles/security-controls-for-blockchain-applications.html
5. What Is Blockchain Sharding?, https://changelly.com/blog/what-is-sharding/#:~:text=%E2%80%9CSharding%20is%20a%20database%20partitioning%20technique%20that%20will,is%20not%20the%20prerogative%20of%20the%20Ethereum%20network
6. Hyperledger Fabric 2.0 Architecture Security Report, file:///C:/Users/ulf.mattsson/Downloads/Hyperledger-Fabric-2.0%20Architecture-Security-Report.pdf
7. Here's Why Quantum Computing Will Not Break Cryptocurrencies, https://www.forbes.com/sites/rogerhuang/2020/12/21/heres-why-quantum-computing-will-not-break-cryptocurrencies/?sh=5424e389167b
8. Adhav, P. (2020-08-25). System Chaincodes in Hyperledger Fabric—VSCC, ESCC, LSCC, ESCC, QSCC. Medium, https://medium.com/coinmonks/system-chaincodes-in-hyperledger-fabric-vsccescclscc-cscc-a48db4d24dc3
9. Albreiki, H., Habib Ur Rehman, M., Salah, K., and Svetinovic, D. (2020). Trustworthy Blockchain Oracles: Review, Comparison, and Open ResearchChallenges. *IEEE Access*. 10.1109/ACCESS.2020.2992698
10. Allianz. (2021). Allianz Risk Barometer, https://www.agcs.allianz.com/news-and-insights/reports/allianz-risk-barometer.html
11. Androulaki, E., Barger, A., Bortnikov, V., Christian, Cachin, Christidis, K., De Caro, A., Enyeart, D., Ferris, C., Laventman, G., Manevich, Y., Muralidharan, S., Murthy, C., Nguyen, B., Sethi, M., Singh, G., Smith, K., Sorniotti, A., Stathakopoulou, C., VukolićJuvoli, M., and Yellick, J. (2018). Hyperledger Fabric: A Distributed Operating System for Permissioned Blockchains. *Proceedings of the Thirteenth EuroSys Conference*, pp. 1–15. 10.1145/3190508.3190538
13. Angelis, S, D., Zanfino, G., Aniello, I., Lombardi, F., and Sassone, V (2019) *Blockchain and Cybersecurity: A Taxonomic Approach*. University of Southampton, https://www.eublockchainforum.eu/sites/default/files/research-paper/wrks-main_1.pdf
14. Baset, S., Desrosiers, L., Gaur, N., Novotny, P., Ramakrishna, V., and O'Dowd, A. (2018). *Hands-On Blockchain with Hyperledger* (ISBN: 9781788994521 ed.). Packt Publishing, https://www.packtpub.com/product/hands-on-blockchain-with-hyperledger/9781788994521
15. Birge, C., Craig, A., Dadoun, D., Glaros, M., Cristin, C., and Chamber of Digital Commerce. (2018). Advancing Blockchain Cybersecurity: Technical and Policy Considerations for the Financial Services Industry, https://query.prod.cms.rt.microsoft.com/cms/api/am/binary/RE1TH5G
16. Carter, H. (2019). Journey to Blockchain: A Non-Technologist's Guide to the Internet of Value. BRI.
17. Chia, V., Hartel, P., Hum, Q., Ma, S., Piliouras, G., Reijsbergen, D., Staalduinen, M. v., and Szalachowski, P. (2019). Rethinking Blockchain Security: Position Paper. ArXiv:1806.04358. http://arxiv.org/abs/1806.04358
18. Threat Modelling and Stride, https://cloudacademy.com/course/module-3-governance-and-risk/threat-modelling-and-stride/
19. Demystifying the Blockchain, https://www.scrygroup.com/blog/2018-07-03/Demystifying-the-blockchain/
20. Everything To Know About Utility Tokenization In Blockchain, https://bizzcoinhub.com/tokenization-in-blockchain/#:~:text=Tokenization%20is%20a%20method%20where%20some%20assets%20are,purchase%20or%20trade%20objects%20that%20aren%E2%80%99t%20easily%20available
21. Copigneaux, B. and European Parliament. (2020). Blockchain for Supply Chains and International Trade: Report on Key Features, Impacts and Policy Options Study. European Parliamentary Research Service, and Scientific Foresight Unit, http://www.europarl.europa.eu/RegData/etudes/STUD/2020/641544/EPRS_STU(2020)641544_EN.pdf
22. How Blockchain will Evolve until 2030 and Today's Hype Versus Reality, https://thepaypers.com/expert-opinion/how-blockchain-will-evolve-until-2030-and-todays-hype-versus-reality--1242127
23. The CIO's Guide to Blockchain, https://www.gartner.com/smarterwithgartner/the-cios-guide-to-blockchain

24. A Beginner's Guide to Answer, What is Data Lineage?, https://www.collibra.com/download/beginners-guide-data-lineage

25. Data and Trending Technologies: Data, https://tdan.com/data-and-trending-technologies-data-in-blockchain-technologies/22447

26. Top 10 Strategic Technology Trends, https://www.openbusinesscouncil.org/top-10-strategic-technology-trends-for-2020/

27. IoT Use Cases, https://www.coursehero.com/file/p22u5cq/9-Smart-Citiesthe-IoT-This-group-includes-use-cases-that-use-blockchain-to/

28. Cloud Security Alliance Hyperledger Fabric, http://maruyama-mitsuhiko.cocolog-nifty.com/security/2021/07/post-fdd305.html

29. DeFi and Web3, https://en.wikipedia.org/wiki/Decentralized_finance

30. Decentralized Finance: On blockchain- and Smart Contract-Based Financial Markets, https://research.stlouisfed.org/publications/review/2021/02/05/decentralized-finance-on-blockchain-and-smart-contract-based-financial-markets

Section V

Platforms

14 Hybrid Cloud, CASB, and SASE

INTRODUCTION

We will discuss the situation where many enterprises have workloads on their physical servers and increasingly need support for Hybrid Cloud (HC). In this situation, logging, management of encryption keys, and policies should ideally work across these environments to effectively control data privacy and security.

Security integration for cloud resources can be supported by Cloud Access Security Brokers (CASBs) and Secure Access Service Edge (SASE). SASE and CASB can be an add-on to a security stack where the organization has already invested in and deployed the other necessary security solutions according to "SASE vs. CASB."

BUSINESSES CONTINUE TO RUN IN PRIVATE DATA CENTERS

McKinsey found that enterprises moved 20% of workloads to the cloud, and 65% continue to run in private data centers. An Uptime Institute survey reported that 58% said most of their workloads would remain in corporate data centers according to "The Potential of Cloud, Part 1."

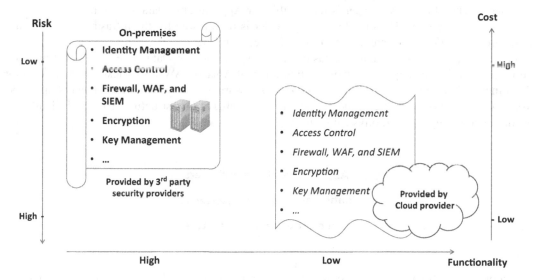

MANAGING DATA ENCRYPTION IN HYBRID CLOUD

Data is moving across multi-cloud and on-premises systems imposing privacy and data residency risks. Encryption requires careful selection from a complex and often incompatible variety of products, according to "The Potential of Cloud, Part 1."

DOI: 10.1201/9781003189664-19

Storing outside a National Jurisdiction—Encryption May Be an Acceptable Control

Data protection can be applied through anonymization or pseudonymization, such as encryption, tokenization, masking, and privacy-enhancing computation (PEC) such as secure multiparty computation (SMPC) and homomorphic encryption. These require specific KM integrations and orchestration of KM policies with different impacts to data residency, protection, and privacy. While storing personal data outside a national jurisdiction may not be allowed, encryption may be an acceptable control to satisfy some of these issues.

BENEFITING FROM CLOUD, BUT BEING RESPONSIBLE WITH DATA

Embrace the cloud must be built on that your data remains secure no matter where it moves, is applied or stored in cloud systems according to "The Potential of Cloud, Part 1."

But Cybercriminals use all sorts of tools and methods—including malware, ransomware, and phishing—to steal and manipulate data from cloud-based applications and systems, according to "The Potential of Cloud, Part 1: First, Businesses Need to Get There."

Shared Responsibility Model in Cloud

Responsibilities Are Split and Not Shared

The shared responsibility model in the cloud is more a model of how responsibilities are split and not shared. The cloud service user is responsible for Applications, Data and users, and configuration as code (software). The cloud service provider is responsible for the infrastructure, including hardware, network, supervisor, and other lower-level components.

In general, my view is that the customer is responsible for Data, Users, Applications, and Configuration. For example, security Configuration of Amazon AWS S3 buckets and Application Containers. Configuration is defined as code in software and may include Containers and other Application components. The Cloud provider is responsible of infrastructure. This can be hardware, communication, hypervisor, physical security:

Applications, Data and Users
Configuration as code (software)
Cloud provider infrastructure

According to "Shared Responsibility Model Explained," in a traditional data center model, you are responsible for security across your entire system." In a cloud environment, your provider shares many operational burdens, including some security but not for the data you collected and probably always will be responsible for. In this shared responsibility model, working together with your cloud provider and sharing portions of the security, you can maintain a secure environment with less operational overhead.

Shared Responsibility Model

With a shared security responsibility model, defining the line is critical for reducing the risk of introducing vulnerabilities according to "Shared Responsibility Model Explained."

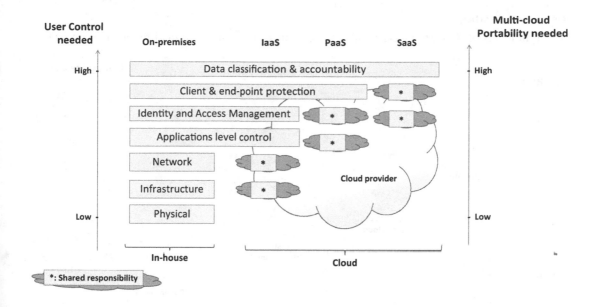

Defining the Lines in a Shared Responsibility

Your security posture in a cloud environment is based on understanding where your provider's responsibility ends and where yours begins according to the "Shared Responsibility Model, what is it?"

- AWS claims responsibility for "protecting the hardware, software, networking, and facilities that run AWS Cloud services."
- Azure claims security ownership of "physical hosts, networks, and data centers."

The agreements are open for interpretation, and security responsibilities vary by provider and introduce complexity and risk for several layers. Each environment, application, and service requires a unique approach for security assessment and monitoring according to the "Shared Responsibility Model Explained."

Contractual mechanisms, together with technical controls, strengthen security and privacy. Security needs to be upfront in the decision-making process regarding shared responsibilities when entering a discussion with a cloud provider.

If your organization collected the data, then you are also liable for that data, even if you outsource the operation or storage of that data to a cloud provider.

Cloud Security Alliance (CSA) discuss more details about security for Data, Users, and Applications for SaaS, IaaS, and PaaS cloud models

Risks

Different levels of risk can be addressed in:

- Multi-cloud Management of Secrets.
- Encryption keys in HSM (Hardware Security Module).
- Protected execution of code in TEE (Trusted Execution Environment).

Risk Considerations

Different levels of Risk and Operational requirements can be addressed in different environments:

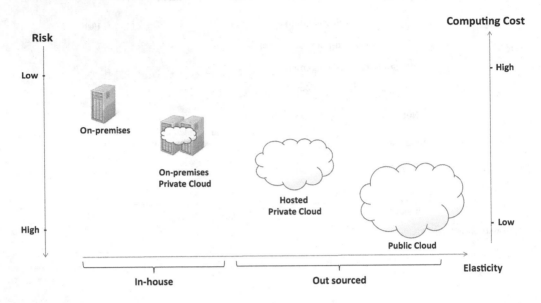

USE CASES

International Bank

One hundred sixty different regions and countries can control encryption and key management by using CASBs across EMEA and APAC with central Enterprise Security Administration for 200 million users. The architecture allows choosing either on-premises or cloud-based encryption and Enterprise Policy Management:

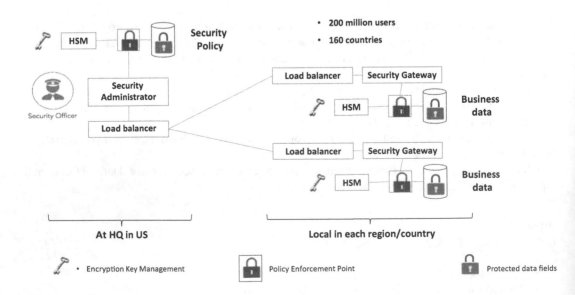

Hosting Service for Data

The same configuration can be implemented with on-premises or cloud encryption and Enterprise Policy Management. Hosted business data is protected by a CASB security gateway that provides encryption or tokenization of sensitive data:

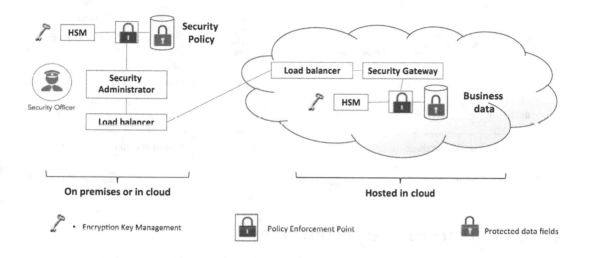

Data Is Protected before Landing in AWS S3

Selected users and applications can use de-identified data in the clear, based on policy rules.

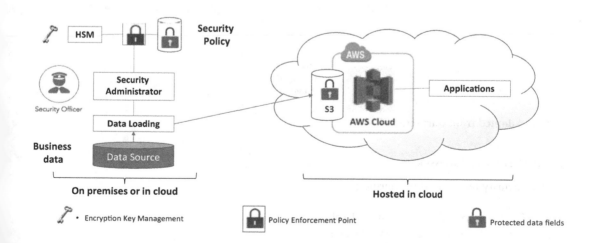

Encryption on Google GCP can be combined with a separated Policy Administration and Key Management for a high level of security.

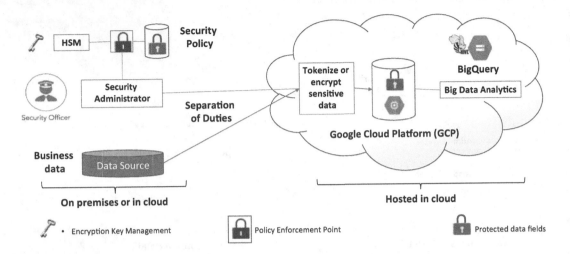

CLOUD SECURITY LOGICAL ARCHITECTURE

The components are a front-end platform (fat client, thin client, mobile), back-end platforms (servers, storage), a cloud-based delivery, and a network refer to the components and subcomponents required for cloud computing according to "Cloud Computing-A Brief Introduction." We will here focus on the usage of CASB and SASE.

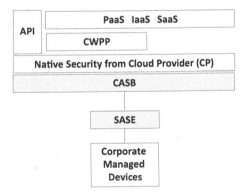

Source: Adopted from GartnerSASE

CLOUD SECURITY GLOSSARY

Cloud Security terms used by Gartner:

- CASB—Cloud Access Security Broker
- SASE—Secure Access Service Edge
- CP—Cloud Providers
- CSPM—Cloud Security Posture Management
- CWPP—Cloud Workload Protection Platform

Cloud Security Layers

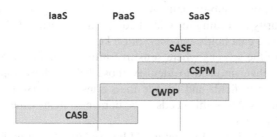

CASB

Cloud Access Security Broker

CASB is an on-premises or cloud-based software that monitors and enforces security policies. A CASB can offer security policy compliance and is used for addressing the weaknesses of legacy systems according to "SASE vs CASB."

Example of Encrypting Data in SaaS with a CASB

A CASB can encrypt data before it is stored in Salesforce or other software-as-a-service (SaaS) where the cloud provider installing and maintaining software in the cloud and users running the software from the cloud over the Internet (or Intranet) according to "Cloud computing architecture":

A CASB encryption gateway may transparently intercept HTTP(S), SFTP, and SMTP:

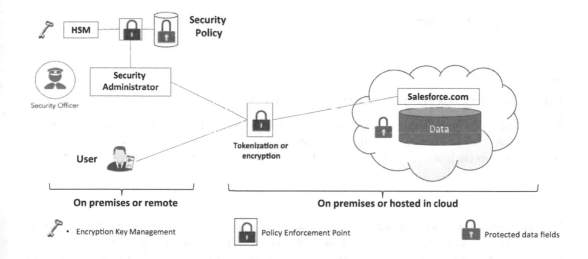

CASB Access via API or as a Proxy

A CASB may deliver security, the management, or both. Broadly speaking, "security" is the prevention of high-risk events, while "management" is the monitoring and mitigation of high-risk events according to "CASB - Cloud Access Security Broker." CASBs that deliver strong security must be in the path of data access, via proxy agents, or without requiring any configuration on each device and allow for rapid deployment and deliver security on both company-managed and unmanaged devices according to "Software: Cloud, access security broker."

CASB Policy and Encryption Key Management

Cloud computing security is a sub-domain of computer security, network security, and, more broadly, information security according to "Cloud computing security." CASB Policy Management controls access to encrypted data fields and encryption keys.

It is tedious to identify the screens where sensitive information is entered, requiring "detective work" to uncover the mechanism used to identify those fields. Many applications use internally developed methods to identify fields and encode their transmission (sometimes compacting them and sometimes signing them). All of this needs to be unraveled many times without access to documentation from the SaaS vendor.

Other times, there are published APIs that could be used to interact with the SaaS platform (for example, to do bulk protection), but other times APIs are not available.

Issues with CASB Deployment

Challenges in decrypting TLS.SSL traffic ranges from performance, limitations in tools to regulatory compliance:

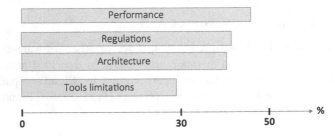

Source: Adapted from (ISC)2

CASB VS. SASE

Which Is Better for Your Organizational Security?

Many businesses need multiple specialized cloud security solutions. A Cloud Access Security Broker (CASB) may not be enough for comprehensive data security but a newer technology or framework approach is increasingly can be added, which is Secure Access Service Edge (SASE).

SASE

Too many siloed security tools that don't integrate with other products and require different knowledge levels and skill sets to operate and maintain can be an issue. According to "Solutions- Cisco SASE Architecture Guide," the Enterprise Strategy Group reports that 31% of organizations use over 50 disparate tools to orchestrate alerts from these different tools according to "Solutions—Cisco SASE Architecture Guide."

Pros and Cons of CASB

Pros

- It provides the capabilities of limited inline threat security.
- It can be used to strengthen the security of your organization's cloud infrastructure.

Cons

- It requires integration with different standalone security solutions.
- Decreases the overall efficacy of the security team since there is a need to acquire, deploy, monitor, and maintain every security solution separately.

PROS AND CONS OF SASE

Pros

- The benefits of SASE technology are that comprehensive visibility is ensured into the traffic that is routed via the corporate WAN.
- It also allows carrying out complete security inspections.
- It is a complete WAN infrastructure solution, so it is impossible to slot into a place like in CASB.

Cons

- It requires network redesign.

Alternatives according to "The Future of Network Security Is in the Cloud":

1. Status quo using a hardware-based branch office.
2. Software-based branch office.
3. Build SASE yourself via service chaining.
4. SD-WAN from one vendor converged network security as a service from another.
5. Provider-orchestrated service chaining.

SASE—Application and Data Protection for Multi-Cloud

Personal data privacy will be the most prominent issue affecting how businesses gather, store, process, and disclose data in the public cloud. GDPR and CCPA drive many companies to focus on data privacy from the legal and security side are missing the focus on data privacy according to "What I learned at Gartner summit."

BENEFITS OF UNIFIED DEFENSES

The benefits of a unified platform App and Data Security Defenses was reported in a study by (ISC)[2]:

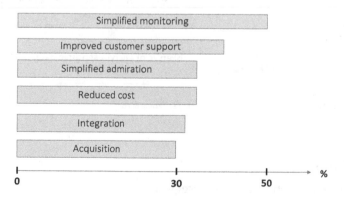

Source: Adapted from (ISC)2

The study included 16 major countries worldwide, with 47% of the input from the United States. The study included Healthcare (42%), Manufacturing, Finance, Retail, and other industries.

DATA SECURITY AND KEY MANAGEMENT FOR HYBRID CLOUD

ISSUES WITH POINT SOLUTIONS

A major problem with encryption is the management of keys that can be an expensive and onerous administrative burden according to "Section 7.2. What Is Encryption?" An organization must protect and monitor the use of the key and may look for key management to be embedded in products according to "Key Management for Enterprise Data Encryption."

A CENTRAL POINT OF CONTROL

A central administration from control for data privacy and security for hybrid cloud according to "Key Management for Enterprise Data Encryption" describes how to use hardware (HSM) and software that combine each technology's benefits. This can give flexibility to deploy encryption at the appropriate place in systems according to "Key Management for Enterprise Data Encryption":

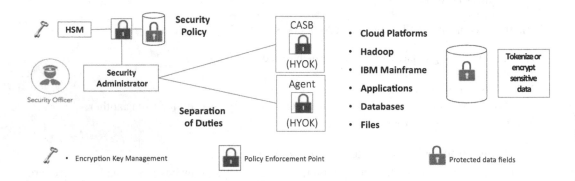

Use Case—Amazon AWS Databases

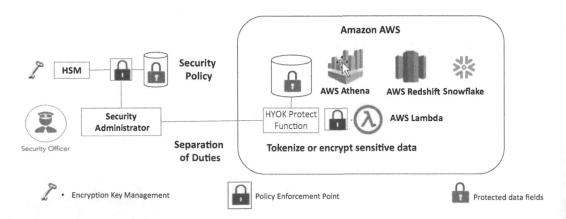

SEPARATION OF DUTIES

Separation of Duties in Each Geographic Region

Separate Responsibilities, Singular Problem Businesses recognize the imperative to separate the duties of those responsible for setting data security policies and granting access to users. By splitting responsibilities, an enterprise ensures that no one person or department has the keys to security, according to "Protegrity Cloud Protect."

Different Hybrid Cloud Policies Slow Innovation

Organizations often can't innovate because they're busy tending to disparate data security policy enforcement across their many on-premises and cloud-native databases and tools. With data security administration decentralized, compliance and security teams scramble to align expectations for data privacy with the data security policies of different vendors.

Local Secrets

Isolation can be created with a strong cryptographic device—the HSM—in each region. This works because the policy is generated along with the data elements and all the other stuff in the policy in a centralized place. The same policy is pulled from each region. A region configured with the HSM will accept the policy and take the codebook created in the United States and reshuffle the tokenization codebook with new key material from the region HSM.

A unique codebook would reside in each region. The nice thing is that once the codebook reshuffling is done, there will be nothing that needs to be done to the protector since it will get a policy as it normally does. The policy is centralized, but data residency will be different and specific to each country, keep the centralized policy for decentralized business authorization/enforcement.

Data Encryption Key Management

There are two basic design approaches for managing your keys in a third-party cloud service: Bring Your Own Key (BYOK) and Hold Your Own Key (HYOK).

Cloud Key Management (KM)

According to "Best Practices for Cloud Data Security and Protection," data residency across cloud services creates complex data security and compliance according to "Best Practices for Cloud Data Security and Protection." This is due to the impacts of access by cloud service providers, government authorities, and staff worldwide. There is a growing number of multi-cloud key management as a service (KMaaS) offerings provided by vendors and natively by each cloud service provider (CSP) that are independent or can integrate with bringing your own key (BYOK) and (HYOK) methods. Growing data residency requirements will affect the choice of KMaaS based on its ability to manage KM policies, misconfigurations, and administrator access.

KM Choices Determine the level of control and risk, Example of HYOK and BYOK (Hold/Bring Your Own Key) vs Amazon AWS Key Management:

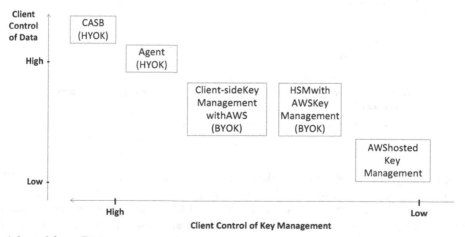

Source: Adapted from Gartner.

KEY MANAGEMENT FOR ENTERPRISE DATA ENCRYPTION

According to "Key Management for Enterprise Data Encryption," often overlooked is providing both operational efficiency and reduced management costs.

Automated Key Distribution Is Challenging

Automated key distribution is becoming more secure and more widely used based on standards for key management developed by the government and by organizations such as ISO, ANSI, and the American Banking Organization (ABA). The key management process should be based on the policy according to "Key Management for Enterprise Data Encryption."

Best Practices for Protecting the Data Flow

Best practices suggest that we must protect sensitive data at the point of capture. The decryption of the data can occur at any point throughout the data flow in an application transparent way with minimum impact to the operational environment, according to "Key Management for Enterprise Data Encryption."

Data Security Policy and Encryption Key Management

A common concern is vendor lock-in and an inability to migrate to another cloud service provider when features or pricing changes and most firms want to have control of policies and keys, so they often prefer to leverage the same tool and skills to leverage the same tool and skills across multiple clouds and for on-premises systems. It can be on-premises or hosted in a private or public cloud.

Bring Your Own Key (BYOK)

With SaaS encryption is built-in and occurs by default for all tenants as part of the service. To keep things simple, encryption and key management interfaces are not exposed. Instead, encryption is handled on the customer's behalf according to "Multi-Cloud Key Management."

Amazon Web Services (AWS) S3 Client-Side Encryption

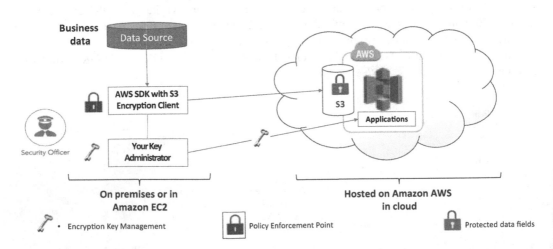

For example, encryption and decryption take place in the Elastic MapReduce File System (EMRFS) client on the cloud customer's cluster. Objects are encrypted by the AWS SDK before being uploaded to S3 and decrypted after they are downloaded. The EMRFS is an implementation of the Hadoop Distributed File System (HDFS) that all Amazon EMR clusters use for reading and writing regular files from Amazon EMR directly to S3 according to "EMR File System (EMRFS)—Amazon EMR."

Your client-side key management software infrastructure needs to be installed where your application is running. Your server-side key management software infrastructure needs to be installed in AWS EC2.

AWS Encryption Key Management

Your application in Amazon Virtual Private Cloud (VPC) can access your own key management infrastructure (KMI) or AWS CloudHSM via an AWS client. Amazon VPC lets you provision a logically isolated section of the AWS cloud, where you can launch AWS resources according to "VPC :: Migration and Modernization Guide." A master key encrypts the data encryption key that is stored with your encrypted data.

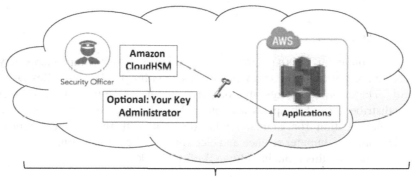

Hosted on Amazon AW SVPC in cloud

Hold Your Own Key (HYOK)

Unlike BYOK, in HYOK, you keep your own encryption keys, and all the encryption and decryption work is done with software or hardware that you control on-premises or in the cloud. The upside to HYOK is that you know no one has access to your data without your approval. You hold all the keys to the kingdom according to "Office 365 Hold Your Own Key."

Keys Should Be Centrally Generated

All data protection system services should be using X.509 certificates and TLS (or old SSL) for secure distribution of encryption keys according to "Key Management for Enterprise Data Encryption." Client-side and server-side certificates should be used and periodically validated by a certificate revocation list.

Your Own Key Management Server in the Cloud

For multi-cloud key management, you can install your own key management server in the cloud. For businesses who do not use advanced hardware for key management on-premises but want to ensure their cloud providers do not own—and cannot be compelled to turn over—keys to decrypt their data, according to "Multi-Cloud Key Management – Securosis."

Security Depends on Where the Keys Are Stored and the Access

Since cryptography is only as good as the protection of those keys according to "Key Management for Enterprise Data Encryption," Security depends on where the keys are stored and who has access to them, and it is essential to include the ability to securely manage keys according to "Key Management for Enterprise Data Encryption."

We will debate more on this topic in Volume II of this book, *Encryption Key Best Practices*.

Selection and Migration

You aren't really working shoulder to shoulder with your cloud vendor. Instead, implement security using the building blocks they provide, possibly filling in gaps where they don't provide solutions, according to "Multi-Cloud Key Management – Securosis."

Leveraging Familiar Tools Also for Cloud

Bring Your Own Keys (and select cloud HSMs), or bring your own software key management stack, can bring familiar tools to the cloud platform but you are signing on for additional set-up. And it's not always simple—the cloud variants of HSMs and software key management services are different than their on-premises counterparts. 3rd party tools can make this easier by adding a layer of abstraction and unity.

Quantum Key Management

Quantum key distribution (QKD) is a secure communication method that implements a cryptographic protocol involving components of quantum mechanics according to "Quantum Key Distribution and BB84 Protocol." The quantum key distribution plays the role of the trusted carrier to augment the symmetric key distribution and competes with public keys. It is secure against unlimited computing power. In the implementation front of quantum key distribution, there is an intersection of fields like quantum physics, optics, computer science and electronics make it more complex.

We will debate more on this topic in Volume II of this book.

A HYBRID OR FULLY REMOTE OFFICE

Flexible remote working was something only the very hip companies implemented, while most others believed it just wouldn't be right for them and 81% of surveyed professionals choose a hybrid schedule and work from home two days of every week. Here are some of the steps to optimize your flexible work strategy according to "5 Tips to Optimize Your Flexible Working System."

SUMMARY

We have discussed the situation where many enterprises have workloads on their physical servers and increasingly need support for Hybrid Cloud and how encryption keys and policies can work across these environments for effective control of data privacy and security.

We also discussed how Cloud Access Security Brokers (CASBs) and Secure Access Service Edge (SASE) can be add-ons to a security stack where the organization has already invested in and deployed the other necessary security solutions.

We will examine more about this topic in Volume II of this book.

BIBLIOGRAPHY

1. HBS Online Survey Shows Most Professionals Have Excelled While Working From Home, https://online.hbs.edu/blog/post/future-of-work-from-home
2. Shared Responsibility Model Explained, https://www.cloudpassage.com/articles/shared-responsibility-model-explained/
3. Quantum Key Distribution and BB84 Protocol, https://medium.com/quantum-untangled/quantum-key-distribution-and-bb84-protocol-6f03cc6263c5
4. Cloud Computing - A Brief Introduction, https://devanshagarwal121.medium.com/cloud-computing-a-brief-introduction-393b7928e964#:~:text=Cloud%20Computing%20Architecture%20Cloud%20computing%20architecture%20refers%20to,based%20delivery%2C%20and%20a%20network%20%28Internet%2C%20Intranet%2C%20Intercloud%29

5. Section 7.2. What Is Encryption?, https://flylib.com/books/en/2.624.1.49/1/
6. American Council for Technology and Industry Advisory Council (2019). Zero Trust Cybersecurity Current Trends. Available at https://www.actiac.org/zero-trust-cybersecurity-current-trends
7. Cloud Access Security Brokers, https://en.wikipedia.org/wiki/Cloud_access_security_broker
8. CASB – Cloud Access Security Broker, https://roi4cio.com/en/categories/category/casb-cloud-access-security-broker/#:~:text=A%20CASB%20may%20deliver%20security%2C%20the%20management%20or,data%20access%2C%20between%20the%20user%20and%20the%20cloud
9. Market Guide for Cloud Access Security Brokers, https://www.gartner.com/doc/3488119/market-guide-cloud-access-security
10. NIST Special Publication 800-207, https://www.nist.gov/news-events/news/2020/08/zero-trust-architecture-nist-publishes-sp-800-207#:~:text=NIST%20announces%20the%20final%20publication%20of%20Special%20Publication,perimeters%20to%20individual%20or%20small%20groups%20of%20resources
11. Hybrid Cloud by the Numbers, https://enterprisersproject.com/article/2020/7/hybrid-cloud-10-statistics
12. Shared Responsibility Model, What Is It?, https://blog.r2ut.com/shared-responsibility-model-what-is-it#:~:text=The%20key%20to%20a%20successful%20security%20implementation%20in,core%20networking%20infrastructure%20that%20enable%20their%20cloud%20services
13. Anderson, B. and McGrew, D. (2017). Machine Learning for Encrypted Malware Traffic Classification: Accounting for Noisy Labels and Non-Stationarity. *Proceedings of the 23rd ACM SIGKDD International Conference on Knowledge Discovery and Data Mining (ACM, Halifax, Nova Scotia, Canada)*, pp. 1723–1732. doi:10.1145/3097983.3098163
14. Department of Defense CIO (2007). Department of Defense Global Information Grid Architecture Vision Version 1.0 June 2007, http://www.acqnotes.com/Attachments/DoD%20GIG%20Architectural%20Vision,%20June%202007.pdf
15. CloudCodes CASB, www.cloudcodes.com
16. The Potential of Cloud, Part 1: First, Businesses Need to Get There, https://www.protegrity.com/protegrity blog/the-potential-of-cloud-first-businesses-need-to-get-there
17. What Exactly Is a Cloud Architect and How Do You Become One?, cloudacademy.com/blog/what-exactly-is-a-cloud-architect-and how do you become one/
18. SASE vs CASB – Which is Better for You, https://www.cloudcodes.com/blog/sase-vs-casb.html
19. Cloud computing architecture – Wikipedia, https://en.wikipedia.org/wiki/Cloud_computing_architecture
20. Software: Cloud access security broker – HandWiki, https://handwiki.org/wiki/Software:Cloud_access_security_broker
21. Solutions – Cisco SASE Architecture Guide – Cisco, https://www.cisco.com/c/en/us/solutions/collateral/enterprise/design-zone-security/sase-arch-guide.html
22. The Future of Network Security Is in the Cloud, https://www.detectx.com.au/the-future-of-network-security-is-in-the-cloud/
23. What I Learned at Gartner Summit, https://www.slideshare.net/ulfmattsson/what-i-learned-at-gartner-summit-2019
24. Protegrity Cloud Protect, https://f.hubspotusercontent30.net/hubfs/5096489/Collateral/Cloud%20Protect/Cloud%20Protect%20Overview.pdf
25. Best Practices for Cloud Data Security and Protection, https://www.itconvergence.com/blog/extend-data-awareness-and-protection-on-public-cloud/
26. Multi-Cloud Key Management – Securosis, https://securosis.com/assets/library/reports/Securosis_MultiCloud_Key_Man_FINAL.pdf
27. VPC :: Migration and Modernization Guide, https://migration-gameday.workshop.aws/en/vpc.html
28. Office 365 Hold Your Own Key, https://www.enowsoftware.com/solutions-engine/office-365-hold-your-own-key
29. Key Management for Enterprise Data Encryption, https://papers.ssrn.com/sol3/papers.cfm?abstract_id=1051481
30. 5 Tips to Optimize Your Flexible Working System, https://www.entrepreneur.com/article/373791

15 HSM, TPM, and Trusted Execution Environments

INTRODUCTION

We will discuss how trusted execution environments (TEEs) can provide a protected environment for running applications and data in the cloud and other platforms.

Hardware security modules (HSMs) can safeguard digital keys and perform limited cryptographic functions required to run in a highly secure environment that may be validated by standards for cryptographic modules, like NIST FIPS 140.

TRUSTED EXECUTION ENVIRONMENTS

Trusted execution environments (TEEs) provide secure computation by combining software and hardware features according to "Trusted Execution Environment (TEE) 101: A Primer."

In general, a process can run without its memory or execution state being visible to any other process on the processor, not even the operating system or other privileged code.

- TEEs are isolated so that the operating system or hypervisor cannot read the code in the TEE.
- TEEs can also protect data "at rest," when it is not being analyzed through encryption.

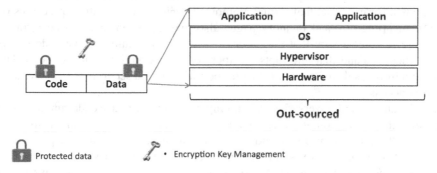

Some business problems require an organization to share data with or analyze data from multiple parties without disclosing their respective information to each other. A trusted hardware environment is often not enough to provide privacy in this type of scenario. This is because of the need to work on multiple parties' data and without disclosing the original data, even to the software that processes it, in case of a compromise of that environment. Privacy-enhanced approaches for this use case rely on data transformation coupled with software that enables secure distributed processing in an untrusted environment.

EXAMPLES OF APPLIED USES

TEEs often perform and scale reasonably well for some use cases. Databases running in TEEs can provide useful performance and scalability. According to "Machine Learning in Trusted Execution Environments," a data provider might provide an encrypted dataset to a user and internally decrypt

DOI: 10.1201/9781003189664-20

the provided data and perform computation as needed according to "Machine Learning in Trusted Execution Environments."

Machine Learning in Trusted Execution Environments

A ML model provider might provide an encrypted dataset to an enclave with the decryption key for the provided data. According to "Machine Learning in Trusted Execution Environments," the enclave can then internally decrypt the provided data and perform computation as needed.

Support for Streaming Data Applications

Enclave computation can also support streaming data applications, where data arrives continuously and is processed through analytics upon arrival. A useful enhancement is that multiple enclaves can be linked together, so that analytics over many data sources can be integrated into one result dataflow without the need to perform all analytics within one enclave. Thus large-scale streaming analysis, such as streaming-rate analytics over sales and shipping data, can be accomplished efficiently. Enclaves also lend themselves to computation "in the small." For example, some server-side banking applications rely on attestation and enclave computation on client-side platforms (such as a user's laptop). For example, a banking server might use a client-side enclave to achieve digital signatures on banking transactions while protecting the signing key from compromise by any malware running on the laptop.

ADVERSARY MODEL AND SECURITY ARGUMENT

The adversary model most typically used for enclave computing includes a privileged adversary running on the same platform as the enclave, seeking to execute code of the adversary's choice outside the enclave in order to access the state of the process running inside the enclave. The security argument against such adversaries is that special-purpose hardware mechanisms prevent any code running outside an enclave from learning any state private to the enclave. Such special-purpose hardware assures, for example, that virtual memory mapping does not allow processes outside an enclave from mapping physical memory pages also mapped to enclave-private virtual memory. Other hardware features assure that the processor cannot jump into enclave code except at predefined legal locations and that interrupts or other control instructions outside the enclave cannot cause execution from inside to branch to outside code without first securing the enclave and preventing disallowed access.

Another relevant class of adversaries may attempt to inject or replace code running in an enclave in order to allow the exfiltration of secrets in the enclave. The security argument against such adversaries combines the protections above and the notion of attestation. Hardware protections assure, for example, that once an enclave is initiated, no change to its code or static data can be achieved from outside the enclave. Once initiated, processes outside the enclave can receive cryptographic attestation that includes a signature of the code inside the enclave so that the outside process can be assured of all code that can run in the enclave.

COSTS OF USING THE TECHNOLOGY

Enclave computation is usually comparable in speed to computing "in the clear." We know of examples that display slowdowns of up to 20% against computing in the clear for relatively small data (on the order of 100MB or so, including application code and data). Other examples show that as data scales toward the Gigabyte range, the slowdown may rise to as much as a factor of 6 or 8 times, still far better than MPC or FHE performance. The use of enclave computation does require the use of specific hardware that includes enclave features. For example, Intel(R) SGX™ features seem to be included in processors of the Skylake™ generation and beyond. Some TEE providers enable virtualization as well, but only virtualization on top of TEE-equipped hardware.

AVAILABILITY

Perhaps the most notable enclave capability today is found in Intel(R) processors. Intel's Software Guard Extensions (SGX)™ provides enclave computing in Skylake™ processors and their successors. Virtualization of SGX is an emerging capability currently (it seems) supported on KVM platforms running on Intel processors. ARM's Trust zone and AMD's Platform Security Processor also offer TEE capability. The software offerings are diverse as well, ranging from implementation support libraries to privacy-preserving data processing platforms. Some frameworks support the application developer by providing convenience and portability, including Baidu's Rust SGX SDK and MesaTEE, Google's Asylo, Microsoft's Open Enclave SDK, Fortanix's Rust Enclave Development platform, and the SGX Linux Kernel Library Others have more focused applications, like SCONE, a container mechanism with SGX support, R3 Corda for Open Source Blockchain and Sharemind HI, an SGX-powered privacy-preserving analytics platform.

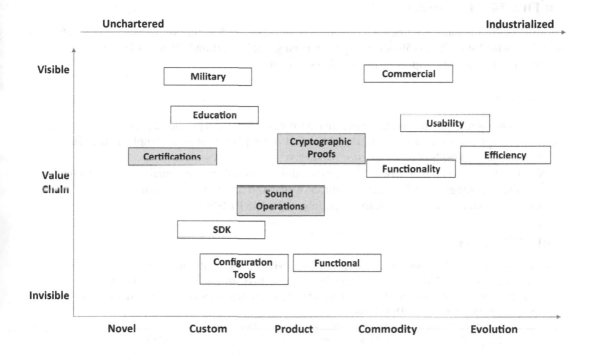

EXISTING STANDARDS

ISO/IEC 29101:2013 (Information technology—Security techniques—Privacy architecture framework) presents how privacy-enhancing technologies such as secure computing, pseudonymization, query restrictions, and more could be deployed to protect personally identifiable information. ISO/IEC 29101 predates the European GDPR and may not include all the latest knowledge on secure computing and its role in regulation according to "Standardisation efforts on secure computing."

ISO/IEC 19592-1:2016 (Information technology—Security techniques—Secret sharing—Part 1: General) covers models of secret sharing, e.g., the homomorphic property. ISO/IEC 19592-2:2017 (Information technology—Security techniques—Secret sharing—Part 2: Fundamental mechanisms) schemes are systematically described using the terms and properties from Part 1 according to "Standardisation efforts on secure computing."

TRUSTED PLATFORM MODULE (TPM)

INTERNATIONAL STANDARD FOR A SECURE CRYPTOPROCESSOR

A Trusted Platform Module complying with the TPM version 1.2 standard Trusted Platform Module (TPM, also known as ISO/IEC 11889) is an international standard for a secure cryptoprocessor, a dedicated microcontroller designed to secure hardware through integrated cryptographic keys according to "Trusted Platform Module."

HARDWARE SECURITY MODULE (HSM)

An HSM is a chip that safeguards and manages digital keys, performs encryption and decryption functions for digital signatures, strong authentication, and other cryptographic functions according to "Hardware security module."

THE FIPS 140-3 STANDARD

The FIPS 140-3 standard defines the module requirements, and testing for these requirements will be in line with ISO/IEC 24759 according to "Cryptographic Module Validation Program."
We will discuss these topics more in Volume II of this book.

SUMMARY

We have discussed how trusted execution environments (TEEs) can provide a protected environment for running applications and data in the cloud and other platforms as a complement to hardware security modules (HSMs).

We also discussed how Hardware security modules (HSMs) can safeguard digital keys and perform limited cryptographic functions required to run in a highly secure environment that may be validated by standards for cryptographic modules, like NIST FIPS 140.

BIBLIOGRAPHY

1. Trusted Platform Module, https://en.wikipedia.org/wiki/Trusted_Platform_Module
2. Hardware Security Module, https://en.wikipedia.org/wiki/Hardware_security_module
3. Cryptographic Module Validation Program, https://csrc.nist.gov/Projects/cryptographic-module-validation-program/fips-140-3-standards
4. International Standard ISO/IEC 20889, https://webstore.ansi.org/Standards/ISO/ISOIEC208892018?gcl id=EAIaIQobChMIvI-k3sXd5gIVw56zCh0Y0QeeEAAYASAAEgLVKfD_BwE
5. ISO/IEC 29101:2013 (Information Technology – Security Techniques – Privacy Architecture Framework).
6. ISO/IEC 19592-2:2017 (Information Technology – Security Techniques – Secret Sharing – Part 2: Fundamental Mechanisms
7. ISO/IEC 19592-1:2016 (Information Technology – Security Techniques – Secret Sharing – Part 1: General).
8. UN Privacy Preserving Techniques Handbook, https://marketplace.officialstatistics.org/privacy-preserving-techniques-handbook#:~:text=UN%20Privacy%20Preserving%20Techniques%20Handbook%20In%20this%20UN,and%20enabling%20Big%20Data%20Collaborations%20Across%20Multiple%20NSOs.ISO/IEC 29101:2013 Information technology – Security techniques – Privacy architecture framework, https://www.iso.org/standard/45124.html
9. Trusted Execution Environment (TEE) 101:A Primer, https://www.securetechalliance.org/wp-content/uploads/TEE-101-White-Paper-FINAL2-April-2018.pdf#:~:text=The%20Trusted%20Execution%20Environment%20%28TEE%29%20is%20designed%20to,devices%20and%20the%20unauthorized%20collection%20of%20sensitive%20data
10. Machine Learning in Trusted Execution Environments, https://www.globalsecuritymag.com/Machine-Learning-in-Trusted,20210610,112686.html
11. Standardisation Efforts on Secure Computing | Sharemind, https://sharemind.cyber.ee/secure-computing-standards/

16 Internet of Things

INTRODUCTION

We will discuss the network of objects called the Internet of Things (IoT). IoT devices are present in the electrical power grid, many mobile devices, and impacting our lives daily. We increasingly rely on IoT for our physical security in cars and medical devices. Many of the devices in industrial control systems are old and hard to upgrade with new security functions.

The Internet of Things (IoT) defines the network of "things" that are embedded with sensors, software, and other devices and systems across the Internet according to "Internet of Things."

Things have evolved due to the convergence of multiple new technologies and traditional fields of embedded systems, wireless sensor networks, control systems, building automation), and others all contribute to enabling the Internet of Things according to "PROJECT PLAN Version 10."

THE CORE OF IoT

IoT involves making physical devices communicate among your smart lights, your bedroom, and kitchen thermostats according to "Robotics vs IoT (Internet of Things) What's the Difference?" You can also control the devices remotely from the cloud once you can access the IoT platform:

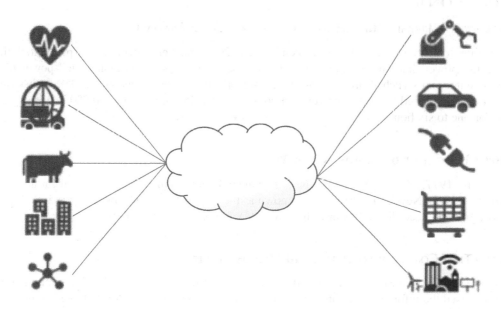

Source: Adapted from IoT ANALYTICS

DOI: 10.1201/9781003189664-21

IoT APPLICATIONS

These are some major industries that are using IoT devices:

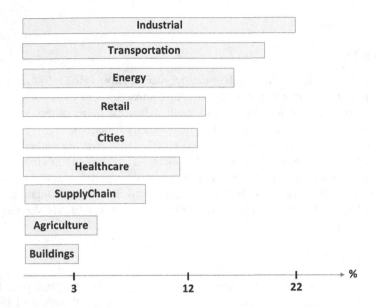

Source: Adapted from IoT ANALYTICS

ATTACKS ON IoT

BLACK OUT IN UKRAINE: BLACKENERGY IN POWER GRID CYBERATTACK

According to Threathunting.se on December 23, 2015, hackers successfully penetrated three Ukrainian power distribution companies. They struck the "Prykarpattyaoblenergo" power distribution center and switched off 30 substations—seven 110kv substations and 23 35kv substations; hackers also attacked two other power grid companies leaving more than 230,000 residents in the dark for one to six hours.

A BRIEF HISTORY OF BLACKOUTS IN NEW YORK CITY

On July 14, 1977, a Strauss Store on Liberty Avenue in Jamaica, Queens, had its metal curtain ripped down by looters. New York City may be known as the city that never sleeps, but that doesn't mean it can't go dark, according to "A brief history of blackouts in New York City."

BREACH THAT COMPROMISED DATA OF 50 MILLION PEOPLE

T-Mobile CEO Mike Sievert announced that the hacker behind the breach of the company that compromised the information of around 50 million individuals had used "brute force" in the attack, according to "T-Mobile CEO apologizes for breach."

HACKERS BREACHED COLONIAL PIPELINE WITH ONE COMPROMISED PASSWORD

The hack that halted the largest fuel pipeline in the United States resulted from a compromised password, according to "Hackers breached Colonial Pipeline with one compromised password."

WATER PLANT HACK LED TO DISCOVERY

A cyberattack on the water treatment plant in Florida led to the discovery of a watering hole attack that initially appeared to be aimed at water utilities according to "Probe Into Florida Water Plant Hack Led to Discovery"

RANSOMWARE ATTACKS ON INDUSTRIAL CONTROL SYSTEMS 2021

No one could easily disrupt day-to-day operations. But industrial control systems (ICS) now interface with a variety of networks and devices, presenting a host of industrial control systems security vulnerabilities according to "Ransomware attacks on industrial control systems (ICS) 2021."

Ransomware Threats for ICS are Growing

The Cybersecurity and Infrastructure Security Agency (CISA) released a fact sheet of ransomware threats in 2021 in relation to operational technology (O.T.).

These attacks are affecting IT networks and operational processes. Ransomware attacks could have severe real-world consequences, and some strategic steps can be taken to avoid and brace for ransomware attacks.

Industrial groups should assess reliance on IT infrastructure.

1. Leaders should develop resilience plans.
2. All players should understand how to execute an incident response plan.
3. Organizations should develop routine data backup procedures for both IT and OT networks.

Expert Cybersecurity Tips

Start with network segmentation and protect devices from zero day attacks through virtual patching and know who needs access and to what degree.

IoT has expanded and changed business, and as 5G with devices with embedded IoT capabilities appear, the problem is almost certain to worsen according to "How to Build a Resilient IoT Framework."

Resilient IoT Framework

IoT security frameworks are different from conventional IT. IoT devices lack a user interface and often attack directly on a device or to gain entry to an enterprise network. According to "How to Build a Resilient IoT Framework," attacks often involve a different dynamic than ransomware and other attacks, according to "How to Build a Resilient IoT Framework."

Seeking Protection

Seventy-four percent of firms surveyed by Ponemon Institute said their IoT risk management programs were failing to keep pace with the risks according to "How to Build a Resilient IoT Framework." The first step to building strong protection is knowing what IoT devices are running on the network, conducting an inventory to identify risk and potential failure points, and using specialized asset management and discovery solution according to "How to Build a Resilient IoT Framework." Visibility and control over the entire IoT landscape is an important starting point.

Playing IT Safe

For example, locking down cloud credentials used to reconfigure devices, ensuring that malware is up to date, and using is a holistic approach with review process as any enterprise application can build a strong security standard.

HOW STRONG ENCRYPTION IMPROVES IoT SECURITY

Billions of different devices introduce enormous security challenges, and locking down all these data flows is a formidable and potentially unrealistic proposition. It's difficult to patch flaws and vulnerabilities, and to replace older and less secure devices might not be practical or cost-effective short term, according to "How Strong Encryption Improves IoT Security."

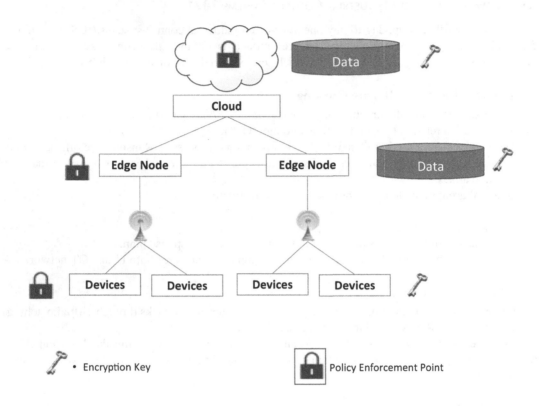

Steps for Security

For example, a gambling casino in the United Kingdom was hacked after cybercrooks entered the company's network through an Internet-connected thermometer in an aquarium and stole the customer database.

According to "How Strong Encryption Improves IoT Security," simple steps like applying patches on lots of devices can be difficult.

Real-world examples in using Advanced Encryption Standard (AES) technology show it can lock down various connected gadgets, and even credit cards and employee badges all use AES.

Protection Is Paramount

Consider multi-factor authentication (MFA) with a basic text message or a physical key or biometric authentication according to "How Strong Encryption Improves IoT Security."

As organizations venture into AI and machine learning, data security can be enhanced by the use of data tokens and data-anonymization techniques.

EDGE COMPUTING

Edge computing that brings calculation closer to data and can improve response times is an architecture rather than a specific technology according to "CloudFormed API":

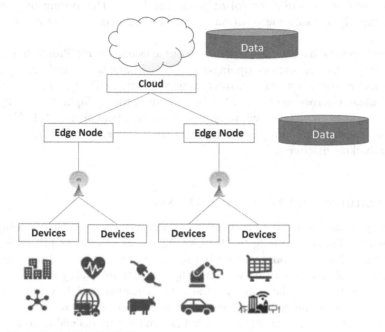

Source: Adapted from IoT ANALYTICS

The first industrial edge computing services that hosted applications such as dealer locators, shopping carts, real-time data aggregators, and ad insertion engines according to "Things That You Must Understand About Edge Computing."

PRIVACY AND SECURITY

The distributed nodes are connected through the Internet and thus require special encryption independent of the cloud. Keeping and processing data at the edge may increase privacy by minimizing the transmission of sensitive information to the cloud, and the ownership of collected data shifts from service providers to end-users according to "CloudFormed API."

ROBOTICS VS. IoT

Explaining and positioning of robotics, IoT, AI, and machine learning can be found in "Robotics vs IoT (Internet of Things) What's the Difference?"

Robotics entails the development of physical devices that undertake production action. The product is a robot, a device that handles tasks in manufacturing, medical, agricultural, and other industrial uses.

The main reason behind robotics is to develop machines that handle tasks that humans can't handle well over time. Mainly, these tasks include repetitive, boring, tedious, and accident-prone tasks. For example, robot assembly helps you to improve precision and consistency in production. To achieve its mission, the arms of a robot move in x, y, z, or circular directions according to "Robotics vs IoT (Internet of Things)."

AI AND ROBOTS

These are some application areas at MIT University:

1. Magnets could offer better control of prosthetic limbs. The system uses tiny magnetic beads to rapidly measure the position of muscles and relay that information to a bionic prosthesis.
2. An inflatable robotic hand gives amputees real-time tactile control. Prosthetics enables a wide range of daily activities, such as zipping a suitcase, shaking hands, and petting a cat.
3. Life in space: Preparing for an increasingly tangible reality by The Space Exploration Initiative supports research across and beyond MIT in two microgravity flights this spring.
4. They were tackling air pollution with autonomous drones. Alumni of the MIT New Engineering Education Transformation Program (NEET) worked together remotely from across the globe to design thinking machines.

TACKLING AIR POLLUTION WITH AUTONOMOUS DRONES

It was developing drones to address pandemic-related challenges to transport biological samples using autonomous vehicles according to "Developing drones to address pandemic-related challenges." Hovering 100 meters above a densely populated urban residential area, the drone takes a quiet breath. Its goal is singular: to systematically measure air quality across the metropolitan landscape, providing regular updates to a central communication module where it docks after its patrol, awaiting a new set of instructions. The central module integrates each new data point a small drone fleet provides, processing them against wind and traffic patterns and historical pollution hot spot information. Then the fleet is assigned new sampling waypoints and relaunched. Alumni of the MIT New Engineering Education Transformation Program (NEET) worked together remotely from across the globe to design thinking machines.

HOW COMPANIES USE ARTIFICIAL INTELLIGENCE IN ROBOTICS

Some companies were already using artificial intelligence in robotics in 2019 according to "A.I. Robots: How 19 Companies Use Artificial Intelligence in Robotics":

Boston Dynamics:
- AI can be used with sensor-based controls that prepare robots for a variety of environments and terrains according to "A.I. Robots: 19 Top Examples Of Artificial Intelligence."
Canvas Technology
- Drones that can be operated manually or autonomously (using technology like AI) to aid fire services, emergency response teams, and law enforcement enable gathering and reporting a wide array of information and data.
iRobot
- AI can be used in a robot vacuum that maps and adapts to its environment as it clears dirt and small debris from floors.
Miso Robotics
- AI can be used in kitchens reportedly decreases food waste and frees up time for human workers to prepare food or help customers.
Neurala
- AI can be used for boosting intelligence in cars, phones, drones and cameras, used by major organizations like NASA, DARPA, Motorola and NVIDIA.

Rethink Robotics
- AI can be used in collaborative robots that can work in the same environment as humans and automatically adjust the amount of force needed for a given task, creating safer environments and widening work capabilities.

SUMMARY

We have discussed IoT devices that are present in the critical electrical power grid, many mobile devices, and impacting our lives daily. When we also increasingly rely on IoT for our physical security in cars and medical devices is hard to upgrade with new security functions. Cloud security and edge computing can help us to control privacy and security to and from these devices since many of the devices, for example, in industrial control systems, are old and hard to upgrade with new security functions.

We will discuss this topic more in Volume II of this book.

BIBLIOGRAPHY

1. Tackling Air Pollution with Autonomous Drones, https://news.mit.edu/2021/tackling-air-pollution-with-autonomous-drones-0624
2. Robotics vs IoT, https://businessingmag.com/12667/equipping/robotics-vs-iot/
3. Robotics, https://news.mit.edu/topic/robotics
4. A.I. Robots: How 19 Companies Use Artificial Intelligence in Robotics, https://builtin.com/artificial-intelligence/robotics-ai-companies
5. Hackers Breached Colonial Pipeline with one Compromised Password, https://www.aljazeera.com/economy/2021/6/4/hackers-breached-colonial-pipeline-with-one-compromised-password
6. A Brief History of Blackouts in New York City, https://www.amny.com/news/blackouts-nyc-1-33881190/
7. Black Out In Ukraine: BlackEnergy in Power Grid Cyberattack, https://www.threathunting.se/2020/05/13/black-out-in-ukraine-blackenergy-in-power-grid-cyberattack/
8. Edge Computing, https://en.wikipedia.org/wiki/Edge_computing
9. Hamilton, Eric (27 December 2018). "What is Edge Computing: The Network Edge Explained". cloud wards.net, https://www.cloudwards.net/what-is-edge-computing/
10. Gartner. "2021 Strategic Roadmap for Edge Computing", https://www.gartner.com/doc/reprints?id=1-24JFAZOO&ct=201104&st=sb
11. Advantages of Edge Computing. Aron Brand. Medium.com. September 20, 2019, https://medium.com/@aronbrand/edge-computing-alexa-and-the-future-of-enterprise-it-51c13268a365
12. Liu, S., Liu, L., Tang, B., Wu, Wang, J., and Shi, W. "Edge Computing for Autonomous Driving: Opportunities and Challenges". *Proceedings of the IEEE*, 107: 8, 1697–1716. Retrieved 2021-05-26., https://ieeexplore.ieee.org/abstract/document/8744265
13. Yu, W.. et al. (2018). "A Survey on the Edge Computing for the Internet of Things". *IEEE Access*, 6, 6900–6919. https://ieeexplore.ieee.org/abstract/document/9403374
14. Gillis, Alexander (2021). "What is Internet of Things (IoT)?". IoT Agenda, https://internetofthingsagenda.techtarget.com/definition/Internet-of-Things-IoT
15. Brown, Eric (20 September 2016). "21 Open Source Projects for IoT". Linux.com, https://www.linux.com/NEWS/21-OPEN-SOURCE-PROJECTS-IOT/
16. "Internet of Things Global Standards Initiative". ITU. https://www.itu.int/en/ITU-T/gsi/iot/Pages/default.aspx
17. How to Build a Resilient IoT Framework, https://www.darkreading.com/edge-articles/how-to-build-a-resilient-iot-framework
18. Hendricks, Drew. "The Trouble with the Internet of Things". London Datastore. Greater London Authorit, https://data.london.gov.uk/blog/the-trouble-with-the-internet-of-things/
19. Laplante, Phillip A., Kassab, Mohamad, Laplante, Nancy L., and Voas, Jeffrey M. (2018). "Building Caring Healthcare Systems in the Internet of Things". *IEEE Systems Journal*, 12: 3, 3030–3037. Bibcode:2018ISysJ.12.3030L. doi:10.1109/JSYST.2017.2662602. ISSN 1932-8184. PMC 6506834. PMID 31080541.

20. "The "Only" Coke Machine on the Internet". Carnegie Mellon University. Retrieved 10 November 2014, https://www.cs.cmu.edu/~coke/history_long.txt
21. Internet of Things, https://en.wikipedia.org/wiki/Internet_of_things
22. Ransomware Attacks on Industrial Control Systems 2021, https://www.cybertalk.org/2021/06/15/ransomware-attacks-on-industrial-control-systems-2021/
23. "Internet of Things Done Wrong Stifles Innovation". InformationWeek, https://www.informationweek.com/executive-insights-and-innovation/internet-of-things-done-wrong-stifles-innovation
24. T-Mobile CEO Apologizes for Breach, https://thehill.com/policy/cybersecurity/569771-t-mobile-ceo-apologizes-for-breach-that-compromised-data-of-50-million
25. Probe Into Florida Water Plant Hack Led to Discovery, https://www.securityweek.com/probe-florida-water-plant-hack-led-discovery-watering-hole-attack
26. How to Build a Resilient IoT Framework, https://www.iotgearbox.com/post/how-to-build-a-resilient-iot-framework
27. How Strong Encryption Improves IoT Security, https://www.protegrity.com/protegrity-blog/how-strong-encryption-improves-iot-security
28. CloudFormed API, https://api.cfd/wiki/Edge_computing
29. Things That You Must Understand About Edge Computing – Sotech, https://sotech.co.id/things-that-you-must-understand-about-edge-computing/
30. Developing Drones to Address Pandemic-related Challenges …, https://news.mit.edu/2021/developing-drones-address-pandemic-related-challenges-scandinavia-0623
31. A.I. Robots: 19 Top Examples of Artificial Intelligence, https://builtin.com/artificial-intelligence/robotics-ai-companies
32. Robotics vs IoT (Internet of Things) What's the Difference?, https://businessingmag.com/12667/equipping/robotics-vs-iot/

17 Quantum Computing

INTRODUCTION

We will discuss quantum computing, its pros and cons, and how it may impact us over time. Cryptographic systems are often built on the premise that certain math problems are, computationally, very hard to solve, according to "The Future of Cryptography." Many of these problems, such as factoring certain large numbers, have been studied by mathematicians everywhere for decades to centuries. In fact, mathematicians often estimate the projected security of such systems by plotting the evolution in "running time" of the best-known attacks according to "The Future of Cryptography." These predictions work well, but only in the absence of major disruptions; new algorithms or technologies drastically improve the expected running time of attacks.

OPPORTUNITIES WITH QUANTUM COMPUTING

Homomorphic encryption and machine learning allow businesses to use sensitive data to fuel advanced analytics, machine learning, and AI—even as those initiatives migrate to cloud environments. Many of these problems have been studied for a long time. We will discuss opportunities and threats with current and future computers.

Quantum computing can speed up the training of ML models and be optimized to speed up some specific ML algorithms.

QUANTUM COMPUTING—THE PROS AND CONS

The figure illustrates expected quantum computing pros and cons over time:

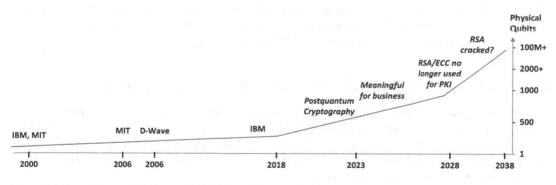

Source: Adopted from CBI Research, 2019 and Gartner, 2018

DOI: 10.1201/9781003189664-22

The figure is illustrating quantum computing and the pros (in gray) and cons (in white boxes):

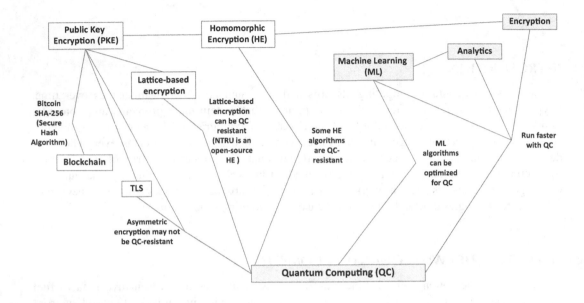

THREATS TO ENCRYPTION

Intel Xeon Computers

"Factoring of RSA-240, an RSA key that has 240 decimal digits and a size of 795 bits." The same team of researchers also computed a discrete logarithm of the same size. The previous records were the factoring in 2010 of an RSA-768 (which, despite its digit, is a smaller RSA key than the RSA-240, with 232 decimal digits and 768 bits) and the computation of a 768-bit prime discrete logarithm in 2016. The sum of the computation time for both of the new records is about 4,000 core-years using Intel Xeon Gold 6130 CPUs (running at 2.1 GHz) as a reference according to "New crypto-cracking record reached." The short-term advice is to move to at least 2048-bit RSA, Diffie-Hellman, or DSA keys as of several years ago, which would keep you safe from improvements in Intel processors and similar. For the short term, use Curve25519 whenever you can; it's very fast, unaffiliated with NIST. It's about equivalent to 128-bit AES encryption.

QUANTUM COMPUTERS CAN BREAK BLOCKCHAIN AND PUBLIC-KEY CRYPTOGRAPHY

One of the biggest challenges surrounding digital technology is securing systems and data. For decades, computer scientists have developed increasingly sophisticated algorithms designed to encrypt data and protect it through frameworks like public-key cryptography (PKE), also known as asymmetric cryptography. Today, these frameworks function relatively well. Billions of transactions and interactions use these algorithms every day.

As quantum computers advance and creep into the mainstream, they introduce a level of computing power that changes the table stakes. While there are many potential benefits, a major disadvantage is the ability to crack today's public-key cryptography, including widely used RSA (Rivest–Shamir–Adleman) and Diffie-Hellman frameworks. This would impact everything from routers and virtual private networks (VPN) to the ability to verify digital signatures according to "Stronger Crypto Algorithms are on the Horizon."

In 2016, the US National Security Agency (NSA) issued an alert and recommended that organizations begin looking at ways to switch to more advanced cryptography. A year later, the US National Institute of Standards and Technology (NIST) began soliciting new and more advanced algorithms that could withstand cracking by quantum computers and become a standard.

Quantum computers lack the processing power to succeed in a brute force assault on classical cryptography algorithms, according to "Preserving Privacy With New Technologies." However, once these machines hit a threshold of approximately 10 million physical qubits within a few years, they will possess this power. The risk is palpable for businesses, universities, the government, and more.

Quantum Computers Can Break Blockchain Security

"Resilience is one of the main motivations for companies to use blockchain technology," although this property may not be as inherent as some believe. Blockchain relies on internet connectivity and PKI based on symmetric encryption like the RSA algorithm. The blockchain framework relies on the security of the cryptographic processes underlying it. Without trusted hash functions and public-key signatures, there are no blockchains. Quantum computers deemed impossible with a classical computer threaten several of the cryptographic primitives used in blockchains. Scalable quantum computers, which are necessary to attack the mathematical problems behind the cryptographic primitives, are not yet available. Small-scale quantum computers have already been built by several companies and world governments. Some are even accessible on the internet and can be used to test quantum algorithms. Quantum supremacy, which describes the point when quantum computers explicitly outperform classical ones, has either been attained or is on the verge of realization. It is therefore of utmost importance to understand the threat posed to blockchains and to outline possible solutions.

POST-QUANTUM CRYPTOGRAPHY

The NIST in the United States launched an international competition to select cryptographic systems for the future, and "these are some of the main proposals for post-quantum systems studied for a decade or more, according to "The Future of Cryptography."

NIST defined security levels for some algorithms

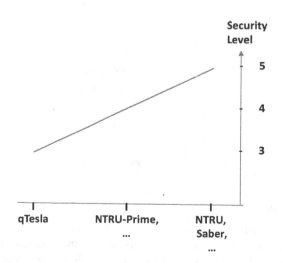

Source: Adopted from NIST

Considerations for different types of algorithms:

Post-quantum cryptography

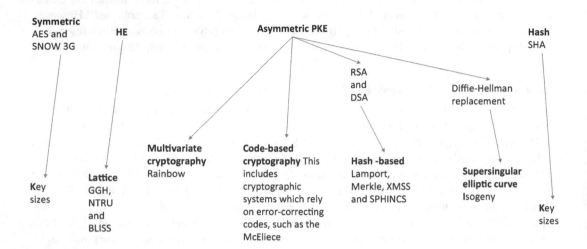

LATTICE-BASED SYSTEMS BASED ON THE HARDNESS OF FINDING SHORT VECTORS IN LATTICES

Lattice-based systems can be based on regularly spaced grids of lattices in thousands of dimensions according to "The future of cryptography." Lattices are typically described as a set of vectors (objects with both a magnitude and direction) that generate the whole lattice (basis vectors). However, it can be exponentially hard to find a short combination of those basis vectors.

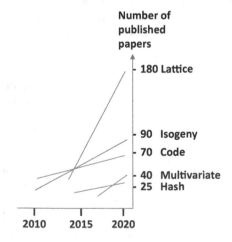

QUANTUM-RESILIENT ALGORITHMS

At present, NIST has narrowed the number of next-generation algorithms, and a group of researchers and computer scientists involved with the project continue to test, refine, and update the algorithms to balance speed and security requirements. They have been studying a number of algorithms that can be quantum-resistant, and it's a good idea to also upgrade older systems like AES to 256-bit keys in order to maximize data protection. Within the next year or two, NIST is expected to finalize new standards. This won't encompass all quantum-resistant algorithms in the future—others may develop algorithms outside the standard—but it's safe to say that this set of algorithms will be widely used in industry and government according to "Stronger Crypto Algorithms are on the Horizon."

Symmetric-Key Cryptography Isn't as Susceptible

Fortunately, symmetric-key cryptography (which relies on private keys) isn't as susceptible to being cracked by quantum computing, and it isn't considered at risk for now. Of course, it's impossible to rely on symmetric crypto to handle many of the interactions and transactions that take place in today's computing environment. So, once quantum-safe algorithms appear, it's wise to migrate to them as soon as possible.

Post-Quantum Cryptography Research

It is mostly focused on six different approaches according to "Post-quantum cryptography."

1. **Lattice-based cryptography** This approach includes cryptographic systems such as learning with errors, ring learning with errors (ring-LWE*), ring learning with errors key exchange, ring learning with errors signature, and the older NTRU or GGH encryption schemes, and the newer NTRU signature and BLISS signatures.
2. **Multivariate cryptography** This includes cryptographic systems such as the Rainbow (Unbalanced Oil and Vinegar) scheme, which is based on the difficulty of solving systems of multivariate equations.
3. **Hash-based cryptography** This includes cryptographic systems such as Lamport signatures and the Merkle signature scheme, and the newer XMSS and SPHINCS schemes.
4. **Code-based cryptography** includes cryptographic systems that rely on error-correcting codes, such as the McEliece and Niederreiter encryption algorithms and the related Courtois, Finiasz, and Sendrier Signature scheme.
5. **Supersingular elliptic curve isogeny cryptography** This cryptographic system relies on the properties of supersingular elliptic curves and supersingular isogeny graphs to create a Diffie-Hellman replacement with forwarding secrecy.
6. **Symmetric key quantum resistance** Provided one uses sufficiently large key sizes, the symmetric key cryptographic systems like AES and SNOW 3G are already resistant to attack by a quantum computer.

HOMOMORPHIC ENCRYPTION AND QUANTUM COMPUTING

"New Homomorphic Encryption algorithms can be secure from Quantum Computer-Based Attacks, and machine-learning algorithm can be optimized for Quantum Computers." Homomorphic encryption, which allows computations on encrypted data, and machine learning are growing in popularity. We will review how homomorphic encryption and quantum computing can be applied to provide privacy and security-sensitive data and confidential machine learning models in vulnerable environments, like different cloud models.

The myriad of regulations already enacted, compounded by the many others that are sure to come, only stresses the need for organizations to protect the data. According to "Privacy-Preserving Analytics and Secure Multiparty," data must move through an enterprise's many cloud-based databases and applications.

The most critical data types in driving innovation—with advanced analytics, machine learning, and AI—are those deemed most sensitive and must be safeguarded. You can shield machine learning models and data in trusted execution environments. This complements encryption of the machine learning models and data for outsourced environments, like different cloud models.

EXAMPLE OF A CRYPTOGRAPHY ROADMAP

The US State Department and several other US government agencies mandated the move from 128-bit AES to 256-bit AES and the cessation of certain secure hashes associated with 256-bit AES a few years back according to "New crypto-cracking record reached." The figure is an example of a cryptography roadmap for QC:

The Future of Cryptography		
Time Frame	Area	Comment
Short	Upgrade to ACE, preferably AES-256 with strong random seed	Immediate-medium step
	Use SHA-512 for hashing	Immediate step
	Use stateful hash-based signatures for signing	Immediate review
	Use hybrid cryptography to protect against both weakness in RSA/ECC and potential weakness in post-quantum algorithms	Immediate steps
Medium	Lattice based algorithms	Tools study and integration plan
	Homomorphic encryption	Tools and partner integration
	Operation on encrypted data	Integration of protocols
	Secure Multi Party Computing (SMPC)	Integration of protocols
	2022 NIST to complete review of quantum safe algorithms	Tools integration
	2022 NIST standards to be released	Tools integration
Long	2024 industry standards based on NIST algorithms from NIST standards	Tools integration
	Analytics and machine learning	ML algorithms optimized for quantum processors
	Full industry adaption 2019+	Tools integration

THE ROAD TO RANDOMNESS

Quantum computers and other strong computers can break algorithms and patterns in encrypted data. We can instead use random numbers to secure sensitive data. Random numbers are not based on an algorithm or pattern that a computer can break.

US NIST RANDOMNESS TEST

Random numbers should be validated, for example, by the NIST statistical test suite for random numbers. NIST SP 800-22 offers 15 statistical tests. These tests assess the presence of a pattern which, if detected, would indicate that the sequence is non-random. The focus is the proportion of zeroes and ones for the entire sequence. The purpose of this test is to determine whether the number of ones and zeros in a sequence is approximately the same as would be expected for a truly random sequence according to "Random Bit Generation." The test suite includes Test For Frequency Within A Block, Runs Test, Test For The Longest Run Of Ones In A Block, Random Binary Matrix Rank Test, Discrete Fourier Transform (Spectral) Test, Non-Overlapping (Aperiodic) Template Matching Test, Overlapping (Periodic) Template Matching Test, Maurer's Universal Statistical Test, Linear Complexity Test, Serial Test, Approximate Entropy Test, Cumulative Sum (Cusum) Test, Random Excursions Test, and Random Excursions Variant Test.

SUMMARY

We discussed quantum computing, its pros and cons, and how it may impact us over time in secure multiparty computation (SMPC), and the threat and promise of quantum computers pushing the field to develop post-quantum cryptographic systems with new algorithms or technologies that drastically improve the expected running time of attacks.

We will talk more about this topic in Volume II of this book.

BIBLIOGRAPHY

1. Amazon, IBM and Microsoft Race to Bring Global Access to Quantum Computing, https://www.cnet.com/news/amazon-ibm-and-microsoft-race-to-bring-global-access-to-quantum-computing/
2. Mattsson, U. New technologies for data protection that arm innovative businesses to win, Apr 21, 2021, ISACA SF, https://engage.isaca.org/sanfranciscochapter/events/eventdescription?CalendarEventKey=7fc789f0-0538-4887-a6e0-8668bcdc68c1&CommunityKey=f510bd50-4fdc-46b1-a329-d6ce8a64bae7&Home=%2Fcommunities%2Fcommunity-home%2Frecent-community-events
3. Mattsson, U. Homomorphic Encryption Will Take on the Challenge of A.I., RSA Conference, February 25, 2021, https://www.rsaconference.com/Library/blog/Homomorphic%20Encryption%20Will%20Take%20on%20the%20Challenge%20of%20AI
4. NIST SP 800-22, https://github.com/greendow/A-variant-of-NIST-SP-800-22-test-suit#:~:text=A%20set%20of%20statistical%20tests%20for%20randomness%20is,Suit%20is%20a%20software%20tool%20released%20by%20NIST
5. Goodin, D. New crypto-cracking record reached, with less help than usual from Moore's Law 795-bit factoring and discrete logarithms achieved using more efficient algorithms, 12/3/2019. Arstechnica, https://arstechnica.com/information-technology/2019/12/new-crypto-cracking-record-reached-with-less-help-than-usual-from-moores-law/
6. The National Academies Press, Decrypting the Encryption Debate: A Framework for Decision Makers, 2018, Chapter: 2 Encryption and Its Applications, https://www.nap.edu/read/25010/chapter/4
7. IBM Quantum, Quantum Computing: Tomorrow's computing today, 2021, IBM Quantum, https://www.ibm.com/quantum-computing/?p1=Search&p4=43700050386405608&p5=b&gclsrc=aw.ds&gclid=EAIaIQobChMIuLe0jcOR8AlVhrLICh1lCQZ0EAAYASAAEgI2avD_BwE
8. NIST, NIST Kicks off Effort to Defend Encrypted Data from Quantum Computer Threat, April 28, 2016, NIST, https://www.nist.gov/news-events/news/2016/04/nist-kicks-effort-defend-encrypted-data-quantum-computer-threat
9. The Future of Cryptography, https://qeprize.org/news/the-future-of-cryptography/
10. Quantum Computing: Progress and Prospects, Quantum Computing's Implications for Cryptography, Quantum Computing: Progress and Prospects, 2019, Chapter: 4 Quantum Computing NAP, https://www.nap.edu/read/25196/chapter/6
11. De Gruyter, Combining a Quantum Random Number Generator and Quantum-Resistant Algorithms into the GnuGPG Open-source Software, October 22, 2019, Degruyter, https://www.degruyter.com/document/doi/10.1515/aot-2020-0021/html#:~:text=Quantum%20resistant%20cryptography%20mostly%20focuses,curve%20isogeny%20and%20symmetric%20key
12. NIST Test, Andrew Rukhin, A Statistical Test Suite for Random and Pseudorandom Number Generators for Cryptographic Applications, 2010, NIST, https://nvlpubs.nist.gov/nistpubs/Legacy/SP/nistspecialpublication800-22r1a.pdf
13. New Crypto-cracking Record Reached, https://arstechnica.com/information-technology/2019/12/new-crypto-cracking-record-reached-with-less-help-than-usual-from-moores-law/
14. Stronger Crypto Algorithms are on the Horizon, https://www.protegrity.com/protegrity-blog/stronger-crypto-algorithms-are-on-the-horizon
15. Post-quantum Cryptography, http://theinfolist.com/php/SummaryGet.php?FindGo=Post-quantum_cryptography
16. Random Bit Generation | CSRC, https://csrc.nist.gov/Projects/Random-Bit-Generation/Documentation-and-Software/Guide-to-the-Statistical-Tests
17. "Privacy-Preserving Analytics and Secure Multiparty", https://engage.isaca.org/swedenchapter/events/eventdescription?CalendarEventKey=dabd556d-0105-4cd9-af8a-55fbf9cbd5c1&CommunityKey=6592afac-ec0b-41ca-b0c4-1e2dbb4d9da3&Home=%2fcommunities%2fcommunity-home%2frecent-community-events

18 Summary

One of the most gratifying outcomes of writing this book is the dialog with people about their view of data privacy and security. I reconnected with people I worked with in the past, and they also introduced me to new people.

We have found that many of life's most useful insights are often quite simple. Good security is also based on simple approaches.

We've helped many clients build data privacy and security into their core business systems throughout the years. Surprisingly, our discoveries have little to do with technical tools. But it has everything to do with how you communicate to find the balance between privacy, security, and compliance that is right for your Business.

A RESPONSIBLE APPROACH TO DATA PRIVACY AND SECURITY

A COMMON LANGUAGE AND FRAMEWORK CAN ENABLE DIALOG

A common language can be based on a risk management framework that can communicate in a common language that is understandable for the different teams that are involved:

A Responsible Approach to Data Assets

Opportunity — Threats — Regulations

Liability — Risk — Cost

Policies — Security — Privacy

A Common Language and Framework can Enable Dialog

Board of Directors — C-level — Teams

FINDING THE RIGHT BALANCE

Risks, Breaches, Regulations, and Opportunities

A common language can enable the dialog for finding the right balance between the two sides:

1. Risks with breaches and compliance to regulations.
2. Finding new and business opportunities.

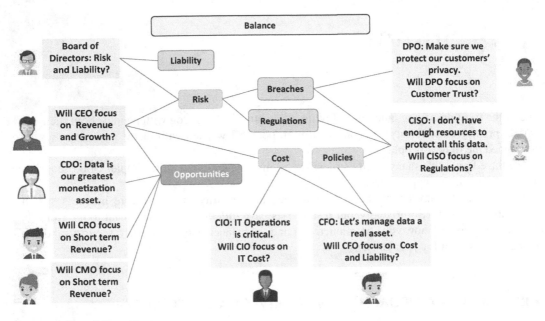

Source: Adapted from Gartner

Risk Management and Solutions

We discussed frameworks for risk management and software development from NIST and other organizations earlier in this book. We also discussed security threats, privacy regulations, implementation aspects, and best practices:

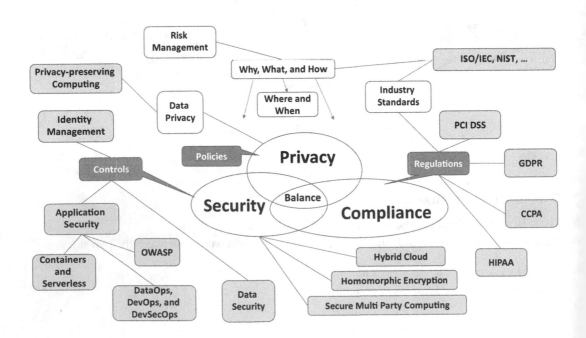

The Roadmap

Start Small with Easy Data Protection Techniques

One implementation approach is to start small with easy data protection techniques for the most urgent use cases and data in your organization:

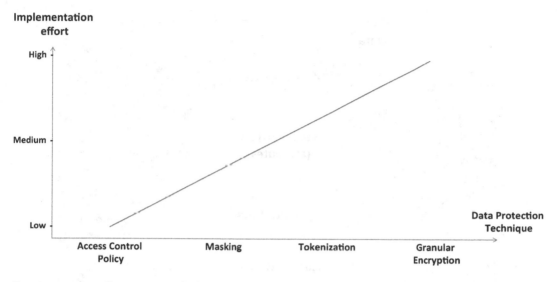

Continuous data discovery can find your evolving data assets across different environments.

Protection That Balances Different Needs

Continue the implementation with granular data protection techniques for the most sensitive data in your organization.

Your data will be protected in a way that provides a balance between different requirements of the organization and before it flows into cloud and mobile, and other distributed environments:

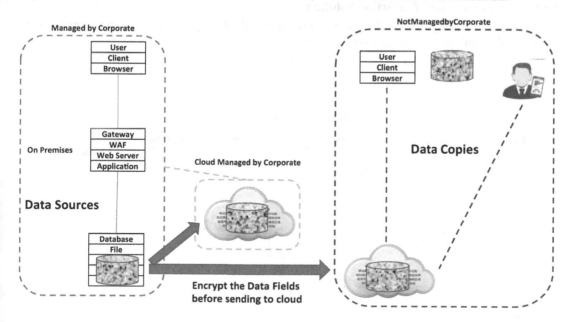

Your sensitive data will be protected from attacks across different environments.

Your analytics databases may be protected by a variety of methods for different use cases and types of data:

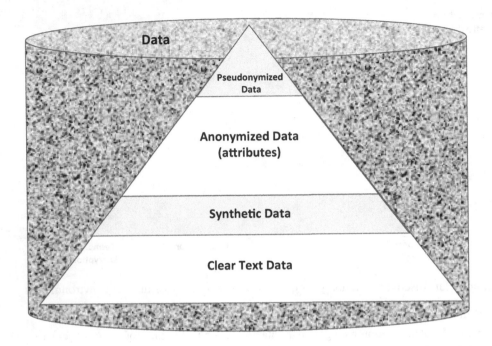

Finding the Right Data Protection Solution

Finding the right data protection for different use cases and data in your organization requires a good understanding of the problem that you want to solve:

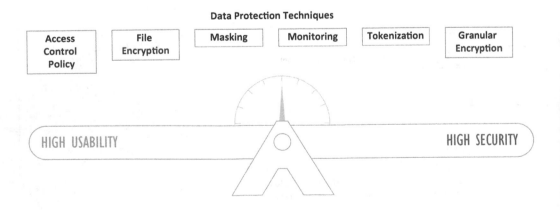

We discussed data protection techniques for different use cases and data in the previous chapters of this book.

BARRIERS TO ESTABLISHING EFFECTIVE DEFENSES

Why are we not more secure? We have the tools, and budget is not a significant issue. Still, awareness among employees and lack of skills are the top barriers to establishing effective defenses, according to a study by (ISC)[2] in 2021:

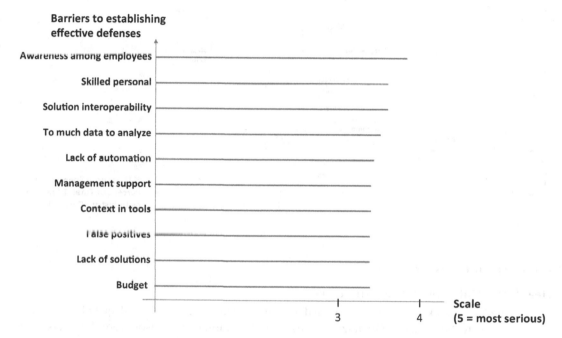

Source: Adapted from (ISC)2

THE COST OF DOING BUSINESS

There is a cost of doing business. For example, the card brands balance easy consumer experience with the cost of security solutions and payment fraud.

Shoplifting and organized retail crime may be higher than computer crime.

The NRSS indicates that the average dollar loss per shoplifting incident was reported as $559 according to "Shedding Light on Retail Theft Statistics."

SECURITY SPENDING AND BREACHES

Is there a correlation between the number of breaches, data leaks, and security spending budget?

DATA LEAKS BY SECURITY SPENDING BUDGET

The number of data leaks compared to security spending budget. Manufacturing, retail, technology (software and internet services), and healthcare are in the upper part:

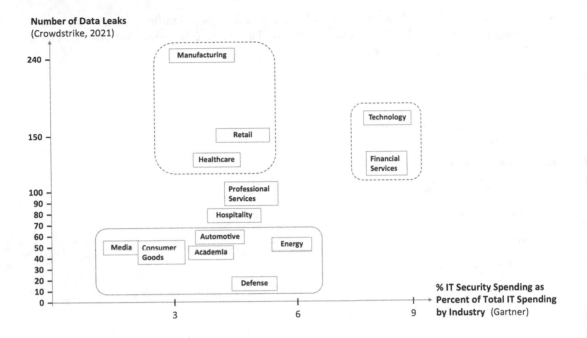

DATA BREACH COSTS INCREASED

Healthcare Data Breach Costs Increased

The healthcare sector keeps very sensitive and private information. Is that data adequately protected?

According to "Healthcare Organizations Are the Top Target for Ransomware Attackers," the healthcare sector was the most targeted vertical for ransomware in 2020. Ransomware attacks seen in the first half of 2021 show a 102% increase from 2020's numbers according to "Ransomware Keeps Healthcare in Crosshairs."

Healthcare data breach costs increased from an average total cost of $7.13 million in 2020 to $9.23 million in 2021, a 29.5% increase. More investments in healthcare data protection can hopefully lower the loss of sensitive data.

The Cost of a Data Breach Is a 10% Rise

The cost of a data breach in 2021 is US$ 4.24 million. This is a 10% rise from the average cost in 2019, which was $3.86 million according to "What is the Cost of a Data Breach in 2021?" The $180 per record cost of a personally identifiable information breach is higher than payment card data.

Awareness Training May Not Be Enough

The attacker only needs to be successful once, but the defenders need to be successful 100% of the time to prevent breaches. Defenders will need a multilayered security approach to be successful and prevent or react to breaches. Each layer can add to the probability to catch an attacker.

Protect Your Data from Ransomware

In many cases, the attack's goal isn't just to encrypt data according to "Detect, Protect, Recover: How Modern Backup Applications Can Protect You From Ransomware."

VOLUME II OF THIS BOOK

I'd like to introduce Volume II of this book.

Volume II will be on emerging tech primarily and include these topics:

Ransomware and other attacks on data
Blockchain and Web3
Cloud-based security services
Quantum computing
Data catalogs and Data provenance
Security assessments and penetration testing
Solutions for small and medium-size businesses
Applications in the cloud
Migration to cloud
Databases in the cloud
Performance overhead
The flow of data
AI and ML, and Metaverse
Privacy and cost
Data protection, strategies, and innovation
Skills, roles, and teams
Dynamic masking, static data masking, and synthetic data
Data privacy protection in healthcare with use cases
Unicode
How to combine security controls
Innovation and vendors
People, process, and technology
Podcasts

BIBLIOGRAPHY

1. Shedding Light on Retail Theft Statistics, https://losspreventionmedia.com/shedding-light-on-retail-theft-statistics/
2. What is the Cost of a Data Breach in 2021? | UpGuard, https://www.upguard.com/blog/cost-of-data-breach
3. Healthcare Organizations Are the Top Target for Ransomware Attackers, https://www.paloaltonetworks.com/blog/2021/08/healthcare-organizations-are-the-top-target/
4. Highlights from the 2021 Unit 42 Ransomware Threat Report, https://unit42.paloaltonetworks.com/ransomware-threat-report-highlights/
5. Ransomware Keeps Healthcare in Crosshairs, https://healthitsecurity.com/news/ransomware-attacks-surge-102-in-2021-as-triple-extortion-emerges
6. Detect, Protect, Recover: How Modern Backup Applications Can Protect You From Ransomware, https://www.gartner.com/doc/reprints?id=1-258HHK51&ct=210217&st=sb

Appendix A: Standards and Regulations

INTRODUCTION

People demand protection of their privacy from lawmakers worldwide, and lawmakers are preparing to meet this demand. People require protection of their privacy from lawmakers worldwide, and lawmakers are preparing to meet this demand.

New technology is helping with more cost-effective and application transparent approaches for compliance to data privacy laws. It's been an exciting journey from where I started in 1994, initially developing data privacy technology based on privacy laws in Sweden and Germany.

We will discuss some major standards and regulations that are driving the need for more data privacy technologies.

MAJOR DATA PRIVACY REGULATIONS

In addition to legal ramifications and reputational damage, breaching data privacy regulations like GDPR can lead to hefty fines—as seen in the recent settlement with WhatsApp.

Companies need to recognize that with such large volumes of consumer data comes great responsibility to uphold privacy. To increase customer trust, leaders need to build a holistic and adapt the privacy program and be more proactive instead of responding to each challenge from different restrictions. California's Consumer Privacy Act's (CCPA) impact is expected to be global, given California's fifth-largest global economy. The New York Privacy Act was introduced in 2019 and is more expansive than CCPA, providing consumers with even greater control over their personal information while at the same time being much more demanding for businesses to comply with. Let's look at the global situation. Year after year, security, risk, and privacy professionals told us that keeping up with evolving privacy requirements is one of their top challenges according to "GDPR vs. CCPA":

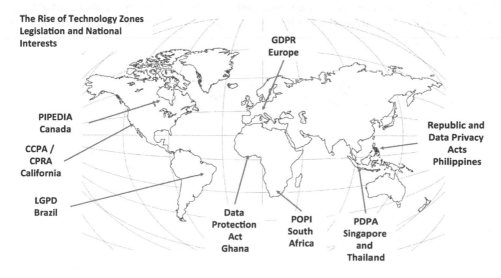

Source: Adapted from Gartner

By 2023, 65% of the world's population will have their personal information covered on the modern privacy regulations, and that is up from 10% today, according to Gartner, since the introduction of GDPR countries like Argentina, Australia, Brazil, Egypt, India and Indonesia, Japan, Kenya, Mexico, Nigeria, Panama, and Singapore, and Thailand has followed. Brazil is passing a comprehensive data protection regulation similar to GDPR. In 1970, Germany passed the first national data protection law, the first data protection law in the world. Sweden's Data Act is a national data protection law that went into effect in 1974. India is passing a comprehensive data protection bill that includes GDPR-like requirements, and Japan implements changes to domestic legislation to strengthen privacy protections in the country.

In March 2020, when the world realized the threat of the pandemic, many believed that privacy would inevitably fall to the bottom of the list of priorities for companies and consumers alike. A year later, we know that didn't happen. Consider that privacy budgets have grown, and in some cases doubled, in 2020 according to "Navigate The 2021 Privacy Landscape With This Global ….":

1. "Companies collected and processed an unprecedented volume of sensitive, personal data."
2. Digital engagement hinged on data. "Digital engagement became the key engagement strategy while consumers were locked in their homes." They were yet designing and delivering superior digital experiences hinged on businesses' ability to collect and process consumer data, such as biometrics, financial data, and behavioral data.
3. Remote working created opportunities and risks. Remote work opened up new opportunities and created new risks. Employers now have access to a worldwide pool of talent. The physical location of a new employee is less important than her skills.

Data and Security Governance (DSG) Converge

According to Gartner, by 2022, more than 100 million organizations will have appointed a privacy officer or a data protection officer (DPO). The increase in regulations will lead organizations to hire capable and powerful senior-level privacy officers to deliver compliance and higher customer satisfaction.

The Evolution of Privacy Regulation Continues at an Aggressive Rate

Privacy regulations are expanding with increased breadth spreading across different geographies and the depth with more types of data covered and additional rules. For example, CCPA covers identity (PI—Personal Information) of a household and not only an individual (PII—Personally Identifiable Information):

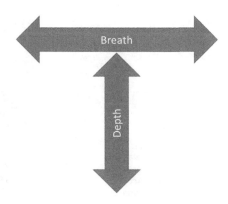

LEGAL AND REGULATORY RISKS ARE EXPLODING

For more than 60 years, regions worldwide have recently enacted or proposed post-modern privacy data protection laws. Across North America, Latin America, and APAC, we see different regulations in the areas of information security, health privacy, financial privacy, education, and more. According to Gartner, already in 2019, different regions enacted the following number of regulations:

Category	North America	Latin America	EMEA	Asia Pacific	Total
Data Protection		1	4	2	7
GDPR			9		9
Security	9		1	3	13
Healthcare	4		2		6
Financial	5				5
Education	3				3
Breach	11	1			12
Privacy	3	1		1	5
Other	8	1	9	2	20
Total	43	4	25	8	80

HOW MANY PRIVACY LAWS ARE YOU COMPLYING WITH?

Organizations are juggling several different regulations to be compliant with. A lot of these organizations are juggling between two and five different regulations.

US-based organizations are juggling these numbers of regulations:

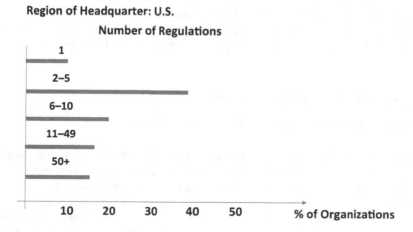

Source: Adapted from IAPP

Europe-based organizations are juggling these numbers of regulations:

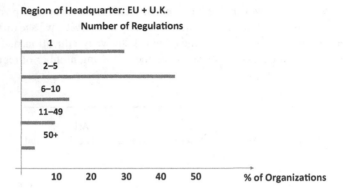

Source: Adapted from IAPP

Summary of all organizations and numbers of regulations:

Source: Adapted from IAPP

This is a study from IAPP, with 47% of the organizations headquartered in the United States, 24% European headquartered, and 13% are United Kingdom based.

One approach that some organizations may take would be to look at the most restrictive regulations in the regions they operate and then implement the plan on how to comply with those standards as a baseline.

Example Rules for a US-Based Organization

Example of basic rules for a financial industry (FI) organization:

- The notion of a "right to privacy" varies across jurisdictions. Therefore, FIs should be aware that they may hold PII and FI about individuals and organizations who reside in places with stronger protection than those afforded to residents of the country or state where the FI has its operations.
- This is a rapidly evolving field. FIs should have a "legal and regulatory watch" function, probably under the legal department or the Chief Data Officer (if there is one) to monitor the evolution of applicable laws and regulations, including GDPR in the European Union, CPRA in California, PIPEDA in Canada, and many more, if they hold accounts for residents of any of those geographical entities.

- All data held by an FI that poses potential privacy issues should be identified and rated for the severity of its potential loss or misuse.
- The adoption of cloud services, and migration between such services, should include a risk assessment about the potential violation of privacy laws, regulations, and customer expectations (the latter because adverse publicity can be as damaging to the FIs business as regulatory or legal penalties).
- FIs should consider encryption, de-identification, or obfuscation techniques for data placed in the cloud to render any exfiltrated data useless for identifying customers and their assets.
- FIs should be aware of the potential costs of data breaches, and if appropriate (as determined by a risk assessment), buy cyber insurance to cover those costs; in particular, parametric insurance should be considered as a way to recover costs without having to debate or prove the actual financial loss, as is required by traditional indemnity insurance policies.

PERSONAL DATA

EUROPEAN UNION

European Union defines the following personal data are considered "sensitive" and are subject to specific processing conditions:

1. personal data revealing beliefs;
2. trade-union membership;
3. genetic data, biometric data processed solely to identify a human being;
4. health-related data;
5. data concerning a person's sex life or sexual orientation.

CALIFORNIA CONSUMER PRIVACY ACT DEFINES PERSONAL INFORMATION

In general, the CCPA defines personal information broadly to include information that can identify, relate to, describe, be associated with, or be reasonably capable of associated with a particular consumer or household according to "Privacy Policy – SignalFire."

GDPR

General Data Protection Regulation (EU) 2016/679 (GDPR) is a regulation in EU law on data protection and privacy in the European Union (EU) and the European Economic Area (EEA). It also addresses the transfer of personal data outside the EU and EEA areas. GDPR was put in effect in May 2018, and the original intention of GDPR was to introduce better control of personal data protection and privacy. Hence, you have control over the ownership of data. You can control the sharing, for what purpose, and other things that are becoming more and more important privacy aspects. It's about integrity that data is kept up today that you have the right to have the data erased. For example, controlling the sharing of the data is the same type of principle that we saw early on in Sweden, Germany, Austria, other countries in Europe. And, as we saw earlier, these laws were implemented and enforced much earlier.

EUROPEAN COUNTRIES

Article 99 outlines the protection requirements.

Failure to Comply and What Are the Consequences?

Companies are liable for a fine of up to four percent (4%) of their global turnover with a maximum fine of ~ USD 25 million. This is for non-compliance with no data breach! We have seen these fines are increasing. Article 5 and GDPR highlight a couple of important aspects.

GDPR Security Requirements Framework

IBM published a framework that helps us comply. Hence, they point to the first step to find what you have to discover your data assets and then ensure that you have security built into your applications built into your data stores by using, for example, encryption and localization.

Data Flow Mapping Under GDPR

Organizations need to look at how the data was captured, who is accountable for it, where it is located, and who has access.

- If there is not already a documented workflow in place in your organization, it can be worthwhile for a team to be sent out to identify how the data is being gathered.
- This will enable you to see how your data flow is different from reality and what needs to be done.

Finding the data is critical. This is an example from BigID that helps you find your data and data flow by using machine learning to make that easier:

GDPR under "Schrems II"

The cloud hosting of data can violate the provisions of the GDPR, considering the risk of access requests by authorities. Several court orders suspended all transfers of personal data to the United States and other third countries since the companies did not implement supplementary measures to provide adequate protection for the data.

- We will discuss solutions hosted by United States cloud hosting providers that were approved by the court to be sufficient to protect data under the EU GDPR.
- We will discuss how to select and apply adequate protection for the data that can satisfy the requirements for cross-border data transfer.

Encrypt Data and Hold Keys by Third Party Allows Cross-Border Transfer under GDPR

On March 12, 2021, the Conseil d'Etat—France's highest administrative court—ruled that personal data on a platform used to book COVID-19 vaccinations, managed by Doctolib and hosted by Amazon Web Services, was sufficiently protected under the EU General Data Protection Regulation because sufficient legal and technical safeguards were put in place in case of an access request from US authorities according to "Encrypt data and hold keys allows Cross Border transfer under GDPR."

BACKGROUND

The hosting of health data by a company bound by US law was incompatible with the GDPR under "Schrems II" and violated the provisions of the GDPR, due to, on the one hand, the possibility of a transfer to the United States of the data collected by Doctolib through its processor, and on the other hand, even in the absence of data transfer, to the risk of access requests by US authorities to the processor, AWS. AWS Sarl is a Luxembourg registered company according to "Encrypt data and holds keys allows Cross Border transfer under GDPR."

The level of protection offered was sufficient due to the many safeguards

The court noted to host its data, Doctolib uses the services of the Luxemburg company AWS Sarl, the data is hosted in data centers located in France and in Germany, and the contract concluded between Doctolib, and AWS Sarl does not provide for the transfer of data to the United States. However, because it is a company's subsidiary under US law, the court considered AWS Sarl in Luxemburg may be subject to access requests by US authorities in the framework of US monitoring programs based on Article 702 of the Foreign Intelligence Surveillance Act or Executive Order 12333.

- Legal safeguards: AWS Sarl guarantees in its contract with Doctolib, a French company, that it will challenge any general access request from a public authority.
- Technical safeguards: Technically, the data hosted by AWS Sarl is encrypted. The key is held by a trusted third party in France, not by AWS.
- Other guarantees are taken: No health data. The data hosted relates only to the identification of individuals to make appointments. Data is deleted after three months.

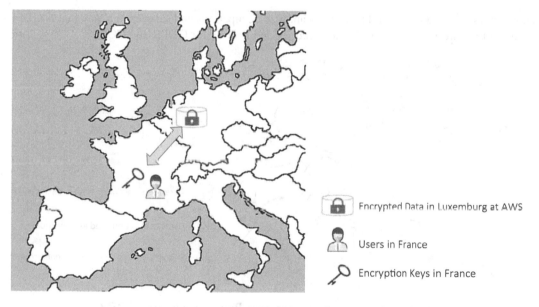

Encrypted Data in Luxemburg at AWS

Users in France

Encryption Keys in France

Companies should consider implementing "additional safeguards" for the transfer of personal data.

EXAMPLE OF INSUFFICIENT PROTECTION OF DATA

Cloudflare is Insufficient to Protect the Data

In April 2021, the Portuguese DPA ordered a public authority to suspend all transfers of personal data to the United States and other third countries. Portugal's National Institute of Statistics (INE) gathers data from Portuguese residents and transfers it to Cloudflare in the United States. Cloudflare was insufficient to protect the data (which included religious and health data), and the parties did not implement any supplementary measures to provide adequate protection for the data. They need to suspend the transfer of data to the United States or any other third country without first establishing adequate protection for the data according to "Encrypt data and hold keys allows Cross Border transfer under GDPR."

International Bank Secures Cross-Border Data

To streamline operations and improve analytical capabilities, a major international bank chose tokenization to remain compliant with data privacy regulations when they consolidated all European operational data from various European bank entities to their Teradata enterprise data warehouse (EDW) at their headquarters:

- Consistently secure the large amount and variety of personally identifiable information (PII) of customers—including names, addresses, phone, email, policy, and account numbers— across multiple systems, end-to-end from the geographically distributed bank entities back to headquarters, where it would be consolidated.
- Protect existing data within all systems.
- Maintain compliance with EU cross-border data protection laws, including the Federal Act concerning the Protection of Personal Data in Austria (Datenschutzgesetz 2000 – DSG 2000) and the Federal Protection Act in Germany (Bundesdatenschutzgesetz), which require that access to Austrian and German customer data at headquarters be restricted to only users in each respective country.

This depersonalized data could be used to analyze occupations and salaries in a way that is GDPR-compliant according to "Practical Data Security and Privacy for GDPR and CCPA":

Tokenized/encrypted data in each country

User access controlled in each country

Encryption keys controlled in each country

GUIDELINES ON THE CONCEPTS OF CONTROLLER AND PROCESSOR IN THE GDPR

"The concepts of the controller, joint controller and processor play a crucial role in the application of the General Data Protection Regulation 2016/679 (GDPR) since they determine who shall be responsible for compliance with different data protection rules," and how data subjects can exercise their rights in practice according to "Guidelines 07/2020 on the concepts of the controller."

Controller

In principle, there is no limitation as to the type of entity that may assume the role of a controller. Still, in practice, it is usually the organization as such and not an individual (such as the CEO, an employee, or a member of the board) that acts as a controller. A controller is a body that decides certain key elements of the processing. Controllership may be defined by law or may stem from an analysis of the factual elements or circumstances of the case.

Processor

A processor is a natural or legal person, public authority, agency, or another body, which processes personal data on behalf of the controller according to "What are 'controllers' and 'processors'?".

Two basic conditions for qualifying as processor exist: it is a separate entity in relation to the controller and processes personal data on the controller's behalf. The processor must not process the data otherwise than according to the controller's instructions.

Relationship between Controller and Processor

A controller must only use processors providing necessary guarantees to implement appropriate technical and organizational measures so that the processing meets the requirements of the GDPR. Elements to be taken into account could be the processor's expert knowledge (e.g., technical expertise about security measures and data breaches); the processor's reliability; the processor's resources, and the processor's adherence to an approved code of conduct or certification mechanism according to "Guidelines 07/2020 on the concepts of controller and processor in the GDPR."

GDPR AND CALIFORNIA CONSUMER PRIVACY ACT (CCPA)

There are many similarities between GDPR and CCPA but also some fundamental differences:

- One big difference is that GDPR focuses more on the person's PII.
- CCPA is focused on medium and larger businesses and introduces PI identifying a household, not just an individual. This includes data that indirectly can identify an individual or even a household. So it's broader than GDPR in that respect.

The CCPA Effect

We can see CCPA affecting regulatory activities in US privacy since 2019, according to Gartner. State-level momentum for thorough privacy bills is at an all-time high. After the California Consumer Privacy Act was passed in 2018, multiple states proposed similar legislation to protect consumers in their states. The IAPP Westin Research Center compiled the below list of proposed and enacted comprehensive privacy bills from across the country to aid our members' efforts to stay abreast of the changing state-privacy landscape according to "US State Privacy Legislation Tracker."

California Privacy Rights Act (CPRA)

The CPRA changes and expands the California Consumer Privacy Act (CCPA). The CPRA becomes a baseline for California consumer privacy law absent a subsequent ballot measure to repeal it because it requires that any amendments be "consistent with and further the purpose and intent of this Act" according to "U.S. State Privacy Legislation Tracker." Most of the CPRA's significant provisions will not take effect until January 1, 2023, providing covered businesses with two years of valuable ramp-up time. The CPRA authorizes the rulemaking process to begin during that same cycle.

DATA PROTECTION

PSEUDONYMIZATION

Tokenization and FPE are forms of pseudonymization are recognized as an important method for privacy protection of PII, including personal health information. Tokenization is one technique for this. Such services may be used nationally and for trans-border communication according to "TECHNICAL ISO/TS SPECIFICATION 25237."

ANONYMIZATION

Anonymization is the process and set of tools used where no longitudinal consistency is needed. The anonymization process is also used where pseudonymization has been used to address the remaining data attributes. Anonymization utilizes tools like redaction, removal, blanking, substitution, randomization, shifting, skewing, truncation, and grouping. Anonymization can lead to a reduced possibility of linkage according to "ISO 25237:2017 – Health informatics – Pseudonymization."

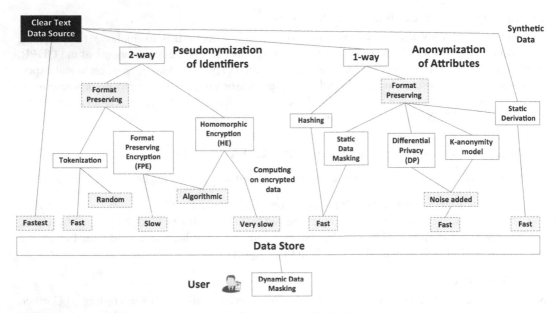

We discuss these techniques more in separate chapters in this book.

SUMMARY

People demand protection of their privacy from lawmakers worldwide, and lawmakers are preparing to meet this demand. And we will discuss GDPR, PCI DSS, ISO/IEC privacy standards, and more in Volume II of this book.

We discussed some major standards and regulations driving the need for more data privacy technologies and helping with more cost-effective and application transparent approaches.

BIBLIOGRAPHY

1. Understanding-the-GDPR-FAQ-Guide, https://www.itworldcanada.com/blog/gartner-predicts-the-future-of-privacy-in-2020/427175, https://www.mdsny.com/gdpr-vs-ccpa/
2. What are 'Controllers' and 'Processors'?, https://ico.org.uk/for-organisations/guide-to-data-protection/guide-to-the-general-data-protection-regulation-gdpr/controllers-and-processors/what-are-controllers-and-processors/#:~:text=%E2%80%98processor%E2%80%99%20means%20a%20natural%20or%20legal%20person%2C%20public,serve%20the%20controller%E2%80%99s%20interests%20rather%20than%20their%20own
3. California CCPA, https://en.wikipedia.org/wiki/2020_California_Proposition_24
4. Rules for the Protection of Personal Data Inside and Outside the E.U., http://ec.europa.eu/justice/data-protection/international-transfers/adequacy/index_en.htm
5. Data Privacy & Cybersecurity, https://lewisbrisbois.com/practices/data-privacy-cyber-security
6. Worldwide: GDPR, Part I: History of European Data Protection Law, https://www.mondaq.com/unitedstates/data-protection/643052/gdpr-part-i-history-of-european-data-protection-law
7. The 18 HIPAA Identifiers, https://www.luc.edu/its/aboutits/itspoliciesguidelines/hipaainformation/18hipaaidentifiers/

8. Data Privacy Laws in Virginia, California and Colorado, https://iapp.org/media/pdf/resource_center/comparison_chart_comprehensive_data_privacy_laws_virginia_california_colorado.pdf

9. ISO 25237:2017 – Health informatics – Pseudonymization, https://standards.iteh.ai/catalog/standards/iso/c32d71a0-fa2f-44b6-8ab4-22ae74c8fbb3/iso-25237-2017

10. TECHNICAL ISO/TS SPECIFICATION 25237, https://cdn.standards.iteh.ai/samples/42807/7f3d18e43d50420ca26506871f1f4c70/ISO-TS-25237-2008.pdf

11. Guidelines 07/2020 on the Concepts of Controller and Processor in the GDPR, https://edpb.europa.eu/our-work-tools/our-documents/guidelines/guidelines-072020-concepts-controller-and-processor-gdpr_en?mkt_tok=MTM4LUVaTS0wNDIAAAF-P842RhinpErpw2fiPKyAZVWLGQu7UKufnGGMx03Kj-UpE0MF5ifV8t1s8oDSEpiih5esfGT_xO37FpJMA-dABlbnNQ-dKAwWwcF47_3gRoAWl

12. FISMA Federal Information Security Modernization Act (P.L. 113-283), December 2014, https://www.congress.gov/113/plaws/publ283/PLAW-113publ283.pdf

13. Privacy Act (P.L. 93-579), December 1974, https://www.govinfo.gov/content/pkg/STATUTE-88/pdf/STATUTE-88-Pg1896.pdf

14. Title 44 U.S. Code, Sec. 3552, Definitions. 2017 ed., https://www.govinfo.gov/app/details/USCODE-2017-title44/USCODE-2017-title44-chap35-subchapII-sec3552

15. California Consumer Privacy Act, OCT 4, 2019, https://www.csoonline.com/article/3182578/california-consumer-privacy-act-what-you-need-to-know-to-be-compliant.html

16. GDPR and Tokenizing Data, https://tdwi.org/articles/2018/06/06/biz-all-gdpr-and-tokenizing-data-3.aspx

17. GDPR Vs CCPA, https://wirewheel.io/wp-content/uploads/2018/10/GDPR-vs-CCPA-Cheatsheet.pdf

18. Privacy Policy – SignalFire, https://signalfire.com/privacy-policy/

19. California Consumer Privacy Act FAQs for Covered Businesses, https://www.jacksonlewis.com/publication/california-consumer-privacy-act-faqs-covered-businesses

20. What Personal Data is Considered Sensitive?, https://ec.europa.eu/info/law/law-topic/data-protection/reform/rules-business-and-organisations/legal-grounds-processing-data/sensitive-data/what-personal-data-considered-sensitive_en

21. Cross Border transfer under GDPR, IAPP, https://iapp.org/news/a/why-this-french-court-decision-has-far-reaching-consequences-for-many-businesses/

22. General Data Protection Regulation, https://en.wikipedia.org/wiki/General_Data_Protection_Regulation

23. IBM Framework Helps Clients Prepare for the E.U.'s General Data Protection Regulation, https://ibm-systemsmag.com/IBM-Z/03/2018/ibm-framework-gdpr

24. International Standard ISO/IEC 20889, https://webstore.ansi.org/Standards/ISO/ISOIEC208892018?gclid=EAIaIQobChMIvI-k3sXd5gIVw56zCh0Y0QeeEAAYASAAEgLVKfD_BwE

25. GDPR vs. CCPA, https://www.mdsny.com/gdpr-vs-ccpa/

26. Navigate the 2021 Privacy Landscape With This Global, https://www.forrester.com/blogs/use-the-brand-new-forresters-global-map-of-privacy-rights-and-regulations-2021-to-navigate-the-evolving-privacy-landscape/

27. Flowcharts and Checklists on Data Protection, https://edps.europa.eu/sites/edp/files/publication/flowcharts_and_checklists_on_data_protection_brochure_en.pdf

28. Encrypt Data and Hold Keys Allows Cross Border Transfer under GDPR - Global Security Mag Online, https://www.globalsecuritymag.com/Encrypt-data-and-hold-keys-allows,20210613,112749.html

29. Practical Data Security and Privacy for GDPR and CCPA, https://sf-prod.isaca.org/resources/isaca-journal/issues/2020/volume-3/practical-data-security-and-privacy-for-gdpr-and-ccpa

30. Guidelines 07/2020 on the Concepts of Controller, https://edpb.europa.eu/system/files/2021-07/eppb_guidelines_202007_controllerprocessor_final_en.pdf

31. US State Privacy Legislation Tracker, https://iapp.org/resources/article/us-state-privacy-legislation-tracker/

Appendix B: Governance, Guidance, and Frameworks

INTRODUCTION

We will discuss evolving governance and guidance from and few important frameworks. We will also discuss skills for different roles. An effective corporate and risk governance framework is essential to maintaining an organization's safe and sound operation and helping to promote public confidence.

CIA—THE HEART OF INFORMATION SECURITY

The CIA triad of confidentiality, integrity, and availability is at the core of information security, and data breaches that can be tied back to a failure to adhere to basic infosec principles have been an unpleasant surprise in a world of modern security frameworks and maturing processes according to "information security":

Confidentiality

Integrity   Availability

CIA—CONFIDENTIALITY, INTEGRITY, AND AVAILABILITY

The CIA triad represents the three pillars of information security: confidentiality, integrity, and availability, according to "Executive Summary – NIST":

Confidentiality:
Being some of the more tech-savvy groups of people in society, security professionals are well aware that data privacy for consumers is close to nonexistent with the last private corners of our digital lives dissipating rapidly, according to "Three Pillars of Infosec."

Integrity:
Most serious breaches take time to develop, with the dwell times of adversaries in a target's environment averaging several weeks and more sophisticated attacks spanning multi-year periods. "The anatomy of a modern attack often begins with the compromise of a less-than-vital system according to 'Three Pillars of Infosec'."

Availability:
As proof that no industry is entirely immune to useful proverbs, aviation aficionados will be familiar with the saying "elevate and then navigate," meaning that while flying, a pilots job number one is to keep the plane in the air at all times, and if a risk appears that jeopardizes the elevation of the plane, troubleshoot that problem first.

DO WE NEED TO USE A COMMON FRAMEWORK AND LANGUAGE?

Do we need to use a common language to discuss data privacy and security across the different teams?

I think it is essential to evaluate and just pick one framework and map it to other frameworks as the basis for our common language:

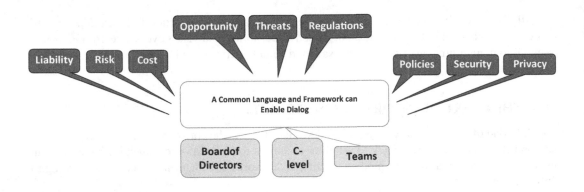

PRIVACY LAWS AND THEIR UNIQUE DEFINITIONS OF PERSONALLY IDENTIFIABLE INFORMATION (PII)

Privacy laws globally govern the collection, use, and disclosure of Personally Identifiable Information, or PII for short. In general terms, PII is any information that could be used to identify a specific person (depending on how you look at it). The fact that each privacy law can define PII in slightly different ways according to "Each Privacy law's definition of Personally."

PRIVACY RISK FRAMEWORKS

Privacy risk frameworks attempt to assess the practical implementation of privacy protection through an approach grounded in risk management. They help organizations calculate or estimate their privacy risk in IT systems and business processes and assess which organizational and technical measurements are possible and appropriate. Because of their broad nature, they have often been extended to a full management framework.

The current praxis is mostly dominated by pragmatic frameworks like Privacy Impact Assessment (PIA)—now known as Data Protection Impact Assessment (DPIA). However, numerous frameworks have, or are being developed, offering a more systematic approach, and their popularity is rising. Below is just an overview with short descriptions of their constellations.

- **DPIA—Data Protection Impact Assessment (aka PIA—Privacy Impact Assessment)**

Privacy Impact Assessment is a type of impact assessment designed to describe the processing, assess the necessity and proportionality of processing, and help manage the risks to the rights and freedoms of natural persons resulting from the processing of personal data according to "What is a DPIA and how to conduct it?"

IT SECURITY POSTURE

IT Security Function Capabilities Adequacy Rating of Your Organization:

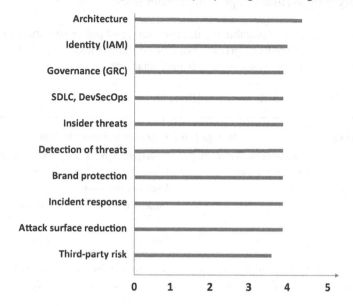

Source: Adapted from (ISC)2

ROADMAP TO REDUCE RISK AND LIABILITY OF UNPROTECTED DATA

Privacy Impact Assessment (PIA)

Privacy Impact Assessment (PIA) Risk roadmap example:

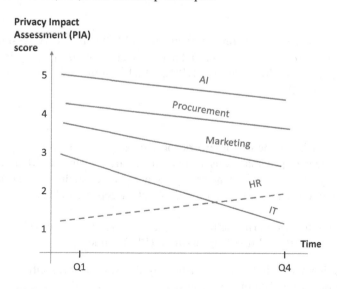

Source: Adapted from U.S. Securities and Exchange Commission, Office of Information Technology

PRIVACY IMPACT ASSESSMENT

A Privacy Impact Assessment (PIA) is a process that helps organizations in identifying and managing the privacy risks arising from new projects, initiatives, systems, processes, strategies, policies, business relationships, and so on, according to "Privacy Impact Assessment."

A PIA is typically designed to accomplish three main goals:

1. Ensure conformance with applicable legal, regulatory, and policy requirements for privacy.
2. Identify and evaluate the risks of privacy breaches or other incidents and effects.
3. Identify appropriate privacy controls to mitigate unacceptable risks.

Example from the Privacy Impact Assessment (PIA) Guide:

Avg. PIA Score	Average Privacy Strategy Deviation by Type		
5	Contravention of consent	Inadequate rights	Excessive exposure
4	Excessive sharing	Excessive use	Disproportion harm
3		Excessive collection	
2		Inadequate protection	Excessive retention
1			
	low	Medium	High

Source: Adapted from U.S. Securities and Exchange Commission, Office of Information Technology.

UNITED STATES

"The E-Government Act of 2002, Section 208, establishes the requirement for agencies to conduct privacy impact assessments (PIAs) for electronic information systems and collections according to 'Privacy Impact Assessment'." The review is a practical method of evaluating privacy in information systems and groups and documented assurance that privacy issues have been identified and adequately addressed.

EUROPE

The European Commission signed its first Framework for Privacy Impact Assessments in the context of RFID Technology in 2011. This served as a basis to later recognize Privacy Impact Assessments in the General Data Protection Regulation (GDPR), which in some cases now mandates data protection impact assessment (DPIA.

PIAF PROJECT

PIAF (a Privacy Impact Assessment Framework for data protection and privacy rights) is a European Commission co-funded project that aims to encourage the EU and its Member States to adopt a progressive privacy impact assessment policy as a means of addressing needs and challenges related to privacy and to the processing of personal data according to "Privacy Impact Assessment – HandWiki."

The following questions describe administrative controls, technical safeguards, and security. Measures according to "Privacy Impact Assessment (PIA) Guide":

1. Has the retention schedule been established by the SEC Records Officer? If so, what is the retention period for the data in the system?
2. What are the procedures for the identification and disposition of the data at the end of the retention period?

3. Describe the privacy training provided to users either generally or specifically relevant to the program or system?
4. Will SEC Contractors have access to the system?
5. Is the data secured by FISMA requirements? If yes, when was certification and accreditation last completed?
6. Which user group(s) will have access to the system?
7. How is access to the data by a user-determined? Are procedures documented?
8. How are the assignments of roles and rules verified?
9. What auditing measures/controls and technical safeguards are in place to prevent data misuse (e.g., unauthorized browsing)?

THE IT ROADMAP FOR CYBERSECURITY

Who needs to be involved?

The most successful companies establish cross-functional teams for their cybersecurity initiatives, according to Gartner. We have outlined the recommended functions and their roles to ensure success in hitting the milestones.

DATA-PROTECTION TIPS FOR BUSINESS AND CONSUMERS

COMPLIANCE WITH GDPR, CCPA, AND HIPAA BY US COMPANIES

The source is a study by FTI Consulting, an independent global business advisory firm. More than 500 leaders of large-sized private sector companies, are based in the United States:

We will discuss best practices in Volume II of this book.

Privacy Officer in Australia

The Code requires all Australian Government agencies (as defined by section 5 of the Code). An agency may have more than one Privacy Officer, according to "Privacy Officer Toolkit."

A Privacy Officer is the first point of contact for advice on privacy matters in your agency and coordinates various functions to help their agency comply with the Code. However, it is ultimately your agency that is required to abide by the Code and the Privacy Act. Your agency is expected to provide you with the necessary resources, time, and support to carry out your role effectively.

Skills

Here are five reasons why adding privacy knowledge to your professional repertoire enhances your capabilities according to "Five Reasons to Add Privacy Knowledge to Your Professional Repertoire":

1. Do you collect, record, organize, structure, store, adapt, alter, retrieve, consult, use, disclose by transmission, disseminate or otherwise make available, align or combine, restrict, erase, or destruct personal data?
2. Are you processing the personal data or providing goods or services to members of the European Union? You may argue that you are not based in the European Union, so GDPR is not applicable.
3. Have you ever heard of the California Consumer Privacy Act (CCPA)? All companies that serve California residents and have at least US$25 million in annual revenue must comply with CCPA.
4. Do you work in a multinational company and regularly transfer personal data across your organization, irrespective of borders?
5. The Luxembourg Data Protection Authority recently fined Amazon €746 million for violations in connection to GDPR.

WHAT SKILLS AND KNOWLEDGE SHOULD A PRIVACY OFFICER HAVE?

SKILLS AND KNOWLEDGE

You will need skills and knowledge in a range of areas to carry out your role effectively.

Most important will be an in-depth understanding of the Privacy Act and the Code and the ability to translate these requirements into practice in your agency according to "Privacy Officer Toolkit – OAIC." You will also need to understand any other legislation that governs the way your agency handles personal information.

Other useful skills and knowledge include:

1. the ability to understand your agency's strategic priorities and key projects involving the use of personal information.
2. understanding the systems and processes your agency uses to handle personal information.
3. strong communication skills to speak with a wide range of stakeholders, including senior executives, staff from other areas such as legal, IT, security, project management teams, and the OAIC.
4. an understanding of private dispute resolution and complaint-handling methods and processes.

THE IT SECURITY SKILLS SHORTAGE

Nine in ten organizations (87%) currently experience IT Security Skills Shortage:

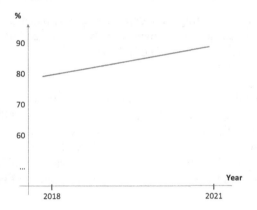

Source: Adapted (ISC)2

IT Security Skills Shortage by Role:

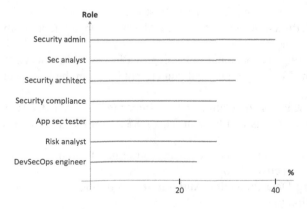

Source: Adapted (ISC)2

What types of certifications are most needed?

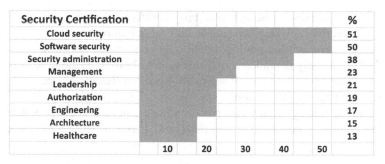

Security Certification		%
Cloud security		51
Software security		50
Security administration		38
Management		23
Leadership		21
Authorization		19
Engineering		17
Architecture		15
Healthcare		13

Source: https://www.isc2.org/-/media/ISC2/Research/Cyberthreat-Defense-Report/2021/CyberEdge-2021-CDR-Report-v10--ISC2-Edition.ashx?la=en&hash=60BC7C7969857E2FF07B714896F079EF5C9C1C39

What skills a most needed for many security roles?

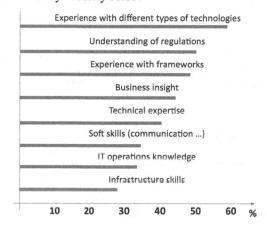

Source: Adapted from Gartner

IT Security Skills Shortage is the #2 barrier to effective defenses:

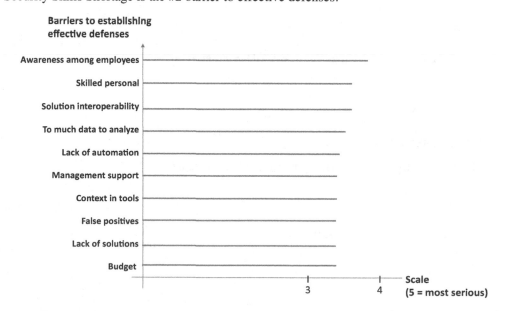

Source: Adapted from (ISC)2

CYBERSECURITY WORKFORCE GAP

There is no near-term solution to the cybersecurity workforce gap on the horizon. There simply aren't enough cybersecurity "All-Stars" available for every organization.

Competing for the same limited pool of talent only perpetuates staff turnover and knowledge drain cycles, which ultimately degrades an organization's ability to respond to cybersecurity incidents according to "Employee Turnover: It's Time to Focus on Retention" according to "Employee Turnover: It's Time to Focus on Retention."

Organizations, hiring managers, and cybersecurity leaders need to adopt new strategies that generate sustainable pipelines of talent, according to "The Cybersecurity Career Pursuers Study."

CERTIFICATIONS AND SKILLS

A CISSP (or similar experience) can be a good entry into the security domain, similar to a driver's license for a car:

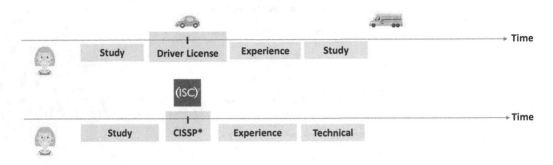

*: Certified Information Systems Security Professional by (ISC)2

Years of experience is needed to become a QSA (Qualified Security Assessor) PCI DSS:

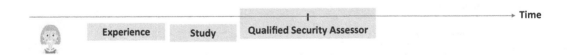

SECURITY ORGANIZATION

Years of business or technical experience is needed to become a CISO:

CISO Role and the Organizational Map

This is an example where the CISO is reporting to the CIO with a dotted line to the chief risk officer (CRO):

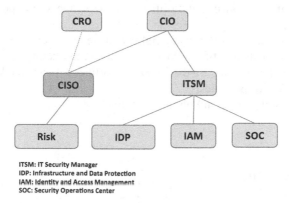

ITSM: IT Security Manager
IDP: Infrastructure and Data Protection
IAM: Identity and Access Management
SOC: Security Operations Center

Virtual CISOs: Security Leader or Security Risk?

Every organization needs a leader dedicated to establishing, executing, and preserving its information security task according to "Virtual CISOs: Security Leader or Security Risk?" For many mature organizations, this leader is the chief information security officer (CISO).

When Are Virtual Chief Information Security Officers the Right Choice?

Cybersecurity executive management and leadership are crucial components to securing an organization's infrastructure and assets properly. However, many organizations may not afford a full-time cybersecurity executive, commonly positioned as the chief information security officer (CISO). Given that reality, one option is for organizations to essentially purchase a CISO as a service in the form of a virtual CISO.

A fundamental understanding of virtual CISOs and how they can be utilized in different organizations is helpful for organizations to understand their options. Virtual CISOs have various benefits and drawbacks depending on the organization's size, industry, funding, and loyalty. For example, although virtual CISOs can provide many benefits without the hefty cost of a traditional full-time CISO, organizations need to consider some of the following questions as well according to "When Are Virtual Chief Information Security Officers":

1. Can the virtual CISO be a security leader for the organization, and at times for multiple organizations operating in a part-time capacity?
2. Can a virtual CISO be used as a complement to larger organizations that can afford a full-time dedicated CISO?
3. When hiring a virtual CISO, how are organizational loyalty and quick response time affected?
4. Can virtual CISOs be used as trainers to incoming full-time CISOs?
5. Is a virtual CISO enough to meet certain compliance requirements, and should they be used solely for that purpose?

DATA PROTECTION OFFICER IN GDPR

DPO, According to GDPR

The GDPR clearly stipulates in which cases the designation of a data protection officer (DPO) is mandatory and their typical responsibilities but only gives vague guidance on how they are appropriately positioned within the organization.

The Role of the DPO

The DPO role is primarily described in Article 39 of the GDPR. They shall monitor compliance, inform and advise data controllers, data processors, and all employees who carry out personal data processing, cooperate with supervisory authorities, and act as the single point of contact for data subjects regarding their rights.

The DPO's role in compliance with privacy rights and creating transparency might significantly impact IT implementation costs and time, product launching, marketing initiatives, and so on. The law also stipulates the independence of the DPO, in particular their freedom to discharge their responsibilities without fear of penalties.

We will debate more on this topic in Volume II of this book.

Office of the DPO

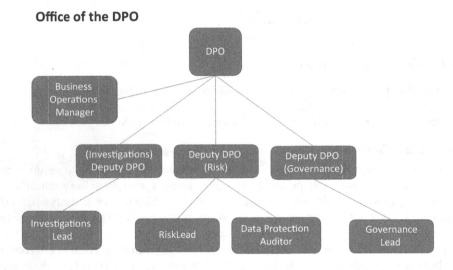

Examples of Data Protection Officers in banks:

DPOs in Banks

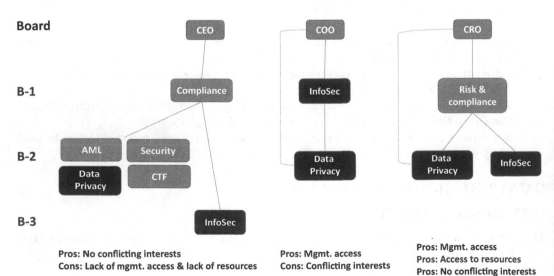

HOW TO APPOINT A DATA PROTECTION OFFICER

Organizations must fill this newly named "superhero" role before Europe's new data privacy law takes effect.

The term of a data protection officer (DPO) has existed for many years. Still, it is now, in most cases, a requirement under the European Union's (EU) General Data Protection Regulation (GDPR), which took effect in May 2018. Failure to meet its regulatory standards could cost organizations millions in legal fees or even more in non-compliance fines. Depending on the nature of the violation, GDPR penalties can be 2% of global revenue—or roughly $10 million, whichever is greater. At the upper end, fines can range up to 4% of global revenue, amounting to billions of dollars for some organizations.

The scope and magnitude of the DPO role make it difficult for organizations to determine how to best fill the position, according to "How To Appoint A Data Protection Officer."

WHERE DO WE PLACE THE PRIVACY FUNCTION?

The question CPOs ask privacy experts most often is where the CPO should report to. The next most common asks are companies like us structuring the privacy organization and how many privacy headcounts they are employing.

But what about Board-level recognition of privacy as a top risk? Privacy has made it onto Board agendas like never before in the last two years. Is it resulting in more CPOs?

SHOULD WE STAY IN LEGAL?

Data privacy began as a legal requirement for the vast majority of companies. As a result, reporting to the General Counsel has been the typical placement for the privacy organization. If this sounds like your business, you have lots of company. But things are changing.

If not legal, then where? Here are a few anecdotal observations of advantages we've seen of placing privacy in various reporting structures:

- CRO and CISO: owning the talent and methodology for rolling out controls aligned with the business strategy.
- IT: managing large budgets and experience rolling out enterprise technology and infrastructure, often needed for privacy programs growing into an automation phase.

CREATING A PRIVACY ENGINEERING CAPABILITY

Companies with a large privacy footprint inevitably face this question: how do we build a discipline around converting our legal and business requirements into products, devices, and software. Just hiring a cadre of privacy engineers is easier than it sounds: we project an ongoing shortage for this in-demand, hard-to-develop skillset.

WHAT DO THESE PRIVACY SUPERHEROES DO?

They're the "arms and legs" of the privacy function typically embedded within product teams. Generally reporting up through the chief product or technology officer, they're assigned to specific products or business functions such as e-commerce, digital, operations, or marketing and can have a dotted reporting line to the CPO.

ALIGNING PRIVACY WITH DATA GOVERNANCE

A number of CPOs have acquired data-governance responsibilities. This is a natural add-on for successful and effective privacy executives who are often the best ones in the organization to know how personal data is collected and used to grow the business. Where this role is divided between a chief data officer and a chief privacy officer, some natural divisions of labor should be considered.

DIFFERENT PRIVACY ORGANIZATIONAL MODELS

With the right CPO leveling, organizational placement, privacy engineering capability, and alignment with the CDO, a key remaining question is an optimal operating model. Most follow one of the following approaches:

1. Advisory: This is where most companies start their privacy programs, a single subject-matter expert, usually in the legal department, reacting to inbound questions and needs from across the business, and in their spare time establishing documented policies and procedures.
2. Center of Excellence for GEOs: In large multinationals that are organized into regional profit-and-loss centers, you will often find a CPO based in one of the company's international headquarters and privacy leaders in the Americas, EMEA, or Asia-Pacific regions who customize programs to local business requirements and needs.
3. Center of Excellence for BUs: Large corporations that are comprised of distinct business units or acquired entities, especially where there are variations of business-to-business and business-to-consumer models, will demand specialized attention and solutions that often result in a core privacy team sitting in a corporate function supporting privacy champions employed by the business.
4. Shared Service for BUs: Where you have business segments that are large enough to be their own Fortune 500 companies and are distinct from each other in terms of geographic and business scope, you can find CPOs over each business segment supported by a CPO in corporate responsible for championing enterprise-wide solutions.

If your company doesn't have a named chief privacy officer, broadly communicated privacy strategy, or target operating model aligned with the latest business strategy, there has rarely been a better time to fill this vacuum.

ROLES IN TRANSITION

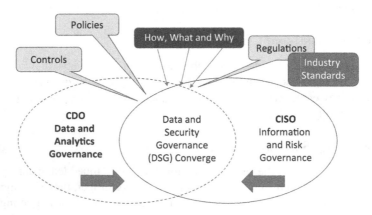

Source: Adapted from Gartner

PRIVACY MATURITY POSTURE

EXAMPLE—MITRE PRIVACY MATURITY MODEL

Elements of a Privacy Program

MITRE is providing a framework of core privacy program capabilities and criteria that can be used to measure progress toward achieving a program's target goal according to "Privacy Maturity Model Version 1 – MITRE Corporation."

The model is based on foundational laws and guidance concepts applicable to US federal government organizations and usable by the private sector. The foundational privacy principles are the same across industries. The core foundation for the framework is a set of seven privacy elements of a privacy program. These elements are provided in the table below (based on Federal CIO Council Privacy Committee).

SECURITY GOVERNANCE

REGULATORY COMPLIANCE

Organizations rarely operate without complying with some standard or regulation, such as the Payment Card Industry Data Security Standard (PCI DSS) or the EU General Data Protection Regulation (GDPR). Compliance is important because failure to be compliant can lead to a security breach and significant fines or impositions, possibly even exclusion from industry or region. Therefore, of the three drivers for security planning shown in the figure below (IT context, risk management, and regulations), regulatory compliance is the "must do" activity.

Security governance provides the authority for security activities and controls, as well as guidance for users. Maturity in security programs depends heavily on the existence of adequate governance. Formal approaches to security architecture enable a tighter alignment of security and business. They achieve this alignment by providing a contextual and conceptual underpinning for logical and technology layers. An organization's technical debt will increase over time, leading to high future reengineering costs. If left uncontrolled, technical debt will inevitably accumulate across the security portfolio and become a substantial burden on the effectiveness of the security function. Using a policy-as-code approach allows organizations to provide demonstrably secure and repeatedly deployable implementations.

We will discuss this topic more in Volume II of this book.

BOARD ASPECTS

RISK MANAGEMENT AND LIABILITY OF UNPROTECTED DATA RESONATES WITH BOARD OF DIRECTORS

How to discuss Risk and Liability of Unprotected Data with Board of Directors
Different audiences have different goals:

- Short-term Revenue at the CEO level. Ransomware should not stop revenue.
- On longer-term Liability at the Board of Directors level.

Who will support longer-term initiatives to protect sensitive data? A CISO may only last for 18 months, a DPO may care about customers long term, and BoD may look at Risk and Liability:

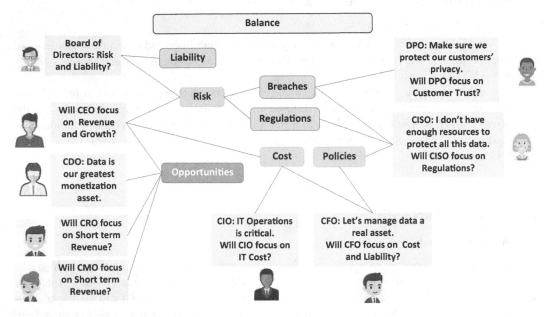

Source: Adapted from Gartner

BOARDS AND PRIVACY

Boards of Directors generally recognize the importance of a solid privacy program. Steep fines for violating privacy regulations have made headlines, and reputational harm from violating customer privacy can be irreparable, according to "Internal Audit and I.T. Audit." However, privacy is not just a cost center; privacy can add value. Enterprises that respect privacy can build trust with their customers and, thus, drive financial benefits. According to "Defense forces survey: Appetite for national defense," just over half (52%) of respondents believe that their board has adequately prioritized privacy according to "Defence forces survey: Appetite for national defense."

Compliance (including the costly penalties of non-compliance) and ethics primarily drive privacy strategy. Thirty-four percent of respondents believe that the board views the privacy program as compliance-driven, 14 percent think that the council sees ethics as the primary driver, and 52 percent believe that the board considers the privacy program to be caused by a combination of compliance and ethics.

Privacy programs do not operate in a vacuum—privacy strategies should align with other enterprise goals. Most respondents (69%) report that their enterprise privacy strategy aligns with organizational objectives, while 14% say privacy strategy does not align with organizational objectives. Sixteen percent respond they do not know.

RISING FROM THE MAILROOM TO THE BOARDROOM

Boards and business leaders expect their key advisors to deliver fresh insights and increasingly expect them to demonstrate foresight. It is crucial to understand the dynamics of conversations in the boardroom and around the audit committee table according to "Internal Audit and I.T. Audit" to achieve what is expected.

MAJOR FRAMEWORKS

A Cybersecurity Framework is a guide on how both internal and external stakeholders of organizations can manage and reduce cybersecurity risk. It is important to start with Risk Management before selecting security controls:

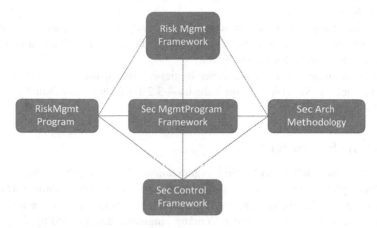

It is important to start with Risk Management before selecting security tools and eventually automating some of the tasks. Mapping to additional frameworks can easily be accomplished when needed. Make sure to understand the problem that you are solving and ask the questions, "Why, What, and How" in that order:

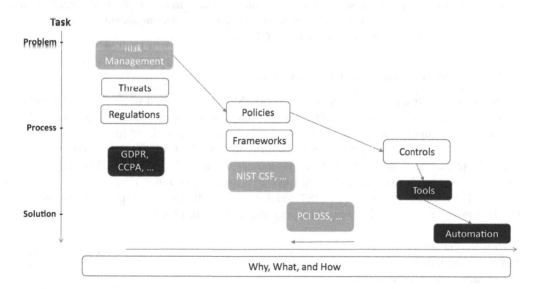

CMMC CYBERSECURITY MATURITY MODEL CERTIFICATION

According to NDIA, the Cybersecurity Maturity Model Certification (CMMC) program collects cybersecurity standards developed by the Department of Defense (DoD) to protect defense contractors from cyber-attacks.

How will CMMC work? DoD will require CMMC certification before any company/business/contractor wins a DoD contract.

The Cybersecurity Maturity Model Certification (CMMC) is a training, certification, and third-party assessment program of cybersecurity in the US government Defense Industrial Base (DIB) aimed at measuring the maturity of an organization's cybersecurity processes (process institutionalization) toward demonstrating compliance with the protection of Federal Contract Information (FCI) and Controlled Unclassified Information (CUI) according to "Osics, LLC - I.T. Risk and Cybersecurity Professional."

The CMMC framework was first developed by a memorandum of understanding and is now under a contract between the United States Department of Defense (DOD) and a non-profit accreditation board composed of industry stakeholders.

The framework, designed to increase cyber hygiene through the maturation of practices and processes, will impact the $712bn defense industry—3.2% of the Gross Domestic Product of the United States of America.

NIST Cybersecurity Framework

NIST Cybersecurity Framework guides how organizations' internal and external stakeholders can manage and reduce cybersecurity risk. It lists organization-specific and customizable activities associated with managing cybersecurity risk, and it is based on existing standards, guidelines, and practices. The framework has been translated into many languages and is used by the governments of Japan and Israel, among others. It provides a high-level taxonomy of cybersecurity outcomes and a methodology to assess and manage those outcomes. It is being used by many businesses and organizations and helps shift organizations to be proactive about risk management according to "The Top 24 Cybersecurity Frameworks."

It is important to review frameworks and select one to follow to cover all basic aspects of your security projects. Mapping to additional frameworks can easily be accomplished when needed.

We will discuss this topic more in Volume II of this book.

NIST Secure Software Development Framework

The NIST Secure Software Development Framework (SSDF) is the latest standard aimed at improving software security according to "NIST SSDF (Secure Software Development Framework)."

According to Synopsis, we've already got the PCI DSS (Payment Card Industry Data Security Standard), the BSIMM (Building Security In Maturity Model), the OWASP (Open Web Application Security Project), the SAMM (Software Assurance Maturity Model), the ISO (International Organization for Standardization), the SAFECode (Software Assurance Forum for Excellence in Code)—the list goes on according to "NIST SSDF (Secure Software Development Framework)."

The framework recommends 19 practices, organized into four groups:

1. Prepare the organization.
2. Protect the software.
3. Produce well-secured software.
4. Respond to vulnerability reports.

Recommendations, Not Mandates

All good. A more-than-worthy goal. Who wouldn't want to mitigate the risks of software vulnerabilities? It's just that it sounds a bit like issuing a framework for controlling the speed of vehicles in public ways when there have been dozens of laws on the books for decades designed to do the same thing.

Beyond that, whatever the specifics of the final version of the NIST Secure Software Development Framework, they will be recommendations, not mandates. NIST is a federal agency under the Department of Commerce but is not a regulatory agency and therefore has no leverage to force compliance with the framework according to Synopsis.

THE PCI SECURITY STANDARDS COUNCIL

The PCI Security Standards Council's mission is to enhance global payment account data security by developing standards and supporting services that drive education, awareness, and effective implementation by stakeholders, according to "The PCI Security Standards Council."

PAYMENT CARD INDUSTRY (PCI) DATA SECURITY STANDARD

Payment Card Industry (PCI) Data Security Standard,

According to "Payment Card Industry (PCI) Data Security Standard," the 12 requirements for building and maintaining a secure network and systems can be summarized as follows:

1. Installing and maintaining a firewall configuration to protect cardholder data. The purpose of a firewall is to scan all network traffic, block untrusted networks from accessing the system.
2. Changing vendor-supplied defaults for system passwords and other security parameters. These passwords are easily discovered through public information and can be used by malicious individuals to gain unauthorized access to systems.
3. Protecting stored cardholder data. Encryption, hashing, masking, and truncation are methods used to protect card holder data.
4. Encrypting transmission of cardholder data over open, public networks. Strong encryption, including using only trusted keys and certifications reduces risk of being targeted by malicious individuals through hacking.
5. Protecting all systems against malware and performing regular updates of anti-virus software. Malware can enter a network through numerous ways, including Internet use, employee email, mobile devices, or storage devices. Up-to-date anti-virus software or supplemental anti-malware software will reduce the risk of exploitation via malware.
6. Developing and maintaining secure systems and applications. Vulnerabilities in systems and applications allow unscrupulous individuals to gain privileged access. Security patches should be immediately installed to fix vulnerability and prevent exploitation and compromise of cardholder data.
7. Restricting access to cardholder data to only authorized personnel. Systems and processes must be used to restrict access to cardholder data on a "need to know" basis.
8. Identifying and authenticating access to system components. Each person with access to system components should be assigned a unique identification (ID) that allows accountability of access to critical data systems.
9. Restricting physical access to cardholder data. Physical access to cardholder data or systems that hold this data must be secure to prevent the unauthorized access or removal of data.
10. Tracking and monitoring all access to cardholder data and network resources. Logging mechanisms should be in place to track user activities that are critical to prevent, detect, or minimize impact of data compromises.
11. Testing security systems and processes regularly. New vulnerabilities are continuously discovered. Systems, processes, and software need to be tested frequently to uncover vulnerabilities that could be used by malicious individuals.
12. Maintaining an information security policy for all personnel. A strong security policy includes making personnel understand the sensitivity of data and their responsibility to protect it.

CIS CRITICAL SECURITY CONTROLS

The CIS Critical Security Controls (CIS Controls) are a prioritized set of Safeguards to mitigate the most prevalent cyber-attacks against systems and networks. It provides a highly practical and useful framework for every organization to use for both implementation and assessment, according to "CIS Critical Security Controls."

CIS CONTROLS MAPPING TO PAYMENT CARD INDUSTRY (PCI)

Mapping of CIS Critical Security Controls to Payment Card Industry (PCI) Data Security Standard v3.2.1, according to "CIS Controls Mapping to Payment Card Industry (PCI)." Major areas in CIS are focused on data, applications and networks, and users. Below are examples of these areas and mapping of CIS to PCI DSS.

This as an example of areas in CIS that are focused on data:

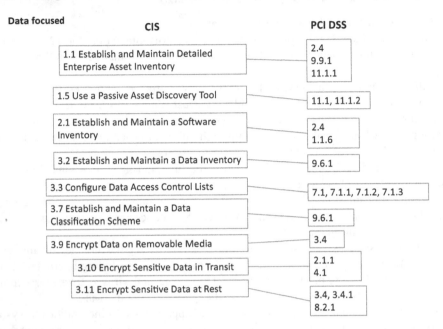

Source: Adapted from https://www.cisecurity.org/white-papers/cis-controls-mapping-to-payment-card-industry-pci/

This as an example of areas in CIS that are focused on applications and networks:

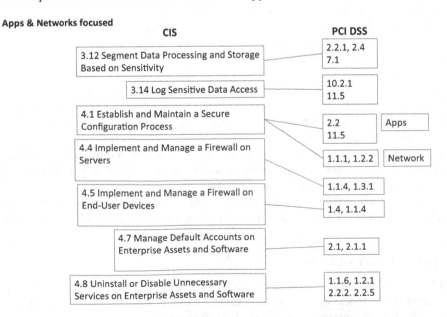

Source: Adapted from https://www.cisecurity.org/white-papers/cis-controls-mapping-to-payment-card-industry-pci/

This as an example of areas in CIS that are focused on users.

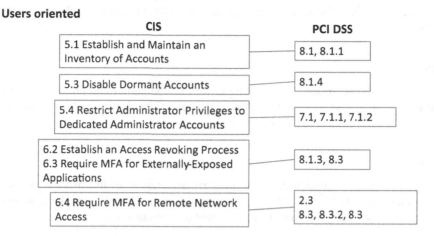

Users oriented

Source: Adapted from https://www.cisecurity.org

DATA RISK ASSESSMENT

Business risks, financial risks, and data privacy risks should be treated and measured just as different risk exposures for the organization. Finance-based data risk assessment (FinDRA) is starting to gain interest.

Gartner is reporting that FinDRA is growing in popularity.

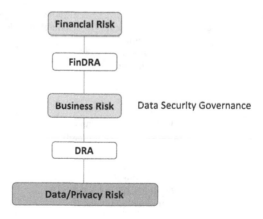

Source: Adapted from Gartner

RED, BLUE, AND PURPLE TEAMS

Purple teams are emerging to increase the effectiveness of the Red and Blue teams according to "The Difference Between Red, Blue, and Purple Teams":

- Red Teams are internal or external entities dedicated to testing the effectiveness of a security program by emulating the tools and techniques of likely attackers in the most realistic way possible. The practice is similar but not identical to penetration testing and involves pursuing one or more objectives—usually executed as a campaign.

- The best Blue Team members can employ Adversarial Empathy, that is, thinking deeply like the enemy, which usually only comes from attack experience.
- Blue Teams refer to the internal security team that defends against both real attackers and Red Teams.

RED TEAM

A red team is a group that plays the role of an enemy or competitor and provides security feedback from that perspective. Red teams are used in many fields, especially in cybersecurity, airport security, the military, and intelligence agencies.

BLUE TEAM

A blue team is a group of individuals who perform an analysis of information systems to ensure security, identify security flaws, verify the effectiveness of each security measure, and make sure all security measures will continue to be effective after implementation.

PURPLE TEAMS

Purple teams exist to ensure and maximize the effectiveness of the Red and Blue teams. They do this by integrating the defensive tactics and controls from the Blue Team with the threats and vulnerabilities found by the Red Team into a single narrative that maximizes both. Ideally, Purple shouldn't be a team, but rather a permanent dynamic between Red and Blue.

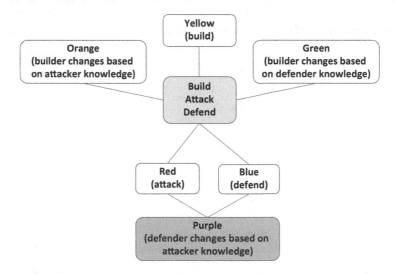

Source: Adapted from danielmiessler.com

CYBER INSURANCE

Cyber insurance is a specialty lines insurance product focused on protecting businesses and individuals providing services for such companies, from Internet-based risks, and more generally from risks relating to information technology infrastructure, information privacy, information governance liability, and activities related thereto according to "Cyber Liability Insurance."

If your organization collected the data, you are also liable for that data, even if you outsource the operation or storage of that data.

Cyber Insurance Does not Protect You from At-Fault Incidents

Cyber insurance does not protect you from at-fault incidents, such as if you used public Wi-Fi when working on sensitive documents. How do you decide which insurance to buy? No two policies are the same, according to "Cyber Insurance: What Is I.T."

Best Practices for Lowering Cyber Insurance Costs and Cyber Risk

Best practices on how to approach cyber insurance to ensure it's a good fit and cost-effective for your company:

Do your homework. Determine what aspects of the cybersecurity framework are most important to your organization, what your organization/team will be responsible for, and what makes sense for your organization to outsource to a cybersecurity insurance provider according to "Best practices for lowering cyber insurance costs and cyber risk."

Taking these proactive steps will not only lower your cyber insurance premiums but also improve your company's cybersecurity position.

SUMMARY

We have discussed evolving governance and guidance and a few important frameworks. We concluded that an effective corporate and risk governance framework is essential to maintaining an organization's safe and sound operation and helping to promote public confidence. We also discussed new skills for different roles, and the importance of an effective corporate and risk governance framework.

We will examine more about this topic in Volume II of this book.

BIBLIOGRAPHY

1. Unique Insights for Governance, Risk, Compliance and Audit Leaders, https://www.routledge.com/Rising-from-the-Mailroom-to-the-Boardroom-Unique-Insights-for-Governance/Turner/p/book/9780367559991
2. Best Practices for Lowering Cyber Insurance Costs and Cyber Risk, https://www.networkworld.com/article/3146519/best-practices-for-lowering-cyber-insurance-costs-and-cyber-risk.html
3. Paul Lucier, 'Six Steps to Start Readying for Quantum', 10 August 2020, https://www.isaca.org/resources/news-and-trends/industry-news/2020/six-steps-to-start-readying-for-quantum (sourced 14 September 2020)
4. Qualified Security Assessor, https://en.wikipedia.org/wiki/Qualified_Security_Assessor
5. ISACA, "Privacy: Beyond Compliance," August 2020, www.isaca.org/bookstore/bookstore-wht_papers-digital/whppbc
6. https://www.bankinghub.eu/banking/finance-risk/general-data-protection-regulation-organisational-alignment-data-protection-officer
7. Securing Software Development: NIST Joins the Parade , https://www.synopsys.com/blogs/software-security/nist-ssdf-secure-software-development-framework/#:~:text=The%20NIST%20Secure%20Software%20Development%20Framework%20%28SSDF%29%20is,we%20need%E2%80%93yet%20another%20%E2%80%9Cframework%E2%80%9D%20for%20improving%20software%20security
8. OWASP SAMM, https://owasp.org/www-project-samm/
9. SAFECode, https://safecode.org/
10. Mitigating the Risk of Software Vulnerabilities by Adopting a Secure Software Development Framework (SSDF), https://csrc.nist.gov/CSRC/media/Publications/white-paper/2019/06/07/mitigating-risk-of-software-vulnerabilities-with-ssdf/draft/documents/ssdf-for-mitigating-risk-of-software-vulns-draft.pdf

11. Newhouse, W., Keith, S., Scribner, B., and Witte, G. (2017) National Initiative for Cybersecurity Education (NICE) Cybersecurity Workforce Framework. (National Institute of Standards and Technology, Gaithersburg, MD), NIST Special Publication (S.P.) 800-181. doi:10.6028/NIST.SP.800-181

12. National Institute of Standards and Technology (2018), Framework for Improving Critical infrastructure Cybersecurity, Version 1.1. (National Institute of Standards and Technology, Gaithersburg, MD). doi:10.6028/NIST.CSWP.04162018

13. McGraw, G., Migues, S., and West, J. (2018) Building Security In Maturity Model (BSIMM) Version 9. Available at https://www.bsimm.com/download/

14. International Organization for Standardization/International Electrotechnical Commission (ISO/IEC), Information technology – Security techniques – Application security – Part 1: Overview and concepts, ISO/IEC 27034-1:2011, 2011. Available at https://www.iso.org/standard/44378.html

15. Five Reasons to Add Privacy Knowledge to Your Professional Repertoire, https://www.isaca.org /resources/news-and-trends/newsletters/atisaca/2021/volume-29/five-reasons-to-add-privacy-knowledge-to-your-professional-repertoire?utm_source=isaca&utm_medium=email-internal&utm_campaign=newatisaca&utm_content=edmi_newatisaca_20210915&utm_term=mc-wk6-article-5-reasons-to-add-privacy&cid=edmi_2008403&Appeal=edmi&utm_source=sfmc&utm_medium=email&utm_campaign=IPWarming_Wk6D1_AtISACA_20210915_edmi_2008393&utm_term=AtISACA_Article_PrivacyKnowlege&utm_id=126635&sfmc_id=98083954

16. ANSI Accreditation Services – International Information Systems Security Certification Consortium, Inc. (ISC)2 Archived July 18, 2012, at the Wayback Machine. ANSI

17. "(ISC)² CISSP Security Credential Earns ISO/IEC 17024 Re-accreditation from ANSI" (Press release). Palm Harbor, FL: (ISC)². September 26, 2005. Archived from the original on March 2, 2010. Retrieved November 23, 2009.

18. The Difference Between Red, Blue, and Purple Teams, https://danielmiessler.com/study/red-blue-purple-teams/#:~:text=Purple%20Teams%20exist%20to%20ensure%20and%20maximize%20the,Team%20into%20a%20single%20narrative%20that%20maximizes%20both

19. "DoD 8570.01-M Information Assurance Workforce Improvement Program" (PDF). United States Department of Defense. January 24, 2012. Retrieved April 12, 2012.

20. NIST Cybersecurity Framework, https://en.wikipedia.org/wiki/NIST_Cybersecurity_Framework

21. Sypris Electronics. "DoDD 8570.1: Blue Team". Sypris Electronics. Archived from the original on April 25, 2016. Retrieved July 3, 2016.

22. Johnson, Rowland. "How your red team penetration testers can help improve your blue team". S.C. Magazine. Archived from the original on May 30, 2016. Retrieved July 3, 2016.

23. Murdoch, Don (2014). *Blue Team Handbook: Incident Response Edition* (2nd ed.). reateSpace Independent Publishing Platform. ISBN 978-1500734756.

24. SANS Institute. "Cyber Guardian: Blue Team". SANS. SANS Institute. Retrieved July 3, 2016.

25. Mateski, Mark (June 2009). "Red Teaming: A Short Introduction (1.0) (PDF)." RedTeamJournal.com. Retrieved 2011-07-19.

26. "Penetration Testing Versus Red Teaming: Clearing the Confusion". Security Intelligence. Retrieved 2020-12-23.

27. When Are Virtual Chief Information Security Officers the Right Choice? https://www.isaca.org/resources/news-and-trends/isaca-now-blog

28. Fenton, Mike (2016). "Restoring executive confidence: Red Team operations". *Network Security*. 2016 (11): 5–7. doi:10.1016/S1353-4858(16)30103-9.

29. Ragan, Steve (12 November 2012). "Thinking Like an Attacker: How Red Teams Hack Your Site to Save It". Slashdot. Archived from the original on 2013-03-02. Retrieved 10 April 2013.

30. An Introduction to Information Security, National Institute of Standards and Technology (NIST) Special Publication (S.P.) 800-12, https://csrc.nist.gov/publications/detail/sp/800-12/rev-1/finalRev 1, An Introduction to Information Security.

31. Red and Blue teams, danielmiessler.com/study/red-blue-purple-teams/

32. U.S. Securities and Exchange Commission, https://www.sec.gov/about/privacy/piaguide.pdf

33. "PrivacyandDataProtectionImpactAssessmentFrameworkforRFIDApplications".EuropeanCommission; Policies, Information and Services; Laws. https://wayback.archive-it.org/12090/20210429105106/https://digital-strategy.ec.europa.eu/en/library/privacy-and-data-protection-impact-assessment-framework-rfid-applications

34. Certified Information Systems Security Professional, https://en.wikipedia.org/wiki/Certified_Information_Systems_Security_Professional

35. CMMC, https://www.acq.osd.mil/cmmc/faq.html

36. Sorin Mustaca Cybersecurity, https://www.sorinmustaca.com/cybersecurity-vs-information-security-infosec/#:~:text=The%20members%20of%20the%20classic%20InfoSec%20triad%20%E2%80%94,criteria%2C%20critical%20information%20characteristics%20and%20basic%20building%20blocks

37. Cybereason, https://www.cybereason.com/blog/three-pillars-of-infosec-confidentiality-integrity-and-availability

38. officer#:~:text=The%20scope%20and%20magnitude%20of%20the%20DPO%20role,for%20data%20subjects%20%28including%20customers%2C%20clients%20and%20employees%29

39. "Privacy Officer Toolkit", https://education.oaic.gov.au/privacy-officer-toolkit/#:~:text=The%20Code%20requires%20all%20Australian%20Government%20agencies%20%28as,to%20help%20their%20agency%20comply%20with%20the%20Code

40. Termageddon, https://termageddon.com/privacy-laws-and-their-unique-definitions-of-personally-identifiable-information-pii/#:~:text=Privacy%20laws%20across%20the%20world%20govern%20the%20collection%2C,of%20PII%20include%20name%2C%20email%20or%20phone%20number

41. Virtual CISOs: Security Leader or Security Risk?, https://www.isaca.org/resources/isaca-journal/issues/2021/volume-5/virtual-cisos-security-leader-or-security-risk#:~:text=Every%20organization%20needs%20a%20leader%20dedicated%20to%20establishing%2C,leader%20is%20the%20chief%20information%20security%20officer%20%28CISO%29

42. MITRE Framework, https://www.mitre.org/publications/systems-engineering-guide/enterprise-engineering/engineering-informationintensive-enterprises/privacy-systems-engineering

43. Internal Audit and I.T. Audit, https://www.routledge.com/Internal-Audit-and-IT-Audit/book-series/CRCINTAUDITA

44. CIS Critical Security Controls, https://www.cisecurity.org/controls/

45. CIS Controls Mapping to Payment Card Industry (PCI), https://www.cisecurity.org/white-papers/cis-controls-mapping-to-payment-card-industry-pci/

46. NDIA, https://www.ndia.org/policy/cmmc#:~:text=What%20is%20CMMC%3F%20The%20Cybersecurity%20Maturity%20Model%20Certification,prior%20to%20any%20company%2Fbusiness%2Fcontractor%20winning%20a%20DoD%20contract

47. The Top 24 Cybersecurity Frameworks – hack_21, https://hack21.sedique.com/the-top-24-cybersecurity-frameworks/

48. Privacy Impact Assessment, https://en.wikipedia.org/wiki/Privacy_Impact_Assessment

49. Daniel Miessler, https://danielmiessler.com/projects/information-security-glossary-of-terms/

50. Patriotic Insurance, https://insuranceleadership.com/

51. Information Security, https://en.wikipedia.org/wiki/Information_security

52. Executive Summary – NIST, https://www.nccoe.nist.gov/publication/1800-25/VolA/index.html

53. Each Privacy law's definition of Personally, https://termageddon.com/privacy-laws-and-their-unique-definitions-of-personally-identifiable-information-pii/

54. Privacy Impact Assessment (PIA) Guide, https://www.sec.gov/about/privacy/piaguide.pdf

55. Privacy Officer Toolkit – OAIC, https://www.oaic.gov.au/s/privacy-officer-toolkit

56. "How To Appoint A Data Protection Officer", https://www.gartner.com/smarterwithgartner/how-to-appoint-a-data-protection-officer

57. "Privacy Maturity Model Version 1 – Mitre Corporation", https://www.mitre.org/sites/default/files/publications/pr-19-3384-privacy-maturity-model.pdf

58. Defence Forces Survey: Appetite for National Defense, https://independentnorth.net/defence-forces-survey-appetite-for-national-defence-and-conscription-has-declined/

59. Cybersecurity Maturity Model Nist, https://www.easy-online-courses.com/course/cybersecurity-maturity-model-nist

60. NIST SSDF (Secure Software Development Framework) | Synopsys, https://www.synopsys.com/blogs/software-security/nist-ssdf-secure-software-development-framework/

61. Privacy Impact Assessment – HandWiki, https://handwiki.org/wiki/Privacy_Impact_Assessment

62. Three Pillars of Infosec, https://reveltech.com.sg/blog/three-pillars-of-infosec-confidentiality-integrity-and-availability/

63. Cyber Liability Insurance – Learn About Commercial …, https://www.oakdaleinsurance.com/cyber-liability-insurance.html

64. When Are Virtual Chief Information Security Officers the …, https://www.isaca.org/resources/news-and-trends/isaca-now-blog/2021/when-are-virtual-chief-information-security-officers-the-right-choice

65. NIST SSDF (Secure Software Development Framework) | Synopsys, https://www.synopsys.com/blogs/software-security/nist-ssdf-secure-software-development-framework/

66. The PCI Security Standards Council, https://www.pcisecuritystandards.org/

67. Payment Card Industry (PCI) Data Security Standard, https://www.pcisecuritystandards.org/documents/PCI_DSS_v3-2-1.pdf?agreement=true&time=1635583482915

68. Privacy Impact Assessment – Wikipedia, https://en.wikipedia.org/wiki/Data_protection_impact_assessment

69. What is a DPIA and how to conduct it? [Video …, https://dataprivacymanager.net/what-is-dpia-a-data-protection-impact-assesment/

70. Osics, LLC – I.T. Risk and Cybersecurity Professional, https://osicsllc.com/

71. Cyber Insurance: What Is IT., https://securethoughts.com/cyber-insurance/

72. Cybersecurity Professionals Stand Up to a Pandemic (ISC)² Cybersecurity Workforce Study, 2020, https://www.isc2.org/-/media/ISC2/Research/2020/Workforce-Study/ISC2ResearchDrivenWhitepaperFINAL.ashx?la=en&hash=2879EE167ACBA7100C330429C7EBC623BAF4E07B

73. The Cybersecurity Career Pursuers Study, https://www.isc2.org/-/media/ISC2/Research/2021/CybersecurityCareerPursuers-Study

74. Employee Turnover: It's Time to Focus on Retention – Hireology, https://hireology.com/blog/employee-turnover-its-time-to-focus-on-retention/

Appendix C: Data Discovery and Search

INTRODUCTION

Discovery is the starting point before protecting our sensitive data, and it can be related to searching for data in an increasingly distributed environment. Having already encrypted or tokenized data fields can increase the challenges of these operations.

We will discuss solutions to find, classify, and catalog data and approaches to encrypting data before outsourcing it to the cloud and enabling discovery and search on data.

SEARCH OVER ENCRYPTED DATA

Use Cases

This is a Use Case of a law enforcement agency that keeps sensitive criminal records and hesitates to use cloud storage according to "Survey on Secure Search Over Encrypted Data on the Cloud." To encrypt data on the local premises before outsourcing it to the cloud preserves data confidentiality. It hinders data processing. We will discuss how to enable searching that is of paramount importance for outsourced data. Also, cloud-based solutions are developed and widely used in different applications. Due to legal regulations, a medical center that owns patients' health records "cannot outsource its data to a cloud that is vulnerable to attacks."

Overcoming the Confidentiality Problem

Search systems do not function when data is encrypted because they cannot compare the query to the encrypted data. Searchable encryption techniques were studied in early 2000 by Song et al.

Approaches to Search Over Encrypted Data in the Cloud

Utilize an Index Structure

Searchable encryption systems commonly implement an index structure to keep track of occurrences of keywords in data records. The process of initializing this index takes the key and a collection of data files as inputs. Then, it extracts keywords from the data records and inserts them into the index structure.

Search Over Encrypted Data in the Cloud

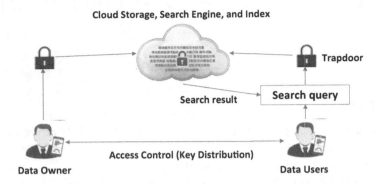

Cloud Storage, Search Engine, and Index

Trapdoor

Search result   **Search query**

Access Control (Key Distribution)

Data Owner   **Data Users**

Source: Adapted from "Survey on Secure Search Over Encrypted Data on the Cloud"

A build-index process will allow the data owner to generate a secure and searchable structure that enables search over the encrypted data. An index structure is generally implemented in a hash table, metadata (markup), or inverted index where each unique keyword is mapped to document identifiers it appears in according to "Survey on Secure Search Over Encrypted Data on the Cloud."

EXPANSION TO THE KEYWORD-BASED SEARCH

One expansion to the keyword-based searchable encryption is to allow users to perform regular expression searches on encrypted data. Song et al. propose to "create all possible variations of a given regular expression." For instance, for ab [a—z] query, it generates all 26 possible search queries that are aba, abb, …, abz. This approach works only for simple regular expressions and is not scalable for those with a high degree of variability, for example, a∗b∗ according to "Survey on Secure Search Over Encrypted Data on the Cloud."

CRYPTOGRAPHICALLY PROTECTED DATABASE SEARCH

According to "Cryptographically Protected Database Search," protected database search systems cryptographically isolate the roles of reading from, writing to, and administering the database according to "Cryptographically Protected Database Search." The design of such systems is a balancing act between security, functionality, performance, and usability. This challenge is made more difficult by ongoing database specialization, as some users will want the functionality of SQL, NoSQL, or NewSQL databases. This database evolution will continue, and the protected search community should quickly provide functionality consistent with newly invented databases according to "SoK: Cryptographically Protected Database Search."

FUZZY SEARCH OVER ENCRYPTED DATA

To meet both ends of security and searchability, search-supported encryption is proposed. Schemes may suffer severe security vulnerability when index data is not well protected. A granular and protected index can support some use cases for "fuzzy search" to overcome such a flaw. This approach can work well for both accuracy and efficiency and will not hurt the fundamental security. A searchable encryption approaches can be divided into three steps:

1) **Represent**: Keywords are extracted from outsourced files or received queries and transferred into word-vectors, a combination of which builds the final representation of files or queries according to "A Novel Fuzzy Search Approach over Encrypted Data with Improved Accuracy and Efficiency."

2) **Encrypt and index**: Data owners usually provide the encryption algorithm and key.

3) **Search**: Users send queries, and data holders perform some searches.

Example of search over encrypted data:

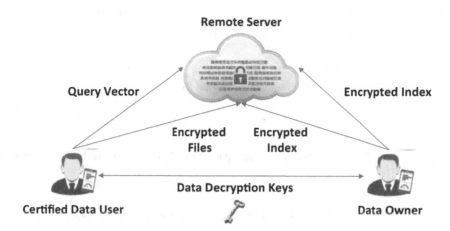

Source: Adapted from "Survey on Secure Search Over Encrypted Data on the Cloud."

Bloom Data Search Filters

A Bloom filter is "a space-efficient probabilistic data structure," conceived by Burton Howard Bloom in 1970, that is used to test whether an element is a member of a set according to "Bloom filter":

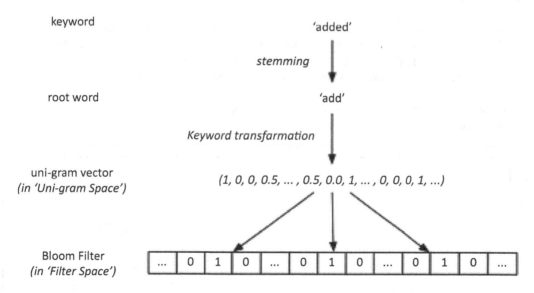

Source: Adapted from "Bloom, Burton H. (1970), Space/Time Trade-offs in Hash Coding with Allowable Errors"

Popular databases are utilizing Bloom filters to operate Bloom pruning of partitions for certain queries. For example, when joining a date dimension table with a large fact table. False-positive matches are possible, but false negatives are not according to "2 Set up of Bloom." False-positive matches with Bloom filters:

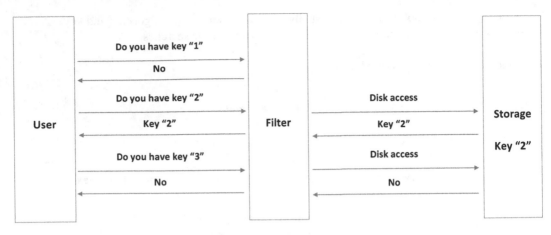

Source: Adapted from "Bloom, Burton H. (1970), Space/Time Trade-offs in Hash Coding with Allowable Errors"

We will discuss "Data Encryption and Fuzzy Search via Encrypted Fabric" in Volume II of this book.

DISCOVERY OF DATA

DISCOVERY OF DATA IN CLEAR

Mature solutions can Find, classify, and catalog the most sensitive data and provide important features, for example:

1. Catalog: Capture technical, privacy and security metadata across any data
2. Cluster Analysis: Find duplicate, similar and redundant data across files and databases
3. Classify: Classify data entities and documents with advanced ML
4. Correlate: Find PI and related data for privacy data rights automation

Discovery via data discovery and data classification tools can use ML to help with the identification of sensitive data:

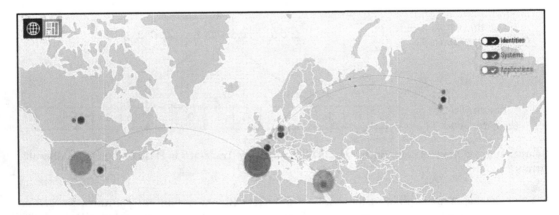

Source: Adapted from BigID

Discovery of Data that is Encrypted

Discovery can be enabled via a data catalog or by adding Meta Data to the data field in preserving the format, type, or length of the original data. Adding meta data to the data field as a prefix or a suffix will not preserve the original data's length. Alternatives can be challenging. Discovery should ideally cover data that is protected by different techniques:

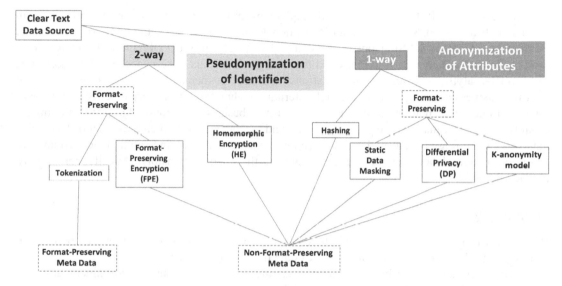

Challenges and solutions:

- It can be a challenge to keep a data catalog in sync with data changes. A data catalog may act as a master for changes to all data definitions.
- It can be a challenge to add Meta Data to the data field in ways that preserve the format, type, or length of the original data. Tokenization via lookup tables or token certificates can help in synchronizing updates.

What Is a Data Catalog?

A data catalog can provide a searchable inventory of all data assets in an organization according to "What is a Data Catalog?" These assets can include these things:

1. Structured (tabular) data
2. Unstructured data
3. Reports and query results
4. Data visualizations and dashboards
5. Machine learning models
6. Connections between databases

A data catalog typically includes capabilities to do the following:

1. Search the catalog
2. Automate the discovery of potentially relevant data for which they didn't specifically search
3. Govern the use of the data in compliance with industry or government regulations

Enable Initiatives With a Data Catalog

It's a challenge to find, understand, and organize it before you can turn it into business value. How an intelligent data catalog accelerates that process by discovering and inventorying data at an enterprise scale is explained in "Build the Data Foundation for Every Digital Transformation."

DATA GOVERNANCE EVOLVES TO ADDRESS COMPLIANCE, COMMERCIALIZATION, TRUST

According to "GDPR, CCPA, and the AI Explainability Question" protection and privacy regulations such as the EU's General Data Protection Regulation (GDPR), the California Consumer Privacy Act (CCPA), and Singapore's Personal Data Protection Act (PDPA) have been significant drivers for data governance initiatives and the emergence of data governance solutions according to "DWBIAnalytics – Blogger." Organizations have an ever-increasing appetite to leverage their data for business advantage, either through internal collaboration, data sharing across ecosystems, direct commercialization, or as the basis for AI-driven business decision-making. While doing so, organizations must maintain employee, partner, and customer trust in their approach of leveraging data (and technology fueled by data). This requires data governance and solutions to step up once again and enable data-driven businesses to leverage their data responsibly, ethically, compliantly, and accountably.

SUMMARY

We discussed approaches to overcome the confidentiality problem by encrypting data before outsourcing it to the cloud and the importance of data lineage and provenance.

We also discussed searching for data in an increasingly distributed environment and how encrypted or tokenized data fields can increase the challenges.

We will discuss these topics further in Volume II of this book.

BIBLIOGRAPHY

1. BigID, https://bigid.com/
2. Data Catalog, IBM, https://www.ibm.com/cloud/learn/data-catalog#:~:text=What%20is%20a%20 data%20catalog%3F%20A%20data%20catalog,include%20%28but%20are%20not%20limited%20 to%29%20these%20things%3A
3. Data Lineage, https://en.wikipedia.org/wiki/Data_lineage#:~:text=Data%20lineage%20and%20prov-enance%20typically%20refers%20to%20the,view%20is%20flawed%20for%20certain%20data%20 management%20cases.
4. The Forrester Wave™: Data Governance Solutions, Q3 2021, https://www.alation.com/forrester-wave-data-governance-q3/?submissionGuid=2dca97b4-2f9b-4196-a49a-0115e06d3fab&utm_ content=ep
5. What is a Data Catalog?, https://www.ibm.com/cloud/learn/data-catalog#:~:text=Data%20catalog%20 and%20IBM%20Cloud%20IBM%20Watson%20Knowledge,their%20relationships%20with%20 other%20members%20of%20your%20organization
6. Your Complete Guide to Answer, What is Data Lineage?, https://www.collibra.com/download/your-complete-guide-to-answer-what-is-data-lineage-ppc?msclkid=f802b71e45951d8860a6d64676f9 4ab1
7. Discover Workshop, https://www.protegrity.com/discover-workshop
8. Bloom, Burton H. (1970). "Space/Time Trade-offs in Hash Coding with Allowable Errors," *Communications of the ACM*, 13(7): 422–426, CiteSeerX 10.1.1.641.9096, doi:10.1145/362686.362692 , https://dl.acm.org/doi/10.1145/362686.362692
9. Song, X., Wagner, D., and Perrig, A. "Practical Techniques for Searches on Encrypted Data". in: *Proceedings of IEEE Symposium on Security and Privacy, 2000. S&P 2000*, 2000, pp. 44–55
10. Cryptographically Protected Database Search, https://arxiv.org/abs/1703.02014

11. A Novel Fuzzy Search Approach over Encrypted Data with Improved Accuracy and Efficiency, https://arxiv.org/abs/1904.12111

12. Singh, J., Pasquier, T., Bacon, J., Ko, H., and Eyers, D. (2016). Twenty security considerations for cloud-supported internet of things, *IEEE Internet of Things Journal* 3: (3), 269–284.

13. Melnik, Sergey, Gubarev, Andrey, Long, Jing Jing, Romer, Geoffrey, Shivakumar, Shiva, Tolton, Matt, and Vassilakis, Theo (2010). "Dremel: Interactive Analysis of Web-Scale Datasets." *Proc. of the 36th International Conference on Very Large Data Bases (VLDB)*.

14. Mattsson, Ulf. "Data Security: On Premise or in the Cloud," *ISSA Journal*, December 2019 – https://www.issa.org/journal/december-2019/

15. Mattsson, Ulf. "Practical Data Security and Privacy for GDPR and CCPA," *ISACA Journal*, May 2020 – https://www.isaca.org/resources/isaca-journal/issues/2020/volume-3/practical-data-security-and-privacy-for-gdpr-and-ccpa

16. Bösch, C., Hartel, P., Jonker, W., and Peter, A. (2014). "A Survey of Provably Secure Searchable Encryption." *ACM Computing Surveys* 47 (2): 18:1–18:51. doi:10.1145/2636328. Poh, G. S., Chin, J.-J., Yau, W.-C., Choo, K.-K. R., Mohamad, M. S. (2017). "Searchable symmetric encryption: Designs and challenges." *ACM Computing Surveys* 50: (3), 40:1–40:37. doi:10.1145/3064005. URL http://doi.acm.org/10.1145/3064005

17. SoK: Cryptographically Protected Database Search, https://ieeexplore.ieee.org/document/7958577

18. Electronic Health Records: Privacy, Confidentiality, and Security, https://journalofethics.ama-assn.org/article/electronic-health-records-privacy-confidentiality-and-security/2012-09

19. Survey on Secure Search Over Encrypted Data on the Cloud, https://arxiv.org/pdf/1811.09767

20. 2 Set up of Bloom, https://people.math.gatech.edu/~randall/AlgsF09/bloomfilters.pdf

21. Build the Data Foundation for Every Digital Transformation …, https://www.informatica.com/lp/build-the-data-foundation-for-every-digital-transformation-priority_3622.html

22. DWBIAnalytics – Blogger, https://dwbianalytics.blogspot.com/

23. What is Data Lineage? Our Complete Guide, https://www.collibra.com/download/beginners-guide-data-lineage

24. Bloom filter – Wikipedia, https://en.wikipedia.org/wiki/Bloom_filter

25. GDPR, CCPA, and the AI Explainability Question, https://www.dataversity.net/gdpr-ccpa-and-the-ai-explainability-question/

Appendix D: Digital Commerce, Gamification, and AI

INTRODUCTION

While traditional companies push into a digital business, the digital giants are also trying to find their TechQuilibirum and shift into conventional business. Gamification is the new means for collaboration and communication and is an instructional strategy to increase motivation and engagement. Customer Engagement programs also increase.

We will discuss digital commerce projects, augmented reality, gamification, and how AI can support.

DIGITAL COMMERCE AND DIGITAL BUSINESS

REACH YOUR TECHQUILIBRIUM

Finding the balance point between being a traditional company and being a digital company can take several years. The right balance will look different for each industry and enterprise. For example, an oil pipeline might not need to be as digital as a bank or retail store, according to "Gartner Keynote: Find Your Digital Business TechQuilibrium."

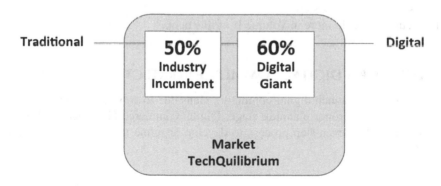

Source: Adopted from Gartner

TECHQUILIBRIUM POINTS WILL SHIFT

While traditional companies push into a digital business, the digital giants are also trying to find their TechQuilibrium and shift into conventional business. For example, Google's move into automotive or Apple's credit card. Like traditional businesses, the digital giants will push as far as the market will accept, according to "Gartner Keynote: Find Your Digital Business TechQuilibrium."

Top Business Objectives in the next two years

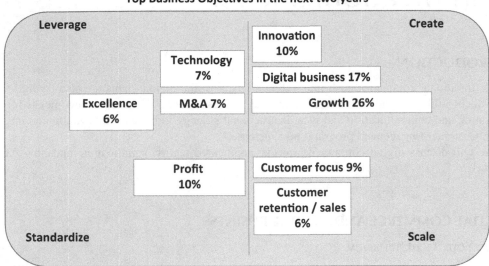

Source: Adopted from Gartner

The most common business objectives mentioned by CIOs can be plotted against the matrix described in the previous section. Ensuring that innovation projects are aligned with corporate business objectives is a critical first step.

We will discuss this topic more in Volume II of this book.

HOW TO DEVELOP A DIGITAL COMMERCE STRATEGY

Companies often hastily launch digital commerce plans due to competitive and growth pressures without going through a proper planning stage. Digital commerce IT leaders and other business sponsors can follow this seven-step process to develop or refine their digital commerce strategy, according to Gartner.

KEY CHALLENGES

1. IT leaders are often tasked with implementing the digital commerce platform but often fail to involve other business stakeholders or align with company goals before kick-starting the process.
2. IT leaders tend to focus on technical functionality when selecting vendor solutions without thinking through the customer experience. Insufficiently designed customer encounter negatively impacts the success of digital commerce services.
3. Digital commerce is a journey rather than a destination. Fast-changing market circumstances and customer preferences often catch companies off guard, and they fail to respond accordingly.

IT leaders supporting digital commerce should:

Recommendations from Gartner include:

1. Establish a cross-functional team before the project kicks off that includes stakeholders from, at least, sales, marketing, operations, supply chain, customer service, and finance. Obtain sponsorship from senior management that has P&L responsibility for digital commerce.
2. Work with the team's marketing and product managers to define digital commerce customer experiences by looking from internal processes and technologies and the outside in as a customer journey. Borrow best practices from other companies, and conduct focus groups to hear the voice of customers.
3. Continuously track performance and adjust the digital commerce strategy and technology platform to quickly respond to changes in business direction and/or customer preferences.

AUGMENTED REALITY

Augmented reality (AR) is the real-time use of information in text, graphics, audio, and other virtual enhancements integrated with real-world objects. It is this "real world" element that differentiates AR from virtual reality. AR integrates and adds value to the user's interaction with the real world, versus a simulation according to "Augmented reality – EDUINDEX NEWS."

AR Three Basic Features

AR can be defined as a system that incorporates three primary features: a combination of real and virtual worlds, real-time interaction, and accurate 3D registration of virtual and real objects. The overlaid sensory information can be constructive (i.e., additive to the natural environment) or destructive (i.e., masking of the natural environment according to "Augmented reality – Wikipedia.")

The Digital World Blend into a Person's Perception

The primary value of augmented reality is how components of the digital world blend into a person's perception of the real world, not as a simple display of data but through the integration of immersive sensations, which are perceived as natural parts of an environment according to "Augmented reality – EDUINDEX NEWS."

Possible Applications

Example application areas described below include archaeology, architecture, commerce, and education. According to "Augmented reality – Wikipedia," some of the earliest cited examples include augmented reality supporting surgery by providing virtual overlays to guide medical practitioners, to AR content for astronomy and welding according to "Augmented reality – Wikipedia."

We will discuss this topic more in Volume II of this book.

GAMIFICATION

Organizations use gamification to encourage participation in apps, workout programs, and even to reward employees. Still, it's now taking center stage for a more unexpected industry: automotive companies, according to "How Gamification Boosts Consumer Engagement."

Companies often hastily launch digital commerce projects due to competitive and growth pressures without going through a proper planning stage. Digital commerce IT leaders and other business stakeholders can follow this seven-step process to develop or refine their digital commerce strategy.

Key Challenges

1. IT leaders are often tasked with deploying the digital commerce platform but often fail to involve other business stakeholders or align with company goals before kick-starting the process.
2. IT leaders tend to focus on technical functionality when selecting vendor solutions without thinking through the customer experience. Insufficiently designed customer experience negatively impacts the success of digital commerce services.
3. Digital commerce is a journey rather than a destination. Fast-changing market conditions and customer preferences often catch companies off guard, and they fail to respond accordingly.

We will discuss this topic more in Volume II of this book.

SUMMARY

We have discussed digital commerce projects and gamification, how AI supports them and finding their TechQuilibirum. We also discussed gamification means collaboration and communication to increase motivation and engagement.

We will talk over more about this topic in Volume II of this book.

BIBLIOGRAPHY

1. Schueffel, Patrick (2017). *The Concise Fintech Compendium*. Fribourg: School of Management Fribourg/ Switzerland. Archived from the original on 24 October 2017. Retrieved 31 October 2017. https://web. archive.org/web/20171024205446/http:/www.heg-fr.ch/EN/School-of-Management/Communication-and-Events/events/Pages/EventViewer.aspx?Event=patrick-schuffel.aspx
2. Augmented Reality, https://en.wikipedia.org/wiki/Augmented_reality
3. Wu, Hsin-Kai, Lee, Silvia Wen-Yu, Chang, Hsin-Yi, and Liang, Jyh-Chong (March 2013). "Current status, opportunities and challenges of augmented reality in education". *Computers & Education*. 62: 41–49. doi:10.1016/j.compedu.2012.10.024.
4. Rosenberg, Louis B. (1992). "The Use of Virtual Fixtures as Perceptual Overlays to Enhance Operator Performance in Remote Environments". https://apps.dtic.mil/docs/citations/ADA292450
5. Steuer. "Defining Virtual Reality: Dimensions Determining Telepresence" https://web.archive.org/ web/20160417163019/http://ww.cybertherapy.info/pages/telepresence.pdf (PDF). Archived from the original (PDF)on 24 May 2016. Retrieved 2018-11-27, Department of Communication, Stanford University. 15 October 1993.
6. Rosenberg, L.B. (1993). "Virtual fixtures: Perceptual tools for telerobotic manipulation". *Proceedings of IEEE Virtual Reality Annual International Symposium*. pp. 76–82. doi:10.1109/VRAIS.1993.380795. ISBN 0-7803-1363-1. S2CID 9856738.
7. Jump up to: [ab] Dupzyk, Kevin (6 September 2016). "I Saw the Future Through Microsoft's Hololens". Popular Mechanics, https://www.popularmechanics.com/technology/a22384/hololens-ar-breakthrough-awards/
8. "How to Transform Your Classroom with Augmented Reality - EdSurge News". 2 November 2015. https://www.edsurge.com/news/2015-11-02-how-to-transform-your-classroom-with-augmented-reality
9. Crabben, Jan van der (16 October 2018). "Why We Need More Tech in History Education". https://jan-vdcrabben.medium.com/why-we-need-more-tech-in-history-education-805fa10a7251
10. Gartner Keynote: Find Your Digital Business TechQuilibrium …, https://www.gartner.com/ smarterwithgartner/gartner-keynote-find-your-digital-business-techquilibrium/
11. Augmented Reality – EDUINDEX NEWS, https://eduindex.org/2021/07/22/augmented-reality/
12. How Gamification Boosts Consumer Engagement, https://www.gartner.com/smarterwithgartner/how-gamification-boosts-consumer-engagement
13. Gartner Keynote: Find Your Digital Business TechQuilibrium …, https://www.gartner.com/ smarterwithgartner/gartner-keynote-find-your-digital-business-techquilibrium/

Appendix E: Innovation and Products

INTRODUCTION

New opportunities with machine learning and big data capabilities increase as data volumes and computing power increase and established new leaders.

In this section, we will discuss the Innovation and Evolution of innovative products and position some vendors.

DATA AND TECHNOLOGY ARE DRIVING BUSINESS CHANGE

New AI, machine learning, and big data capabilities increase as data volumes and computing power increase, and established leaders need to adapt and grow according to "Legacy Companies Need to Become More Data Driven—Fast." The insurance industry is beginning to make the transition from traditional data and analytics to machine learning, in contrast to traditional insurance companies, according to "Legacy Companies Need to Become More Data Driven—Fast," and reflect these five high-value tactics:

1. **Know your business**, and prioritize which data is most valuable to your firm. One of the greatest assets that any business maintains is its unique customer data set—customer interactions, transactions, and behavioral history.
2. **Link technology investments** to high-value business objectives. Organizations often equate success with leading-edge technology investments while often straying from the core business strengths that have made a firm competitive and unique.
3. **Centralize data** infrastructure, decentralize customer management. Business units naturally tend to feel a strong sense of ownership of "their data," but successful companies manage data as a team sport in a collaborative manner.
4. **Educate C-Suite** executives on the business value of machine learning and AI. It is long past the time when C-executives can profess ignorance of these new technologies.
5. **Start small** and demonstrate measurable business outcomes while recognizing that transformational change often takes decades, according to "Legacy Companies Need to Become More Data Driven—Fast."

ORGANIZATIONS THAT SAW OPPORTUNITIES WERE ABLE TO ACCELERATE

"How can organizations accelerate in the turns? They must find their TechQuilibirum," according to "Gartner Keynote: Find Your Digital Business TechQuilibrium." In 2008, during the last major recession, organizations that saw opportunities where others saw risk were able to accelerate into the turn and come out further ahead. Those that panicked and cut costs, or pulled back investment, fell behind.

LEGACY COMPANIES NEED TO BECOME MORE DATA-DRIVEN

Many data-rich companies have reigned as market leaders over the years. "However, business conditions evolve, and today, these companies face new challenges that threaten their hard-won leadership positions" according to "Legacy Companies Need to Become More Data Driven—Fast."

Too many organizations focus on cure-all solutions, home runs, moonshots, or major transformational initiatives.

INNOVATION

THE DILEMMA

The dilemma is simple; innovations that satisfy a brand's need for growth require taking risks that are unacceptable to that brand, and most brands don't have these qualities; driven by quarterly results, most brands will eschew long-term growth for short-term profitability according to "The Innovator's Dilemma."

EIGHTY-FIVE PERCENT OF THE JOBS HAVE NOT BEEN INVENTED YET

Eighty-five percent of the jobs today's students will be doing in 2030 have not been invented yet, according to The Institute for the Future.

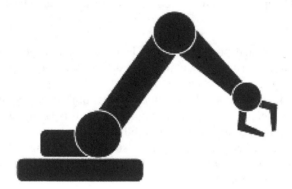

DISRUPTIVE INNOVATIONS

Most companies achieve success by responding to what their customers want and consistently pursuing higher profits. However, these strategies that help companies thrive under normal circumstances instead can lead to their demise when confronting certain innovations.

These disruptive innovations don't come along very often, but when they do, they change how companies make and market products, the types of customers who buy them, and how they use them. The Innovator's Dilemma explains how to recognize disruptive innovations, why they cause industry-leading organizations to fail, and how to avoid the same fate according to "The Innovator's Dilemma."

INNOVATION ALIGNED WITH BUSINESS OBJECTIVES

The figure below highlights the most common business objectives mentioned by CIOs. These objectives are plotted against the matrix described in the previous section. Ensuring that innovation projects are aligned with corporate business objectives is a critical first step.

Top Business Objectives in the next two years

Leverage			Create
	Technology 7%	Innovation 10%	
		Digital business 17%	
Excellence 6%	M&A 7%	Growth 26%	
	Profit 10%	Customer focus 9%	
		Customer retention / sales 6%	
Standardize			Scale

Source: Adopted from Gartner

DATA INNOVATION SLOWED BY COMPLIANCE AND OTHER CONCERNS

We always want to know how organizations align data-driven progress with the strengths and constraints of their technologies, to understand how we can continue to safeguard data as businesses continue to explore new and not-so-new technologies according to "Survey Says: Data Innovation Slowed by Compliance."

DATA SECURITY VIEWED AS NECESSARY

For some, though, investment doesn't always mean easy implementation. Despite having a strong interest in pursuing data security technologies, hurdles get in the way according to "Survey Says: Data Innovation Slowed by Compliance":

- 47% believe an excessive amount of time is required to deploy new data security technologies.
- 39% think their employees have insufficient skills to implement the technologies.
- And, of those who worry about the skills gap, 42% were privacy and security executives, while 35% were data and AI executives.

An Answer to Innovation Worries

Compliance indeed tends to paralyze innovation. Share data too freely, without regard to data privacy regulations, and a business will eventually find itself the focus of regulators and disappointed customers and partners. Hold data too tightly, and a business will eventually find itself losing ground to data-driven competitors. Over the past two decades, we've created solutions that solve the critical challenges of safeguarding data and keeping individuals' sensitive information private by listening to our customers. We have an effective, comprehensive data-protection platform that relieves the burden of compliance by continuously classifying and discovering data so that sensitive data within the scope of regulations do not go undetected, according to "Survey Says: Data Innovation Slowed by Compliance."

DATA PROTECTION HISTORY AND INNOVATION

MAJOR INNOVATIONS IN DATA PROTECTION

Examples of major patent application filings for data protection that resulted in 86 awarded (granted, issued) US Patents:

Granular Database Encryption

	Data Protection Policy	

	Tokenization	

	Cloud Encryption Gateway

| 2000 | 2005 | 2010 | 2015 | 2020 |

MAJOR MILESTONES IN DATA PROTECTION TECHNOLOGY

1997
- Launching of the first granular Database Encryption product with a separated centrally managed policy. It generated audit log records of selective operations on sensitive data and sent them to separate central reporting. The product provided Separation of Duties between Database Administration and Security Administration. Agents locally enforce the centrally managed policy.

1999
- A major beverage company encrypted sensitive HR and IP data.

2000
- Microsoft, IBM, Informix, and Sybase integrated with this database encryption platform, and it was used by Visa USA, Mastercard Worldwide, American Express, and Goldman Sachs. Teradata started to resell the Platform and first introduced our technology to Airlines Reporting Corporation (ARC) and major retailers in the United States.

2004
- PCI DSS (Payment Card Industry Data Security Standard) became an important driver for Database Encryption products.

2010
- A better approach to tokenization was invented. It was called Vaultless Tokenization and provided increased performance and scalability limits. It was a paradigm shift avoiding costly real-time replication service.

2014
- Some Database Encryption vendors agreed to license several of the Database Encryption patents.

2015
- Data Security Gateways introduced a less intrusive way to secure sensitive enterprise data on-premise and in the cloud with tokenization, encryption, and activity monitoring.

2018
- Requirements from data privacy legislation worldwide started to become an increasingly important driver for protecting sensitive data. GDPR became a model for data privacy regulations.

2021
- It provided A new Granular Tokenization approach of Unicode data. It enabled the preservation of length, types, languages, and high performance.

DATA PRIVACY TECHNOLOGY VENDORS

This is an example of smaller data privacy technology vendors with between 5 and 200 employees.

US PATENT APPLICATIONS

The number of US Patent Applications filed by 15 of these smaller data privacy technology Vendors:

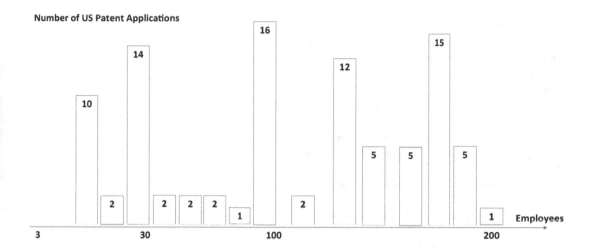

Another eight vendors of this size had no patent applications filed.

SUPPORT FOR DIFFERENT DATA PRIVACY FEATURES

The figure illustrates the number of vendors with support for different data privacy features:

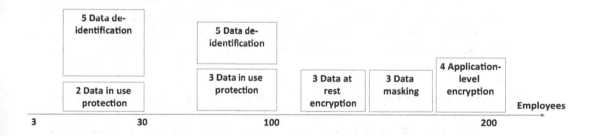

A VENDOR COMPARISON TOOL

Maturity of data protection solutions:

1. Some vendors have limited protection features focused on PCI DSS data (payment data) and not PII.
2. "API" will need programming by a developer or as a configuration definition?
3. Some vendors gravitate or just have a focus on APIs.
4. Tokens may be vaulted or not, and even FPE.

These categories can be the basis of comparison.

Comparison Capability	Competitor 1	Competitor 2	Competitor 3
Does the competitor protect the data itself?			
If the competitor protects the data itself, can it be reversed?			
What method of protection is offered? Encryption, Tokenization, Access Control, Static Data Masking, etc.			
Does the vendor focus on a silo or on an enterprise solution?			
Does the competitor have the ability to control and monitor across the enterprise with a single pane of glass?			
Doe, the competitor, has a policy-based solution that delivers on Least Privileges?			
Does the vendor have a solution that can enforce the Separation of Duties?			
How long has the vendor been involved in protecting the data itself?			
How easy is it to implement the competitor solution vs. Mature Vendors?			
For a given opportunity, is the buyer interested in an enterprise or siloed solution?			
With the competitive solution, find out what the security is at rest, in transit, and in use.			
Does the competitor protect the data at rest?			

- **Most vendors do not protect the data itself**. When you hear that the cloud is secure because they use encryption by default, this is not protecting the data itself. This is why cloud vendors point you to a shared responsibility model where they are not responsible for the data—you, their customer, is.
  - We have called this the difference between fine-grained and coarse-grained protection. Fine-grain refers to what I described above with data de-identification. It's the individual values of identifiers that we make unreadable with tokenization. Coarse-grained encryption uses encryption (never tokenization) to encrypt artifacts like files or a database. Coarse-grained encryption does not protect the data itself. This is a key concept in differentiating what we do and what others do.
- **Most vendors cannot reverse the data they protect**. Reversing means changing the protected data back to its original state or making it readable or "in the clear," or re-identifying it as described above. Some new vendors pop up and offer data protection at the data level. Sometimes they call it anonymization, but there are so many terms out there that it's confusing. What most or all of these vendors cannot do is to un-protect the data. Suppose you cannot reverse the protected data to its original state. How can you deliver it to people who need that data to perform their job function, like the doctor or practitioner in the earlier example?
  - This prevents these competitors from protecting operational or transactional systems, which is a big part of what customers need to do.
    - Many years ago, when we started protecting customer data, our product innovation focused on databases, particularly analytical databases like Teradata. We would be tasked with protecting only a handful of business systems.

- Over the last few years, organizations have been asking to protect hundreds of systems. Many of these systems are operational or transactional systems. Since they cannot reverse protected data, these new competitors cannot deliver on data protection for a large part of what customers are now asking for.
- **Most vendors focus on a single type of silo.** When you start looking at the competition, you find database vendors that offer access control and tablespace encryption (coarse-grained encryption), you find disk encryption (coarse-grained encryption), you find Hadoop protection like Privacera (access control), etc. These products are focused on a single business platform like the customer business system on Oracle or the customer business system on Cloudera. Protection relies on the security capabilities offered by these business systems. What these solutions ignore is that data in an enterprise flows from business system to business system. When data travels from Oracle to Cloudera, you may need to unprotect data in Oracle and protect it again in Cloudera. This is very inefficient and does not model what is happening with data in enterprises.
- **Mature Vendors focus on the enterprise.** The corporate governance organization requires that a set of data must be protected across all silos. This is a major differentiator that Mature Vendors have on almost all competitors. We can protect data across siloed business systems that make up the enterprise.

  The Mature Vendors Enterprise Security Administrator (ESA) is the central command and control for creating rules for protecting this data across all business systems. Agents called protectors might perform two major functions across all silos in the enterprise.
  - Protectors enforce the rules for protecting the sensitive data specified by the corporate governance organization. The rules are encapsulated in the data security policy. These policies are distributed across all silos.
  - Protectors record any security operations that are required by business processes on sensitive data; protect, un-protect, re-protect. This enables customers a view of what's happening to the set of sensitive data specified by governance across all silos.
- **Single pane of glass:** Given the Mature Vendors enterprise reach, we can use a single pane of glass to control and monitor the protection of sensitive data across silos.
- **Policy-Based Security:** Remember that most vendors cannot reverse protected data? Most vendors cannot deliver on the NIST best practice of Least Privileges.
  - This is the capability that enables those who need to see the data in the clear or readable to perform their job function. Data at rest is de-identified and rendered unreadable must be reversed to achieve NIST's Least Privileges.
- **Separation of Duties:** If you examine how companies protect their data today, you will find that System Administrators and DBSs are responsible for implementing who should have readable access to protected sensitive data. This is an awful practice that NIST identifies as Separation of Duties. You must separate the team that implements security from the group that administers security, and it should not be the same team
  - A Mature Vendors platform enables the security team to administer security by creating security policies. These policies determine the rules for security data and also who can see the data in the clear. IT should never be able to see sensitive data in the clear.

Most vendors have not innovated in the area of protecting the data itself.

- Mature Vendors has the most robust tokenization product.
- Mature Vendors Data Security Gateway is unlike any other product in the market.

Most vendors have not been in the space as long as Mature Vendors. In fact, when you look at the CASB vendors, this area is hard to develop.

SUMMARY

We have discussed the evolution of products and that product innovation and how product innovation can come in three different forms. New opportunities with machine learning and big data capabilities increase as data volumes and computing power increase and established new leaders.

We also discussed the evolution of innovative products and positioned some vendors.

We will discuss this topic more in Volume II of this book.

BIBLIOGRAPHY

1. Legacy Companies Need to Become More Data Driven—Fast, https://hbr.org/2021/06/legacy-companies-need-to-become-more-data-driven-fast?utm_campaign=Oktopost-Rick+Farnell+General+Industry+News&utm_content=Oktopost-linkedin&utm_medium=social&utm_source=linkedin
2. How Forward-thinking Organizations Are Becoming Data-driven, https://www.ey.com/en_us/consulting/how-forward-thinking-organizations-are-becoming-data-driven
3. The Innovator's Dilemma, https://makemeread.in/the-innovators-dilemma-book-summary/#:~:text=%20The%20Innovator%E2%80%99s%20Dilemma%20%E2%80%93%20Book%20Summary%20,do%20big%20brands%20solve%20the%20Innovator%E2%80%99s…%20More
4. ICPID 2020 | Product Innovation and Design / Singapore, http://icpid.org/
5. Legacy Companies Need to Become More Data Driven—Fast, https://hbr.org/2021/06/legacy-companies-need-to-become-more-data-driven-fast
6. Survey Says: Data Innovation Slowed by Compliance, https://www.protegrity.com/protegrity-blog/survey-says-data-innovation-often-slowed-by-compliance-and-other-tech-concerns
7. Gartner Keynote: Find Your Digital Business TechQuilibrium, https://www.gartner.com/smarterwithgartner/gartner-keynote-find-your-digital-business-techquilibrium/
8. Augmented reality – Wikipedia, https://en.wikipedia.org/wiki/Augmented_reality
9. Legacy Companies Need to Become More Data Driven—Fast, https://hbr.org/2021/06/legacy-companies-need-to-become-more-data-driven-fast

Appendix F: Glossary

Access Control: The process of granting or denying specific requests to: (1) obtain and use the information and related information processing services; and (2) enter specific physical facilities (e.g., federal buildings, military establishments, border crossing entrances)

Actuarial Pricing: The discipline that applies mathematical and statistical methods to assess risk and price policies in insurance, finance, and other industries and professions.

Advanced Encryption Standard (AES): AES is a block cipher encryption algorithm.

Advanced Persistent Threat: An adversary with sophisticated skills and resources provides opportunities to achieve its goals using multiple attack vectors (cyber, deception, physical, malware.)

Advanced Threat Prevention (ATP): A cybersecurity tool that identifies malware, quarantines it, and allows it to be analyzed and identified in and between organizations.

Alert: A notification that can detect an incident, vulnerability, or finding.

Annual Revenue: The amount of yearly income of an organization before taxes.

Antivirus Software: A program that monitors the network to detect malicious code and to prevent malware insertion.

API: Application programming interface.

Architecture: A highly structured specification of an acceptable approach within a framework for solving a specific problem according to "Glossary of Terms, Acronyms, and Notations."

Assumption of Breach: Assumption of a breach is a model that dictates that you have been breached and will be breached again. Robert Mueller defined it at the RSA security conference in 2013.

Attack: An assault perpetrated by a threat source that attempts to exfiltrate data, interrupt processes, or alter data or system operations.

Audit: Independent review and examination of records and activities to assess the adequacy of system controls and ensure compliance with established policies and operational procedures.

Authentication: Verifying the identity of a user, process, or device.

Authorization: The ability to determine if a user has the right to create, read, update, or delete specific data.

Availability: The ability to ensure the data is available to users.

Backdoor: An undocumented way of gaining access to a computer system. A backdoor is a potential security risk.

Backup: A copy of files and programs made to facilitate recovery if necessary.

Board of Directors: In a public company, a board of directors (BoD) is a group of individuals elected to represent the shareholders. A board's mandate is to establish corporate management and oversight policies and make decisions on major company issues, including Cybersecurity. Every public company must have a board of directors.

Botnet: A collection of computers compromised by malicious code and controlled across a network.

Breach: A data breach is an incident where information is stolen or taken from a system without the knowledge or authorization of the system's owner. A security breach is an incident that results in unauthorized access to networks, devices, or data without knowledge or authorization of the system's owner.

Bug: An unexpected detect in a system or device.

Business Continuity Management (BCM): The process of creating systems of prevention and recovery to deal with potential threats to a company.

Business Interruption: Business interruption is when business as usual is interrupted when the authorized users cannot access an application. In cyber, it is typically a result of a denial of service attack.

Business Process: A set of digital rules utilized by one or more systems to take inputs, transform them, and produce outputs reported or utilized by other systems.

BYOD: Bring Your Own Device

Capability Maturity Model Integration (CMMI): Impact and likelihood information can be obtained by using the CMMI as the basis for the answer ratings developed at Carnegie Mellon University (CMU). CMMI is used in terms of process level improvement training and appraisal programs. CMMI defines the following maturity levels for processes: Initial, Managed, Defined, Quantitatively Managed, and Optimizing.

Category Domains: In risk modeling, category domains are subsets of data that can be allocated into further categorization.

Chief Information Security Officer (CISO): A senior-level executive within an organization responsible for establishing and maintaining the enterprise vision, strategy, and cybersecurity program to ensure digital assets are adequately protected.

Click jacking: An attack that unwittingly has a user click a web page element disguised as another element. Typically, this results in malware being deployed unknowingly.

Cloud: Technology services and software that run on the Internet instead of on-premises computers.

Cloud Computing: Cloud computing provides on-demand work access to a shared pool of computing capabilities or resources that can be provisioned rapidly with minimal management effort.

Compliance Manager or Officer: A Compliance Manager or Officer is an employee whose responsibilities include ensuring the company complies with its outside regulatory requirements and internal policies. A compliance officer may craft and update internal policies to mitigate the risk of the company breaking laws and regulations and lead internal audits of procedures. In cyber there are many regulations based on type of data processed, geography, and industry that a compliance manager must be familiar with.

Common Vulnerability Exposure (CVE): A database of vulnerabilities published by NIST. The Common Vulnerabilities and Exposures (CVE) system provides a reference-method for publicly known information-security vulnerabilities and exposures.

Confidentiality: The ability to ensure that only authorized and approved users have access to the data.

Consensus: This refers to a Majority of participants of a network agreeing on the validity of a transaction. In the context of Hyperledger Fabric Consensus, a network of nodes provides a guaranteed ordering of transactions and validates the block of transactions.

Consensus Security: An application of security protocols, such as encryption and hashing, to protect data integrity and safeguard Consensus Algorithm against proof of work, proof of Stake etc.

Container image: A package of software that can run within a container.

Control Assessment: A security assessment that uses policies, and control tests to ascertain the effectiveness of a cybersecurity control both organizationally and technically.

Cookie: A small text file that is placed on your computer by some websites you visit. Cookies can then be used to track you through the site, or when you revisit. Some cookies will allow you to save information about yourself, to prevent you re-entering it. When used correctly cookies can be very useful; however, some websites use them to track you without your consent.

Critical Infrastructure: Critical Infrastructure represents the digital assets that are instrumental for society to function without a debilitating impact on the security, economy, health, safety or environment.

CVE: Short for Common Vulnerabilities and Exposures, is a list of publicly disclosed computer security flaws.

Cyber Budget: Cyber budgets are a combination of fixed and variable costs and delineated by capital and operational expenses. The cyber budget should be aligned with the fixed operational costs (the security team personnel), the capital fixed costs (the tools and their licensing costs), and the variable costs.

Cybergeddon: A term defined by the author to indicate the worst-case scenario of inherent risks analysis in terms of zero percent effectiveness of controls of an organization.

Cyber Insurance: A risk transference mechanism to reduce business interruption, data exfiltration and regulatory losses due to cyber-attacks.

Cyber Legal Team: The legal team that will be involved in cyber when a breach occurs. All communications will likely be run by legal before they are released to the media or a regulator. The communications team usually crafts any breach notifications with the CISO and legal collaborating.

Cyber Resiliency: Cyber resilience measures an entity's ability to continuously deliver the intended outcome despite adverse cyber events. It can be used to benchmark and define organizations goals in terms of cybersecurity.

Cyber Risk: The risk at the digital asset level; system, process, technology, and data can have reputational, organizational, legal, and/or financial impacts. It is the cornerstone of measuring cyber resiliency.

Cybersecurity: The body of technologies, processes, and practices designed to protect networks, computers, programs, and data from attack, damage, or unauthorized access.

Cybersecurity Posture: Refers to the maturity and effectiveness of the various cybersecurity control measures.

Cyber Simulation (SIM): An automated approach to train Cybersecurity Operations (SOC) teams to adequately respond to evolving threats.

Cyber Threat: A malicious attempt to damage or disrupt a computer network or system.

Cyber Threat Intelligence (CTI): A cybersecurity tool that works in the deep and dark web to identify hackers and track their malicious activities. CTI provides detailed information about potential or current attacks that threaten an organization.

Data: The information that is processed and stored. Data can be classified into different types including privacy, credit card, intellectual property, customer data, supply chain data, etc.

Data Breach: The unauthorized movement or disclosure of information.

Data Exfiltration: Data Exfiltration is when cyber criminals steal data. This can be due to many causes including and not limited to misconfigured systems, poor access controls, from insiders or external actors. Specifically, it is the unauthorized copying, transfer or retrieval of data from a computer or server. Data exfiltration is a malicious activity performed through various techniques, typically by cybercriminals over the Internet or other networks.

Data Loss: Data Loss can happen due to theft, deletion, or misplacement of data.

Data Loss Prevention (DLP): A cybersecurity tool that provides rules to identify when data is accessed by authorized users and sent outside the organization and add additional rules to prevent unauthorized data leakage. Found mostly in large organizations and those with privacy issues.

Data Privacy Officer (DPO): A senior-level executive within an organization responsible for data privacy. The DPO must ensure that the organization complies with GDPR if it processes EU citizen privacy data regardless of where it is located.

Data Type: The classification of data processed. This can be one or more types including but not limited to privacy, personally identifiable (PII), patent, formula, healthcare, federal, business, credit card, etc.

Deepfake: A video of a person in which their face or body has been digitally altered so that they appear to be someone else, typically used maliciously or to spread false information.

Detect: Detect is the third of the five NIST functions. The Detect Function defines the appropriate activities to identify the occurrence of a cybersecurity event. The Detect Function enables timely discovery of cybersecurity events.

Digital Asset: Refers to the systems, business processes, technologies, and data type used to automate work using computer technology.

Disaster Recovery (DR): A discipline to recover from a disaster using a redefined plan tested and ready to execute.

Distributed Denial of Service (DDOS): Distributed Denial of Service (DDOS) happens when a cyber-offender takes action that prevents legitimate users from accessing targeted computer systems, devices or other network resources.

DLT: Distributed Ledger Technology (DLT) is technological infrastructure and protocols that operate a decentralized network allowing simultaneous secure access, validation, and record updating using cryptographic signatures and with no central authority.

Domain: In cyber risk modeling, domain is a specific set of data. In this invention it is related to the cyber risk engine. However, other domains can be created.

Encryption: A process used in Cybersecurity that provides data scrambling so that only authorized parties can access it.

Enterprise Risk Management: A business program that combines risk management disciplines across several operational, credit, cyber, etc.

Event: An event is a suspicious occurrence that may be an indication that an incident is occurring.

Exploit: This term is used generally to represent any method deployed by unauthorized users to gain access to computers or networks.

Exposure: A condition where the system is unprotected, and an attacker can obtain access to the system or network.

FERPA: The Family Educational Rights and Privacy Act (FERPA) is a federal law that protects the privacy of student education records by the US Department of Education.

FI: Financial institutions.

Financial Cyber Impacts: Financial Cyber Impacts are defined in three categories: data exfiltration, business interruption, and regulatory loss and are aligned to what cyber insurance companies will pay out claims against.

Finding: A finding is a result of a control assessment.

Firewalls: A cybersecurity tool that that prevents unauthorized access to or from a private network. This a basic cybersecurity tool and most SMEs will also have firewalls.

Fully homomorphic encryption (FHE): FHE has numerous applications. For example, it enables private queries to a search engine—the user submits an encrypted query and the search engine computes a succinct encrypted answer without ever looking at the query in the clear.

GDPR: GDPR is the General Data Protection Regulation that came into effect May 25, 2018, protecting EU citizen privacy data.

GWAS: A genome-wide association study (GWAS) is used in genetics research to associate specific genetic variations with particular diseases.

Hacker: A hacker is someone who makes things. In this context, it's someone who makes things by programming computers. This is the original, and purest definition of the term, i.e., you have an idea and you "hack" something together to make it work. It also applies to people who modify things to significantly change their functionality, but less so.

HIPAA: The Health Insurance Portability and Accountability Act of 1996 (HIPAA) is a US federal law that required national standards to protect sensitive patient health data.

Homomorphic encryption (HE): HE allows operations on encrypted data.

Hyperledger: This umbrella project of open source blockchains and community focused on developing a suite of stable frameworks, tools, and libraries for enterprise-grade blockchain (DLT) deployments.

Hyperledger Fabric: Distributed ledger software that can be used as a foundation for developing blockchain based solutions or applications.

Hypervisor: Virtual machine monitor software that virtualizes physical resources and allows for running virtual machines.

IAPP: International Association of Privacy Professionals, https://iapp.org, is the largest and most comprehensive global information privacy community and resource. Founded in 2000, the IAPP is a not-for-profit organization that helps define, promote, and improve the privacy profession globally.

Identify: Identify is the first of the five NIST functions. The Identify Function assists in developing an organizational understanding to managing cybersecurity risk to systems, people, assets, data, and capabilities.

Identity Access Management (IAM): A cybersecurity tool that provides authorization and authentication of users to systems.

Impact: Impact is the degree to which a cyber-issue may have an adverse outcome on the organization. Several factors can influence impact in Cybersecurity.

Incident: An occurrence that may result in a loss or adverse consequence to the digital asset.

Incident Response: Refers to cybersecurity remediation work where an incident is confirmed, and resources respond to mitigate and repair the damage to the digital assets.

Inherent Cyber Risk: The cyber risk without controls in place or as if there was zero percent effectiveness of cybersecurity controls. It is the worst-case scenario and is also called "cybergeddon" risk.

Innovation: The act or process of introducing new ideas, devices, or methods.

Insured: Insured is a first- or third-party organization that has purchased cybersecurity insurance to transfer risk and increase cyber resiliency.

Integrity: Integrity ensures that the data is unaltered and is consistent, accurate, and trustworthy over its entire life cycle.

Inter-cloud computing: Paradigm for enabling the interworking between two or more cloud service providers.

Interconnectivity: The term defines the electronic connections between businesses, systems, processes, vendors, suppliers, governments, and the like.

International Standards Organization (ISO): ISO is the International Standards Organization. It publishes the ISO/IEC 27001, an information security standard, part of the ISO/IEC 27000 family of standards. ISO/IEC 27001 specifies a management system intended to bring information security under management control and gives specific requirements. Organizations that meet the requirements may be certified by an accredited certification body after completing an audit.

Intrusion Detection System (IDS): A cybersecurity tool that monitors systems for malicious activity or policy violations.

IP Address: An Internet Protocol is a numerical label connected to a computer network used for communications.

IT Auditors: IT Auditors are responsible for developing, planning, and executing IT audit programs based on risk assessments in a highly integrated audit environment. This includes documenting and communicating risks, providing counsel on control issues and recommended process changes, and monitoring corrective actions to improve the organization's existing practices reducing cyber risk.

Lattice-based cryptosystems (LBE): LBE can build systems that securely and privately handle computation on encrypted data. Some homomorphic encryption schemes use it. LBE can be Quantum resistant. Lattice-based cryptography is based on cryptographic systems such as Learning With Errors, LWE. Lattice-based cryptography has been published and analyzed increasingly during 2011–2020.

Likelihood: A probability a cyber-attack will cause damage.

Malware: Software that is intended to damage or disable computers and computer systems.

Mergers and Acquisitions (M&A): The area of corporate finance, management and strategy that deals with purchasing and/or joining with other companies. Two organizations join forces to become a new business in a merger, usually with a new name. In terms of digital assets, not all digital assets will be acquired or utilized in the merger or acquisition.

Microsharding: Microsharding splits a file up into multiple pieces, but the pieces are extremely small. Theoretically, as small as a single byte, each microshard tends to be just a few bytes in practice. Each of these microshards is stored in different locations.

Mitigation: Mitigation uses measures to reduce the likelihood of risk or implement risk reduction controls based on the impacts.

MLOps: MLOps (machine learning operations) is a discipline that enables data scientists and IT professionals to collaborate and communicate while automating machine learning algorithms.

National Institute of Standards and Technology (NIST): NIST is the National Institute of Standards and Technology, a unit of the US Commerce Department. The NIST Cybersecurity Framework (CSF) is a set of 98 control tests that. The CSF provides a policy framework of computer security guidance for how private sector organizations in the United States can assess and improve their ability to prevent, detect, and respond to cyber-attacks.

New York State (NYS) Part 500 regulation: New York State (NYS) Part 500 regulation establishes cybersecurity requirements for financial services companies.

Non-personal data: A class of data objects that does not contain PII Personal data objects that were originally made anonymous are non-personal data.

OPD: Organizational data whose protection is required based on the policies established by governance of data process. Organizations have policies that govern the data under their control. ISO/IEC 38505-1 identifies and examines higher-level governance concerns regarding the use of data which is relevant from the perspective of governance of data.

Operational Risk: The prospect of loss resulting from inadequate or failed procedures, systems, or policies.

Opt-in/Opt-out: An important distinction in the privacy debate concerns the terms under which e-mail marketers (legitimate ones, not spammers that ignore ethical and legal concerns) can contact users. Opt-in is the consumer-friendly position, where companies can send e-mail only to people who have directly given their consent for such communications, typically by signing up at a Web site.

Partially homomorphic encryption (PHE): PHE allows only one operation on the encrypted data (i.e. either addition or multiplication but not both). PHEs **are in general more efficient than SHE/SWHE and FHE, mainly because they are homomorphic with respect to only one type of operation addition or multiplication**.

Payment Industry Data Security Standard (PCI-DSS): PCI-DSS is the Payment Industry Data Security Standard. It applies to banks, merchants, and data processors who process credit card data.

Penetration Testing: A method that searches for vulnerabilities and attempts to circumvent the system's security features.

Phishing: The fraudulent practice of sending emails from reputable companies to induce users to reveal personal information, such as passwords and credit card numbers.

Physical Security: Controls for physical access to the organization. These controls are locks, cameras, doors, fire suppression systems, personnel identification (badges), visitor security, etc. All organizations usually have some level of physical security. More mature have electronic means.

Privacy: Related to the confidentiality and integrity of data.

Privacy Policy: A disclaimer placed on a website informing users about how the website deals with a user's personal information.

Process Revenue: The amount of revenue based on the use of a particular process.

Programmer: A programmer is someone who can solve problems by manipulating computer code. They can have a wide range of skill levels—from just being "ok" with basic scripting to being an absolute sorcerer with any language.

Protect: The second of the five NIST functions. The Protect Function outlines appropriate safeguards to ensure delivery of critical infrastructure services. The Protect Function supports the ability to limit or contain the impact of a potential cybersecurity event.

PHI: Protected Health Information

Pseudonymity: This concept originated in the field of cryptography. Pseudonymity can provide a consistent identity without revealing one's actual name, instead of using an alias or pseudonym. Pseudonymity combines many of the advantages of both a known identity and anonymity.

Public domain data: A class of data objects over which nobody holds or can hold copyright or other intellectual property rights. Data can be in the public domain in some jurisdictions, while not in others.

Qualitative: Qualitative data is information about qualities; information that can't actually be measured from a subjective viewpoint.

Quantitative: Quantitative research is used to quantify the problem by generating numerical data or data that can be transformed into usable statistics. It is objective.

Ransomware: A type of malicious software intended to block access to network systems until the target pays some form of ransom to the deployer.

Recover: The fifth of the five NIST functions. The Recover Function identifies appropriate activities to maintain plans for resilience and to restore any capabilities or services that were impaired due to a cybersecurity incident. The Recover Function supports timely recovery to normal operations to reduce the impact from a cybersecurity incident.

Regulatory Loss: Regulatory loss happens when a regulator fines an organization for a cyber-breach. The costs of the fines are defined by the regulator(s).

Regulatory Risk: Regulatory risk is defined as having privileges withdrawn by a regulator, or having conditions applied by a regulator that adversely impact the economic value.

Reputational Risk: Reputational risk is a matter of corporate trust. The loss can be demonstrated in lost revenue; increased operating, capital or regulatory costs, or destruction of shareholder value.

Residual Cyber Risk: The cyber risk with controls in place. It is the best-case scenario.

Respond: The fourth of the five NIST functions. The Respond Function includes appropriate activities to act regarding a detected cybersecurity incident. The Respond Function supports the ability to contain the impact of a potential cybersecurity incident.

Resources: Resources are an operational or capital item. Operational resources are personnel and capital resources are equipment.

Risk: A risk, in plain language, is a chance of something bad happening combined with how bad it would be if it did happen.

Risk Accumulation: Risk Accumulation or Amplification is the aggregation of losses from a single event due to the concentration of cyber risk exposed to that single event. In cyber risk this based on the digital assets. Some examples are cloud compromise and data exfiltration.

Risk Amplification: The aggregation of financial losses from a cyber event due to reputational, operational, or legal impacts.

Risk Calculation: In risk modeling, it is a mathematical determination of the risk exposures.

Risk Names: In risk modeling, they are measurable exposures that use algorithms to express their value.

Risk Parameters: In risk modeling, they are specific numerical or other measurable factors forming one of a set that defines a digital asset risk or sets the conditions of its operation.

Risk Qualifications: In risk modeling, they are calculations that use subjective data from the business.

Risk Quantifications: In risk modeling, they are calculations that use objective financial metrics derived from the business and cyber-related metrics derived from metric-based organizations.

Risk Questionnaire: In risk modeling, it is a set of questions that are used in the risk qualification metrics

Rootkit: A rootkit is a set of software tools that enable an unauthorized user to gain control of a computer system without being detected.

Secure multi-tenancy: A type of multi-tenancy that employs security controls to explicitly guard against data breaches and provides validation of these controls for proper governance.

Securities and Exchange Commission (SEC): A US governmental agency that oversees securities transactions and the activities of financial professionals and mutual fund trading to prevent fraud.

Security Control Measures: Refers to the means taken by organizations to identify, protect, detect, recover, or respond to cybersecurity. This includes people, process, and tools.

SIEM: Security Incident Event Management (SIEM) is a cybersecurity tool that provides real-time analysis of security alerts generated by applications and network hardware to identify brute force, viruses, and firewall attacks.

Somewhat homomorphic encryption (SWHE): SWHE allows a limited number of either addition or multiplication operations of the data, but not both. SHE (Somewhat Homomorphic Encryption also called SWHE) is more general than PHE because it supports homomorphic operations with additions and multiplications.

Spam: Spam is any unsolicited electronic message. Often spam messages will be commercial in nature. "Spammers" usually harvest email addresses from websites, or buy them from other companies.

Spyware: Any technology that aids in gathering information about persons or organizations without their knowledge. On the Internet, spyware is programming that's secretly installed in a computer to gather information about the user and relay it to advertisers or other interested parties. Spyware can infiltrate a computer as a virus or as a surprise result of installing a new program.

System: A consolidated set of technologies that provides the basis for collecting, creating, storing, processing, and distributing information.

Tabletop Exercise: A discussion-based exercise where resources meet and work through a scenario to validate plans, procedures, policies regarding an incident.

Technology: Technology is computer-related components that typically consist of hardware and software, databases, messaging, and devices.

Threat: A negative event can lead to an undesired outcome, such as damage to or loss of an asset. Threats can use—or become more dangerous because of—a vulnerability in a system.

Threat Actor: An entity that is partially or wholly responsible for an incident that impacts—or has the potential to impact—an organization's cybersecurity. In threat intelligence, actors are generally categorized as external, internal, or partners.

Unicode: The Unicode Standard provides a unique number for every character, no matter what platform, device, application, or language. It has been adopted by all modern software providers and now allows data to be transported through many different platforms, devices, and applications without corruption. Support of Unicode forms the foundation for the representation of languages and symbols in all major operating systems, search engines, browsers, laptops, and smart phones—plus the Internet and World Wide Web (URLs, HTML, XML, CSS, JSON, etc.).

Vendors: Third parties that provide goods or services to an organization.

Vendor Cyber Risk: The measurement of cyber risk that a third party possesses in relationships to digital assets of the first party.

Vendor Cyber Risk Management: The measurement and management of cyber risk that deals focuses on of third-party products (such as cloud service providers) and services (system integrators, management consultants, and the big 4) and the digital assets they provide or work with.

Verizon Data Breach Report (VRR): The VRR is annual security report from Verizon that provides vast statistics on data breach information.

VPN: A virtual private network is an encrypted connection over the Internet to protect it from unauthorized access. It allows for the safe transmittal of data from one location to another.

Virtual machine (VM): Isolated execution environment for running software that uses virtualized physical resources.

Virus: A piece of code capable of negatively affecting computer systems and networks by corrupting or destroying data.

Vulnerability: Vulnerabilities are weaknesses in a system. They make threats possible and/or more significant.

Vulnerability Management System (VMS): A VMS is a cybersecurity tool that cyclically uses software to identify and classify vulnerabilities. VMS vendors include Qualys, Rapid7, Tripwire, Saint, Tenable, Core Security, Critical Watch, Beyond Security, and many others.

Web Bug/Beacons: A web beacon is a clear image (you cannot usually see it). They are often placed in email messages. When you open the message, the bug will notify the sender. Web bugs are often used by services such as MSGTag.

Weights: Cyber risk refers to probability weighting used for percent complete metrics and maturity weighting to define which parameters are more critical than others.

White Hat/Black Hat: White hat hackers (also known as ethical hackers) are the polar opposite of their black hat counterparts. They use their technical skills to protect the world from bad hackers according to "Different Types of Hackers: The 6 Hats Explained."

Willful Neglect: In cybersecurity it means conscious, intentional failure or reckless indifference to the obligation to comply with cybersecurity measures.

BIBLIOGRAPHY

1. Glossary of Terms, Acronyms, and Notations, https://pages.nist.gov/FIPS201/glossary/
2. Privacy Glossary, https://www.privacytrust.com/guidance/privacy_glossary.html
3. Different Types of Hackers: The 6 Hats Explained – InfoSec…, https://sectigostore.com/blog/different-types-of-hackers-hats-explained/

Index